# INTRODUCTION TO
# CIVIL LITIGATION

# INTRODUCTION TO
# CIVIL LITIGATION

**MARK I. WEINSTEIN**
Associate Professor of Law
California Western School of Law

**THE PHILADELPHIA INSTITUTE**

**WEST PUBLISHING COMPANY**
Minneapolis/St. Paul     New York     Los Angeles     San Francisco

## WEST'S COMMITMENT TO THE ENVIRONMENT

In 1906, West Publishing Company began recycling materials left over from the production of books. This began a tradition of efficient and responsible use of resources. Today, up to 95 percent of our legal books and 70 percent of our college texts are printed on recycled, acid-free stock. West also recycles nearly 22 million pounds of scrap paper annually—the equivalent of 181,717 trees. Since the 1960s, West has devised ways to capture and recycle waste inks, solvents, oils, and vapors created in the printing process. We also recycle plastics of all kinds, wood, glass, corrugated cardboard, and batteries, and have eliminated the use of styrofoam book packaging. We at West are proud of the longevity and the scope of our commitment to our environment.

**Composition:** Carlisle Communications, Ltd.
**Copyediting:** Bonnie Gruen
**Text Design:** Lois Stanfield/Light Source Images
Production, Prepress, Printing and Binding by West Publishing Company.

Photo Credits: 1 Charles Gupton, Stock Boston; 17 © The Photo Works, Photo Researchers, Inc.; 41 © James L. Shaffer; 65 © Barbara Ries, Photo Researchers, Inc.; 91 © James L. Shaffer; 103 © James L. Shaffer; 235 Courtesy of Wang Laboratories, Inc., Frost Publishing Group, Ltd.; 261 © Day Williams, Photo Researchers, Inc.; 273 Jim Pickerell, Stock Boston; 309 © Photo Researchers, Inc.; 333 Jim Pickerell, Stock Boston.

**Library of Congress Cataloging in Publication Data**

Weinstein, Mark I.
    Introduction to civil litigation / Mark I. Weinstein, the
Philadelphia Institute. — 3rd ed.
        p.   cm. — (West's paralegal series)
    Includes index.
    ISBN 0-314-93380-8 (hard)
    1. Civil procedure—United States.   2. Pre-trial procedure—United
States.     I. Philadelphia Institute.   II. Title.   III. Series.
KF8840.W45 1993
347.73'5 — dc20
[347.3075]
                                                          92-42903
                                                          CIP

# CONTENTS IN BRIEF

# CONTENTS

## CHAPTER 7

## DISCOVERY 185

## CHAPTER 8

## DISCOVERY SUPPORT SYSTEMS 235

# PREFACE

This book is intended for students who are learning about the process of civil litigation for the first time. My approach in this book centers on two major concerns: first, paralegals need to know the theory underlying the practice of law in the context of civil litigation; second, visual methods concerning the fundamental drafting tasks of paralegals are critical to the process of learning. Therefore, I have explained the role and context of each paralegal task, and have provided concrete examples of the many documents paralegals must draft.

The major theme of this book is that the role of the paralegal in the area of civil litigation is far from static. It is hoped that paralegals will experience an expansion in their role both in scope and recognition. This book is written with the notion that, wherever possible, paralegals can perform all the vital tasks involved in civil litigation but for the constraints imposed by the Code of Professional Responsibility and the Model Rules of Professional Conduct written by the American Bar Association and adopted by the various states.

There are certain issues that due to time, scope and priorities have been left out of these materials. For example, the process of developing legal research skills is not addressed in this book. Although very important, these skills should be taught either prior to or as a supplement to this course. In addition, because emphasis has been placed on the role of the paralegal, the materials on the whole process of civil litigation have been deliberately shaped and limited; this book is not intended to be an exhaustive study of all the issues that can arise in civil litigation.

My goal in writing this new edition has been to update the material to reflect the major changes that have occurred in the field. In addition, new material has been added and existing material has been revised and reorganized in order to make this book more "user friendly" for students.

The major changes include the addition of a chapter on evidence, the separation of the material on interviewing and fact investigation into separate chapters, the restructuring of the materials on discovery support systems and preparation for trial into separate chapters, and the inclusion of more discussion throughout the book concerning the role of the paralegal.

A chapter outline, a summary list of key terms, and additional questions have been included in each chapter. Further, the material has been updated to reflect the recent changes in jurisdiction and procedural rules. New forms have been added and existing forms have been revised to help illustrate the points raised in the text.

The new edition of the text is accompanied by several supplements:

- The updated *Instructor's Manual* contains chapter outlines, teaching tips, suggested projects and additional problems, a test bank, and transparency masters.

- *Westest Computerized Testing* provides the entire test bank on disk.

- The new *Student Study Guide,* prepared by Gail Krebs of Commonwealth College, contains true/false, multiple choice, and definition questions to help test the student's knowledge of the material. Practice Exercises provide hands-on experience with drafting documents, researching state codes, preparing interview questions, and analyzing ethical situations. Answers are provided.

- New *State Supplements* for California, Florida, New York and Texas provide summaries of state procedures and rules where they differ from those discussed in the text.

I wish to thank my editor, Elizabeth Hannan, and my developmental editor, Patricia Bryant, at West Publishing for their support and guidance throughout this project. In addition, I wish to thank the reviewers of the previous edition. Their insightful comments were very helpful to me. Also a special thanks to my new colleague, Professor Chin Kim, who took the time to carefully review the previous edition and provide me with valuable feedback.

I must acknowledge my colleagues of many years at the Philadelphia Institute: Arnold Rosenberg, Bob Lee, Suzanne Brady, Cathy Branscom, and Rita Hunter. They have been very supportive of my various teaching and writing endeavors at the Institute. A special thanks goes to Henry Keiser for his support as well.

I gratefully acknowledge the assistance of Deborah Pummer. While in private practice in Allentown, Pennsylvania, Deborah's skills, enthusiasm and loyalty were extraordinary. I also wish to thank Cindy Bonney, Debbie Galm and Karen Hunter for their assistance and support.

Saving the best for last, I dedicate this edition to my wife Barbara and my daughters Lauren and Kayla. Their love, support, encouragement, understanding, and sense of adventure gave me the strength to write this book and afforded me the luxury of giving up my private practice to fulfill my dream of returning to law teaching. Thank you.

Mark I. Weinstein
San Diego, CA

# CHAPTER 1
# GENERAL INTRODUCTION

**INTRODUCTION TO CIVIL LITIGATION**

Definition of Litigation

Regulation of the Litigation Process

Remedies Available in Civil Litigation

Settlement of Civil Disputes

**INTRODUCTION TO THE ROLE OF THE PARALEGAL IN CIVIL LITIGATION**

Tasks and Skills

Ethics

**SUMMARY**

**KEY TERMS**

**QUESTIONS**

## I. INTRODUCTION TO CIVIL LITIGATION

The purpose of this chapter is to provide some general background information and insight into the system of noncriminal dispute resolution provided by the state and federal court systems for private parties and the government. We will examine the process of civil litigation first by attempting to define it, second by looking at its sources of regulation, and third by exploring the remedies it provides.

This chapter also defines the role of the paralegal in this system of dispute resolution. Some obvious limitations are that a paralegal cannot dispense legal advice, conduct a trial, or conduct a deposition. While this chapter provides a general introduction to the role of the paralegal, the chapters that follow discuss the tasks of the paralegal in more particularity and detail.

## A. Definition of Litigation

**Litigation** is the use of the legal process to settle disputes between people, businesses, and government entities. It is a mechanism provided by government to allow for impartial decision making that is not based on acts of violence, coercion, or economic disparity.

Litigation in the United States usually takes one of three forms. Each has its own procedures for resolving disputes. In addition, each has its own body of principles for determining the rights and responsibilities of the parties or people affected by it. These three forms are criminal litigation, administrative litigation, and civil litigation.

**Criminal litigation** is the process by which an individual is prosecuted for committing an act that our society, through its legislature, has deemed to be antisocial. An example of criminal litigation would be where a person is charged with committing a murder. The state prosecutes the individual charged (the **defendant**) for allegedly violating a criminal statute defining what constitutes a murder. The purpose of this prosecution is to determine whether the defendant is guilty of the crime charged. If the defendant is determined to be guilty, the court hearing the criminal case must then decide the appropriate sentence that will be imposed on the defendant. An example of a sentence would be incarceration for a certain period of time. In addition, the court can impose a fine and/or costs upon the defendant. Further, in some instances, the court can order the defendant to make restitution to the victim of the criminal activity.

**Administrative litigation** is the process by which private individuals, businesses, and administrative agencies resolve disputes before an administrative agency concerning the applicability, eligibility, and the enforcement of an administrative agency's regulations. An example of such litigation might involve a federal administrative agency like the Federal Communications Commission determining whether a television station's license should be renewed in accordance with the agency's standards. Such a process is typically called a license renewal proceeding. Another example might involve two cable television companies competing for a license in a certain municipality so that they would have the exclusive rights to service customers in that community. Another example would be a state environmental protection agency prosecuting a company alleged of polluting a waterway by dumping toxic chemicals, for the purpose of obtaining a cease and desist order against the alleged polluter.

**Civil litigation** is the process by which private individuals, businesses, and governments resolve disputes that are neither criminal nor administrative, concerning the payment of money, ownership and possession of property, marital obligations, the prevention of injury to a party, and declarations of rights and responsibilities of the various parties involved. Civil litigation concerns itself predominantly with the following topical areas of law: contracts, torts, property, matrimonial, equity, and antitrust. **Contract law** is concerned with the wrongs or injuries arising from the violation of an obligation or duty created by consent of the parties involved. **Tort law** involves private injuries or wrongs arising from a breach of duty created by law. **Property law** is concerned with the rights and responsibilities of ownership and possession of real and personal property. **Matrimonial law** involves the rights and responsibilities of marriage, divorce, custody of children, support and alimony, and division of marital property. **Equity** is concerned with providing relief and remedies for parties who would otherwise have no other recourse. **Antitrust law** involves the protection of trade and commerce from monopolies, restraints of trade, and other anticompetitive schemes.

## B. Regulation of the Litigation Process

From the moment litigation is commenced until its final determination, its course is channeled and regulated by detailed procedural rules. These **rules of civil procedure** define the issues of law and fact that are in dispute and control the methods by which the opposing parties may present factual and legal arguments in support of their respective positions. The sources of these rules vary. The most important for our purposes are comprehensive codes and court decisions that govern in minute detail each step of the litigation process.

In modern times courts have established comprehensive rules, without reference to particular cases, governing virtually every phase of the litigation process. In establishing these rules, courts have acted either pursuant to authority expressly granted to them by statute, or pursuant to their inherent authority to regulate their own activities. In most jurisdictions, the highest court writes these rules both for itself and for lower courts in the same jurisdiction. In addition, the local courts are permitted to promulgate rules concerning certain limited details of procedure before them. The only restriction placed on these local rules is that they may not be inconsistent or in conflict with the higher court rules.

We will spend a large portion of the remainder of this book studying the content and operation of the Federal Rules of Civil Procedure. Although these rules apply only to the federal courts in the United States, they have been adopted either totally or in part by many states. Although some states have rules that are not based on the federal rules, there are enough common threads between the federal rules and the divergent state rules to make the study of the federal rules worthwhile. The traditional notions of law school education assume that if students fully understand the Federal Rules of Civil Procedure, they can apply that knowledge to help them understand the variations and unique nuances of different state or local rules. In addition to focusing on the Federal Rules, we will examine the Pennsylvania Rules of Civil Procedure, for they illustrate how different systems attempt to resolve similar procedural problems and situations.

Rules of civil procedure establish and regulate, stage by stage, the nature and requirements of the litigation process, especially in the time-consuming pretrial stages. Virtually every move a litigation lawyer makes should be checked against provisions of the rules. Although these rules govern only procedure (as distinguished from the substantive rights of a party), virtually every right of a litigant may be lost if proper procedure is not followed. For example, while the constitution may provide that a **plaintiff** (a party who initiates a civil lawsuit) in a particular kind of civil case is entitled to a trial by jury, the rules of procedure may require that the plaintiff make a formal demand for trial by jury within ten days after receiving defendant's answer to the complaint. (A **complaint** is the name of the document by which civil litigation is commenced by a plaintiff.) Despite the constitutional provision, the plaintiff may lose the constitutional right to a trial by jury unless the requirements of the rules of civil procedure are complied with.

For the novice entering the field of civil litigation, it is imperative to learn and master the applicable rules of civil procedure for the geographical area of your paralegal practice. This will facilitate the orderly progression of your client's claims. If you neglect to either research or learn the applicable rules of procedure, you may find your client's claim bogged down in a quagmire of procedural issues that may thwart the ultimate resolution of the claim.

### 1. The Sources of Law

All rules of civil procedure such as those described above must be consistent with the following sources of law: constitutional law, legislative law, and court-made law. Therefore, we will now turn to a brief discussion of each of these sources.

*a. Constitutional Law.*   The federal government, and every state, has a **constitution** that not only establishes the framework of its governmental institutions but also sets forth a number of simple but important principles of law. Examples of where the U.S. Constitution and typical state constitutions have established important principles of law include such concepts as the prohibition against cruel and unusual punishment (such as described in the Eighth Amendment to the United States Constitution), and the right to due process of law and the equal protection of law as described in the Fifth and the Fourteenth Amendment to the United States Constitution. The provisions of all other laws in the jurisdiction are limited by the constitution.

*b. Legislative Law.*   Congress and every state legislature make laws that are referred to as **statutes.** In addition, most states vest municipal and county governments with limited legislative power. The laws passed by such local governments are generally called **ordinances.**

A hypothetical example of legislative law would be if Congress adopted a statute that prohibited the burning of the American flag. Once a majority in the

House of Representatives and the Senate agreed on the language of the statute, it would then be sent to the President for review and approval. Assuming that the President approves of the language, he or she would then sign the legislative enactment. The President's signature approving the legislation transforms the legislative enactment into a statute. Accordingly, the statute now has become a law.

     ***c. Court-Made Law.***   When a judge resolves disputes concerning important legal issues, an opinion is usually written setting forth the essential facts of the case, the judge's view of the law as applied to those facts, and the reasoning that led to this view. The opinions of courts, especially those of appellate courts, have been collected and compiled for hundreds of years.

     The early English settlers in America brought with them a body of well-defined legal principles that had evolved in the opinions of English courts over the centuries since the Norman conquest. This body of law is known as the **common law** and is still used in both federal and state courts in this country. In the course of the two hundred years since American courts have been independent from the formal authority of English law, the common law originally received by American courts has undergone great changes, both through the hundreds of thousands of opinions in which judges have shaped, developed, and interpreted the common law to resolve modern problems, and through statutes, ordinances, and regulations that have changed it. An example of court-made law and how it operates can be best explained by once again referring back to the hypothetical example of the statute that was passed by Congress and approved by the President prohibiting the burning of the American flag. Assuming that a defendant was charged with the crime of burning the American flag, part of the defendant's defense to the charge would assert that the statute was unconstitutional in that it violated his or her rights to the expression of free speech as guaranteed by the First Amendment to the United States Constitution. Upon judicial review of this defense, if the court decides that the statute indeed violates the defendant's rights to expression when free speech is guaranteed by the First Amendment, such a decision has the force of law. Accordingly, the statute would no longer be viable for purposes of prosecuting individuals burning the American flag.

## 2. The Relationships among the Sources of Law

     Before discussing the relationships among different sources of law, it must be understood that there are fifty-one constitutions in the United States—those of each state and the United States Constitution. Similarly, there are fifty-one legislative bodies passing statutes. As a result, conflicts exist over whether certain matters should be the subject of federal legislation, state legislation, or both. For example, if the federal government makes laws controlling the sale of corporate stocks and bonds to the public, may a state also control sales of these securities within its boundaries? While the answer in this particular situation is yes, the resolution of this question is complex, involving issues of federal constitution law that go to the heart of our federal system of government. Such problems are beyond the scope of this book. The discussion that follows concerns the constitution, statutes, common law, regulations, and ordinances of one state.

Constitutions are the paramount source of law. Any legal principle in a statute or ordinance or in the common law that conflicts with legal principle in the constitution is invalid and unenforceable. For example, if a state constitution prohibits any support of parochial education, a state legislature may not adopt a law that grants money to parochial schools. Further, to the extent that a particular statute regulates a certain area of activity, that statute normally supersedes any rules of common law applicable to that area of activity. For example, while common law includes the legal principle of **caveat emptor** (buyer beware) giving no relief to a buyer who purchased a defective product, statutes have imposed responsibilities on sellers who sell defective products.

In our system of government, it is the courts rather than the legislative or executive branches of government that are charged with the final responsibility for interpreting constitutions and legislation. If, for example, a legislature decides that a certain statute is permitted by the constitution (that is, the statute is constitutional), the courts can still decide that the statute is unconstitutional. Once the highest court of a state decides that a statute is unconstitutional or determines the proper interpretation of the language of the statute, neither the state legislature nor the governor may change this decision. All that the legislature is empowered to do is to amend the statute to eliminate its unconstitutional aspects or change the wording of the statute so as to change its interpretation.

Although there are hierarchies in the above-named sources of law, all three have one thing in common: they all take precedence over procedural rules concerning the orderly disposition of civil disputes. This is consistent with the notion that form should not take precedence over substance.

### 3. The Application of Legal Principles in Court Decisions

*a. Precedent.*    Unlike legislatures, which may make laws as they see fit, courts may develop the law only by deciding disputes that are the subject of litigation. In deciding a controversy before it, a court will look to see if the same, or similar, question has ever been decided in that jurisdiction before. This is known as looking for **precedent.** If the highest court has decided an issue that is now the subject of another lawsuit, the first determination will be binding on the later case. This doctrine of adhering to precedent serves to apprise the public of the law and to make its application uniform. For example, if the highest court has held that children under the age of seven may not be held liable for acting negligently it would make for great confusion if each lower court decided for itself in various cases whether such children could or could not be held liable.

This doctrine of following earlier cases on the same point now in dispute is also known by the Latin words, **stare decisis** (let the decision stand).

In the event that a judge can find no precise precedent in that jurisdiction for a given point of law, the next step is to find opinions in cases where the legal issues resolved are most closely analogous to the case now at issue. In this way, the legal principle that is most appropriate may be determined. Finally, the judge may find it necessary or desirable to consider decisions of courts of other jurisdictions, which are not binding, as persuasive factors in deciding the case.

*b. Overruling.* From time to time courts consciously depart from stare decisis and explicitly decline to follow the precedents of previous opinions within their state or jurisdiction. When such a departure from precedent occurs, a court is said to have **overruled** a previous decision or decisions.

Overruling should not be confused with reversal. **Reversal** describes the action of a higher court when it determines that the result reached in a lower court in the same case and with the same parties was incorrect. Overruling, on the other hand, involves only changing the legal principle for which a case stood—the actual result between the original parties does not change.

For example, assume a lower court finds that Smith committed fraud against Jones and awards Jones $10,000. If, on appeal, a higher court in the jurisdiction disagrees with the lower court, it may reverse—so that Jones does not recover anything. If, however, ten years later a court decides that the legal principles that the court used in finding fraud in the case of Smith v. Jones are no longer (or never were) valid, the court may overrule the legal principle for which Smith v. Jones stood, thus destroying the "precedential value" of Smith v. Jones but not changing the actual result of that case, namely, Jones's $10,000 recovery from Smith.

Precedent is usually overruled for either of two reasons. Sometimes, especially in cases of precedent developed in the court of constitutional and statutory interpretation, the court recognizes a mistake in its logical development of the legal principle. On other occasions, most often in the development of common law, overruling occurs because the court concludes that changes in social conditions have deprived the legal rule of any utility.

## C. Remedies Available in Civil Litigation

Every party who commences a civil litigation lawsuit has some specific goal in mind. This goal can be defined simply as what the plaintiff expects as a result of the litigation. Another way of viewing this is by examining the benefits a party can achieve in proving the correctness of his or her position. These benefits or goals can be described as **remedies** that a court may grant a successful plaintiff or claimant. The following is a short list of the more common remedies available in civil litigation.

### 1. Money Damages

The most frequent type of remedy or relief in civil litigation is an award of a specific amount of money in favor of one party and against another. However, it is important to note that before the court can award a specific amount of money, it must determine whether a defendant is **liable,** or responsible, to the plaintiff. After liability has been established and after an award of a specific amount of money has been made, it is incorporated by the court into a judgment. If the judgment is not paid, the winner is entitled to have court personnel seize and sell the loser's property to obtain the cash required to satisfy the judgment.

*a. Compensatory Damages.* **Compensatory** (money) **damages** are calculated to compensate the winner for all economically measurable and legally recognized harm directly resulting from the loser's wrongful conduct.

Accordingly, a plaintiff suing in a tort case such as a personal injury action (and assuming the plaintiff can prove a breach of duty by the defendant) will be entitled to money damages equal to medical expenses, lost wages, and pain and suffering. Attorney's fees and most other costs of litigation are not, however, compensable except in a few, specific types of cases where statutes allow them. In addition, the spouse of a successful plaintiff in a personal injury action may be entitled to join in the action and recover an award for "loss of consortium," that is, the injured spouse's inability to provide normal marital companionship and care.

*b. Punitive Damages.*    In certain types of civil litigation, **punitive damages** may be awarded in addition to compensatory damages. The purpose of these damages, where authorized by the common law or statute, is to punish a party who has indulged in wrongful conduct that the law deems particularly reprehensible, for example, defamation, or assault and battery.

An example of statutory punitive damages is the federal antitrust laws that permit a successful plaintiff to recover in damages three times the amount of compensable harm shown to have resulted from defendant's illegal conduct. The purpose of this augmented recovery is not only to punish, but also to provide incentive for enforcement of the antitrust laws by private parties.

### 2. Restoration of Possession of Property

Sometimes civil litigation involves a dispute over the right to possess a certain piece of property. In such cases, the relief sought may be a judgment ordering the defendant to turn over possession to the plaintiff. An example could be the return of a borrowed item from a neighbor who refuses to give it back.

### 3. Declarations of Rights and Responsibilities

Examples of declarations of rights and responsibilities include divorces, annulments, paternity actions, custody and visitation rights, and declaratory judgments. The court can determine the legal status of the parties involved in divorce, where the court terminates a marriage, in annulment, where the court declares a marriage null and void, in paternity, where the court determines the legal parentage of a child, and in custody, where the court determines with whom a child will reside. A declaratory judgment might, for example, involve a court determination of the meaning of specific language in an insurance policy, when an insurance company differs with an insured (plaintiff) over what kinds of situations may be excluded from coverage under a policy. This kind of dispute is typically resolved by the courts in the form of a declaratory judgment.

### 4. Equitable Remedies

*a. Injunction.*    An **injunction** is a decree of a court of equity that generally orders the defendant to cease some activity. It is designed to prevent "irreparable injury" to the plaintiff, that is, injury that is not easily compensated by the award of money damages. An example would be where a court orders picketers of a store to stay in a certain area and be limited to a certain number of participants. Occasionally an injunction may be in the form of requiring the defendant to perform some act (mandatory injunction) to prevent irreparable injury to the plaintiff. One example of this would be a court order requiring striking teachers to go back to work.

*b. Specific Performance.* **Specific performance** is a court order that compels a party to perform in accordance with the terms of a contract. Because of the extraordinary nature of this remedy (that is, forcing a party to do something he or she does not want to do), the subject matter of the performance has to be such that awarding compensatory damages would not adequately resolve the problem. If, for example, two parties have entered into a contract for sale of a piece of real estate and thereafter one of the parties refuses to perform, a court of equity will issue a decree ordering specific performance of the contract, which requires the owner to sell the real estate to the buyer. On rare occasions, specific performance may also be ordered of a contract for sale of property other than real estate if such property is so unique that no comparable substitute can be purchased, for example, an original work of art.

Specific performance is similar to a mandatory injunction in that a court can order a defendant to perform an act. However, specific performance involves a court ordering a defendant to perform his or her obligations under a contract. A mandatory injunction can be ordered wherein the parties have no agreement or contract, in order to prevent an injury from occurring.

*c. Reformation.* When the terms of a written contract or other legal instrument to which one or more parties are bound have been set forth as a result of a mistake by a party or as a result of fraud used against one of the parties, a court of equity will issue a decree, rewriting the instrument in the language it deems the parties would have employed in the absence of mistake or fraud. This remedy is called **reformation.**

## D. Settlement of Civil Disputes

Disputes may reach their final resolution by voluntary agreement of the parties or by a decision rendered by a court. The overwhelming majority of civil disputes are terminated by voluntary agreements of the parties rather than by judgment after a trial. This is because of the time and expense involved in litigating a dispute and the gamble that a trial always presents, no matter how sure one party is of being in the right. Furthermore, judges encourage parties to settle their disputes without trial as this helps reduce the burden on the court system. Many more cases are started than could ever be heard, and even though large numbers of cases are settled outside of court, backlogs still exist.

Thus it is frequently in the best interests of the parties as well as of the judicial system for disputes to be resolved without trials. Settlement negotiations, although most common before trial, may take place at any time: before the suit is filed; after the suit is filed, but before the trial; during the trial; or even after the trial while an appeal is pending.

Typically, the parties may have had discussions among themselves before consulting attorneys. If they have not, the attorney or the paralegal acting under the attorney's supervision as part of a litigation team may initially try to explore the possibility of an amicable settlement before starting a lawsuit. Sometimes it is necessary to start a lawsuit because the opponent does not take the dispute seriously. Once a lawsuit has been filed, the subject of making a settlement is bound to arise. Whether a settlement will be reached depends on the relative strengths of each party's case and the willingness of the parties to compromise. Later in this book, we will explore this process and the role of the paralegal in more detail.

## II. INTRODUCTION TO THE ROLE OF THE PARALEGAL IN CIVIL LITIGATION

One of the basic assumptions about civil litigation in this book is that except for the actual direct involvement in the formal participation of a trial, the taking of a deposition, the arguing of motions and applications to judges, oral argument on appeal to the various courts, or the dispensing of legal advice to a client, there is very little that a lawyer can do that a skilled paralegal cannot do. Because they have different educational and licensing requirements, paralegals cannot practice law. However, a paralegal has the authority to use acquired legal skills based upon the supervision received from the supervising attorney. Therefore, the paralegal's role in civil litigation is directly related to the amount of authority and discretion that a supervising lawyer is willing to entrust to the paralegal within the constraints mentioned above.[1]

Included below is Rule 5.3 of the Rules of Professional Conduct, which involves responsibilities regarding nonlawyer assistants:

"With respect to a nonlawyer employed or retained by or associated with a lawyer:

(a) a partner in a law firm should make reasonable efforts to ensure that the firm has measures in effect giving reasonable assurance that the person's conduct is compatible with the professional obligations of the lawyer;

(b) a lawyer having direct supervisory authority over the nonlawyer should make reasonable efforts to ensure that the person's conduct is compatible with the professional obligations of the lawyer; and

(c) a lawyer shall be responsible for conduct of such a person that would be a violation of the Rules of Professional Conduct if engaged in by a lawyer if:

(1) the lawyer orders or, with the knowledge of the specific conduct, ratifies the conduct involved; or

(2) the lawyer is a partner in the law firm in which the person is employed, or has direct supervisory authority over the person, and in either case knows of the conduct at a time when its consequences can be avoided or mitigated but fails to take reasonable remedial action."

---

[1]See Code of Professional Responsibility, EC 3-6. Please note that many states have adopted a new code of conduct called the Rules of Professional Conduct, which were derived from the Model Rules of Professional Conduct adopted by the American Bar Association in 1983, as amended. Please check in your state how the appropriate sanctioned code of conduct for lawyers impacts on paralegals.

**COMMENT²**

Lawyers generally employ assistants in their practice, including secretaries, investigators, law student interns, and paraprofessionals. Such assistants, whether employees or independent contractors, act for the lawyer in rendition of the lawyer's professional services. A lawyer should give such assistants appropriate instruction and supervision concerning the ethical aspects of their employment, particularly regarding the obligation not to disclose information relating to representation of the client, and should be responsible for their work product. The measures employed in supervising nonlawyers should take account of the fact that they do not have legal training and are not subject to professional discipline.

A partner in a law firm should make reasonable efforts to ensure that the firm has measures in effect giving reasonable assurance that the person's conduct is compatible with the professional obligations of the lawyer.

A lawyer having direct supervisory authority over the nonlawyer should make reasonable efforts to ensure that the person's conduct is compatible with the professional obligations of the lawyer.

Certain codes of conduct are directly aimed at paralegals. An example of such a code is that which has been promulgated by the National Association of Legal Assistants. However, unlike the Rules of Professional Conduct governing lawyers, adopted by the various states and enforced as part of the licensing procedure, the paralegal codes of conduct are voluntary associational regulations.

## A. Tasks and Skills

In spite of the discretionary process used to define the role of the paralegal, certain tasks and skills are fairly common to the role of a skilled civil litigation assistant. A list of the tasks and skills required of a litigation assistant is provided below (see Exhibit 1.1), but you should be aware of several cautions: the listing is very general and will be more clearly defined in the balance of the book; it contains terms not yet defined; and it is based on a notion of general civil litigation practice (each specialty area has its own unique set of skills and tasks).

## B. Ethics

Also crucial to the role of the paralegal in civil litigation is the concept of professional responsibility or legal **ethics.** Although lawyers are bound by the standards of professional conduct as articulated by the Code of Professional Responsibility, or the Rules of Professional Conduct, there is no code of conduct for paralegals. Although some states have recently promulgated guidelines for paralegals, they are typically directed at lawyers who use paralegals in their legal practice, not at the paralegals themselves. However, since lawyers are responsible for the work product of their paralegals and the actions of their employees

---

²The comments that accompany each rule are not part of the rules themselves. Instead the comments included with the rules attempt to explain and illustrate the meaning of the rules.

**EXHIBIT 1.1**

## Tasks and Skills of the Litigation Assistant.

### LITIGATION ASSISTANT

1. Commencement of action
   a. Conduct initial client interview
   b. Organize and analyze files, including preparation of chronologies
   c. Investigate and analyze facts
      i. Interview witnesses
      ii. Investigate, perform corporate checks, previous litigation, and deed checks
      iii. Analyze medical reports, wages
   d. Draft summons, marshal's service, civil cover sheet
   e. Draft complaint
   f. Draft answer

2. Discovery
   a. Draft request for admissions
   b. Draft request for production
   c. Draft interrogatories
   d. Digest/analyze answers and responses to same
   e. Set up depositions
      i. Draft notice, subpoena, arrange for reporter
      ii. Prepare questions
      iii. Take notes of testimony
      iv. Prepare digests
   f. Organize and analyze documents
      i. Prepare for production of documents
      ii. Conduct production of documents
      iii. Organize/catalog documents produced
      iv. Organize/catalog documents for retrieval systems

3. Trial
   a. Organize trial exhibits
   b. Arrange trial settings
   c. Prepare trial subpoena
   d. Organize trial book
   e. Prepare witnesses
   f. Take notes and handle exhibits at trial

4. Post-trial
   a. Summarize trial testimony
   b. Check appeal record
   c. Organize appendix
   d. Prepare collection documents, i.e., garnishment, levy
   e. Satisfy judgment

> **EXHIBIT 1.1**
>
> ## Tasks and Skills of the Litigation Assistant (continued)
>
> 5. Settlements
>    a. Draft releases
>    b. Draft motions and stipulations for dismissal
>    c. Draft motions re. jury fee refunds
>    d. Draft settlement sheets
>
> 6. General
>    a. Draft motions and stipulations, i.e., dismissal, extensions of time
>    b. Draft notices, i.e., to set, to continue, deposition
>    c. Shepardize and check cites
>    d. Perform legal research: specific points, briefing cases
>    e. Keep up correspondence
>    f. Maintain tickler systems, master docket, calendars
>    g. Maintain files: form files, legal memos, experts

(within the scope of their employment), any violation of the Code of Professional Responsibility or the Rules of Professional Conduct can have a negative impact on the entire law office in which the paralegal is employed. Therefore, by implication, paralegals are also bound by the norms established in the Code of Professional Responsibility or the Rules of Professional Conduct. Again, because of the preliminary nature of the discussion of role at this juncture of the book and the vastness of the topic at hand, only a few generalized notions of legal ethics are discussed below.[3]

The relationship between lawyer and client must be one based on trust. Only then will an attorney be able to properly represent a client. A paralegal must be aware of this relationship and act to foster it. When given the responsibility of working with clients or with matters that vitally concern clients, a paralegal must do nothing to cause the client to question whether this relationship of trust is well founded. In addition to conducting oneself in a professional manner, a paralegal should observe some other precepts. A few of them are listed below, and from time to time throughout this book reference will be made to other ethical considerations. The propriety of all a paralegal's actions will reflect on his or her employer. When in doubt about any action, the paralegal should check in advance with the lawyer or other person in charge.

### 1. Confidentiality

The cornerstone of any law office is the concept of client **confidentiality.** As a general rule what a client tells his or her lawyer is privileged communica-

---

[3]Every paralegal should study and become familiar with the Code of Professional Responsibility and the Rules of Professional Conduct and the comparisons between both documents.

tion. This privilege involves the concept of lawyer/client confidentiality, which extends to all employees in a law office including the paralegal. Although much of the information with which a lawyer's assistant is concerned is highly confidential and extremely private in nature, it will not always be easy to recognize what information is confidential. Often a client will be extremely offended if he or she learns that a lawyer, a lawyer's assistant, or other employee of the law firm has discussed his or her business in public, even if the information mentioned is public knowledge. The best rule to observe in order to avoid problems is: Do not discuss a client's or your firm's business with any outsider no matter how close a friend. Furthermore, do not discuss any such business in a public place such as an elevator or restaurant.

### 2. Dealing with Clients

Some clients have reservations about dealing with someone who is not a lawyer. This problem should be overcome in time. However, it is very important that the paralegal remember to obtain the lawyer's permission before writing or calling a client. When doing so it is a good idea to mention that the lawyer has asked you to call or write.

### 3. Letters

The legal assistant may not in any way represent him- or herself to the public as a lawyer. A letter signed by the legal assistant on law firm stationary could be misleading. Therefore, the lawyer in charge should be asked to decide the best way of identifying the role of the legal assistant. You may be asked to put the words "Legal Assistant" or some other appropriate title below your signature so that clients or other lawyers will understand your position with the law firm.

### 4. Communicating with Persons Represented by Counsel

It is important that the legal assistant understand the constraints and prohibitions involved in communicating directly with a party who is represented by another lawyer or law firm. Rule 4.2 of the Rules of Professional Conduct is essentially the same as Disciplinary Rule 7-104(A)(1) of the Code of Professional Responsibility. Rule 4.2 provides as follows: "In representing a client, a lawyer shall not communicate about the subject of the representation with a party the lawyer knows to be represented by another lawyer in the matter, unless the lawyer has the consent of the other lawyer or is authorized by law to do so." Although this rule speaks in terms of lawyer communication, a legal assistant is bound to the same proscription.

## III. Summary

This chapter has defined civil litigation as the process by which private individuals, businesses, and governments resolve disputes that are neither criminal nor administrative. It typically is concerned with the payment of money, ownership and possession of property, prevention of injuries, and status questions.

Litigation is regulated by rules of procedure. The purpose of these procedural rules is to establish and regulate, stage by stage, the nature and requirements of the litigation process.

There are basically three sources of law: constitutional, legislative, and court-made. Constitutions are the primary sources of law. However, it is the role of the courts to interpret constitutions and legislation. A system of precedence aids courts in their decision making process. However, in the appropriate circumstances, courts can overrule a previous decision.

The remedies typically available in civil litigation are monetary damages, restoration of property, and declaration of rights and equity. Every lawsuit has as its goal a particular remedy.

For strong systemic reasons, the vast majority of civil cases filed result in settlement.

The latter part of this chapter focused on the skills and ethics involved in role of the paralegal. With respect to the skill and task areas, paralegals play an important role in the prelitigation phase, including pretrial, trial, and appeal and in accomplishing settlement. With respect to ethics, paralegals must understand the concepts of confidentiality, unauthorized practice of law, and dealing with persons represented by counsel.

## IV. Key Terms

Administrative
   litigation
Antitrust law
Civil litigation
Compensatory
   damages
Complaint
Confidentiality
Constitution
Contract law
Court-made
   (common) law

Criminal litigation
Defendant
Equity
Ethics
Injunction
Legislation
Liability
Litigation
Matrimonial law
Overrule
Plaintiff

Precedent
Property law
Punitive damages
Reformation
Remedies
Reversal
Rules of civil
   procedure
Specific performance
Stare decisis
Tort law

## V. Questions

1. Distinguish common law and legislative law.
2. Determine the hierarchies in the listed sources of law:
   a. ordinance
   b. state constitution
   c. state legislation
   d. federal legislation
   e. federal constitution
3. Which branch of government is charged with the responsibility of interpreting law? Why?

4. What is the difference between compensatory damages and punitive damages?
5. Compare and contrast the remedies of injunctions with specific performance.
6. Compare and contrast the remedies of compensatory damages with injunctions.
7. Compare and contrast the remedies of compensatory damages with specific performance.
8. Compare and contrast criminal litigation with civil litigation.
9. Compare and contrast reversal and overruling.
10. Based on current events or recent history, provide an example where a court has declined to follow a previous court decision.
11. Generally, what constitutes the unauthorized practice of law by a paralegal?
12. Does your state have a statute that deals with the unauthorized practice of law? If yes, find the statute and bring a copy of it to class.
13. Should paralegals be licensed? If yes, what criteria should be established to determine qualifications?

# CHAPTER 2

# OVERVIEW OF COURT SYSTEMS FOR CIVIL LITIGATION

## I. Introduction to Court Systems

The purposes of this chapter are to provide a general overview of how court systems are set up to resolve civil disputes and to explore some of the considerations necessary when choosing a court for litigation. We will examine the basic structure of the federal court system and the Pennsylvania state court system.[1] In addition, you will learn the basic vocabulary used in describing court systems to help you understand the process of deciding where to file a particular civil lawsuit.

Every state in the United States has its own court system.[2] These systems are set up by state constitution, state statute, or a combination of both. In addition to these state court systems, there is a federal court system. The authority for the federal court system is based on Article III of the United States Constitution. In addition, federal legislation has been enacted that elaborates and expands the authority and scope of the federal court system. State and federal court systems exist side by side. As a result of these separate and different systems, many questions can arise involving the interplay of the federal and state courts concerning authority to hear cases, supremacy of systems, and finality of decisions made in each system.

From a systemic perspective, the federal and state court systems are very similar. Both derive their heritage from the legal system of England and have similar procedures for initially hearing cases and reviewing those initial decisions. Although the terminology describing the various courts within a given system (either federal or state) may vary, the basic functions of these courts are the same.

However, in spite of the overall similarity of the court systems, each state has its own unique brand of civil dispute resolution. No two states have exactly the same laws or the same court procedures. In addition, the federal system is not exactly like that of any of the states.

In order to understand all these court systems, it is important to learn their common characteristics. Every court system is divided into at least two classes of courts: trial and appellate courts. **Trial courts** are where a civil dispute is heard initially. In trial courts witnesses testify, a judge presides, and a jury may render a decision (verdict). In **appellate courts,** the losing party at a trial seeks to have the decision of the trial court reviewed and overturned.[3] Typically, appellate courts decide their cases on the basis of the stenographic record of the testimony at trial, documents presented at trial, pleadings filed, briefs submitted by the parties pointing out the legal authority for the positions they assert, and oral argument where the attorneys seek to clarify and amplify their respective positions. Generally speaking, no new evidence is presented to the appellate courts. The basic mandate of appellate courts is to review the trial proceedings upon request of one of the parties to ensure that the parties received a fair trial with respect to the applicable law involved and that the decision was supported by the evidence (testimony and documents) presented at the trial.

---

[1]Pennsylvania was chosen because of its similarity to other state court systems.
[2]This includes the District of Columbia.
[3]A losing party includes a party who wins a judgment but is not awarded as much as had been hoped.

Another distinction between trial and appellate courts is that trial courts are generally **inferior** to appellate courts. Inferior refers to the concept that decisions of an appellate court of a state are deemed binding on the trial court within its jurisdiction. Thus, a trial court judge is required to follow the decision of the appellate court even if he or she disagrees. If a state has an intermediate appellate court and a highest appellate court, the decision of the highest appellate court is binding on both the intermediate appellate court(s) and the trial court(s) of the same state.

## A. Federal Court System

The federal court system is divided into three different kinds of courts as shown in Exhibit 2.1: the U.S. District Courts, U.S. Courts of Appeals, and the U.S. Supreme Court.[4] It is a three-tiered system that provides a trial court and two levels of appeal. Each court has a distinct role in the process of civil dispute

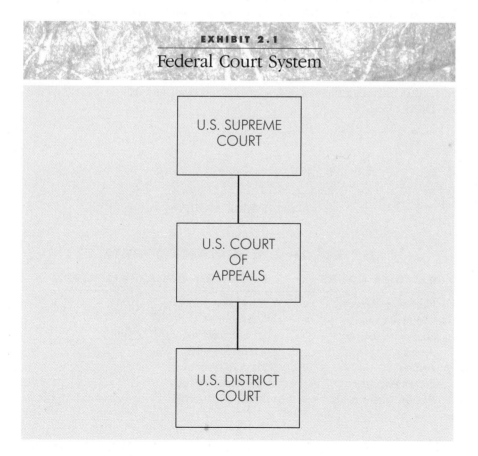

**EXHIBIT 2.1**

## Federal Court System

U.S. SUPREME COURT

U.S. COURT OF APPEALS

U.S. DISTRICT COURT

---

[4]There are also certain specialized courts such as the Court of Claims, the Tax Court, and the Bankruptcy Court.

resolution in the federal court system. Since litigation starts first with the trial court, we will examine the role of the U.S. District Court.

### 1. District Court Organization

In the federal system, the district court is the trial court. It is also the court of **original jurisdiction,** which refers to the fact that it has the authority to decide a case when it is first instituted by one of the parties. The district court can also be described as a court of **limited jurisdiction,** meaning that it has the authority to adjudicate only cases that fall within a particular class of cases. In other words, these courts have the power to hear only cases that have been prescribed by Congress. Unless a case falls within the limits set up by Congress, the federal courts do not have the authority to decide it.

As a way of organizing the district courts, the United States is divided into **districts.** Some states have only one district while other states have two or more districts.[5] For example, Montana has only one district, which is called the U.S. District Court for Montana. Pennsylvania has three districts: the U.S. District Court for the Eastern District of Pennsylvania, the U.S. District Court for the Middle District of Pennsylvania, and the U.S. District Court for the Western District of Pennsylvania. The number of federal districts for a given state is related to the state's population. Accordingly, the larger the state in terms of population, the more districts the state will have. However, every state has at least one district regardless of how sparsely it is populated. Exhibit 2.2 lists all the U.S. District Courts.

**EXHIBIT 2.2**

## U.S. District Courts

### LISTING OF U.S. DISTRICT COURTS

| DISTRICT COURT | LOCATION OF CLERK'S OFFICE |
|---|---|
| Northern Alabama | Birmingham, Alabama |
| Middle Alabama | Montgomery, Alabama |
| Southern Alabama | Mobile, Alabama |
| Alaska | Anchorage, Alaska |
| Arizona | Phoenix, Arizona |
| Eastern Arkansas | Little Rock, Arkansas |
| Western Arkansas | Fort Smith, Arkansas |

---

[5]The District of Columbia and territories of the United States also have their own district courts. No district contains more than one state.

---

**EXHIBIT 2.2**

## U.S. District Courts (continued)

---

### LISTING OF U.S. DISTRICT COURTS

| DISTRICT COURT | LOCATION OF CLERK'S OFFICE |
| --- | --- |
| Northern California | San Francisco, California |
| Central California | Los Angeles, California |
| Southern California | San Diego, California |
| Eastern California | Sacramento, California |
| Colorado | Denver, Colorado |
| Connecticut | New Haven, Connecticut |
| Delaware | Wilmington, Delaware |
| District of Columbia | Washington, D.C. |
| Northern Florida | Tallahassee, Florida |
| Middle Florida | Jacksonville, Florida |
| Southern Florida | Miami, Florida |
| Northern Georgia | Atlanta, Georgia |
| Middle Georgia | Macon, Georgia |
| Southern Georgia | Savannah, Georgia |
| Guam | Agana, Guam |
| Hawaii | Honolulu, Hawaii |
| Idaho | Boise, Idaho |
| Northern Illinois | Chicago, Illinois |
| Central Illinois | Peoria, Illinois |
| Southern Illinois | East St. Louis, Illinois |
| Northern Indiana | South Bend, Indiana |
| Southern Indiana | Indianapolis, Indiana |
| Northern Iowa | Cedar Rapids, Iowa |
| Southern Iowa | Des Moines, Iowa |
| Kansas | Wichita, Kansas |
| Eastern Kentucky | Lexington, Kentucky |
| Western Kentucky | Louisville, Kentucky |
| Eastern Louisiana | New Orleans, Louisiana |
| Middle Louisiana | Baton Rouge, Louisiana |
| Western Louisiana | Shreveport, Louisiana |
| Maine | Portland, Maine |
| Maryland | Baltimore, Maryland |
| Massachusetts | Boston, Massachusetts |
| Eastern Michigan | Detroit, Michigan |
| Western Michigan | Grand Rapids, Michigan |
| Minnesota | St. Paul, Minnesota |
| Northern Mississippi | Oxford, Mississippi |
| Southern Mississippi | Jackson, Mississippi |

**EXHIBIT 2.2**

## U.S. District Courts (continued)

## LISTING OF U.S. DISTRICT COURTS

| DISTRICT COURT | LOCATION OF CLERK'S OFFICE |
| --- | --- |
| Eastern Missouri | St. Louis, Missouri |
| Western Missouri | Kansas City, Missouri |
| Montana | Billings, Montana |
| Nebraska | Omaha, Nebraska |
| Nevada | Las Vegas, Nevada |
| New Hampshire | Concord, New Hampshire |
| New Jersey | Newark, New Jersey |
| New Mexico | Albuquerque, New Mexico |
| Northern New York | Albany, New York |
| Southern New York | New York, New York |
| Eastern New York | Brooklyn, New York |
| Western New York | Buffalo, New York |
| Eastern North Carolina | Raleigh, North Carolina |
| Middle North Carolina | Greensboro, North Carolina |
| Western North Carolina | Asheville, North Carolina |
| North Dakota | Bismarck, North Dakota |
| Northern Ohio | Cleveland, Ohio |
| Southern Ohio | Columbus, Ohio |
| Northern Oklahoma | Tulsa, Oklahoma |
| Eastern Oklahoma | Muskogee, Oklahoma |
| Western Oklahoma | Oklahoma City, Oklahoma |
| Oregon | Portland, Oregon |
| Eastern Pennsylvania | Philadelphia, Pennsylvania |
| Middle Pennsylvania | Scranton, Pennsylvania |
| Western Pennsylvania | Pittsburgh, Pennsylvania |
| Puerto Rico | San Juan, Puerto Rico |
| Rhode Island | Providence, Rhode Island |
| South Carolina | Columbia, South Carolina |
| South Dakota | Sioux Falls, South Dakota |
| Eastern Tennessee | Knoxville, Tennessee |
| Middle Tennessee | Nashville, Tennessee |
| Western Tennessee | Memphis, Tennessee |
| Northern Texas | Dallas, Texas |
| Southern Texas | Houston, Texas |
| Eastern Texas | Beaumont, Texas |
| Western Texas | San Antonio, Texas |
| Utah | Salt Lake City, Utah |
| Vermont | Burlington, Vermont |
| Virgin Islands | Charlotte Amalie, St. Thomas |

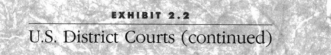

### EXHIBIT 2.2
## U.S. District Courts (continued)

### LISTING OF U.S. DISTRICT COURTS

| DISTRICT COURT | LOCATION OF CLERK'S OFFICE |
| --- | --- |
| Eastern Virginia | Norfolk, Virginia |
| Western Virginia | Roanoke, Virginia |
| Eastern Washington | Spokane, Washington |
| Western Washington | Seattle, Washington |
| Northern West Virginia | Elkins, West Virginia |
| Southern West Virginia | Charleston, West Virginia |
| Eastern Wisconsin | Milwaukee, Wisconsin |
| Western Wisconsin | Madison, Wisconsin |
| Wyoming | Cheyenne, Wyoming |

### 2. Subject Matter Jurisdiction in Federal District Court

In order to invoke the authority of the federal district courts, a plaintiff or party instituting a civil action must affirmatively demonstrate that the case falls within one of the bases set out by Congress for federal court jurisdiction. This is called **subject matter jurisdiction.** The main statutory authority for jurisdiction usually involves one of the following:

Cases arising under the Federal Constitution or laws and treaties of the United States (28 U.S.C. §1331)

Cases between citizens of different states involving a claim worth $50,000 or more (28 U.S.C. §1332)

Civil cases of admiralty and maritime jurisdiction (28 U.S.C. §1333)

Civil suits brought by and against the United States (28 U.S.C. §1345 and §1346)

Proceedings under the copyright, patent, and trademark laws (28 U.S.C. §1338)

Federal Tort Claims Act cases (28 U.S.C. §1346(b))

Civil rights cases (28 U.S.C. §1343).

Although this list is far from comprehensive, it provides a basic notion of the kinds of cases federal district courts commonly are called upon to adjudicate.[6]

---

[6]Readers interested in more detail concerning federal jurisdiction should refer to Charles Wright, *Federal Courts,* 3d ed. (St. Paul: West Publishing Company), 1976.

Later in this chapter we will examine in more detail the concepts of jurisdiction with respect to the parties of the lawsuit.

*a. Federal Question Jurisdiction.*   One of the major areas of federal subject-matter jurisdiction involves **federal question jurisdiction.** This category of subject-matter jurisdiction covers cases arising under the Federal Constitution, Federal Statutory Law, and Treaties of the United States. An example of a case arising under the United States Constitution might involve a lawsuit challenging a state's right to enforce a statute that violates the U.S. Constitution. For instance, if a state were to establish a minimum size for trucks using the highways within its state borders, and that size was inconsistent with neighboring states, an adversely affected trucker could claim that the state violated the interstate commerce provisions under the United States Constitution. Such an action could clearly be brought to Federal Court under this type of subject-matter jurisdiction.

Further, certain federal statutes provide subject-matter jurisdiction in the statute itself. An example would be the Federal Truth and Lending Law, which provides that Federal Courts have subject-matter jurisdiction to hear any case or controversy arising under that statute. The statute deals with requiring lenders to make certain disclosures to potential borrowers or consumers of credit designed to reveal the true cost of credit financing. A lawsuit concerning the failure to make proper disclosures can be brought in federal court.

*b. Diversity of Citizenship Jurisdiction.*   This category of subject-matter jurisdiction typically involves a case between citizens of different states. Both individuals and businesses are considered to be citizens under this section of the law.

Two requirements must be satisfied in order to obtain federal jurisdiction under this category. The first requirement is that there be **diversity of citizenship** between the parties. Specifically, the plaintiff and the defendant must be citizens of different states. For instance if a plaintiff was a citizen of New Jersey and the defendant was a citizen of California, the diversity requirement would be satisfied. On the other hand if the plaintiff and defendant were citizens of the same state, the diversity requirement would not be satisfied.

In addition to the diversity requirement, there is a further requirement that the amount in controversy must exceed $50,000. This threshold amount must be met exclusive of interest and costs.

In essence there is really nothing federal about diversity of citizenship jurisdiction other than the fact that the parties are from different states and that there is a threshold amount in controversy that has been satisfied. Accordingly, the kinds of cases that can arise under this category of subject-matter jurisdiction can involve contracts, torts, and other matters that are more typical of state court proceedings. For example, a breach of contract claim might involve a plaintiff from Pennsylvania entering into a contract with a defendant from California. The subject matter of the contract is a project to be built in the state of Minnesota. Plaintiff alleges that defendant has breached the contract and further claims damages in the amount of $75,000. Since the diversity requirement has been met and the amount of controversy threshold has been met, this case would be the proper subject of federal subject-matter jurisdiction.

Another example of diversity of citizenship jurisdiction could be a car accident case. Assume a driver of a motor vehicle from Texas collides with a driver of a motor vehicle from Illinois in the state of Colorado, and further assume that the amount of damages claimed exceeds $50,000, a lawsuit covering this subject matter could be filed in the federal courts. The parties are citizens of different states, and the amount of controversy exceeds $50,000.

### 3. United States Court of Appeals

The U.S. Court of Appeals is the intermediate-level appellate court in the federal court system. For organizational purposes, the United States is divided into twelve geographical areas, known as **circuits,** that are numbered from one to eleven. The twelfth district is the District of Columbia Circuit. There is a court of appeals for each circuit, which is identified by the number of the circuit. Federal statute (Title 28 U.S.C.) establishes the circuits and their geographic jurisdiction. The circuits are constituted as shown in Exhibit 2.3. The number of judges on the court of appeals of each circuit depends upon the volume of litigation in the federal courts in that circuit.

**EXHIBIT 2.3**

## Circuit Courts

| CIRCUITS | COMPOSITION |
| --- | --- |
| District of Columbia | District of Columbia |
| First | Maine, Massachusetts, New Hampshire Puerto Rico, Rhode Island |
| Second | Connecticut, New York, Vermont |
| Third | Delaware, New Jersey, Pennsylvania Virgin Islands |
| Fourth | Maryland, North Carolina, South Carolina, Virginia, West Virginia |
| Fifth | Canal Zone, Louisiana, Mississippi, Texas |
| Sixth | Kentucky, Michigan, Ohio, Tennessee |
| Seventh | Illinois, Indiana, Wisconsin |
| Eighth | Arkansas, Iowa, Minnesota, Missouri, Nebraska, North Dakota, South Dakota |
| Ninth | Alaska, Arizona, California, Idaho, Montana, Nevada, Oregon, Washington, Guam, Hawaii |
| Tenth | Colorado, Kansas, New Mexico, Oklahoma, Utah, Wyoming |
| Eleventh | Alabama, Florida, Georgia |

As the intermediate appellate court in the federal court system, this court has only appellate jurisdiction. It is empowered to hear the final decisions of the district courts. District court decisions are appealed to the court of appeals for the circuit in which the district is located. Absent an appeal to the U.S. Supreme Court, the decision of the court of appeals is considered a final one.

### 4. United States Supreme Court

The U.S. Supreme Court is the highest court in the country. It has an interesting mix of appellate jurisdictions with respect to both federal and state court cases, as well as original jurisdiction in certain classes of cases.[7] There are two different methods of appellate review in the Supreme Court concerning the decisions of the lower federal courts. The usual method of reviewing the decisions of the courts of appeals is by the statutory **writ of certiorari.** This is a discretionary review process by which the members of the Supreme Court can determine what cases they wish to review. If the court declines to exercise its discretion (refuses to allow an appeal), the decision of the court of appeals becomes final. If the court allows a petition for review (i.e., grants a writ of certiorari) it can exercise the same kind of appellate review as described earlier in this chapter. Whatever the outcome is in this appellate review, the decision is final. There is no further review or appeal from the Supreme Court. It is the court of last resort.

Besides the discretionary review process described above, there is a non-discretionary review process called **appeals as of right.** This process involves direct appeals to the Supreme Court that are usually limited to matters set out by statute arising in the lower federal court. These direct appeals are becoming less and less desirable to the Supreme Court. An example might involve an appeal from the judgment of a federal court holding an act of Congress unconstitutional in any civil action to which the United States or any of its agencies is a party.

In addition to the review process of the decisions of the lower federal courts, the Supreme Court has the authority to review decisions of the highest courts of the various states where issues involving the U.S. Constitution and federal law are at stake. For example, if the highest court of the state of Ohio decides that police officers in Ohio can stop and search every person with long hair for drugs and weapons without violating the Fourth Amendment to the U.S. Constitution concerning search and seizures, upon granting a petition for a writ of certiorari from that Ohio decision, the U.S. Supreme Court can review and override the Ohio Supreme Court decision. Because the Supreme Court is the final arbitrator of federal constitutional law, its decision is binding on all states whose decisions it chooses to review.

## B. State Courts

Although the Pennsylvania court system will be used as the primary example, it should be noted at the outset that the state court systems are organized similarly

---

[7]Original jurisdiction in the Supreme Court occurs in all cases in which a state is a party and in cases affecting ambassadors, other public ministers, and consuls. See Article III, Section 2 of U.S. Constitution.

to the federal court system, with differences occurring in such areas as names of courts, number of courts, and jurisdiction of courts. Also, although a few states have a two-tiered system (Vermont, for example), wherein there is a trial court and one appellate court, most states have a three-tiered model.

### 1. Trial Courts

In Pennsylvania, as well as in most states, there are two types of trial courts: small claims courts and general trial courts. Quite typically, there is a **court of general jurisdiction,** which handles a broad range of cases and is presumed to have the right to hear all cases unless the right is specifically taken away from it. This is in direct contrast to the trial courts in the federal court system where there is no presumption of jurisdiction. In Pennsylvania this court is called the Court of Common Pleas.[8] It has original jurisdiction as well as appellate jurisdiction concerning matters that may arise from appeals from an inferior trial court called the District Justice Court in Pennsylvania (small claims court). This District Justice Court also has original jurisdiction but it is a court of limited jurisdiction. It can handle only certain kinds of civil cases wherein the amount in controversy is small.[9] The party who appeals a decision of a District Justice Court gets a whole new trial in the Court of Common Pleas in the judicial district in which the District Justice Court is situated. This appeal process is called a **trial de novo.**

Many state court systems have special trial courts to entertain such matters as criminal cases (criminal courts), juvenile proceedings (juvenile courts), family disputes, such as divorce, support, and child custody (family courts), matters relating to estates and trusts (orphans', surrogates', or probate courts), and civil cases (civil trial courts). In theory, this specialization permits judges who preside in specialized courts to develop a greater degree of expertise within confined areas of the law.

In some states, the distinction between courts of general jurisdiction and courts with special competence has been abolished to a certain degree in favor of a single court that consolidates the functions of various specialized courts. For example, in Philadelphia there is a unified court system called the Court of Common Pleas of Philadelphia County. However, this court is divided into specialty areas such as criminal court, civil trial court, motions court, family court, and orphans' court. This arrangement allows for the central administration of the court. At the same time, the advantages of specialized judicial expertise are not lost because judges may be assigned on a full-time basis to one of the internal divisions of the court.[10]

---

[8]Examples of names for similar courts in other states are circuit courts, district courts, county courts, or superior courts.

[9]Examples of names for similar courts in other states are Justice of the Peace Court, Associate Circuit Court, Magistrate's Court, Small Claims Court, Landlord-Tenant Court, District Court, and Municipal Court.

Quite typically the amount in controversy is $2,000 or less in matters concerning contracts and torts.

[10]In some jurisdictions the judges rotate among the various divisions for prescribed periods of time instead of being permanently assigned to one division.

### 2. Appellate Courts

The losing party in a civil lawsuit in a court of general jurisdiction may always appeal the decision to an appellate court. In those states that have a two-tiered appellate system (similar to the federal system), most cases will have to be heard by the intermediate appellate court before appeal to the highest court is possible. State statutes usually articulate what types of cases are appealable directly to the highest court and which must first go to the immediate appellate court system.[11] A plaintiff in a car accident case concerning money damages for personal injuries sustained as a result of the accident who is dissatisfied with the decision rendered in the trial court (Court of Common Pleas), may appeal this decision to the Superior Court of Pennsylvania (intermediate appellate court) as a matter of right. Should this same plaintiff be dissatisfied with the decision of the Superior Court, he or she may seek review of this decision by filing a petition for allowance of appeal with the Pennsylvania Supreme Court (the highest court).[12] The Pennsylvania Supreme Court would then decide if it wishes to hear the case. In other words, the last level of appeal in this state is generally at the discretion of its highest court.

As mentioned earlier in this chapter, if the case involves federal rights, a party who wishes to appeal a state Supreme Court decision (or its equivalent in states other than Pennsylvania) may request that the U.S. Supreme Court hear the case. Absent some claim of violation of a federal right, the state's highest court is the final authority concerning all matters of state law and procedure.

One final point needs to be made before leaving the discussion of state appellate courts. State intermediate and highest appellate courts may also have original jurisdiction in certain kinds of cases. For instance, if a private citizen in Pennsylvania sues the state or a state public official, the litigation must be commenced in the Commonwealth Court of Pennsylvania (also an intermediate appellate court) instead of following the usual procedure in the Court of Common Pleas. In some states certain types of actions such as a Writ of Prohibition filed against a lower trial court judge would be instituted in the first level appellate court.

## C. Arbitrations

Another form of civil dispute resolution that may be provided by the federal and state trial courts is the system of **arbitration.** This is a system whereby parties litigate a civil dispute in front of a panel of lawyers (usually three lawyers) who render a decision. This procedure may be voluntary or involuntary depending on the court system involved. For example, by local rule in the United States District Court for the Eastern District of Pennsylvania, parties to civil actions for money damages filed in that district must have the case conducted before a panel of three arbitrators. Local Rule 8 provides that the amount in controversy

---

[11]An example of direct appeal might be a first-degree homicide conviction involving the imposition of a death sentence.
[12]In Pennsylvania this petition for allowance of appeal functions similarly to a petition for a writ of certiorari in the federal system.

(money damages) not exceed $75,000. Arbitrators are attorneys who have been in practice at least five years and who are admitted to practice in this federal court. Any party may appeal this decision and will be provided with a trial de novo in the district court. This is a relatively new procedure and has not been adopted by all the federal district courts; the Middle and Western Districts of Pennsylvania do not have a similar procedure.

In civil matters, Pennsylvania has adopted a system of compulsory arbitration whereby any lawsuit in which the amount in controversy is less than $20,000 in the larger counties and $10,000 in the smaller counties must be submitted to a board of three lawyers who are members of the bar of the court for decision. Again, any party may appeal this decision; this appeal is in the form of a trial de novo in the Court of Common Pleas. The statute authorizing this system is set out below:

### §7361. COMPULSORY ARBITRATION

a. General Rule—Except as provided in subsection (b), when prescribed by general rule or rule of court such civil matters or issues therein as shall be specified by rule shall first be submitted to and heard by a board of three members of the bar of the court.

b. Limitations—No matter shall be referred under subsection (a):

1. which involves title to real property; or

2. where the amount in controversy, exclusive of interest and costs, exceeds:

i. $20,000.00 in judicial districts embracing first, second, second class A, or third class counties or home rule charter would be a county of one of these classes; or

ii. $10,000.00 in any other judicial district.

c. Procedure—The arbitrators appointed pursuant to this section shall have such powers and shall proceed in such manner as shall be prescribed by general rules.

d. Appeal for trial de novo—Any party to a matter shall have the right to appeal for trial de novo in the court. The party who takes the appeal shall pay such amount or proportion of fees and costs and shall comply with such other procedures as shall be prescribed by general rules. In the absence of appeal then the judgment entered on the award of the arbitrators shall be enforced as any other judgment of the court. For the purposes of this section and section 5571 (relating to appeals generally) an award of arbitrators constitutes an order of a tribunal. [1976, July 9, P.L. 586, No. 142, §2, effective June 27, 1978. As amended 1980, April 6, P.L. 100, No. 38, §1, effective in 60 days.]

The philosophy underlying this type of dispute resolution system by the courts is an attempt to alleviate the tremendous backlogs that have occurred in the civil trial courts by providing a system whereby disputes can be handled in a more expeditious and informal basis. At the same time the courts are attempting to comport with notions of a fair hearing procedure by having lawyers conduct the hearing and guaranteeing a trial de novo appeal process in case a party is dissatisfied with the result of the arbitration process.

In addition to systems of compulsory arbitrations, the parties themselves may agree, either informally or by written contract, to voluntarily submit their dispute to a third party for resolution. This voluntary system is frequently used in labor/management, insurance, and construction disputes.

## II. Choosing the Proper Court

Because there are different state and federal legal systems in the United States, and so many different courts within the same legal system, it is important for the litigation paralegal to know in which court or courts a lawsuit may be commenced. The question of where a particular lawsuit may be filed is usually divided into two threshold questions: What court has jurisdiction over the subject matter and the parties to the lawsuit? What court has proper venue or geographical location to hear the lawsuit? The concepts of jurisdiction and venue will be discussed in more detail below. Certain practical considerations concerning the choice of court will also be discussed.

## A. Subject Matter Jurisdiction

A court that has jurisdiction over the subject matter of the litigation is authorized under the laws and constitution of the state (if it is a state court) or the laws and Constitution of the United States (if it is a federal court) to hear and resolve the dispute before it because of the nature of the claim, the parties involved, or the legal issues being raised. As stated earlier in this chapter, trial courts in the state systems are generally courts of general jurisdiction, that is, the presumption exists that the court can hear a case on any subject matter unless a statute exists, either on the state or federal level, to the contrary. In the federal court system, the opposite presumption exists, since it is a court of limited jurisdiction. That is, unless a statute exists that grants jurisdiction over the subject matter, it is presumed that the federal courts do not have the authority to hear and decide the case. Even in states in which courts are divided by subject matter (for example, family court, probate court), the assumption still exists that you can file your lawsuit in state court. The question then is, Which of the existing state courts is authorized to hear your case?

### 1. Exclusive or Concurrent Jurisdiction

In many instances, the fact that the federal courts have been granted the authority to hear certain cases does not negate the right of state courts to hear the same type of case. This concept of both federal and state courts having jurisdiction to resolve the same kind of dispute is known as **concurrent jurisdiction.**

An example of concurrent jurisdiction would be a case that involves a "federal question." The fact that such a case may be brought in federal court does not preclude the states from also hearing it. Unless stated otherwise in the federal statute, state courts have concurrent jurisdiction of actions even though they may be a result of a federal law. Thus, a plaintiff with a claim arising under federal law may elect to bypass the federal system and sue in a state court. In such an instance, the state court must apply the same federal law that the federal courts would have to follow.

Many federal claims may be heard only in the federal courts, however. Some federal statutes require that the action be brought only in the federal courts. This is known as **exclusive jurisdiction.** State courts may not entertain this type of case. Examples of such statutes are admiralty and federal security laws.

### 2. Removal from State Courts to Federal Courts

Where there is concurrent jurisdiction in both federal and state courts, the defendant may choose to litigate in the federal court, even though the plaintiff brought the action in the state court. The federal court's jurisdiction in this instance is called **removal jurisdiction** and is governed in part by the following sections of Title 28, Section 1441:

a. Except as otherwise expressly provided by Act of Congress, any civil action brought in a State court of which the district courts of the United States have original jurisdiction, may be removed by the defendant or the defendants, to the district court of the United States for the district and division embracing the place where such action is pending.

b. Any civil action of which the district courts have original jurisdiction founded on a claim or right arising under the Constitution, treaties or laws of the United States shall be removable without regard to the citizenship or residence of the parties. Any other such action shall be removable only if none of the parties in interest properly joined and served as defendants is a citizen of the State in which such action is brought.

c. Whenever a separate and independent claim or cause of action, which would be removable if sued upon alone, is joined with one or more otherwise non-removable claims or causes of action, the entire case may be removed and the district court may determine all issues therein, or, in its discretion, may remand all matters not otherwise within its original jurisdiction. [28 U.S.C.A. §1441.]

An action may be removed to federal court after its commencement in state court only when the action could originally have been brought in the federal court. The purpose of this statute is to afford the defendant the same option that a plaintiff has in selecting between state and federal forums.

If plaintiff, a citizen of Idaho, sues defendant, a citizen of Montana, in Idaho state court for $55,000, the action may be removed to the federal district court of Idaho upon petition of the defendant. The district court of Idaho had original jurisdiction to hear the case (diversity of citizenship and an amount in controversy exceeding $50,000). Note that removal is always to the federal district court in the locale where the state action was started.

Subsection (b) of the 28 U.S.C. §1441 makes an exception to the removal rule for causes of action that do not arise under federal law. In such instances a case may not be removed if any of the defendants are citizens of the state in which the action was brought.

## B. Jurisdiction over the Parties

Much of this chapter has dealt with the problem of subject matter jurisdiction, which relates to the right of a particular court to entertain different types of lawsuits. But an equally important aspect of jurisdiction is jurisdiction over the parties, or **personal jurisdiction.** Broadly speaking, this concept of jurisdiction deals with the circumstances under which a state or federal court may make a binding decision affecting the legal interests of a person. In this context, the term "person" includes entities, such as corporations and partnerships, which may be parties to a lawsuit.

The objective of the litigation process is the final resolution of controversies between parties. In order for the process to be effective, the parties must be bound by the outcome of the litigation. If the parties were not bound, the losing party could refuse to accept an unfavorable decision, and a losing plaintiff might start a new lawsuit or a losing defendant might refuse to pay a judgment ordered by the court.

### 1. Individual Defendants

Conceptually, there should be little difficulty in understanding why the plaintiff should be bound by the decision of a court. Having initiated the case and selected the court, the plaintiff is deemed to have consented to be bound by its decision, subject to the right of appeal. This rationale does not apply to the defendant, who is an involuntary participant in the case. If given the choice, no defendant would elect to be subject to the personal jurisdiction of a court and little, if any, litigation could take place.

To meet the problem of binding an unwilling defendant, the law developed the concept of personal jurisdiction over the defendant. To establish the personal jurisdiction of courts, certain rules have evolved. These rules, frequently in the form of statutes, deal with the issues of when, where, and under what circumstances a person may be made a party to a lawsuit and compelled to defend at the risk of being bound by an adverse decision.

The question of a court obtaining personal jurisdiction over a defendant is resolved, in part, by whether proper **service of process** may be made on the defendant. Service of process is the delivery of the document initiating a lawsuit (usually a "complaint") to the defendant. Service may also be made on someone either authorized directly by the defendant or presumed to have been authorized by the defendant by law to receive service on behalf of the defendant.

To illustrate, if a plaintiff wishes to sue a defendant, formal notification of the commencement of the action must be made. Under the federal rules, service of the complaint is now permitted by mailing it to the defendant and requesting that the defendant sign a written acknowledgment of receipt. If mailing cannot be successfully accomplished, private process servers or state officers, such as a sheriff or constable, must serve the complaint. The federal rules, and most states, also allow service to be made at the "domicile" or "place of abode" of the defendant by leaving a copy with a competent adult. The place of abode or domicile of any individual is one's regular, full-time place of residence—what a person considers to be his or her home.

Generally speaking, valid service of process may be made only within the geographical area where a court is empowered to act. Therefore, if an action is brought in the state courts of Georgia, service of process may be made only within the state of Georgia unless some statute allows for service outside the state. If no statute specifically authorizes service outside the state, service of process on a defendant outside of the state would not give a court power or jurisdiction over the defendant. These rules apply equally for the courts of all states and for the courts of the federal system as well.

### 2. Corporate Defendants

Corporations are "artificial persons" that for many purposes have the same rights and responsibilities as natural persons. They do not, however, have all the same rights as individuals. For example, they do not have the same constitutional protections as natural persons. They are bound by the corporate laws of the state that has allowed the particular corporation to have an existence by granting it a "charter." This is known as the state of incorporation. A corporation can be incorporated in only one state.

A corporation may always be served in its state of incorporation at the office it has designated. (One of the requirements in applying for a corporate charter is indicating a "registered office" in the state.) This office is analogous to an individual's place of abode.

Corporations that do business in more than one state normally get approval from the various states to do business there. This is known as being **licensed to do business** in a state (other than the state of incorporation), or "qualifying to do business" in a state. When qualifying or getting a license to operate in a state, a corporation must list an office in that state. Corporations chartered by one state that do business in other states are known as "foreign" corporations in all states other than the state of incorporation. A foreign corporation that is licensed to do business in a state must always be served with process at its registered office in that state because one of the requirements of qualifying to do business in a state is agreeing to submit to the jurisdiction of the state's court.

## C. Long-Arm Statutes

Under certain circumstances it is appropriate to give a court the power to adjudicate a dispute even if the defendant, whether an individual or corporation, is not present, domiciled, registered to do business, or incorporated in the state at the time the suit is commenced. Most states have passed **long-arm statutes,** so called because they operate figuratively to reach out and make nonresidents amenable to suits in states foreign to their presence or domicile. In other words, the long-arm statute reaches out beyond the state line and snags a defendant and brings him or her within the territory and power of its courts. An example of this situation is the nonresident motorist who is involved in an automobile accident while passing through a state. If the other party to the accident is a local resident, the issue presented is whether the local resident may sue in the state in which the accident occurred or whether suit must be brought in the state in which the nonresident lives. This issue has been resolved by legislation making such non-resident motorists subject to personal jurisdiction in the state in which the accident occurred.

In addition to nonresident motorist statutes, states also have long-arm statutes in the area of foreign corporations.[13] These corporations often do business in the state, even if they do not maintain an office or other place of business there. For example, a California insurance company may issue policies to residents of Iowa without having any place of business in Iowa or without qualifying to do business in Iowa. All transactions could take place by mail. Under a long-arm statute, service may be made on the foreign corporation by reason of the fact that it has done business within a state. The corporation has not qualified to do business but that is not necessary. The importance of the long-arm statute is that it makes the foreign corporation subject to personal jurisdiction of a state's courts without any voluntary action on the part of the corporation except the act of doing business in that state.

In most cases in which jurisdiction is based on a long-arm statute, process is served by mail. Though the exact procedures required to ensure proper and effective service vary from state to state, the plaintiff is usually required to mail a copy of the complaint or other process to a state official in the state in which the action is brought.

If a suit begun in the federal court is based on a long-arm statute, whereby the plaintiff brings the defendant to a district court in the plaintiff's state, the method of service of process is governed by the law of the state in which the district court is located (Rule 4(d)(7), Federal Rules of Civil Procedure).

In addition to the state requirements set out in long-arm statutes themselves, notions of personal jurisdiction over foreign or out-of-state defendants must comport with the United States Constitution's concept requiring a defendant to have minimum contact with a forum state (the state where a lawsuit is instituted), such that maintenance of a suit does not offend traditional notions of fair play and substantial justice. The requirement that defendants have "minimum contacts" acts to ensure that states, through their courts, do not reach beyond the limits imposed on them by their status as coequal sovereigns in a federal system[14]

## D. In Rem Jurisdiction (Jurisdiction over the Property)

In certain situations suit may be brought even though the defendant is beyond the reach of the court's process (even long-arm service) and personal jurisdiction does not exist. In lawsuits relating to the title or ownership of property located within a state, the presence of the property within the state is sufficient to give the court jurisdiction over the "res" or "thing." This type of jurisdiction is called **in rem jurisdiction,** meaning that only controversies with respect to the property within the state may be resolved by the decision. A judgment in rem affects the interests of all persons in a specified property.

A modified version of in rem jurisdiction is "quasi-in-rem" jurisdiction. It involves two types of cases: a plaintiff attempting to apply the property of a defendant to the satisfaction of a claim unrelated to the property; and a decision

---

[13]Many states have long-arm statutes for matters other than foreign corporations or nonresident operators of motor vehicles, planes, etc.

[14]See International Shoe Company v. Washington, 326 U.S. 310 (1945) and Hanson v. Denckla, 357 U.S. 235 (1958).

resolving conflicting claims to a specified property (for example, lawsuits to quiet title to property).[15]

When an action is started by means of in rem jurisdiction, notice of the action is served on the defendant by mail. If, however, the whereabouts of the defendant are unknown, notice may be given by putting a notice on the property (called posting) and/or by placing an advertisement in newspapers of general circulation in the area where the property is located, in addition to attempting service by mail.

## E. Venue

**Venue,** which focuses on the question of where within the state or in what district within the federal system the action should be heard, is related to jurisdiction. The concept of jurisdiction is designed to deal with the problem of whether a court has the authority to entertain a lawsuit and render a binding decision over the parties. Venue, on the other hand, deals with the place of trial within a given state of the federal system and is designed to ensure that the action is brought in the location that will cause all the parties and especially the defendant the minimum inconvenience. By way of an example of the difference between jurisdiction and venue, assume the following: a breach of contract case in which the plaintiff resides in Philadelphia, Pennsylvania (Philadelphia County), the defendant resides in Allentown, Pennsylvania (Lehigh County), and the cause of action arose in Norristown, Pennsylvania (Montgomery County). Jurisdiction over the subject matter would be in the Pennsylvania Court of Common Pleas (trial court of general jurisdiction); jurisdiction over the person would be where service of process could be had over the defendant, which is Lehigh County, venue would be either where the defendant resides (Lehigh County) or where the cause of action arose (Montgomery County). To simplify matters, jurisdiction determines that the case can be brought in the Court of Common Pleas. Venue determines which County Court of Common Pleas can be used.

Normally, the plaintiff picks the place of trial (venue) by reference to statutes and court rules. As an example, a portion of the Federal Venue Statute is set out below. The plaintiff should always try to find a district or county where both personal jurisdiction and venue may be satisfied (assuming, of course, that subject matter jurisdiction already exists).

### TITLE 28 SECTION 1391

§ 1391. Venue generally

a. A civil action wherein jurisdiction is founded only on diversity of citizenship may, except as otherwise provided by law, be brought only in the judicial district where all plaintiffs or all defendants reside, or in which the claim arose.

b. A civil action wherein jurisdiction is not founded solely on diversity of citizenship may be brought only in the judicial district where all defendants reside, or in which the claim arose, except as otherwise provided by law.

---

[15]McLaughin and Mark, "Recent Trends in Personal Jurisdiction," *ALI-ABA Resource Materials, Civil Practice and Litigation in Federal and State Courts* (1982), p. 4.

c. For purposes of venue under this chapter, a defendant that is a corporation shall be deemed to reside in any judicial district in which it is subject to personal jurisdiction at the time the action is commenced. In a State which has more than one judicial district and in which a defendant that is a corporation is subject to personal jurisdiction at the time an action is commenced, such corporation shall be deemed to reside in any district in that State within which its contacts would be sufficient to subject it to personal jurisdiction if that district were a separate State, and, if there is no such district, the corporation shall be deemed to reside in the district within which it has the most significant contacts.

d. An alien may be sued in any district.

e. A civil action in which a defendant is an officer or employee of the United States or any agency thereof acting in his official capacity or under color of legal authority, or an agency of the United States, or the United States, may, except as otherwise provided by law, be brought in any judicial district in which (1) a defendant in the action resides, or (2) the cause of action arose, or (3) any real property involved in the action is situated, or (4) the plaintiff resides if no real property is involved in the action. Additional persons may be joined as parties to any such action in accordance with the Federal Rules of Civil Procedure and with such other venue requirements as would be applicable if the United States or one of its officers, employees, or agencies were not a party.

The summons and complaint in such an action shall be served as provided by the Federal Rules of Civil Procedure except that the delivery of the summons and complaint to the officer or agency as required by the rules may be made by certified mail beyond the territorial limits of the district in which the action is brought.

f. A civil action against a foreign state as defined in section 1603(a) of this title may be brought—

1. in any judicial district in which a substantial part of the events or omissions giving rise to the claim occurred, or a substantial part of property that is the subject of the action is situated;

2. in any judicial district in which the vessel or cargo of a foreign state is situated, if the claim is asserted under section 1605(b) of this title;

3. in any judicial district in which the agency or instrumentality is licensed to do business or is doing business, if the action is brought against an agency or instrumentality of a foreign state as defined in section 1603(b) of this title; or

4. in the United States District Court for the District of Columbia if the action is brought against a foreign state or political subdivision thereof.

A party (most likely a defendant) may consent to litigate in a district or county where venue is not otherwise proper. Also, if none of the involved parties objects to an improper venue, the defect of improper venue is waived or lost. Further, parties may also consent to personal jurisdiction where none exists. In contrast, subject-matter jurisdiction is not amenable to the will of the parties.

## F. Other Considerations

In addition to the questions of jurisdiction and venue with respect to the choice of court, there are other very real practical factors that should be considered in making this determination.

Normally the plaintiff must initially pick the court in which to institute a civil lawsuit. When there is a choice of courts, part of the plaintiff's determination should include the following factors:

Court delays and backlogs in bringing civil cases to trial

Size and composition of juries

Special pleading requirements

Judge(s) most likely to be assigned to the case

Differences in rules of evidence

Differences in rules of procedure

Local customs

Size of jury awards

Procedure of appeal

Personal convenience for witnesses, parties, and counsel

Although this list is not exhaustive, it does highlight some of the major factors that a plaintiff should consider before filing a lawsuit.

If you are a defendant, obviously your choices are more limited. Unless the plaintiff has made an error in judgment with respect to jurisdiction or venue, the main option available to you is to remove the case from state to federal court, if applicable, under the removal statute previously discussed. Another available option, assuming the case is already in federal court, is that even when a case is filed in a court of proper venue, a defendant may file a motion to transfer the case to another federal district court that is a more convenient forum.[16]

## III. Summary

All court systems are divided into two kinds of courts: trial courts and appellate courts. Trial courts hear the disputes initially. Appellate courts review the decisions of trial courts to ensure the parties received a fair trial.

The federal court system has three tiers. In order to invoke the authority of the federal courts, there must be subject-matter jurisdiction. The main categories of federal jurisdiction are federal questions and diversity of citizenship.

The three tiers of the federal system are district court, court of appeals, and Supreme Court. The district court is where the trial takes place. The court of appeals has solely an appellate function and reviews the decisions of the district

---

[16]See Title 28 U.S.C §1404(a), which authorizes these transfers under the doctrine of forum non conveniens. See also Title 42 Pa.C.S. §5103, §5106 and PRCP 1006(d).

court. The Supreme Court has primarily an appellate function and reviews the decisions of the courts of appeals and highest courts of a state. In exercising its appellate function, the Supreme Court can decide which cases it wishes to hear based on the writ of certiorari.

State courts are organized similarly to the federal courts. However, state trial courts are usually courts of general jurisdiction. Depending on the size of the state, a state court system can be two- or three-tiered. If a question of federal rights is involved, a party who wishes to appeal a decision of the highest state court may request the U.S. Supreme Court to hear the appeal.

Arbitration is a form of dispute resolution that can be voluntary or compulsory. Voluntary systems are based on the agreement of the parties and typically are found in contracts. Compulsory systems are imposed by courts as a way of diverting cases from requiring judges and juries as the sole method of resolution.

A plaintiff must understand various concepts in selecting the system and court. Subject-matter jurisdiction determines whether a court can hear and determine a specific type of case. Personal jurisdiction determines whether a court can bind a defendant to its decision. In rem jurisdiction determines whether a court can determine a case based on where the property (which is the subject matter of the suit) is located. Venue determines where within a court system is the proper court for hearing a case. Although the plaintiff can generally pick the place of trial and system, the defendant can remove a case from state court to federal court where there is concurrent jurisdiction.

---

## IV. Key Terms

Appeal as of right
Appellate courts
Arbitration
Circuit
Concurrent
    jurisdiction
Court of general
    jurisdiction
District
Diversity of
    citizenship
    jurisdiction

Exclusive jurisdiction
Federal question
    jurisdiction
In rem jurisdiction
Inferior
Licensed to do
    business
Limited jurisdiction
Long-arm statute
Original jurisdiction
Personal jurisdiction

Quasi-in-rem
    jurisdiction
Removal jurisdiction
Service of process
Subject matter
    jurisdiction
Trial courts
Trial de novo
Venue
Writ of certiorari

## V. Questions

1. Define and distinguish the roles of trial courts and appellate courts.
2. What is the name of the court of general jurisdiction in your state?
3. What is the trial court in the federal system?
4. What is meant by the concept that a court has limited jurisdiction?
5. What is the intermediate court in the federal court system? Define its jurisdiction.

6. Give examples of the different ways a case can reach the U.S. Supreme Court.
7. Name the appellate courts in your state and define their jurisdiction.
8. What is the difference between exclusive and concurrent jurisdiction?
9. Compare and contrast jurisdiction-over-the-parties (personal jurisdiction) with venue.
10. Why have states enacted long-arm statutes?
11. What is the difference between a voluntary system of arbitration and a compulsory system?
12. Define the method by which judges are selected in your state.
13. Using the federal venue statute provided in this chapter provide the options a plaintiff has with respect to choosing a court:
    (a) A citizen of Ohio has an auto accident with a citizen of Oklahoma in Nevada and suffers damages in excess of $75,000.
    (b) A citizen of Oregon has an auto accident with a citizen of Texas in New Orleans, Louisiana, and suffers damages in the amount of $25,000.
    (c) A citizen of Pennsylvania has an auto accident with another citizen of Pennsylvania in New Jersey and suffers damages in excess of $100,000.
    (d) A New Jersey corporation enters into a contract with a California corporation to build a commercial development in Arizona. A breach of contract took place in Arizona and the amount in controversy is $45,000.
14. A plaintiff files a lawsuit in the circuit court of St. Louis County, Missouri. Plaintiff is from St. Louis. The defendant is a citizen of Illinois. The lawsuit is based on an auto accident and the amount requested is $75,000. What are the defendant's options with respect to the proper court?

# CHAPTER 3

# LEGAL INTERVIEWING

## I. INTRODUCTION

The focus of this chapter is to examine the role of the paralegal in the process of gathering initial information from the client. Paralegals can and often do play an important role in doing the initial client interview. The information in this chapter will help the paralegal gain insight into the dynamics of the interviewing process and develop skills in questioning techniques.

## II. LEGAL INTERVIEWING

**Legal interviewing** as used in this chapter refers to the paralegal's interaction with a client for the purpose of identifying the client's problem, and for the purpose of gathering a sufficient amount of information on which a solution to that problem can be based. Interviewing in the civil litigation context usually involves gathering factual data concerning the following: the nature of the client's problem, the client's legal position, and the assessment of the chances of success of adopting litigation as a strategy to resolve the problem.[1] Depending on the complexity of the case, the paralegal may or may not be directly involved in conducting the interview.

Although the subject of legal interviewing has only recently begun to be taught in the law school education curriculum (usually in the context of a clinical program centered on the study of lawyering), numerous articles and books address the many issues that can arise in this initial process of gathering information from a client. It is far beyond the scope of this chapter to address all the issues that can or should be discussed in this context. Instead, we will highlight only a few of the major issues.

Although at times legal interviewing appears to be instinctual, intuitive, and dependent on one's interpersonal dynamics, it is actually a skill to be learned and developed. In order to be successful at this craft, a paralegal needs to develop a relationship with the client that facilitates the flow of information necessary to understand the client's problem and to perhaps eventually resolve the client's situation. There are certain tools or techniques that a paralegal can use to help in this process of gathering information, such as questioning techniques and active and passive listening techniques.

Basic to the discussion of interviewing is the issue of communication. Communication can be both verbal and nonverbal (gestures, proximics, and so on). In addition, communication in a legal interview setting can be both content laden and emotion laden. A client who has been "traumatized" by some prior incident (which may be the basis for using a lawyer's services) will very rarely convey direct information concerning this prior event without interjecting emotions or feelings. Therefore, in developing strategies for facilitating this information flow, a paralegal must recognize the importance of both nonverbal

---

[1]See Binder and Price, *Legal Interviewing and Counseling* (St. Paul, West Publishing Co., 1977), p. 5. This book is highly recommended for readers interested in studying a model for a client-centered approach to legal interviewing.

communication and feelings exhibited by the client. The failure to identify and somehow acknowledge the importance of the client's emotions, displayed either verbally or nonverbally, can act as a barrier to effective communication with the client.

Before engaging in legal interviewing, paralegals should define the role they wish to assume during the course of the interview. Just as an interviewer assesses the information he or she receives both with respect to content and the manner in which it is conveyed, so too will the client engage in a similar process of assessing the interviewer. Since the legal interviewer usually controls the setting for the interview, he or she give thought to such things as seating arrangements, appearance, demeanor, furniture, and decorations with respect to creating an atmosphere that is consistent with the role or message that the paralegal wishes to convey. Also, the paralegal should consider the impact such a setting is likely to have on the client. Obviously, the more uncomfortable a client feels during the interview, the more likely this discomfort will act as a barrier to information gathering. In addition to creating a comfortable physical setting, the paralegal should communicate on a verbal level that is comfortable to the client.

The paralegal has two central goals when conducting an initial client interview. The first goal is to gather enough information to identify the client's problem, identify legal issues inherent in the client's problem, and begin to identify other sources of information that may either prove or disprove the client's version of events. The second goal is the development of a working relationship between the interviewer and the client in which both parties feel comfortable. This goal is often called establishing rapport (trust and confidence). These two goals overlap and are not mutually exclusive. In other words, gathering information from a client should be done in such a way that maximizes the flow of quality information and establishes mutual respect, confidence, and trust between paralegal and client.

Before learning some of the actual techniques that a paralegal can use in interviewing, consider this word of caution: Although theoretical and practical interviewing models of behavior can be presented in textbooks, these models are not a substitute for experiential learning. Through the process of experience, skilled interviewers learn that no one model of behavior works in the variety of situations that can arise during client interviews. In fact, one of the most challenging aspects of interviewing is for the interviewer to learn how to adjust his or her style to meet the immediate needs dictated by a new situation. Therefore the maxims articulated here should be taken as merely an expression of some possible techniques available to the paralegal as the situation warrants and as defined by the interplay between paralegal and client.

## A. Questioning Techniques

As part of the process of obtaining full and complete information from a client, an interviewer will have to use a variety of different questioning techniques. The way you ask a question affects the way the client will answer it. Questions can be classified in terms of the breadth of information they seek to elicit. There are basically four different categories of questions: open-ended questions, leading questions, yes/no questions, and narrow questions.[2] Each form of question and its advantages and disadvantages will be discussed in the following paragraphs.

### 1. Open-Ended Questions

**Open-ended questions** are ones in which the client selects the subject matter or information for discussion.[3] Examples of open-ended questions are:

What is the nature of your problem?

How are you today?

Clients can choose to respond to these questions in their own way without the form of the questions narrowing such topics as time, place, or subject. The advantages of this form of question are that clients are permitted to tell their stories in their own words without any or much interruption, they can select the topics of importance to them, and they may feel more comfortable initially in an interview after they have had a chance to "unload" their problem. On the other hand, there are some disadvantages associated with this form of question: clients might leave out specific important details, clients who are initially reluctant to talk might become more uncomfortable, and clients can become unfocused, ramble, or provide far too much detail on relatively minor points.

### 2. Narrow Questions

**Narrow questions** can be contrasted with open-ended questions in that they not only select the subject matter, but also can select specific aspects of the subject matter to be discussed. An interviewer asking narrow questions must determine what information is important. Examples of narrow questions are:

On what corner did the accident occur last Sunday?

Who was present in the room when the plaintiff fell down?

As you will note in both examples, the questions restrict possible responses to very narrow issues. In the first example, the event, the date, and the general location are all restricted. In the second example, the event and the location are restricted. The major advantage of narrow questions is that they elicit detail by focusing the client on a specific topic. The major disadvantages are that when the interviewer chooses specific topics clients may not discuss important items because they feel that the interviewer does not think they are important, and clients may feel they are being cut off by the interviewer's use of narrow questions.

### 3. Yes/No Questions

Obviously, **yes/no questions** are framed in such a manner that the response calls for a simple yes or no. Examples include:

---

[2]Binder and Price, p. 38–40.
[3]Binder and Price, p. 38.

Did you go to work Tuesday?

Have you ever been to St. Louis in the summer?

Yes/no questions are narrow questions. In addition they are very similar to leading questions (which will be discussed next) except that the response is not suggested by the question.

### 4. Leading Questions

**Leading questions** are very narrow questions that call for a yes or no response, and suggest the desired response. This is the most narrow type of question an interviewer can ask. Examples are:

You were late for work today, weren't you?

He drove the car through the stop sign, isn't that correct?

In both examples, the suggested response is yes. The major disadvantage of this form of question is that it does not accurately test the validity of the response and presents a danger of distortion. Also, the form of question tends to verify that which you may already assume rather than being a useful tool to elicit new information. The major advantage is that it may elicit information from a client that the client would be otherwise reluctant to discuss.

During the course of an interview, a skilled interviewer will use both open-ended and narrow questions. Rarely will an interview in a legal setting consist of only one form of question. It is the ability to ask the appropriate form of question for the type of information that is needed that separates the skilled interviewer from the novice.

## B. Listening Techniques

Although most novice interviewers concentrate on questioning techniques, they also must develop listening techniques. In addition to ensuring that the interviewer hears and comprehends what has been conveyed by the client, listening techniques can provide the client with the motivation to provide full and complete information.[4] Listening techniques usually fall within two categories: passive listening and active listening.

**Passive listening techniques** are used primarily to encourage a client to keep talking. For instance, silence that creates a pause may be a strong motivator for the client to continue with his or her story. Noncommittal responses such as "please continue," "I see," or "Mm-hmm" indicate that the interviewer is listening.[5] Even an affirmative head nod can be used as a passive listening technique.

**Active listening** is when the interviewer reflects back what the client has said.[6] It is not simply a process of repeating, but rather a manner of communi-

---

[4]Binder and Price, p. 21.
[5]Binder and Price, p. 24.
[6]Binder and Price, p. 25.

cating back to the client the essence of what the interviewer hears.[7] Active listening demonstrates that the listener understands what has been said by the client, while passive listening only implies that the interviewer hears and understands. It is often reassuring for a client to hear a short summary of the thoughts he or she has just conveyed, indicating that the interviewer understands. This valuable technique not only enhances the flow of information but also is quite helpful in developing rapport.

## C. Models of Interviewing

Although there is a wide body of literature concerning interviewing, there are surprisingly few books or articles that suggest a concrete model of legal interviewing. Some authors suggest either "do's or don'ts" or checklists for eliciting information relevant to a particular legal subject matter.[8] Others provide a theoretical basis for understanding the interpersonal dynamics involved in the legal interview process. However, as the novice paralegal approaches that first legal interview, it is helpful to have some idea how to structure the interview. One such model is provided in *Legal Interviewing and Counseling,* by Binder and Price. Although the authors are writing about law students or lawyers conducting an interview with a client, the model is equally applicable to the paralegal.

In their book, Binder and Price provide a three-stage model of a client interview, some of which is excerpted below.[9]

> The lawyer–client dialogue typically begins with the lawyer attempting to gain a preliminary understanding of the client's problem. The lawyer's goal is to determine in a general way what relief the client seeks and what concerns the client faces. When the client's problem has been preliminarily identified, the lawyer usually proceeds to gather information about the client's legal position. Before there can be any meaningful discussion of what alternatives are available to solve the client's problem, there must usually be at least a tentative determination of the client's legal position.

### A Three-Staged Interview

> There are undoubtedly several ways of approaching the task of ascertaining the client's problem and legal position. What we will describe is a general approach we have found to be useful. Under this approach, the process of ascertaining the client's problem and legal position is divided into three stages: (1) Preliminary Problem Identification, (2) Chronological Overview and (3) Theory Development and Verification. [A case may require one or more interviews for the lawyer to complete these three stages.]

> ***Preliminary Problem Identification Stage.*** In the Preliminary Problem Identification stage, the lawyer asks the client to provide a general

---

[7]Binder and Price, p. 25.
[8]More information on the usefulness of checklists will be provided later in this chapter.
[9]Binder and Price, ch. 5.

description of at least the following: (1) the underlying transaction that caused the problem, and (2) the relief the client desires. During this stage, the lawyer encourages the client to describe the foregoing matters in whatever way seems comfortable. The lawyer refrains from imposing any particular order on the client's presentation and allows the client to proceed in a free-flowing narrative. The lawyer asks only for a general description and refrains from asking for any details.

*Chronological Overview Stage.*    During the Chronological Overview stage, the client is encouraged to provide a step-by-step chronological narrative of the past transaction which underlies the client's problem. The client is asked to proceed from the point where the client believes the problem began, and follow through, step-by-step, up to the present. During the Overview, the lawyer does not attempt to obtain a detailed elaboration of the various points mentioned by the client during the chronological narration.

*Theory Development and Verification Stage.*    At the conclusion of the Overview stage, the lawyer mentally reviews the entire story to determine what potential causes of action and potential defenses are possibly applicable. Using his/her knowledge of the substantive law, the lawyer consciously asks himself/herself, "What are all of the possible legal theories that are potentially applicable given this factual situation?"

When this tentative diagnosis has been made, the lawyer commences the Theory Development and Verification stage. Here the lawyer conducts a detailed examination to determine how many of the potentially applicable causes of action and defenses actually seem viable. The examination, as it relates to any particular theory, attempts to determine whether or not there are facts which will establish the existence of each of the substantive elements needed to invoke the causes of action and defenses which the lawyer has seen as potentially applicable. Thus, if one cause of action seen as potentially applicable is that of breach of contract, the lawyer's inquiry will be devoted to determining in detail whether or not there are facts to establish: (1) the making of an agreement, (2) performance by the plaintiff, (3) breach by the defendant, and (4) damages.

The Theory Development and Verification stage is a phase devoted to *exploring consciously* in *a systematic manner,* whether or not the specific legal theories suggested by the Overview are indeed viable. It is a stage which is begun with several tentative diagnoses, and carried out with a goal of verifying, refining, and perhaps rejecting and replacing these diagnoses.

## The Purpose of the Three-Staged Interview: The Problem of Premature Diagnosis.

Why divide the process of ascertaining the client's problem and legal position into three stages? The purpose of the division is to increase the thoroughness with which cases are analyzed by encouraging lawyers not to prematurely decide what the client's problem is, and what should be done to solve it.

In legal interviewing, it is very common for lawyers to analyze cases on the basis of inadequate information. One common omission involves the lawyer's failure to make an initial inquiry about what relief the client desires to obtain. On hearing the client's initial description of his/her problem, the lawyer fails to inquire about what the client wants done. Rather, the lawyer assumes he/she knows what relief the client desires. Armed with this assumption, the lawyer proceeds to ask the client for information that would be needed in order to bring about the assumed desired result. The questioning, however, often turns out to be largely a waste of time since the information obtained is irrelevant in terms of the relief the client actually desires.

## Techniques for Conducting the Three-Staged Interview

*The Preliminary Problem Identification Stage.*   The process of Preliminary Problem Identification is usually begun with open-ended questions calling for a narrative description of the client's situation. Questions such as the following are typical:

"How can I help you?"

"What brings you here today?"

"What can I do for you?"

These open-ended questions leave the client free to set forth his/her dilemma in any manner which feels comfortable, and in as much detail as seems appropriate. The questions do not, however, explicitly suggest that the lawyer is interested in obtaining a general description of the past transaction which underlies the problem, and the relief which the client desires. To encourage the client to include each of these factors in the description, it is sometimes useful to provide a structural guide which outlines the information the lawyer desires. A structural guide can be worked somewhat as follows:

"Give me a brief description of your problem, how it arose, and what solutions you hope to find."

"Tell me what your problem is, how it came about, and what you think you'd like to have done about it."

Such guides can be inserted into the dialogue either immediately after the initial open-ended questions, or after receiving the client's initial reply.

*Chronological Overview Stage.*   The principal form of question used during the Overview is an open-ended question which encourages the client to continue the narration. Thus, a typical question is one such as, "What happened next?" The use of the term "next" suggests the client proceed with the story in chronological sequence but in all other respects the question is open-ended. The client is left free to describe the incident in any way the client sees fit. Thus, the client can state what he or she observed, felt, thought, etc.

Given the purposes of the Overview and the restrictions against detailed probing, this form of question seems quite appropriate as the chief form of interrogatory. The question attempts to keep the client focused along a chronological track, and hopefully minimizes risks of interrupting normal paths of association. Additionally, the question permits the client to use his/her sense of relevancy without being confined in any way to what the lawyer may see as potentially relevant. This form of questioning gives the client an opportunity to provide clues that might be lost if the lawyer were to try to discover all significant facts through a series of narrowly focused questions. As will be repeatedly noted in this chapter, the lawyer will not have the capacity to develop all the facts concerning a particular transaction by sitting back and thinking about how such an event might have occurred, and then asking, did this, that, and the next thing happen. There will almost always be too many factual possibilities for the lawyer to be able to think of every one of them.

*Theory Development and Verification Stage.* The objective of the Theory Development and Verification Stage is to conduct an investigation which will reveal what legal theories can reasonably be relied upon to provide the client with legal relief. To accomplish this objective, the lawyer should undertake at least two tasks. There should be an endeavor to determine (1) what legal theories are possibly applicable, and (2) which of the possibly applicable theories are potentially viable.

Why the distinction between possibly applicable and potentially viable? As noted earlier, one of the major defects that occur in legal interviewing is premature diagnosis. The lawyer recognizes facts which suggest the possible applicability of one or two theories, investigates these, and concludes the inquiry. The lawyer fails to look into theories other than those that immediately "leap to mind." If the lawyer can learn to think of Theory Development and Verification as requiring, first of all, an effort to see how many theories might be applicable before trying to determine which are viable, then the likelihood of premature diagnosis may be reduced.

Determining what theories may possibly be applicable requires a very specific focus. At the conclusion of the Overview stage, the lawyer must consciously ask, "Given these facts and what I know of the client's desires and concerns, what legal theories, regardless of how weak or strong they may now appear, might entitle my client to the relief he/she seeks?" Certain causes of action or defenses will perhaps be obvious, but the lawyer's mental effort must be geared toward the development of the maximum number of possibilities. Critical to the success of this endeavor will be the lawyer's knowledge of the substantive law; the more substantive knowledge the lawyer has in his/her head, the more successful the lawyer will be in executing this task.

What about the situation where the lawyer, for one reason or another, has little or no substantive knowledge of the legal theories that are potentially relevant? [By our definition, a lawyer has substantive knowledge of a legal theory when the lawyer has general familiarity with the basic substantive elements of the cause of action or defense involved.] Where the lawyer lacks adequate substantive knowledge the available choices seem to be: (1) adjourn the meeting and research the law; (2) go back through the Overview to learn more detail about the story in general since the additional detail might aid subsequent research; (3) refer the client to another lawyer or associate counsel who is familiar with the area. Which option the lawyer should choose is dependent upon many factors, but time will not permit an analysis of these factors here. What must be noted, however, is that if the client appears to need immediate help, the latter choice will probably be called for.

If the lawyer had knowledge of some, but only a limited number of, causes of action or defenses, an additional option is available. The choice is: (4) investigate the theories with which the lawyer has familiarity, deferring until later investigation of those theories which require legal research. Indeed, this choice might be combined with option number 2, a general review for more facts. Again, time will not permit an analysis of what factors should be considered in reaching a decision. What is important to remember is that the decision should be made in the client's best interest.

Finally, it must be remembered that any diagnosis of which theories are possibly applicable must be considered tentative. During the Theory Development and Verification stage, the lawyer may come upon information suggesting that the initial theories are invalid, but additional legal theories are possibly applicable.

The reader should keep in mind that the above-mentioned model is just that, a model. As paralegals develop more confidence and skill in the interview setting, they will develop their own style, which may not conform to this model but may still be effective. In addition, due to interview time constraints, paralegals may not have the amount of time necessary to adopt this three-layered approach. Instead, a skilled interviewer can combine the chronological overview stage with the theory development and verification stage in order to save time.

## D. Specific Interview Issues

### 1. Identifying Yourself as a Paralegal

At the beginning of an initial interview with a client, the paralegal must identify him- or herself. This is important for two reasons: one, the client understands that the paralegal is not a lawyer;[10] and two, the client is given the option to discuss the problem with the paralegal's supervising attorney, should the client make such a request. Although most clients come to a law office and expect to meet with an attorney, a skilled and confident paralegal should have little or no problem handling the situation. The paralegal should take a positive approach in describing his or her role. If the paralegal describes this role in the negative, such as "I am not a lawyer," instead of the positive, such as "I am a trained or certified legal assistant," the client is more likely to resist. Keep in mind that the client is most likely looking for assistance, so that as long as the paralegal seems confident in his or her role of providing help, the client will, in most situations, be satisfied.

### 2. Fees

Depending on the structure of the law office and the responsibility delegated by the lawyer to the paralegal, the paralegal may have to discuss the issue of fee for services rendered during the interview. Fees generally take one of three different forms:

- Flat fees for discreet services rendered (for example, $150 to provide representation at a small claims hearing)

- Hourly rate fees (based on a set amount per hour and number of hours worked on the case)

- Contingent fees (based on an agreed-upon percentage of recovery in a case)

---

[10]This avoids problems concerning the authorized and unauthorized practice of law under the Code of Professional Responsibility.

In the context of civil litigation, any one of these three forms (or combinations of the three) can be used. Normally, the supervising attorney will set the fee structure that the paralegal uses in the initial interview.

It is important to remember that when the paralegal has the responsibility to discuss fees, he or she should take the initiative in the interview to raise this issue. No client should leave an interview without an understanding of how much it is going to cost to use the services of the law firm. Also, depending on the fee arrangement, certain forms will have to be prepared and executed by the client. More information will be provided on this later in the chapter.

### 3. Ending the Interview

Given the time constraints involved in the operation of a busy office, initial interviews cannot go on indefinitely. Normally, paralegals and lawyers allot time periods ranging from forty-five minutes to one hour for initial interviews. This time allotment system provides a systematic way of scheduling appointments. In addition, interviewer and client attention spans may dwindle the longer an interview continues. Therefore, the paralegal must learn to develop an approach for ending an interview without offending a client. Sometimes it is quite helpful to tell the client at the outset of the interview how much time has been allotted. Then the client will not be surprised later in the interview when the paralegal has to terminate the meeting. Keep in mind that subsequent meetings can be arranged to gather more information and discuss the client's concerns in more detail.

Certain tasks should be performed before the initial interview is ended. Documents, such as retainer agreements, authorization forms, and take-home questionnaires, need to be discussed and prepared. In addition, the paralegal should inform the client as to what future action the paralegal will be taking and should set a time, if possible, when they will discuss the matter again. Also, if the paralegal needs more information from the client, such as documents the client did not bring to the interview, he or she should assign the client the responsibility of providing that additional information to the paralegal, also within a certain time frame if possible.

### 4. Note Taking

Information gathered during an interview will not be of much value unless it is somehow recorded by the interviewer. If the interviewer doesn't take notes during the interview, important information may get lost. However, if the paralegal is too busy taking notes during an interview, the client may feel that the interviewer is more concerned with taking notes than with dealing with him or her as a person.[11] Here are a few suggestions with respect to note taking.[12]

- Explain to the client that you will be taking notes during interview, and explain the purpose of taking notes.

---

[11] Interviewers who constantly look down at their notepaper lose eye contact with their clients. This lack of eye contact can act as a negative barrier to establishing rapport with the client.
[12] Binder and Price, p. 77.

◆ Unless there is a specific need for recording detailed information, write down key words and dates that will serve as a reminder of what was communicated (try not to write full sentences).

◆ Shortly after the client has left, prepare a detailed memo of the facts (if you wait too long, you will forget the details).

Other forms of information recording include video-recording or audio-recording interviews. Make sure the client understands that you are using these recording methods and consents to their use.[13] These methods of tape recording can be very useful in preparing comprehensive notes, analyzing the client's behavior during the interview, and in self-critiquing your own performance in the interview.

## E. Using Checklists and Preparing Documents

Checklists can play a very important role in the initial interview. They provide any easy way to record information and serve as a way of ensuring that all relevant lines of inquiry will be developed concerning specific legal issues. They can help ensure that inexperienced paralegals will obtain useful information on which to assess and develop the client's case.

However, learning to interview clients based on checklists can be dangerous. Checklists should not be used as a crutch during the interview process. A paralegal who cannot interview a client without a checklist doesn't have good interviewing skills, and the checklist will not make up for that deficiency.

Exhibits 3.1 and 3.2 are examples of different approaches to checklists for a personal injury case.

**EXHIBIT 3.1**

## Interview Form

Interviewer:

REPORT—INTERVIEW FORM

NAME:                              DATE OF ACCIDENT:
PARENTS OR SPOUSE:                 TIME:
HOME ADDRESS:    Tel. No.          PLACE:
BUSINESS ADDRESS:  Tel. No.

AID OF POLICE REPORT:

NATURE OF ACCIDENT:                WHERE LOCATED:
Employer (School):                 Date of Birth:
Address:                           Place:
Occupation:                        Marital Status:
Earnings:                          Social Sec. No.:
Time Lost:                         V.A. or Military Coverage

---

[13]A written consent form should be prepared and signed by the client authorizing the use of the electronic recording device.

---
**EXHIBIT 3.1**
## Interview Form (continued)
---

No.:WEATHER:                          STREET CONDITIONS:
Name, address, tel. no., and relationship of person(s) to contact:
PLAINTIFF VEHICLE:  Make:  Model:  Year:  Damage:  Repairer:
         Tag No:     Serial No.     Color     Present Location
INSURANCE COVERAGE FOR CLIENT:       Liability
Collision (deductible amount)              Med. Pay.              U.M.C.
Blue Cross No.              Blue Shield No.              Union Benefits
Employment Benefits (incl. sick time)
Accident Ins.                   Other:
DEFENDANT: NAME              ADDRESS              Tel. No.
DRIVER OR OTHER DEFENDANTS:
DEFENDANT VEHICLE: Make    Model    Year    Color    Tag No.
   Deft. Vehicle Damage                   Other Info.
   Defendant's Injuries          Persons in deft. vehicle & injuries if any
PLAINTIFF'S INJURIES: Nature of Injuries:         Unconsciousness?
Hospital:         X-rays:         Admitted:         Out-Patient:
(Include dates)
Physician at Hospital:  Address:    Tel. No.:
Private Physician:     Address:    Tel. No.:
Date of First Visit     No. of Visits    Regular Physician
PREVIOUS MEDICAL HISTORY       PREVIOUS ACCIDENTS
WITNESSES: Names    Address    Tel. No.    What Witness Knows

---
**EXHIBIT 3.2**
## Interview Outline
---

## INFORMATION CONCERNING NEGLIGENT ACT

In a personal injury case, the facts of the occurrence giving rise to the claim should be discussed fully and carefully. It may be sufficient for purposes of drafting a complaint to know only that the client fell on a slippery ice patch in front of the defendant's home. In order to make full use of witnesses, outside sources of information, requests for admission of facts and interrogatories, however, the lawyer must know all of the operative facts of the occurrence. For example, if the client was injured in an automobile accident, the lawyer should know the departure time, route of travel, intended destination, lanes of travel, speeds, positions of passengers, locations of traffic signals, point of impact, nature of surrounding buildings and terrain,

EXHIBIT 3.2
## Interview Outline (continued)

location of vehicles after impact, and all statements at the accident scene by any and all persons. No fact should be considered too insignificant to note or examine. Even if a fact appears irrelevant to the effective presentation of the client's case, it might later become crucial for purposes of impeachment of the testimony of opposing witnesses or the opposing party or for purposes of corroboration of the client's or witnesses' testimonies. The following outline provides a rough description of the facts that should be explored with the client in a personal injury case.

1. All prior movements of the client that placed him or her in a position to be injured, such as place and time of departure and route of travel in the case of an automobile accident; decision to visit a specific home or business and movement thereto in the case of an injury on property of another; prior work experience and job status in a case involving an injury sustained on the job.

2. A complete and graphic description of the accident scene and all its pertinent features. (Use a diagram if necessary.)

3. All prior contact with the defendant, whether by a glimpse before collision or a two year association as the family doctor.

4. The exact locations and lines of vision of all possible witnesses, whether or not known by name.

5. The exact conduct of the plaintiff, the defendant, and all other people involved up to the time of injury.

6. The exact locations and descriptions of all persons, instrumentalities, and other relevant conditions immediately after the accident.

7. All statements made at any time by the defendant or anyone with whom the plaintiff might have spoken.

8. All statements made by the plaintiff or any witnesses.

9. The names of any witnesses who might have seen the incident itself or any part of its prologue or aftermath and a description of what they might have seen.

To avoid improper identification of a doctor, nurse, hospital, or witness by the client, it is good practice to use a telephone book or medical directory to verify the name and address while the client is present. The same information is relevant to the defendant's lawyer in a personal injury action.

**EXHIBIT 3.2**

## Interview Outline (continued)

### DAMAGES—PERSONAL INJURY CASE

Obtaining detailed information on the client's medical history from the moment before the accident until the time of the interview constitutes an important part of the initial interview. An outline of the areas that should be covered follows:

1. Any difficulty of plaintiff prior to the accident with any part of his or her body injured in the accident and the details of such difficulty, including treatment, cause, duration, etc.

2. The exact nature of all movements of plaintiff's body during the occurrence. For example, head hitting the windshield, etc.

3. The first injuries after the accident that the plaintiff recalls, such as unconsciousness, dizziness, nausea, or pain.

4. The date of, and reason for, plaintiff's first attempt to seek medical attention.

5. The names of all hospitals, doctors, therapists, and nurses who treated plaintiff, the nature of the treatment given by each such person, the dates of treatment, and the cost of each treatment.

6. The location and nature of any X-ray reports, medical report, and the like.

7. A description of the location, duration, and intensity of all pain, and of the effects of such pain on plaintiff's daily life, such as loss of sleep, inability to perform duties or recreational activities, loss of availability to spouse and/or children and/or parents, inability to engage in special interests, etc.

8. Costs and places of purchase of all drugs; appliances such as collars, braces, and heat lamps; travel expenses; and other expenditures incurred as a result of injuries sustained in the accident.

9. The client's employment and wage history, including current employer, previous employers, length of employment with each employer, positions held, and salaries at each job, and the amount of time lost from work as a result of the injury.

10. With regard to any property damaged (e.g., car smashed, clothing destroyed), the costs or estimated costs of repairs or replacements.

Most law firms develop their own checklists. However, if no such checklists or outlines are available, or if they are ripe for revision, one of the paralegal's roles will be to develop or revise checklists for the law firm.

As mentioned previously in this chapter, **authorization forms** and **retainer agreements** are typically prepared and used during the initial interview. See Exhibits 3.3 through 3.8 for examples of forms commonly executed by clients during the initial interview: medical record authorization forms (Exhibits 3.3 and 3.4), employment history record authorization forms (Exhibit 3.5), education record authorization forms (Exhibit 3.6), and retainer agreement forms (Exhibits 3.7 and 3.8).

---

**EXHIBIT 3.3**

## Medical Records Authorization

(Letterhead of Law Firm)

Dr. K. D. Jones
10 Pine Hill
City, State   zip code

  Re: (Name of Client)

This letter authorizes you to forward to the office of (Name of Law Firm) at the above address, or to permit the photocopying of all records you may have covering treatment of (Name of Client) on (date of first visit) 19___, and thereafter.

Please indicate the medical history; the analytical and curative steps taken; the report of X-rays, if any were taken; the current medical status and need for future treatment; and any other relevant information you may have.

Please indicate also the amount of your bill, and whether it has been paid in part or in full.

Please forward the above requested information promptly upon receipt of this authorization.

Sincerely,

(Signature) _____
(Name of Client)

**EXHIBIT 3.4**

## Medical Records Authorization

*MEDICAL AND/OR HOSPITAL AUTHORIZATION*

To Whom It May Concern:
   Patient_____
   I hereby give my permission, and this is your authority, to permit
_____ or their designated representative
to examine, make, or be furnished copies of any records or information,
X-rays, and X-ray reports in connection with any illness or injury requiring
confinement and/or treatment by you.
   I agree that a photocopy of this authorization shall be considered as
effective and valid as the original.

Dated: _____      Signed: _____

                                Address: _____

                                         _____

Exhibit 3.3 and 3.4 provide examples of a medical records authorization. If the subject of the interview involves an injury sustained by the client that necessitated medical treatment by a physician and/or hospital, it is important to obtain copies of the medical records. If appropriate, a report by a treating physician articulating the medical condition of the client, treatment rendered, and an opinion as to the prognosis of the client's condition should also be obtained. However, due to physician–patient privilege and the privacy issues surrounding this relationship, medical providers will not give out any information about their patients without a release signed by the patient authorizing and directing the release of information. Accordingly, to facilitate this process, the client will be given an authorization to sign during the interview.

Likewise, if the subject of the interview involves either verification of employment, verification of days missed from employment, or verification of a client's rate of pay earned from employment, the client should be provided with an employment history authorization form for signature. This authorization allows an employer to provide the requested employment information to the law firm. An example of this form is provided below:

**EXHIBIT 3.5**

## Employment History Authorization Form

ABC Corporation
1000 Boulevard
City, State   zip code

Attention: Ms. Smith
            *Director of Personnel (Payroll)*

    Re: (Name of Client)

Dear Ms. Smith:
    This letter authorizes you to release to my attorney, Elmer Jones, Es-
quire, any and all information he may request concerning my employment
by ABC Corporation.

                            Sincerely,

                            (Signature) _____
                            (Name of Client)

If the need for obtaining school records should arise during the interview,
the client should sign a school record authorization. This allows a school district
to provide the law firm with the requested information. An example of a school
record authorization is provided below:

**EXHIBIT 3.6**

## School Record Authorization

School Record Authorization

To Whom It May Concern:
    I hereby give my permission, and this is your authority, to permit
_____ or their designated representative
to examine, make, or be furnished, copies of any records or information
(including psychiatric and psychological reports) which pertain to my child.
_____ who is a student in the
_____ School District.

Dated: _____        Signed: _____
                                 Address: _____

At the end of the interview, if the client wishes to retain or hire the law firm to provide legal representation, the paralegal will typically ask the client to sign a fee agreement or retainer form. This document outlines in writing the specific terms under which the law firm will provide legal representation, including the scope of representation and the fee arrangement. The document outlines the formal relationship between the client and the law firm.

Examples of retainer agreements are provided below. Exhibit 3.7 is a contingent fee arrangement, which is typically used in personal injury actions on behalf of a plaintiff. The benefit to the client of such an arrangement is that the client can gain access to legal services without having to pay anything at the outset and unless the case is successful in recovering money.

Exhibit 3.8 is used in situations where a firm will charge a client on the basis of a set hourly rate. Litigation cases that do not lend themselves to contingent fee agreements are typically of this format. For example, a law firm representing a defendant in civil litigation will use this method of engagement.

The final document a paralegal should prepare with respect to the interview is a memo to the client file summarizing the information presented by the

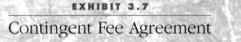

**EXHIBIT 3.7**

## Contingent Fee Agreement

Date

I (we) hereby constitute and appoint (Name of Attorney) of the law firm of (Firm Name) as my (our) attorney to prosecute a claim for (type of action) against (Name). The claimant (deceased) is (Name) and the cause of action arose on (Date).

I (we) hereby agree that the compensation of my (our) attorney for services shall be determined as follows:

Out of whatever sum is secured from the above defendant, either by way of settlement or verdict, the expenses of suit, investigation, or fees of witnesses, if any, shall first be paid in full, and of the balance so remaining, the said attorney shall retain 33 ⅓ percent. All medical bills incurred as a result of the accident shall be chargeable to the client's share exclusively. Counsel reserves the right to withdraw if after complete investigation he or she determines that there is no merit to the claim. I hereby authorize the said attorney to pay bills for medical and hospital treatment by payment directly to the physician or hospital concerned.

(Signature) _____
(Name of Client)

**EXHIBIT 3.8**

## Sample Fee Letter for Cases in Which Fee Cannot Be Specified (Hourly Rate)

Dear. . .

This letter will confirm our recent discussion in which I agreed, at your request, to represent you in the above-captioned matter.

As I explained to you, because of the nature of the matter, and because of the possibility of the occurrence of presently unpredictable and unforeseen circumstances, I am not in a position to quote you a specific fee for my professional services. However, I indicated to you that I would represent you on an hourly (or per diem) basis. My fees for office and telephone consultations are $ _____ per hour, with fractions of hours computed in periods of not less than _____ (e.g., tenths) of an hour, and taken into account interruption of other work. Each such hour is based upon actual work on your particular case.

My absence from my office in your behalf will be charged at the same hourly rate, although I shall minimize travel expenses and travel and courthouse time, if any, whenever I am able.

(OR)

My absence from my office in your behalf will be charged at a rate of $ for a half-day, and of $ _____ for a whole day, if in the county. Trips out of the county will call for a half-day charge of $ _____ and a whole day charge of $ _____ , which takes into account in part my unavailability to my other clients during such periods. I shall minimize travel expenses and travel time, if any, whenever I am able.

Any out-of-pocket expense directly attributable to your matter, including travel expenses, will be charged to you at cost, in addition to the fee. This will acknowledge receipt of $ _____ as a retainer, which will be credited against the fee.

I am pleased to represent you in this matter, and I assure you that I will pursue your matter as diligently and expeditiously as possible.

Very truly yours,

_____
(Lawyer)

Date: _____        Confirmed: _____
(Client)

client and any impressions the interviewer might have with respect to the client. Since the memo will be examined and used by other members of the law firm, it should be typed, organized chronologically, and be concise. See Exhibit 3.9 for an example of such a memo.

**EXHIBIT 3.9**

## Interoffice Memo

## INTEROFFICE MEMO

TO: Attorney X                                      DATE: 7/27/91
FROM: Paralegal Y

IN RE: Joan Smith v. Tanglewood Pie Company

I interviewed Joan A. Smith, 432 B. Street, Dry Gulch, 98765, 382-6103, D/B 2/4/51. She is married to John Smith, and has three children, ages 2, 7, and 8, living at home with her.

On 9/10/90 she went into Jim's Restaurant, 435 Main Street, Dry Gulch, to order lunch. She sat at the booth nearest the cashier in front. With her were Mr. Engels who is a watchman at C Corporation, Broad and Snyder Streets, Dry Gulch (243-7703), and "Sam," who is a friend of Mr. Engels. She was served by a dark-haired woman, glasses, about 35 years of age. She ordered a cheeseburger, coke, and apple pie.

She finished her cheeseburger, and began to eat the pie. As she was chewing on a small piece, an apple core stuck in her throat. She began to choke, felt that she was going to vomit, and rushed outside holding her mouth. She does not know whether Jim's had a bathroom, since this was the first time she had eaten there.

As she rushed outside, still gagging, she tripped over a box that was located outside near the door, falling to her knees and striking her head. She was not knocked unconscious. Mr. Engels followed her out and saw her fall. A traffic officer located at the corner of Main and South immediately came to her assistance and may have seen her fall.

She was taken to Angel of Mercy Hospital, X-rayed in the emergency ward, and admitted into the hospital at approximately 1:15 P.M. with a broken kneecap and nausea. No surgery was performed, but she was casted and remained in traction until 9/18/90 when she was discharged to her home. The treating doctor was Susan Sweet, M.D., 611 Suede Road, Dry Gulch, and a consulting neurologist, Samuel Carson, M.D., 34th and Sycamore Streets, Dry Gulch, examined her for recurring headaches.

She remained at home in bed until 10/13/90, and then was confined to her home until the middle of November. The cast was removed by Dr. Sweet on 10/14/90.

After she returned home, her husband called Jim, the proprietor of Jim's Restaurant. Jim told him that all his pies are ordered from Tanglewood Pie Company, Tanglewood, N.J., and that this is the first time anything has happened to any of his customers while eating pie in his restaurant. Jim contacted Tanglewood, and they sent someone down on the afternoon of the accident to pick up the pie. Tanglewood has the pie.

On 9/11/90, an investigator appeared in Ms. Smith's hospital room to talk to her about the accident. Ms. Smith said the man took notes, but she does not remember signing anything. (This should be checked as soon as the defendant is notified of our representation.)

After the accident, Ms. Smith's nausea continued for about two weeks. The pain in right knee was appreciable for four weeks, but the pain in the left knee and leg disappeared shortly after the accident.

Today, Ms. Smith still favors her left leg, and her right knee is stiff for days if she has to stand for any length of time or walk for more than four blocks. The headaches trouble her from time to time.

**EXHIBIT 3.9**

## Interoffice Memo (continued)

Ms. Smith bought a heat lamp ($41.95) and purchased about $20.00 worth of pain killers, which she used through November 1990.

While Ms. Smith was in the hospital, Mr. Smith hired Rita Cory, 733 Winter Street, Dry Gulch, to do the housework and take care of the youngest child while he was at work. She also cooked the meals. She worked six days a week at $60.00 per day until the middle of November 1990, and thereafter worked one day a week until June 1991, doing the heavy housework that Ms. Smith used to do. During the summer, Ms. Smith has tried to do all the housework, but she thinks it is too much for her, and she plans to contact Ms. Cory in a few weeks.

Prior to the accident, Ms. Smith was employed part-time as a nurse's aid in Public Hospital. She worked during the day, between two and four days a week as needed. She thinks she was paid $6.35 per hour. She had had the job on and off for two years. While she was working, she left her youngest child with her mother-in-law, and the two older kids were in school. She has not returned to her job because "she does not feel up to it."

Before the conclusion of the interview or shortly thereafter (depending on the arrangement between the supervising attorney and the paralegal), the paralegal should consult with his or her supervising attorney about the client's situation. The paralegal should present a summary of facts adduced during the interview to see if the lawyer has any helpful thoughts or insights about the client's situation. This form of collaboration reduces the possibility of incorrectly diagnosing a client's problem and helps develop better follow-up procedures.

## III. Summary

The main purposes of a client interview are to gather a sufficient amount of information on which a solution to that client's problem can be based and to build client rapport. These purposes can be accomplished through various questioning and listening techniques.

Questioning techniques can be divided into four categories: open-ended, narrow, yes/no, and leading. Each category will shape the range or choice of responses provided to the client.

Listening techniques fall into two categories: passive and active. Passive techniques encourage a client to keep talking. Active techniques provide feedback to the client and assure the client that the interviewer understands what he or she has said.

The model of interviewing provided in this chapter consists of three stages: preliminary problem identification, chronological overview, and theory development and verification. In the preliminary problem identification stage, the interviewer attempts to learn why the client is there and what solution the client wants. The overview helps the interviewer get a step-by-step chronology of the clients problem or transaction. In the theory development and verification stage, the interviewer conducts a more detailed examination to determine the viability of potential theories of recovery or defenses.

Either during the interview or at the end, the paralegal may have the client review and sign various documents. These documents may involve authorization forms to help gather information and/or retainer agreements that form the contract between law firm and client. The paralegal should also take notes during the interview so that he or she can prepare a memo outlining what went on during the interview.

---

## IV. KEY TERMS

Active listening        Legal interviewing        Passive listening
    techniques          Narrow questions              techniques
Authorization forms     Open- ended               Retainer agreements
Leading questions           questions             Yes/No questions

## V. QUESTIONS

1. What are the two main goals of an initial client interview?
2. What are the four basic forms of questions? Give examples of each.
3. What is the difference between active and passive listening?
4. What are the main types of retainer agreements?
5. What are the differences between a contingent fee arrangement and a set hourly arrangement?
6. Why do you have clients sign information authorization forms?

# CHAPTER 4

# CASE PREPARATION: FACT INVESTIGATION AND FILE PREPARATION; MAINTENANCE AND DOCKET CONTROL

## I. INTRODUCTION

The focus of this chapter is to examine the role of the paralegal in the initial fact-gathering process that is the foundation for all civil litigation.[1] In most lawsuits, establishing the facts is the most important part of the case. At trial a judge or jury can evaluate only information (evidence) that is brought into the courtroom. Therefore, when a lawyer undertakes to represent a party in a dispute, it is imperative to ascertain as many facts surrounding the dispute as possible. This investigation of facts (factual development) is necessary to enable the lawyer and/or the paralegal to form an opinion at an early stage of the strength or weakness of the client's case. From such an evaluation, decisions will be made as to whether a lawsuit should be filed, whether the case should be settled before trial, and the manner in which to prepare for trial.

The first part of this chapter focuses on the factual development of a client's case (after the initial interview) from sources other than the client. The second part discusses the process of systematically developing a case file.

The process of gathering factual information through the use of formal devices is discussed in chapter 7. The reason for creating this distinction in the fact-gathering process is that, generally, in order for a party to use a discovery device, he or she must be a party to a lawsuit. For the purposes of this chapter, the reader can assume that a lawsuit does not have to be filed in order to develop strategies for the kinds of fact-gathering processes discussed here.

This chapter is based upon the assumption that paralegals can and often do play a central role in the case-preparation process. Although individual law firms may differ in how they define the role of paralegals and how they delegate responsibility to paralegals in the areas of informal fact development (as distinguished from use of discovery devices) and file organization, litigation paralegals can play a significant and useful role in these areas. Therefore, this chapter will focus on issues that directly concern the paralegal when doing factual investigation and file organization.

## II. FACTUAL INVESTIGATION

After the interview with the client, the paralegal begins the process of constructing the client's case. In other words, the paralegal must start to make decisions as to what steps should be performed next. This decision-making process is usually done by collaborating and exchanging ideas with the paralegal's supervising attorney. The information obtained from the client is usually insufficient to provide a complete factual database to resolve the client's potential litigation problem. As a result, testimony of witnesses, details that support the client's position, documents, and reports can be very helpful. Also, the paralegal should explore all potentially contradictory sources to the client's position (that is, unfavorable witnesses) to be prepared to rebut the potential opposition to the client's position.

---

[1]Although legal research skills are equally important to the successful outcome of any civil lawsuit, it is assumed that legal research skills are taught in either a different course or as a supplement to this course. The topic of legal research is outside the scope of this textbook.

The following reprint taken from *The Lawyering Process: Materials for Clinical Instruction in Advocacy* is helpful in identifying specific lines of inquiry:

1. *Imagine arguing your client's story to a judge or jury.* Assume, at the start, that your client's perceptions, recollections and interpretation are essentially accurate. Then develop (or write out) an argument that resolves inconsistencies and fills in gaps in your client's favor. Rework the story until it is consistent with the most desirable outcome the rules permit.

2. *Ask yourself, "If my client's story as I just argued it were true, what else would be true?"* The purpose here is to move from your conclusions and interferences to the "data" that would support them. For example, suppose you represent a client who claims she was defrauded in the door-to-door sale of a food freezer plan. She understood the salesman to say that she was leasing the freezer and could cancel at any time. She tried to cancel, but the company now insists that no such option was offered and is suing her for the balance. If the client's story were true, what else would be true? The following possibilities come immediately to mind: (i) the freezer, not the food plan, would be the money-maker for the company; (ii) the salesman might have been "working" the area and made similar representations to other purchasers; (iii) there may be company training manuals or written instructions to salesmen on the sales "pitch," (iv) complaints about similar practices may be on file with better business or consumer protection agencies; (v) the salesman may have been under some particular pressure to make sales at the time he visited your client. Each of these suggests possible lines of inquiry and could lead to facts that corroborate your client's story.

3. *Imagine you are counsel for your opponent and argue his or her "best" case to a jury. . .* Partisan investigation requires that you plan for and adjust your story to rebut or avoid counter-explanations. In order to do this, you need to put yourself in the place of opposing counsel and construct an argument as you did for your client. This act of imagination, aided by some preliminary inquiries, will begin to give you a sense of the case you have to undermine or explain away.

4. *Ask yourself, "If my opponent's story were true, what else would be true?"* This is the same thought process that you used in analyzing your client's story. The lines of inquiry developed here points you to facts you hope are not there. If you do find them, you will have to revise your client's story to explain them or find ways to discredit or undermine them. Generally it is preferable to incorporate what seem to be unfavorable facts into your story or explain them rather than attempt the risky, inherently uncertain task of trying to contradict them. This means, for example, that your primary goal in interviewing most hostile witnesses is to establish as much congruence as possible between their recollections and what you can prove to be true. Eliciting material for impeachment becomes the main focus only when all else has failed.

5. *List sources of information for all the lines of inquiry that seem worth pursuing.* Sometimes there won't appear to be any good ways of pursuing a line of inquiry. At other times, the possibilities will be so numerous you

will find it difficult to choose among them. Part of this problem is resolved as you get more deeply into the case, or as circumstances change, but even at the planning stage there are many ways to be more creative about investigative possibilities. For example, some of the following suggestions may be helpful:

◆ Brainstorm, i.e., in a group of two or three people let your imagination run free. Don't criticize any suggestion until you have a full list and don't stop to explore the details of any particular possibility. Use each idea as a jumping off place for another.

◆ Visualize each piece of evidence you would like to have and where it might be located. Identify the obstacles you would encounter if you went directly to each source and focus on how you could avoid these barriers.

◆ Ask a friend or stranger who is "outside" your problem or frame of reference. Sometimes a fresh, more distant view is the most creative one.

◆ Use libraries and research guides, and ask research people (journalists, reference librarians, research firms, claims adjusters, police investigators) how they develop leads in analogous areas.

◆ Forget the problem for a while—go to a movie, think about something else—and come back to it later. A rest period often permits you to begin again in new ways.

6. *Select the lines of inquiry you will pursue and the order in which you will pursue them.* Identifying a line of inquiry doesn't necessarily mean you will pursue it. Sometimes costs will be prohibitive, time will be a problem, or other considerations will be more important. You will often need to decide which lines of inquiry to pursue, and when. Comparing and choosing among alternatives is difficult and inevitably dependent on the particular case and context. For example, in many cases you will do a great deal of investigation and preparation before a deposition, in order to maximize the likelihood of obtaining the statements or admissions you want. At other times, it is best to depose or interview a witness quickly, before many facts are known, and before he or she can be "prepared" by the other side.

The most we can offer here are some general criteria for choosing among or sequencing lines of inquiry: (i) How much information (that you would not otherwise choose to divulge) will you have to disclose in order to get what you want? Generally, you disclose least when you investigate physical evidence—documents, photographs, objects, scenes, etc.—and more when you seek testimony. (ii) Who has the advantage of delay or avoidance? (iii) Is your choice reversible? That is, if the inquiry is not successful, have you committed yourself to propositions you can't back up or have you closed off options that would otherwise be available? (iv) Have you expanded possibilities for further inquiry? (E.g., collecting documentary evidence and obtaining a few admissions from an opponent may improve your chances of getting assistance from an expert.) (v) Is the information likely to become available without expensive and time-consuming investigation? The rule of thumb, not surprisingly, is to select and sequence your inquiries so as to maximize the information you get and minimize costs and risks.

7. *Inquire-Assess-Revise story—Develop new lines of inquiry—Inquire-Assess-Revise...* In this spiral fashion you will build your case—that is, you will refine and adapt your original story, enlarge the base of solid facts, and progressively eliminate alternative unfavorable explanations.

Through some such means you will learn to analyze your case, develop lines of inquiry, and devise some method of deciding whether and when to pursue them. Each time you thoroughly investigate a case you will expand your knowledge of what to look for the next time, because in this area, as in others, experience accumulates and informs your subsequent choices and actions. You will also become more adept at seeking and shaping the facts you need to meet your clients' purposes, going down fewer "blind alleys" and reducing the amount of irrelevant information you collect.[2]

Also crucial in the process of developing factual lines of inquiry is the concept of getting the **givens.** This refers to those factual items, such as documents, that both sides of a case must acknowledge and account for in their construction of their theory of case. It is another way of saying facts that cannot be controverted by either side. The failure to obtain and discover the givens can significantly affect the factual foundation upon which all lines of inquiry should be developed and pursued. A potential theory of the case is always more effective if it relies on what cannot be controverted and can account for opposing views of what the case involves.[3]

## A. Witnesses

The testimony of independent witnesses is often needed to corroborate a client's version of the facts or to contradict an opponent's version.[4] Witnesses forget things as time passes. Therefore it is important to contact and interview witnesses as quickly as possible.

Locating witnesses who will support a client's position is a prime concern of the investigator of facts. A client may be able to supply the names of witnesses, but often the client is able to say only that there was a passenger in the other car or that there is a coworker named "Joe." Police reports, employees, and other witnesses are frequently good sources of information about previously unidentified witnesses. It is normal to ask in interrogatories about the identity of witnesses of whom the opponent has knowledge.[5] The lawyer or paralegal should keep complete records of the names, addresses, and telephone numbers of all possible witnesses and notes on any communication with such witnesses.

Interviewing witnesses is an art. Usually, if the witness is a friend or relative of the client, he or she will readily speak to the attorney or investigator. Otherwise, the job of the interviewer will be not only to get a statement but to get the

---

[2]Gary Bellow and Bea Moulton, *The Lawyering Process: Materials for Clinical Instruction in Advocacy,* (Minneola, NY: The Foundation Press, Inc.), 1978, pp. 321–23.

[3]Bellow and Moulton, p. 356.

[4]Independent witnesses should be distinguished from witnesses who may be family members or employees of a party and thus have a particular point of view. Independent witnesses are more likely to be unbiased and therefore are usually more persuasive to the fact finder at the trial.

[5]Interrogatories are one of the discovery techniques to be discussed in chapter 7. They are written questions addressed to the opponent.

witness to speak at all. Many people do not want to become involved in someone else's troubles, especially if it may mean testifying in court. Therefore the interviewer may first have to overcome a certain reluctance, if not outright resistance of the witness. By giving a statement, the witness is doing you a favor and this should be acknowledged.

Listed below are some suggestions for interviewing witnesses:

- Try to interview the witness as soon as possible, preferably before your opponent does.

- Obtain all the germane facts the witness possesses about the case you are investigating.

- Obtain leads to other witnesses and potential sources of information.

- Attempt to reduce the witness's statement to writing and, if possible, have the witness sign the statement.

- Try to instill in the witness a willingness to help you or your client.

- After the interview, give the witness your card, and ask him or her to contact you in the event of a change of name or address.

Bear in mind that once a party is represented by an attorney, it is unethical for the paralegal or attorney to contact the party directly. Any attempt to interview a party who is represented by counsel should be done only by first contacting the party's attorney and seeking permission to talk to the party. If permission is refused, then a deposition can be arranged with counsel for all parties present once the lawsuit has been filed.[6]

## B. PHOTOGRAPHS

Photographs can be very valuable in depicting a visual representation of a fact or view that is relevant to a client's case. Photographs that accurately depict a scene can serve many purposes at trial. For example, they may help establish liability or lack of it by showing the angle of impact of cars or the extent of a depression in a sidewalk; they can describe better than testimony the nature of a road or intersection; they can show the amount of damage to the car and the force of impact; and they can be used to bring to the attention of the jury any disfigurement or restriction suffered by a client. Not all photographs may be used, however. The trial judge has the authority to disallow photographs if (1) they are so graphic and gory that they might prevent a jury from making a reasoned decision, or (2) they could be misleading, because pictures can look completely different than the actual scene at the time of the incident depending on the angle of the photographs, the time of day they were taken, or the presence of conditions that were not present at the time of the incident (for example, a traffic light in the photo that was not there when the incident occurred).

Certain pictures should be taken as soon as possible. In "slip and fall" cases, pictures should be taken of the accident scene before repairs can be made.

---

[6]A deposition is one of the discovery procedures that will be discussed in chapter 7. It is simply an interview of someone before a court reporter, who records all questions and answers.

Pictures should also be taken of noticeable wounds or casts and of scars and disfigurements. In automobile cases, pictures of all cars and of the scene of the collision should be taken immediately so that the road conditions at the time of the incident will be documented.

Enough cannot be said about the value of good pictures in demonstrating a case to a jury or to the judge. Imagination is critical when contemplating the use of photographs to demonstrate some aspect of the client's case. But the time element involved is equally important; if the accident scene has been changed, the car repaired, or the wound healed, photographs will be useless and ordinarily inadmissible.

## C. Medical Information

In a personal injury case, it is important that the lawyer or paralegal obtain complete documentation of the physical injuries of the plaintiff and the medical costs incurred as a result of such injuries. Such information as well as information on lost wages will enable the plaintiff's attorney to prepare for settlement negotiations and to document the special damages that will be asserted if the plaintiff is successful in establishing liability. Insurance companies are most likely to evaluate a case on the basis of the special damages. The more they are thoroughly documented, the more accurate the settlement figure is likely to be.

### 1. Information from Doctors

All doctors who have treated the plaintiff for injuries should be promptly contacted for their reports and copies of their bills. A patient authorization should be signed and sent to the doctors with any request for information. While a form letter requesting a summary of diagnosis, prognosis, and methods of treatment is adequate, it often leads to a form report that is brief, lacking in clout, an incomplete. Most doctors will write genuinely useful reports if given appropriate assistance and approached properly.

Sometimes doctors may not recall all the problems of a particular patient. Their office notes may be minimal, perhaps listing only one or two words for each visit, such as "neck pain" or "upset stomach." The investigator who has talked with the client in detail about each complaint and its cause is usually able to assist the doctor in recalling the patient's specific problems and to elicit a more helpful report.

A letter requesting a report should therefore specify all the subjective complaints of the client and their relationship to the accident. It should request a definitive diagnosis and prognosis and a brief description of the treatment rendered. Above all, it should be courteous. See the sample letter in Exhibit 4.1.

It is important to ascertain that the client has in fact mentioned the listed problems to the doctor. Otherwise, the doctor may send back a report stating, for example, "He never complained of nausea to me, and I never treated him for it."

Upon receipt, the report should be studied to see if it is complete and accurate. Even typographical errors (for example, "the patient is employable" rather than the "the patient is not employable") can be devastating. Courteous and prompt requests for clarification should be made whenever there are any ambiguities.

Many doctors will send follow-up reports as a matter of course; others need prompting. If a second letter to the doctor is necessary see Exhibit 4.2 for an example.

**EXHIBIT 4.1**

## Sample Letter Requesting Medical Information

Benjamin A. Casey, M.D.
100 Medical Building
City, State zip code

Re: Mr. J.M. Brown

Dear Dr. Casey:

This office represents Mr. Brown, who was severely injured in an automobile accident on March 3, 1992. As you know Mr. Brown hit his head against the door post, was knocked unconscious, and shortly thereafter began to experience sharp pains in his neck and lower back, frontal headaches, nausea, and dizziness. He was unable to return to his job until March 28 because of these injuries. He informs us that since March 6 you have been treating him for these injuries.

We would be grateful if you could provide us with a report concerning your diagnosis and treatment of Mr. Brown's injuries together with your prognosis of his future medical course. We would also appreciate an itemized bill listing all visits and charges for your services.

An authorization for the release of this information is enclosed. Any fee for the preparation of the report will be promptly paid by our office.

Thank you for your cooperation.

**EXHIBIT 4.2**

## Sample Letter Requesting Additional Medical Information

Dear Dr. Casey:

Thank you for your detailed report on April 8, 1992, concerning Mr. Brown. Mr. Brown informs us that since the date of your report he has seen you nine times (4/11;4/18, etc.) for persistent neck pain and a dull ache in the lower back.

We would be most appreciative if you could send us a report confirming the treatment on these dates and an updated prognosis.

If it would not be too great an imposition, we would also request that your secretary send us a copy of the final bill when Mr. Brown is finally discharged from your care.

Thank you for your continuing cooperation.

In the initial interview with a client, the paralegal should explore possible sources of payment for these bills, such as Blue Cross, major medical plan, or medical payments coverage in an automobile insurance policy. In many cases the doctor will be willing to postpone payment of the bill until the conclusion of the case if the patient is unable to pay. Nevertheless, the unpaid bills represent losses to the plaintiff that must be paid and therefore are included in the list of special damages. Immediately after the recovery of damages, the law firm should pay all outstanding medical bills.

Many insurance policies that provide for payment of medical bills require the substitution of the insurance company for the plaintiff to the extent of the insurance payments. Such substitution is called **subrogation.** In subrogation cases, the insurance company usually pays the attorney a fee based on the total recovery less the amount distributed to the insurance company.

### 2. Information from Hospitals

Copies of hospital records and bills may be obtained by writing the medical records librarian of the treating hospital with specific reference to those portions of the hospital record desired. Emergency or outpatient records should be specifically identified since they are kept in files separate from inpatient files. The librarian will send a synopsis of the treatment upon request in return for a nominal fee. If more detail is required, the paralegal can request the discharge summary, prepared by the attending physician after discharge; admission notes, usually prepared by the admitting intern; operating room notes; progress notes, prepared by the attending physician or resident; X-ray reports; lab reports; order sheets listing medication and other nursing care ordered; consultation reports, prepared by specialists requested to perform specific examinations; and nurses' notes. In most cases in which the discharge summary is too brief, progress notes, operating room notes, consultation reports, and X-ray reports should serve to fill out the picture of hospital treatment.

If the case involves the cause of a death, the autopsy report, which may be obtained from the local medical examiner's or coroner's office can provide helpful information.

The paralegal should read all medical reports with the assistance of a good medical dictionary so that he or she can translate into lay language for the convenience of everyone involved with the case.

## D. Wage Loss

In addition to medical bills and compensation for pain and suffering, an injured plaintiff may be entitled to recover an amount equivalent to the gross wages he or she would have earned but for the accident. The amount of lost wages is usually calculated by multiplying the daily or hourly wage by the number of days or hours missed from work. The amount of this loss may be confirmed by writing to the personnel office of the client's employer. (See Exhibit 3.5.)

Despite the apparent routine nature of most wage claims, the investigator should be alert to possible additional losses. Such additional losses may exist if the client normally works overtime, has a second source of income, is self-employed, or is disabled for an extended period of time.

Overtime is a source of considerable revenue for many wage earners. The investigator should ask the client specifically about overtime work and rate of pay and should confirm this recollection by a letter to the employer. If the client's employer provides seasonal overtime, such as construction work in the summer or sales work in December, these periods should be calculated separately.

The client or the client's accountant should verify loss of income in cases of partial or full self-employment. Income tax returns are not a totally accurate gage. A better measure of loss is average gross weekly revenue (obtainable from the client's books for past periods of time) minus costs that were not actually incurred during the client's disability such as cost of products sold, telephone costs, and car mileage. Fixed costs (expenses that must be paid in spite of the client's disability) such as rent, salaries, and insurance should not be deducted in computing loss of income.

In cases of permanent or lengthy disability, any wage loss calculation must include probable future wage increases, future promotions, and fringe benefits. Past or present union contracts might provide a basis from which to prove wage increases, or a worker who has similar seniority could be asked to divulge his or her wage increases since the time of the accident. If no concrete comparison is possible, an economist might be asked as an expert witness to demonstrate the average inflationary wage increases in a given occupation for a given period.

## E. Other Sources of Factual Information

Factual investigation requires research skills separate and apart from legal issue research skills. The first problem encountered in factual investigation is locating helpful information. The following excerpt from *Effective Factual Research for Lawyers, A Guide to the Location and Use of Information Sources* provides techniques for gathering factual information.

There are at least eight types of resources a researcher should systematically check each time factual information is sought:

1. *Libraries and Information Centers* One of the easiest ways to locate special collections libraries is through the Special Libraries Association (SLA), an organization of librarians who work at these libraries. When there is no SLA Chapter directory, there are other directories or guides to libraries by subject available at your public library (i.e., *Subject Directory of Special Libraries and Information Centers).*

2. *Trade and Professional Associations* Most associations gather and disseminate specialized information to their members. They publish newsletters, reports, surveys, studies, membership lists, technical articles, and journals. Many even maintain libraries. . . Several lists of associations have been compiled, the most popular being the *Encyclopedia of Associations* (available at any library).

3. *Government Agencies* Several guides to federal government information sources are available. They are:

   a. *Researchers' Guide to Washington Experts*

   b. *Federal Information Sources and Systems*

   c. *United States Government Manual*

A few indexes to government documents include:

    a. *The Monthly Catalog of U.S. Government Publications*

    b. *Government Reports Announcements & Index (GRA & I)*

    c. *The Public Affairs Information Service (PAIS Bulletin)*

    d. *State Publication Index*

There are two bookstores organized to sell federal government publications to you once you have determined what you want. They are:
National Technical Information Service,
Springfield, Virginia; and
Government Printing Office, bookstores in regional federal centers throughout the United States

4. *Private and Academic Institutions*    There are private research groups that collect, organize, and disseminate information. Listed below are directories to help find these research organizations and academic institutions:

    a. The Research Center Directory

    b. Industrial Research Laboratories

    c. World of Learning

    d. Statistical Reference Index

5. *Commercial and Private Services for Lawyers*    There are now commericial services for lawyers to retrieve and analyze information. Listed below are some directories to these services:

    a. *Information Sources,* the Information Industry Association's membership directory.

    b. *Law and Legal Information Directory and Encyclopedia of Business Information Sources,* both published by Gale Publishing Co.

    c. *Document Retrieval,* published by The Information Store.

    d. *Forensic Services Director,* list of experts compiled by The National Forensic Center

6. *Colleagues and Experts*    Your own colleagues in the business community can be used as sources of information. Experts can also be used as a source of factual information. With the use of specialized indexes and computer databases, articles and authors which discuss your topic can be easily retrieved. Here is a list of a few of these indexes:

    a. Dissertation Abstracts

    b. Accountants Index

    c. Insurance Periodicals Index

    d. Engineering Index

    e. Psychological Abstracts

    f. Abstracts on the Health Effects of Environmental Pollutants

    g. Chemical Abstracts

    h. Work Related Abstracts

7. *Periodical and Newspaper Publishers*    To identify publishers by topics, you can use these directories to periodical literature. Here are some of them:

    a. *Ulrich's International Periodical Directory*

    b. *Standard Periodical Directory*

    c. *Guides to Special Issues and Index of Periodicals*

    d. *Ayer Directory of Publications*

    e. *The Directory of Newspaper Libraries*

8. *Computer Databases*    There is a vast array of nonlegal, factual databases attorneys can use in their research. These fall into two categories: bibliographic and numeric.... Many of the bibliographic databases are accessible through the same equipment provided for the LEXIS and WESTLAW systems.... Numeric databases contain data and statistics drawn from research such as census surveys, financial reports, market research, and opinion polls.[7]

When planning a research strategy, it is helpful to use a research worksheet listing the eight types of resources with space provided for filling in the specific names under each. Exhibit 4.3 is an example of one type of worksheet.

Another way to identify different sources of factual information is with the checklist shown in Exhibit 4.4.

---

**EXHIBIT 4.3**

## Research Strategy Work Sheet

TOPIC:_____

LIBRARIES

ASSOCIATIONS

GOVERNMENT AGENCIES

PRIVATE/ACADEMIC INSTITUTIONS

COMMERICIAL FIRMS

EXPERTS/COLLEAGUES

PUBLISHERS

COMPUTER DATABASES

Source: *Effective Factual Research for Lawyers* (The Information Store, Inc., 1981), p. 43. Reprinted with permission.

---

[7]*Effective Factual Research for Lawyers A Guide to the Location and Use of Information Sources* The Information Store, Inc, 1981, pp. 8, 9, 12, 13, 15, 18, 20, 21, 23, 24, 26, 27, 29, 30, 32, 33.

**EXHIBIT 4.4**

# Checklist on the Standard Sources of Evidence and Leads

| | | |
|---|---|---|
| 1. Statements of the client | 2. Documents the client brings with him or can get | 3. The attorney for the other side (may be willing to provide information) |
| 4. Attorneys involved with case in the past | 5. Interrogatories, depositions and letters requesting information | 6. Pleadings (e.g., complaint) filed thus far in the case |
| 7. Newspaper accounts and notices in the media requesting information | 8. Records of municipal, state, and federal administrative agencies, generally | 9. Business records, (e.g., canceled receipts) |
| 10. Employment records | 11. Photographs | 12. Hospital records |
| 13. Informers or the "town gossip" | 14. Surveillance of the scene | 15. Police reports and law enforcement agencies |
| 16. Fingerprints | 17. School records | 18. Military records |
| 19. Use of alias | 20. Bureau of vital statistics and missing persons | 21. Court records |
| 22. Office of Politicians | 23. Records of Better Business Bureaus & other consumer groups | 24. Telephone book and directories of organizations |
| 25. Accounts of eye-witnesses | 26. Hearsay accounts | 27. Automobile registrar |
| 28. Object to be traced (e.g., auto) | 29. Asking a more experienced investigator if he or she can think of any leads | 30. Credit bureaus |
| 31. Reports of investigative agencies written in the past | 32. Resources of public library | 33. Associations—trade or otherwise |
| 34. "Shots in the dark" | | |

Source: William P. Statsky, *Introduction to Paralegalism* (St. Paul, West Publishing Co., 1974) p. 312. Reprinted with permission.

## III. FILE PREPARATION, MAINTENANCE, AND DOCKET CONTROL

### A. File Maintenance

As part of the task of preparing for trial, a lawyer and paralegal will assemble a wide range of papers and documents, including pleadings, investigative reports, memoranda of law, motions, transcripts of depositions, and other information obtained through discovery. In large lawsuits, the number of papers and documents can run into the hundreds. Yet when it is time for trial and during the discovery phase it is absolutely essential that the trial lawyer be aware of every important paper in the file and be able to locate each paper quickly. In order for the paralegal to participate on a meaningful basis in this aspect of preparation, it is important that he or she acquire some understanding of the case. Therefore the paralegal should consult with the supervising attorney during this stage of trial preparation if he or she is unsure about any aspect of the case.

In addition to making sure that the files are well organized so the attorney can locate a particular document with a minimum of effort, paralegals must also make sure that files, or portions of them, are readily transportable so that necessary documents can be moved to the courtroom or to a deposition room if necessary.

#### 1. Arrangements of Files

For most cases, lawyers and paralegals find it convenient to keep all their papers in a file jacket, usually made of heavy cardboard. Within that jacket, the papers are segregated in manila file folders. For purposes of convenience, we will refer to the manila folders as "subfiles."

The various subfiles that might be kept in a small personal injury case, in which the law firm represents the plaintiff and which will not involve a lengthy trial, might consist of the following:

- Correspondence

- Pleadings

- Billing

- Settlement discussions

- Legal and factual memoranda

- Expert reports and special damages

- Documents

With such a breakdown, all the writing involved or created by the case could probably be placed in one of the above subfiles without any subfile containing an excessive number of documents. Using the subfiles, documents should be easily and quickly found.

Some lawyers and paralegals include copies of the same document in different subfiles, if the document relates to more than one matter. For example, a letter written to defendant's counsel discussing the possibility of settlement might be included in the general correspondence subfile and the settlement subfile. Moreover, attorneys often require an index of all documents contained in a certain subfile to be included in the subfile and request that each item in the subfile be separated with a blank sheet containing a tab that is coded to the index. This procedure is normally followed in the pleadings subfile, where the index will list all pleadings by number in the order in which they were filed with the court, and each pleading will be preceded by a tab sheet with the number listed in the index.

## 2. Complicated or Lengthy Cases

Complex cases usually require that the pleadings, general correspondences, and documents subfiles be broken down even further as discussed below.

*a. Pleadings.*     The pleadings file is the most likely subfile to be further broken down. If it not broken down, all the interrogatories, answers to interrogatories, depositions, factual pleadings (Answer and Complaint), motions, and briefs will be in the same file. Obviously, this makes it very difficult to locate the documents quickly. Therefore, in a big case the pleadings file will often be broken down into separate subfiles for factual pleading, depositions, interrogatories and answers, and so on. In a very large case, the pleadings subfiles would be broken down even further. For example, the depositions subfile might be divided into separate subfiles for each deposition so that a copy of the deposition and digests of the deposition would be kept together.

In multiparty litigation, discovery of a particular party in the form of interrogatories might also be kept by party or by subject matter, or both, in order to make the information readily available.

At the outset of a complex lawsuit, the attorney and paralegal will attempt to establish the categories of files that will be needed for the lawsuit and will arrange for their preparation. As work on the case develops, better ways to file all the papers and documents relating to the case may be conceived, and files will be rearranged accordingly. While substantial time may be devoted to the process of organizing and reorganizing files, such time is well spent since it ensures that all relevant papers will be readily available.

In very large cases, a single file may have so many papers in it that it will take up an entire file cabinet. In these large cases, it might be necessary to prepare an index of the subfiles so that the attorney can quickly find where a particular paper is located. There is no special nomenclature used in indexing and captioning subfiles, and each law firm or lawyer may have special preferences.

The only relevant filing guidelines are that papers and files should be kept easily accessible and manageable and that the captions used for subfiles should be descriptive of the papers that are lodged within them.

*b. General Correspondence.*     In a voluminous case, the maintenance of a general correspondence file without further breakdown might make it impossible to find particular correspondence when it is needed. This file can be broken down by year or by date so that all correspondence for a particular period is in a separate subfile, with the most recent at the top. Thus, there might be a subfile called "General Correspondence—1983."

General correspondence can also be broken down by subject matter so that all correspondence relating to a particular subject is segregated in a separate subfile, for example, "Correspondence—Insurance Coverage" or "Correspondence—Transmittals," which could contain correspondence that does no more than transmit documents and pleadings. There may also be a dual correspondence system, a chronological file and a subject matter file.

***c. Documents.*** A document subfile can be broken down in many ways. In a large case, it may be broken down in several different ways so that the same document is contained in more than one subfile. Documents are usually organized by subject matter or source. In less voluminous cases, documents tend to be segregated according to source. For example, documents secured from the client's files might be in a subfile called "Documents—Client's Papers," while documents secured from one of the adverse parties might be in a subfile called "Documents Produced by Defendant." See Exhibit 4.5 for a sample index to a relatively large case.

## B. Keeping Track of Case Progress

In any practice with a volume of litigation, file organization can greatly simplify matters. One method of organizing is shown in Exhibits 4.6 through 4.8.[8] These three forms are: Case Sheet, Case Summary Sheet, and Pretrial Preparation Sheet.

Whenever a litigation file is opened, the **case sheet** is prepared. It is distributed as follows:

- statute of limitations binder
- attorney in charge of the case
- paralegal assigned to case
- litigation master binder
- attorney who brought client to office (optional)
- file

The statute of limitations binder is keyed to months and years and is maintained by the senior litigation paralegal. Six-month, 90-, 60-, and 30-day notices are given, simply by photocopying the case sheet and circling the statute expiration date. It is distributed to the attorney in charge, the head of the litigation group, and the attorney who brought the clients to the office.

The **case sheet** is also used as a running log of phone calls and for quick reference for phone numbers, file numbers, settlement history, and so on. Each

---

[8]This method of organization and Exhibits 4.6, 4.7, and 4.8 were prepared by Wilbur Bourne Ruthrauff for use at the Institute for Paralegal Training and at his firm, Gratz, Tate, Speigel, Erwin & Ruthrauff in Philadelphia, Pennsylvania.

**EXHIBIT 4.5**

## Index to Files

INDEX TO FILES
Scott Peterson v. Black's Trustees

I.     GENERAL CORRESPONDENCE
       .1   1957–1959
       .2   1960–1969
       .3   1970–1972
       .4   1973–1974
       .5   1975–1976

II(a).   LITIGATION FILE
       .1   Information Letters to Opposing Counsel
       .2   Pleadings
       .3   Extra Pleadings
       .4   Supreme Court Pleadings
       .5   Second Supreme Court Pleadings

II(b).   LITIGATION FILE
       .1   Transcripts
       .2   Chronology
       .3   Briefs
       .4   Notes and Memoranda Testimony of Doug Shrugg
       .5   Notes and Memoranda Testimony of Pilfer
       .6   Notes and Memoranda Testimony of Erickson
       .7   Notes and Memoranda Testimony of Henry Schmitt
       .8   Transcripts of Hearings dated 1/24/77, 1/25/77, and 1/26/77
       .9   Supreme Court Exhibits

II(c).   LITIGATION FILE
       .1   Legal Memoranda
       .2   Materials for Trial Preparation
       .3   Drafts and Work Papers
       .4   Factual Memoranda

II(d).   LITIGATION FILE
       .1   Deposition of Sarah Neal
       .2   Computation of Possible Damages
       .3   Schedules Re Analysis of Damages
       .4   Settlement Negotiations
       .5   Ernst & Ernst Special Schedules
       .6   Pilfer Report

**EXHIBIT 4.5**

# Index to Files (continued)

III(a).  DOCUMENTS
    .1  Trusts for Children (1/1/50 and 1/1/53)
      (1)  Herbert
      (2)  William
      (3)  John
    .2  Trust for Herbert (4/11/56)
    .3  Trust for William (5/27/56)
    .4  Trust for I. David, Mortimer F., Henry T., Dorothy . (8/12/56)

III(b).  DOCUMENTS
    .1  1964 Employee Difficulties
    .2  Agreement of Sale of Stock from Trust to A.L. (12/28/64)
    .3  1965 Recapitalization
    .4  Sample Debentures
    .5  Bank Loan Agreements
    .6  Salaries

III(c).  DOCUMENTS
    .1  Analysis of Ownership
    .2  Revocation of Trusts (6/29/70)
    .3  (a)  Restrictive Stockholders Agreements
      (b)  Restrictive Stockholder Agreements, Affiliated Companies,
         1976
    .4  Will of Herbert
    .5  Debentures

attorney handling litigation has a binder with a case sheet for every matter for which he or she is responsible

The **case summary** sheet is prepared by the paralegal assigned to the case and is updated as new information is developed. It is distributed the same way as the case sheet, except it is not included in the statute of limitations binder. It provides a capsule summary of the case and the contentions of the various parties and experts.

The **pretrial preparation sheet** is distributed to the same places as the case summary. It serves as a record of completion of trial preparation.

## C. Docket Control

Keeping track of time limitations is a crucial part of the litigation process. If the client is prevented from bringing a lawsuit because the statute of limitations has expired, the lawyer will not only be less one client but may also face a claim of malpractice. Similarly, once litigation has begun, many dates must be tracked. The paralegal is often responsible for keeping the attorney aware of these time requirements and making sure that the lawyer's file is complete and orderly.

**EXHIBIT 4.6**

# Case Sheet

COURT, TERM, NO.: _____

CLIENT: _____
_____

VS/ATS:_____
_____

CO/ORIG. DEFTS:_____
_____

120 Days Expire/
Arbitration Scheduled For:_____
Jury Trial Demanded:_____
Client File No.:_____
Individuals to Contact at Clients (Include telephone
numbers)_____

C/A Arose:_____
Stat. Lim. Expires:_____
Type of Case:_____

Client of:_____
Attorney in Charge:_____
Paralegal:_____

**********************************************************************************

Client's Insurance Carrier:_____
File Number:_____
Policy Number: _____ Claim Number:_____
Individual to Contact and Telephone:_____
_____

Opposing Party's Carrier:_____
File Number:_____
Policy Number: _____ Claim Number:_____
Individual to Contact and Telephone:_____

**********************************************************************************

Attorneys for Other Parties and Telephone Numbers:
_____
_____

**********************************************************************************

Settlement Evaluation: $ _____
Conveyed to Client (Date):_____

Date:_____
Accepted: Yes ( )        No ( )

Settlement Demand: $ _____
Conveyed to Client (Date):_____

Date:_____

Negotiations:_____
_____
_____
_____

Telephone Log

_____
_____
_____

Source: Wilbur Bourne Ruthrauff.

**EXHIBIT 4.7**

# Case Summary Sheet

CLIENT_____ vs./ats_____

Our File No._____

Description of Complaint (and counterclaims):_____
_____
_____

Nature of Case:_____
_____

Plaintiff's/Our Theory—(Expert?):_____
_____

Deft's/Our Theory—(Expert?):_____
_____

Plaintiff's TOTAL Specials: $_____ Lost Earnings: $_____
P.D.: $_____ Medical: $_____ Hospital: $_____
Housework: $_____ Other: $_____

Plaintiff's/Client's Injuries/Diagnosis:_____
_____

Hospitalizations:_____
_____

Prognosis:_____
_____

Our/Defendant's Exam Shows:_____
_____

Lost Earnings (Substantiation):_____
_____

Witnesses:_____
_____

Witnesses to be Subpoenaed (with telephone numbers):_____
_____
_____

Records (Duces Tecum):_____
_____
_____

Exhibits:_____
_____

Source: Wilbur Bourne Ruthraff.

**EXHIBIT 4.8**

# Pretrial Preparation Sheet

CLIENT _____ vs/ats _____

Our File No._____

PRETRIAL PREPARATION

| | Assigned to | Completed |
|---|---|---|
| Complaint Served: ___/___/___ | _____ | _____ |
| Answer Due: ___/___/___ | _____ | _____ |
| Jury Demand:_____ | | |
| Joinder of Add'l Defts—Due By: ___/___/___ | | |
| Carrier File Obtained:_____ | _____ | _____ |
| Interrogs. to Us—Ans./Obj. Due: ___/___/___ | _____ | _____ |
| Interrogs. to Opposing Parties: | | |
|    Basic: | _____ | _____ |
|    Expert Witness: | _____ | _____ |
| *Depositions:* | | |
|    Plaintiff/Defendant | _____ | _____ |
|    Plaintiff's (or Deft's) Employer | _____ | _____ |
|    Witnesses: | | |
|    _____ | _____ | _____ |
|    _____ | _____ | _____ |
| Requests for Admission: | _____ | _____ |
| Police/Other Gvt./Report: | _____ | _____ |
| Photographs (Injuries, Scene, Equipment): | _____ | _____ |
| Medical/Hospitals Reports: | | |
|    Client: | _____ | _____ |
|    Opposing Party: | _____ | _____ |
| Medical Exam of Opposing Party: | _____ | _____ |
| Employment Records: | | |
|    Client: | _____ | _____ |
|    Opposing Party: | _____ | _____ |
| Tax Returns: | _____ | _____ |
| Workman's Comp File: | _____ | _____ |
| Legal Issues to be Researched:_____ | | |
| _____ | | |
| Other Investigation:_____ | _____ | _____ |
| _____ | _____ | _____ |

Source: Wilbur Bourne Ruthrauff.

In order to keep track of all cases in the office and be prepared for dead-lines, a method must exist (usually called **docket control**) for keeping track of all relevant dates in all active and potential lawsuits.

Dates and deadlines in the litigation process are generally of two types: (1) dates imposed by statutes or court rules and (2) dates established by action of the court or by agreement of the parties. Attorneys and paralegals must pay careful attention to the statutes, rules, orders, and agreements noted below to ascertain the appropriate dates and to ensure that whatever action is required of the office by each of the respective dates has been taken.

### 1. Dates Imposed by Statute or Court Rules

The following is a summary of the deadlines imposed by statutes or court rules.

*a. Expiration of Statute of Limitations Period.*   For each possible lawsuit, there is a date after which the commencement of the lawsuit is barred by the **statute of limitations.** When a lawyer agrees to represent a client in bringing a lawsuit, he or she must immediately determine the date on which the statute of limitations will run out in order to avoid the very substantial problems (including a possible malpractice action against the lawyer) that can arise out of a failure to file a timely complaint or to commence the lawsuit on time.

For instance, a personal injury action may have a statute of limitations of two years from the date of injury. If the law firm waits beyond the two year period from the date of injury, the plaintiff may lose the claim because it is now time barred.

Another example involves a breach of contract claim. Assuming there is a four year statute of limitations that begins to run from the date of breach (failure to perform in accordance with the terms of a contract), a lawsuit instituted beyond the four year period may be time barred.

*b. Dates to Respond to Pleadings and Discovery.*   Court rules es-tablish the number of days allowed to answer or otherwise respond to a com-plaint or other pleading or to answer or object to interrogatories or to produce or object to the production of documents. In some instances, a lawyer's failure to respond in the required time may result in the adverse termination of a lawsuit (for example, failure to answer a complaint within the required time period may result in the entry of a default judgment).

*c. Dates by which Motions Must Be Made.*   Court rules govern the time by which certain posttrial motions must be made. For example, a motion for judgment n.o.v. (notwithstanding the verdict) must be made within ten days after the entry of judgment in federal court.

*d. Dates by Which Appeals Must Be Taken.*   Statutes or court rules will establish the date on or before which certain necessary steps must be taken to perfect an appeal from the decision of a lower court. Failure to act properly within the required time period may cause the right of appeal to be lost.

## 2. Dates Established by Court Order or by Agreement of the Parties

The most common types of dates established by a court are dates for preliminary hearings, for arguments on certain motions, for submission of papers (for example, motions, supporting memoranda, and proposed pretrial orders) for pretrial or settlement conferences, and for trial. Usually these dates are established by an order or letter from the judge or clerk of the court.

In many situations, especially in connection with the trial of a case, a court may follow a **pool system,** which involves the scheduling of cases in the order they are listed in the "pool." There may be a common case pool for all trial judges in a particular court (for example, a county trial court), or each judge may be assigned a list or pool of cases (the procedure followed in most of the United States District Courts). The lawyers concerned will be notified by the judge or clerk of the court of the assignment of their case to a trial pool and the relative position of the case in the pool. Such information may also be obtained from legal newspapers.

Once a case is assigned to a trial pool, the lawyer or paralegal will be able to estimate the time before the case is likely to be called for trial by keeping frequent and regular track of the disposition of the cases ahead (closer to the top) in the trial pool and by gaining a growing familiarity with the average rate of case disposition by the particular judge or court.

In addition to dates imposed by courts, dates will also be established or reestablished (normally extended) by agreement of counsel. Sometimes court approval is necessary; most often, it is not. For example, lawyers may establish a date for an oral deposition. They may extend a date for answering pleadings or responding to discovery requests. They may also establish dates for settlement discussions or resolving discovery problems.

## 3. Keeping Track of Dates

The preceding description of relevant dates in a lawsuit is not exhaustive and is intended only to highlight some of the important ones. Each lawsuit may have its own special dates.

Once the relevant deadlines are ascertained (this is really an ongoing practice, depending on the development of the particular case), it is essential that the lawyer be made aware of them in plenty of time to complete whatever action must be taken before the particular date. This is a task to which a lawyer's assistant may be assigned.

*a. The Calendar.* One method of tracking dates is to use a **calendar** with an entire month to a page with spaces large enough to write in the relevant dates. This is often combined with an "early warning" or "tickler" system so that well in advance of a deadline the matter will be brought to the attention of the lawyer's assistant and the lawyer. The amount of notice necessary will vary, depending upon the matter. For example, if a complicated trial is involved, the attorney may require three or four weeks' notice, or even more, in order to review depositions and answers to interrogatories, prepare witnesses for trial, research and write trial briefs, subpoena witnesses, and otherwise prepare for trial. The deadline and early warning dates should be calendared as soon as the document giving rise to the imposition of the deadline has arrived. If this is not done immediately, the deadline may be forgotten.

*b. The "Tickler" System.* An alternative to and more often a desirable supplement to the calendar is the **tickler** or follow-up file system. For example, suppose a lawyer grants another lawyer's request for extension of time in which to file an answer and sends a confirming letter. An extra copy, or follow-up copy, of each letter (or memorandum) that requires future action is often made. Frequently, the follow-up copy may be a different color from the original or file copy so as to readily distinguish it. The follow-up copy would be marked with a specific date and kept in a special accordion file (often called a "tickler" file) that is separated by days and months.

Suppose the above letter to the lawyer advising of the extension of time is written on February 15 and the new deadline for answering is March 25. The date March 25 would be inserted by hand on the follow-up copy of the letter, which then would be inserted in the tickler file in the March 25 slot. As part of the daily routine, the tickler file must be checked; on March 25, the letter will surface and be called to the attention of the lawyer or paralegal. If the answer has already been filed, the follow-up copy may then be discarded. If it has not been filed, the lawyer should be notified and the appropriate action taken.

### 4. The Legal Periodical

Nearly every major metropolitan area has at least one newspaper that is the official instrument of notice to the legal community of many types of court proceedings. Through the legal newspaper, lawyers may learn when a pretrial conference is scheduled, when a case will come to trial, and so on. The lawyer's assistant is often responsible for regularly checking the daily or weekly legal newspaper.

The newspaper usually reports trial schedules and conference schedules of the various courts. This may be the sole means of notice for hearings and conferences. Ordinarily, the cases are listed by name under the court in which they are pending and often the names of the attorneys are also listed. When the attorneys are listed, one can simply check for the names of the appropriate lawyers. On the other hand, when the cases are listed solely by case name, the assistant must know all the names of pending cases in which the law firm is involved. In a large law firm with pending cases it is impossible for any single person to know and be familiar with all the current cases, and more than one person will have to check the newspapers.

The legal newspaper may also be source of information for sheriff's sales and bankruptcies as well as other information that could be pertinent depending upon the type of practice of the law firm. A good assistant will be able to read through the legal newspaper and point out any important matters, for example, that someone your office has sued is also being sued by someone else or that a judgment has been entered in a case bearing on one in your office.

### 5. The Firm's Litigation Docket

Another important function often assigned to a lawyer's assistant is the task of maintaining a docket file of all active or inactive cases in which the law firm

**EXHIBIT 4.9**

## Client Card

CLIENT: W. Simon Smith

TIME RECORD CHARGE:
  Contingent Fee

CAPTION AND COURT:
Smith v. Brian Goodheart
U.S. D.C., N.D. of N.Y.

TYPE OF CASE:
  Horseback riding accident

DATE: 12/20/81

FILE NO.: 39114-00

#77-401

ATTORNEYS HANDLING:
  John Deerling

ATTORNEYS TO BE ADVISED:
  Gregory Von Twill

is or has been involved. This can be accomplished by having a card for every file. Computerized records can list the same information. The card would be cross-referenced not only be the name of the client (see Exhibit 4.9) but also by the names of all the litigants. The purpose of the card is to allow a law firm to initially answer any inquiries concerning a case or a client by referencing one file system and not questioning all the litigation lawyers within the firm. The litigation docket file should also disclose the name of the attorney handling the matter and, if the records are kept properly, the status of the same case. When someone asks a law firm for representation, such a system helps identify possible conflict of interest. Firms that have computer capability process the information contained on the client card into the computer to produce a list of clients by type of case and a computer docket control system that is easily accessible to the paralegal or litigation attorney.

## IV. SUMMARY

After the initial interview, the paralegal begins gathering additional information by creating a theme for the client's story and then creating the opponent's theme. Then the paralegal gathers information to support the client's theme and refute the opponent's theme. If the information acquired does not support the client's theme, the paralegal must rework the theme. Also, he or she must make sure that the theme is supported by factual information called the "givens" that must be acknowledged by both parties.

Witnesses should be interviewed as soon as possible. Photographs should also be arranged. Medical information, if appropriate, should be obtained from treating doctors and hospitals. Wage loss information, if appropriate, should be obtained.

The paralegal is typically responsible for file preparation, maintenance, and docket control. Files should be organized so that the information they contain can be located easily and files can be transportable. Breaking a file down into subfiles called correspondence, pleadings, billing, settlement discussions, legal and factual memoranda, expert reports and documents can be very helpful.

The paralegal is also typically responsible for keeping track of the case progress. It is vital that certain time deadlines and dates are noted. The deadlines are statutes of limitations, court rules for filing or responding to pleadings and motions, appeals and dates established by court order or agreements of the parties. Also the paralegal should monitor the legal newspapers and other methods of notice to the legal community for pretrial conferences and trial notices.

## V. Key Terms

Calendaring system
Case sheet
Case summary sheet
Docket control
File maintenance
Givens

Medical records
Photographs
Pool system
Pretrial preparation
    sheet

Statute of limitations
Subrogation
Tickler system
Wage loss

## VI. Questions

1. What is meant by the process of getting the "givens"?
2. Give some examples of sources typically used to locate witnesses.
3. What are the two main considerations in organizing and maintaining a client file?
4. What is a case summary sheet? How does it differ from a case sheet?
5. What is a statute of limitations?
6. What is the applicable statute of limitations in your state for the following types of cases?
   personal injury
   breach of contract
   libel or slander
7. What happens if a case is filed one day after a statute of limitations has expired?
8. Name two ways that a paralegal can systematically keep track of important dates in a lawsuit?

# CHAPTER 5

# EVIDENCE

## I. INTRODUCTION

In order to gather information when preparing a case for trial one must understand the basic precepts of **evidence.** Evidence involves the presentation of information at a trial. Since the paralegal often plays an important role in the pretrial processes of informal discovery, fact investigation, and preparation for trial, it is important for him or her to become familiar with certain key concepts of evidence. Knowing what information can be presented during a trial will help guide the litigation team in making decisions as to what information to seek prior to litigation and after litigation has begun such as during discovery.

Although trials are real events, the information presented during trials is typically an articificial recreation of a past event or series of events. In order to reconstruct the past in a manner acceptable to the court, the litigation team must master the rules of evidence.

The rules of evidence in the United States have either been codified by statute or rule such as the Federal Rules of Evidence or have been delineated from previous court rulings under the source of common law. For purposes of consistency this chapter will cite only the Federal Rules of Evidence. However, the issues discussed are the kind typically found under either a state common law system of evidence or state/federal codified system of evidence.

The trial judge administers the rules of evidence. It is part of the judge's responsibility to make sure a party receives a fair trial. Evidentiary questions are questions of law and are raised by a party objecting to the introduction or admissibility of certain information being presented during trial. Once an objection has been made the judge must rule on it. The failure of a party to raise an objection concerning admissibility during a trial will waive the objection. In other words, the failure to object can result in inadmissible evidence being allowed into evidence.

## II. TYPES OF EVIDENCE

Evidence can be broken down into the following four categories:

a. witness testimony

b. documentary evidence

c. real evidence

d. demonstrative evidence

Each category will be discussed in some detail below.

## A. Witness Testimony

There are two types of witnesses: lay and expert. Simply stated, a **lay witness** is any witness who does not qualify as an expert witness. An **expert witness** is any witness who has specialized knowledge in an area. The kind of testimony a witness may provide to the court depends on which type of witness he or she is.

Before testifying in court, every witness is required to <u>take an oath</u> to present truthful testimony. Rule 603 of the Federal Rules of Evidence provides the following:

> Before testifying, every witness shall be required to declare that he will testify truthfully, by oath or affirmation administered in a form calculated to awaken his conscience and impress his mind with the duty to do so.

This oath also informs the witness that willful false testimony or perjury is punishable by the court.

### 1. Personal Knowledge

A witness is required to testify about facts that are within the witness's personal knowledge. Rule 602 of the Federal Rules of Evidence provides the following:

> A witness may not testify to a matter unless evidence is introduced sufficient to support a finding that he has personal knowledge of a matter. Evidence to prove personal knowledge may, but need not, consist of the testimony of the witness himself. This rule is subject to the provisions of Rule 703, relating to opinion testimony by expert witnesses.

Accordingly, personal observations such as identity, distance, color, time, and description of an event or object is generally allowed.

### 2. Competency

In order to testify, a witness must have sufficient **competency,** or the physical and mental capacity to understand the duty to tell the truth and the capacity to observe, recollect, and communicate. Questions of a witness's competency to testify are decided by the trial judge. If a witness is so deficient mentally or physically, the court may find the witness incompetent to testify. However, under Rule 601 of the Federal Rules of Evidence, every witness is presumed competent to testify. Rule 601 provides the following:

> Every person is competent to be a witness except as otherwise provided by these rules.

Witness competency questions can arise when testimony of minor children, retarded persons, and severely physically and mentally deficient individuals is proposed.

### 3. Expert Witnesses

An expert witness is one who has special experience, knowledge, or skill that allows him or her to give opinions, not merely facts. Such a witness may testify only if the court first accepts his or her qualifications as an expert. Then the expert witness must show the factual basis on which an opinion is rendered. The opinion must be based only on the perception of the witness and the opinion must lead to a clearer understanding of the determination of a fact at issue. Rule 702 of the Federal Rules of Evidence provides as follows:

> If scientific, technical, or other specialized knowledge will assist the trier of fact to understand the evidence or to determine a fact in issue, a witness qualified as an expert by knowledge, skill, experience, training, or education may testify thereto in the form of an opinion or otherwise.

Thus, the court must decide that some special knowledge will aid the jury (or the judge in a trial without a jury) to understand the evidence presented in the case.

The trier of fact is not obliged to accept the opinion of the expert, but may weigh the evidence of the expert just as all other evidence in the case is evaluated. An expert may never say who is liable in a lawsuit. For example, a traffic engineer used as an expert witness could not testify that "the defendant was negligent." It would be proper, however, for the expert to say that "the defendant was going at a speed faster than was safe for conditions."

Doctors are often used as expert witnesses in personal injury cases. Typically, doctors are requested to testify as to the extent of injuries sustained by a party and the prognosis or likelihood of complete recovery for someone who has sustained serious physical injury.

## B. Documents

Evidence in a trial is presented by **documents** as well as by witnesses. When a document is offered into evidence, it must become an exhibit to be considered by the court. An exhibit must be authenticated; that is, it must be shown to be what it purports to be before it can be introduced into evidence.

Traditionally, courts have required that only the original of a document be offered into evidence, as Rule 1002 of the Federal Rules of Evidence specifies:

> To prove the content of a writing, recording, or photograph, the original writing, recording, or photograph is required, except as otherwise provided in these rules or by Act of Congress.

The **Best Evidence Rule** embodies the requirement that when a document is sought to be proved, the original is required. This rule developed through common law to provide a safeguard against inaccurate and fraudulent documents. However, when the original is lost or cannot be produced, this rule allows certain types of substitutes in lieu of the original to be offered into evidence.

Under Rule 1003 of the Federal Rules of Evidence, duplicates may be admissible:

> A duplicate is admissible to the same extent as an original unless (1) a genuine question is raised as to the authenticity of the original or (2) in the circumstances it would be unfair to admit the duplicate of the original.

In essence the rules provide a system of preference. The original document is always best. However, if the failure to produce the original is satisfactorily explained, duplicate documents may be admissible.

## C. Real Evidence

**Real evidence** involves the real thing. In essence it provides the court with an opportunity to view an actual object or thing that is germane to the issues in the trial. Examples of real evidence are exhibiting a physical injury such as a scar to the jury, exhibiting a damaged object, or exhibiting a weapon that caused injury to a party.

Real evidence must be properly authenticated. In other words, a witness must testify and lay a foundation that the object is what it purports to be.

In addition, real evidence may be excluded by the court if it unfairly inflames the sympathy of the jury or the probability of jury prejudice outweighs the object's relative value in deciding the case. If, for example, a party has lost an arm as a result of claimed negligence by the defendant and wants the jury to examine the actual preserved severed arm, the trial judge, upon objection by the defendant's attorney, might properly conclude that the possible jury prejudice outweighs the probative value and necessity for the jury to examine the arm firsthand.

## D. Demonstrative Evidence

**Demonstrative evidence** is different from real evidence in that it is not a real object directly connected to the case. In essence demonstrative evidence is a visual aid to the court that accurately depicts the real thing. Witness testimony is often necessary to determine accuracy.

Demonstrative evidence can include maps, models, drawings, charts, photographs, videotapes, and courtroom demonstrations. When a photograph is used as an example, a witness must establish that the photograph accurately depicts the subject. For instance, a picture of the scene of an accident or damage to a vehicle or object serves as a visual image to clarify a witness's testimony. Another example of demonstrative evidence might be to have a witness use a chart or diagram to help explain how he or she perceived an automobile accident.

## III. Relevance

## A. Definition and Rule

One of the main requirements of the law of evidence is that only relevant evidence is admissible and anything that is relevant may be brought before the court. Rule 402 of the Federal Rules of Evidence defines the general rule of relevance:

> All relevant evidence is admissible, except as otherwise provided by the Constitution of the United States, by Act of Congress, by these rules, or by other rules prescribed by the Supreme Court pursuant to statutory authority. Evidence which is not relevant is not admissible.

Although Rule 402 defines the general rule of evidence, it does not define what constitutes relevant evidence.

One must look to Rule 401 of the Federal Rules of Evidence in order to obtain a working definition of relevance:

**Relevant evidence** means evidence having any tendency to make the existence of any fact that is of consequence to the determination of the action more probable or less probable then it would be without the evidence.

The basic test is one of logic. Does the evidence offered have a direct relation to a matter important in the trial?

Some examples may be helpful:

### EXAMPLE 1

Father and Mother are engaged in a child custody battle. Mother wants to offer evidence that Father is employed full-time and has no appropriate caretaker for the parties' two young children. This is relevant because it tends to show the ability or disability of Father to be the person best able to care for the children. If Mother wanted to offer evidence that Father is a poor executive at his job, this would not be relevant because it has nothing to do with his ability to provide a proper home for the children.

### EXAMPLE 2

Smith has sued Jones for breach of a contract of employment. Smith claims he was fired by Jones without cause and that he is entitled to damages for the time he could not find another job. Jones's defense is that Smith could not perform the work assigned to him and was, therefore, terminated properly. Jones tries to present evidence through the testimony of Smith's coworkers about Smith's work habits and difficulties on the job. This would be relevant. Smith offers evidence that Jones owns forty-five factories. This would not be relevant because it has nothing to do with Smith's work performance.

### EXAMPLE 3

A and B are involved in a car collision. A claims B ran a red light, causing the collision. A offers evidence that B must drive with glasses and was not wearing them at the time the collision took place. B objects on the grounds of relevancy. B's objection will be "overruled" (not allowed) because the question of B's ability to see is relevant to the cause of the collision.

A next tries to submit evidence that B was involved in another collision two weeks following the incident with A. B objects again on grounds of relevancy. B's objection will be "sustained" (granted) because a collision that occurred after the one that is the subject of the lawsuit has nothing to do with whether a driver was negligent in the particular incident being discussed.

## B. Exclusions

In some circumstances evidence may be excluded although it is relevant. These situations usually involve a court attempting to balance the value of receiving the information against the potential harm of unfair prejudice or emotionalism that the evidence might generate and that would improperly taint the jury's deliberation process. Rule 403 of the Federal Rules of Evidence sets out this relative standard:

> Although relevant, evidence may be excluded if its probative value is substantially outweighed by the danger of unfair prejudice, confusion of the issues, or misleading the jury, or by considerations of undue delay, waste of time, or needless presentation of cumulative evidence.

The Federal Rules of Evidence also specifically elaborate several situations where relevant evidence will be held inadmissible or rejected because of other strongly held policy considerations that override the potential probative value of the relevant evidence. Examples include the following:

1. offers to compromise a claim (Rule 408);

2. evidence of furnishing or offering to furnish medical, hospital, or similar expenses (Rule 409);

3. plea discussions in a criminal case to be used in a civil case (Rule 410); and

4. evidence that a person was or was not insured against liability is not admissible upon the issue of whether a person acted negligently or otherwise wrongfully (Rule 411).

## IV. HEARSAY

### A. Definition and Rule

Rule 801 of the Federal Rules of Evidence defines hearsay as follows:

> **Hearsay** is a statement, other than one made by the declarant while testifying at the trial or hearing, offered in evidence to prove the truth of the matter asserted.

The **declarant** is the person who makes a statement. A **statement** can be oral or written and even sometimes a gesture.

The key concept to remember is that hearsay is more than an out-of-court statement being offered into evidence at trial; it is an out-of-court statement whose substance is being offered as true.

**EXAMPLE**

Fred is testifying on the witness stand. Fred states that Barbara said that she was going eighty-five miles per hour at the time of the accident. Is this statement hearsay?

If the statement is being offered to prove that Barbara was going eighty-five miles per hour at the time of accident, then such a statement is hearsay. However, if the statement is being offered to show that Barbara can speak the English language, then such a statement would not be hearsay. The substance of the statement is not being offered for the truth.

The hearsay rule is very simple. Rule 802 of the Federal Rules of Evidence mandates that hearsay is not admissible. However, in order to try to understand the complexity of this topic, it is important to master the exceptions to the hearsay rule and situations articulated by the Rules of Evidence that do not constitute hearsay. In other words, unless hearsay falls within an exception to the rule or it is not specifically defined as hearsay in accordance with rule 801(d) of the Federal Rules of Evidence, it is inadmissible. However, the failure of a party to make a timely objection to hearsay at trial will allow hearsay to be admitted into evidence.

In order to understand why the rules concerning hearsay exist, one must understand the inherent dangers involved in allowing hearsay evidence and the impact that such information can have on the normal safeguards allowed during a trial. Every time a witness testifies in court certain risks and factors must be considered in evaluating his or her testimony. These factors are perception, memory, narration, and sincerity.[1] In order to test the weight to give to the witness's testimony, he or she is required to testify under oath, in person, and is subject to cross-examination.

The problem with hearsay lies in determining the validity or weight to give testimony. The hearsay declarant is not in court, not under oath, and not subject to cross-examination. Therefore, certain dangers exist in allowing into evidence such untested information. The exceptions to the hearsay rule involve situations where the information is found to be generally reliable in spite of the deficiency. Otherwise, hearsay is excluded because of the absence of these tests for ascertaining trustworthiness.

**EXAMPLE**

Observation of a car accident. A testifies that B told him that Defendant's car struck Plaintiff's car.

A is testifying in court. How do you evaluate whether A's testimony is accurate? How do you evaluate whether B's testimony is accurate?

## B. Exceptions to the Hearsay Rule

In order to understand the full range of exceptions to the hearsay rule, you must study rules 803 and 804 in their entirety. However, rather than provide an exhaustive analysis of each exception, we will highlight only the major exceptions. In addition, although technically not an exception to the hearsay rule under the Federal Rules of Evidence, we will discuss admissions by party/opponent under this category for convenience purposes.

### 1. Admission by Party/Opponent

An out-of-court statement made by a party/opponent being offered for the truth of the matter asserted therein is admissible. Although it certainly looks like hearsay, rule 801(d) provides that such a statement is not hearsay and is admissible. Under the traditional common law of evidence, this category of hearsay was considered an exception to the hearsay rule and admissible.

---

[1]The Advisory Committee's (Federal Rules of Evidence) Introductory Note. See also: Morgan, "Hearsay Dangers and the Application of the Hearsay Concept," *Harvard Law Review* 62 (1948): 177.

**EXAMPLE**

Plaintiff calls A to the witness stand. A testifies that the Defendant told him that the Defendant was not wearing his required glasses at the time of the accident. Is such a statement hearsay?

Under the Federal Rules of Evidence such a statement is not hearsay and is admissible.

## 2. Declarations against Interest (Rule 804(b)(3))

This exception to the hearsay rule allows hearsay to be admitted into evidence when the following criteria are met:

(a) the declarant is unavailable to testify

(b) the statement is against the declarant's pecuniary, proprietary, or criminal liability interest.

**EXAMPLE**

Issue: Did Defendant strike the Plaintiff? A testifies that B said that B struck the Plaintiff, causing injury to the Plaintiff.

Clearly B's testimony is against B's own interest. If B is unavailable to testify, the testimony of A would be allowed. However, if B was available to testify, A's statement would not fall under this exception and would therefore be inadmissible.

## 3. Business Records (Rule 803(6))

Records, documents, reports, and other written compilations may constitute an exception to the hearsay rule. However, in order for records to qualify under this exception they must have been made at or near the time of the matter recorded, and, they must have been made and kept in the regular course of business.

## 4. Excited Utterance (Rule 803(2))

This exception provides that a statement relating to a startling event or condition made while the declarant was under the stress of excitement caused by the event or condition is admissible. This exception is based on the notion that the excitement reduces the prospect of fabrication, and the contemporaneous nature allows for reliability.

**EXAMPLE**

A testifies that mother of child watching her son get hit by a car stated "I should have kept him closer to me so I could have prevented him from running out in the street."

A's testimony as to what mother said would fall within this exception to the hearsay rule.

### 5. Past Recollection Recorded (Rule 803(5))

This exception involves records or memos made by a witness previous to a trial. The writing will be admitted as an exception to the hearsay rule if

(a) the witness once had knowledge about the substance of the writing but now has insufficient memory;

(b) the witness prepared the writing when it was fresh in witness's memory; and

(c) the writing accurately reflects witness's knowledge.

Critical to this exception is the fact that the witness has no present memory concerning the actual substance of the writing. If the witness has some memory of the substance of the writing, he or she must testify without the writing, and the writing is excluded from evidence.

### 6. Present Sense Impression (Rule 803(1))

A statement describing or explaining an event or condition made while the declarant was perceiving the event or condition, or immediately thereafter, is admissible as a hearsay exception. The reliability is provided by the spontaneity.

This exception is similar to the excited utterance exception in that it requires spontaneity. However, statements made under this exception need not be made under stress or while witnessing a startling event.

### 7. Dying Declarations (Rule 804(b)(2))

A statement made by a dying declarant concerning the cause of what the declarant believed to be his or her impending death is admissible.

**EXAMPLE**

On his death bed A states that he ran a red light causing the accident that led to his fatal injury. A's statement would be admissible as a dying declaration.

## V. Summary

Evidence involves the presentation of information at a trial. Rules determine what information can be presented. Questions of evidence are questions of law and are decided by a judge during a trial.

There are four main categories of evidence: witness testimony, documents, real evidence, and demonstrative evidence. Witness testimony can be given by lay witnesses and expert witnesses. A lay witness must have personal knowledge of the basis of his or her testimony and must be competent. An expert witness has special experience or knowledge in an area. With respect to documents, the courts generally require the original document to be produced at trial. Real evidence involves producing the real thing at trial. Demonstrative evidence is a visual aid to the court.

One of the main requirements of the law of evidence involves relevance. Only relevant or logical evidence is admissible. The court determines whether the offered information is directly related to a matter important in the trial.

Another rule of evidence involves hearsay, or an out-of-court statement being offered as truth. Although hearsay evidence is inadmissible, there are several major exceptions to the hearsay rule where, although the statements are made out of court and are being offered for their truth, the courts have found sufficient independent reasons to overcome the reliability risks inherent in hearsay. Examples of the exceptions are admissions by party opponents, declarations against interest, business records, excited utterances, past recollection recorded, present sense impression, and dying declarations.

---

## VI. KEY TERMS

| | | |
|---|---|---|
| Best Evidence Rule | Documents | Real evidence |
| Competency | Evidence | Relevance |
| Declarant | Expert witness | Relevant evidence |
| Demonstrative evidence | Hearsay | Statement |
| | Lay witness | |

## VII. QUESTIONS

1. What is the difference between a lay witness and an expert witness?
2. Who determines whether a witness qualifies as an expert witness?
3. What is an objection?
4. What qualifications must a lay witness possess in order to provide testimony?
5. What is the Best Evidence Rule?
6. Compare and contrast real evidence and demonstrative evidence.
7. When can real evidence be excluded?
8. When can relevant evidence be excluded?
9. Why should offers to compromise a claim be excluded?
10. Define the hearsay rule.
11. Why is an admission by a party opponent an allowable exception to the hearsay rule?
12. What is the basis of reliability for the following:
    a. dying declaration
    b. business records
    c. excited utterances
    d. past recollection recorded
    e. present sense impression

CHAPTER 6

# COMMENCEMENT OF THE LAWSUIT: PLEADINGS AND PRETRIAL MOTIONS

# I. Introduction

The purpose of this chapter is to discuss the role of the paralegal in preparing the documents necessary to commence and defend a lawsuit. Specifically, we will focus on the purpose and drafting requirements of various pleadings and pretrial motions. **Pleadings** are documents filed with a court that set out the parties' respective positions in a lawsuit. Pleading also describes the process of preparing certain documents used to either commence or defend a lawsuit. A **pretrial motion** is an application or request to a court for an order prior to a trial.

Consistent with the assumptions stated in previous chapters, we will focus primarily on drafting pleadings and motions commonly used in federal civil practice. Therefore, the Federal Rules of Civil Procedure will be the procedural guide. In addition, we will also focus on the civil pleading and motion practice used in the courts of Pennsylvania. Because the two systems are different but yet representative of a large number of state pleading and practice requirements, the issues raised in this chapter should have universal application.

Primary attention in this chapter is paid to the kinds of documents and pleading issues that paralegals are most likely to encounter. Because attorneys are usually directly involved in the more sophisticated drafting and pleading problems, much of this chapter is devoted to the more routine pleadings and motions that paralegals commonly encounter. However, some of the more difficult pleading issues are also raised and briefly discussed.

Pleadings are the mechanics of the litigation process. They control how and when a case proceeds through its various stages; that is, commencement of the lawsuit, pretrial discovery, trial and post-trial procedures. Without pleadings a lawsuit could not proceed in an orderly fashion because parties would not know the claims of their opponents.

The rules of pleading are intended to show the real dispute between the parties. By adhering to the rules, matters on which there is no dispute may be disposed of quickly, not requiring the time of the judge. Pleading rules confine the parties to relevant matters and thus are a timesaving device.

Every jurisdiction has its own pleading rules. In federal trial courts, as stated earlier, the rules are known as the Federal Rules of Civil Procedure. Each state also has its own rules. In addition each separate court within a system may set out special rules to be followed in that court. For example, each district court in the federal system will have its own "local" rules that pertain to matters not controlled by the Federal Rules of Civil Procedure. The rule books that are appropriate to an action should be frequently consulted before and during the litigation process.

## II. The Commencement of a Lawsuit

### A. Federal Court

A civil action in federal district court is commenced by the plaintiff's filing of a **complaint.**[1] A complaint is one of the pleadings authorized by Rule 7(a) of the

---

[1] Rule 3, Federal Rules of Civil Procedure.

Federal Rules of Civil Procedure (hereafter referred to as FRCP) and its purpose is to initiate a lawsuit. The function of a complaint is to give an opposing party (defendant) **notice** of the nature and basis or grounds for a claim and a general indication of the type of litigation involved.[2] No technical forms of pleadings are required.[3] However, pursuant to the procedural rules, a complaint should follow a particular format.

Paralegals must include the following in the drafting of the complaint:[4]

- name of court

- name and address of both parties in caption form

- title of the action

- a short and plain statement of the grounds upon which the court's jurisdiction depends

- a short and plain statement of the claim showing that the pleader is entitled to relief

- a demand for judgment for the relief to which the plaintiff deems him- or herself entitled

- demand for jury trial

- name, address, and signature of plaintiff's attorney

In addition, the complaint submitted for filing must be on 8½-by 11 inch paper.

### 1. Caption

The complaint begins with the **caption,** which contains the name of the court, the title of the action, the names of the parties (and perhaps also their addresses), the file number, and the designation of the pleading as a complaint.[5] See Exhibit 6.1 for an example of a caption.

### 2. Statement of Jurisdiction

Next the complaint must contain a short and plain statement of the grounds upon which the court's jurisdiction depends, called a **statement of jurisdiction.**[6] Official Form 2 contains examples of allegations of jurisdiction based upon diversity of citizenship, the existence of a general federal question, the existence of a question arising under a particular statute, and the admiralty or maritime character of the claim.[7] Form 2 is reprinted in Exhibit 6.2.

---

[2] Rule 8(a), FRCP.

[3] Rule 8(e)(1), FRCP.

[4] See FRCP 8(a), 10(a) and 11.

[5] FRCP 10(a).

[6] FRCP 8(a)(1). Also remember that federal district court is a court of limited jurisdiction. Therefore the plaintiff is required to affirmatively state the grounds for federal jurisdiction.

[7] At the end of the FRCP, there is an appendix of forms intended for illustration only. These forms are quite helpful in providing a suggested format as to how to draft certain pleadings in a way that is approved by the federal courts.

**EXHIBIT 6.1**

## Sample Caption

UNITED STATES DISTRICT COURT FOR THE EASTERN
DISTRICT OF PENNSYLVANIA

| | |
|---|---|
| JOHN SMITH<br>4 Linden Street<br>Allentown, PA | : |
| | : |
| | : |
| Plaintiff | : |
| | : |
| v. | : CIVIL ACTION NO. _____ |
| | : |
| TOM JONES<br>1 Main Street<br>Philadelphia, PA | : JURY TRIAL<br>: DEMANDED |
| | : |
| Defendant | : |

COMPLAINT

### 3. Statement of the Claim

After the allegation of jurisdiction the pleading must contain a short and plain **statement of the claim** showing that the plaintiff is entitled to relief. The decision concerning what constitutes a short and plain statement is determined on the basis of the nature of the action. All the essential elements of the claim should be included in the complaint, preferably by specific allegations. In addition, the complaint should contain an allegation of money damages, if claimed.[8]

In order to determine what elements should be included in your complaint, it can be helpful to look at standard jury instructions concerning the kind of claim that is the basis of your lawsuit.[9] These instructions provide you with all the elements necessary to establish liability. Although the federal rules do not always require this kind of specificity, following these jury instructions will at least ensure that you have included enough information to satisfy this "notice" pleading requirement.

Official Forms 3 through 18 are examples of sufficient statements of claims in various types of actions. They illustrate the simplicity and brevity of a complaint in federal court. See Exhibits 6.3 through 6.11 for some examples.

---

[8] See Official Form 9 or Exhibit 6.4, which is based on it.
[9] Jury instructions will be discussed in more detail in the chapters on pretrial preparation and trial.

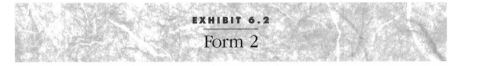

**EXHIBIT 6.2**

# Form 2

## ALLEGATION OF JURISDICTION

(a) Jurisdiction founded on diversity of citizenship and amount.[10]

Plaintiff is a [citizen of the State of Connecticut][1] [corporation incorporated under the laws of the State of Connecticut having its principal place of business in the State of Connecticut] and defendant is a corporation incorporated under the laws of the State of New York having its principal place of business in a State other than the State of Connecticut. The matter in controversy exceeds, exclusive of interest and costs, the sum of fifty thousand dollars.

(b) Jurisdiction founded on the existence of a Federal question and amount in controversy.

The action arises under [the Constitution of the United States, Article , Section ____]; [the ____ Amendment of the Constitution of the United States, Section ____]; [the Act of ____ , ____ Stat. ____; U.S.C., Title ____ , § ____]; [the Treaty of the United States (here describe the treaty)],[2] as hereinafter more fully appears.[3]

(c) Jurisdiction founded on the existence of a question arising under particular statutes.

The action arises under the Act of _____ , _____Stat. _____; U.S.C., Title _____ , § _____ , as hereinafter more fully appears.

(d) Jurisdiction founded on the admiralty or maritime character of the claim.

This is a case of admiralty and maritime jurisdiction, as hereinafter more fully appears. [If the pleader wishes to invoke the distinctively maritime procedures referred to in Rule 9(h), add the following or its substantial equivalent: This is an admiralty or maritime claim within the meaning of Rule 9(h).]

As amended April 17, 1961, eff. July 19, 1961; Feb. 28, 1966, eff. July 1, 1966.

---

[1]Form for natural person.

[2]Use the appropriate phrase or phrases. The general allegation of the existence of a federal question is ineffective unless the matters constituting the claim for relief as set forth in the complaint raise a federal question.

[3]The requirement of an amount in controversy in excess of $30,000 is no longer required for federal question jurisdiction. Therefore, the reader should note that the reprint of Form 2 has been modified to reflect this change.

---

[10]The amount in controversy has been changed from $10,000 to $50,000.

**EXHIBIT 6.3**

## Complaint on a Promissory Note

(Caption)

1. Plaintiff is (name), an individual residing at (street address, city and state).

2. Defendant is (name), an individual residing at (street address, city and state).

3. Jurisdiction of this court is based on diversity of citizenship. The matter in controversy, exclusive of interest and costs, exceeds the sum of $50,000.

4. On or about June 1, 1991, defendant executed and delivered to plaintiff a promissory note in the amount of $50,000 payable with 6% interest on June 1, 1991. A true and correct copy of the note is attached hereto and made part hereof as Exhibit "A".

5. Defendant owes to plaintiff the amount of said note and interest.

WHEREFORE, plaintiff demands judgment against defendant for the sum of $50,000 plus interest* and costs.

(signed)
_____
Attorney for plaintiff

*Further interest may be due from the date the note became payable.
Based on Official Form 3.

### 4. Demand for Judgment

Following the statement of the claim, the complaint must contain a **demand for a judgment** for the relief to which the plaintiff feels he or she is entitled.[11] Relief of several different types may be demanded. This demand for relief is sometimes referred to as a "prayer for relief" or as the "WHEREFORE" clause.[12]

Here is an example of a demand for relief:

WHEREFORE, plaintiff demands judgment against defendant in the amount of $25,000, interest and costs.

### 5. Signature of Attorney

The **signature of the plaintiff's attorney,** along with the address, is placed after the demand for relief.[13] A party who is not represented by counsel must sign his or her own pleading. The signature of an attorney is deemed to be

---

[11] FRCP 8(a)(3).

[12] Demands for relief usually begin with the word "WHEREFORE."

[13] FRCP 11.

**EXHIBIT 6.4**

## Complaint for Negligence

(Caption)

1. Plaintiff is (name), an individual residing at (street address, city and state).

2. Defendant is (name), an individual residing at (street address, city and state).

3. Jurisdiction of this court is based on diversity of citizenship. The amount in controversy, exclusive of interest and costs, exceeds $50,000.

4. On or about March 1, 1991, in a public highway known as Boyle Street in Boston, Massachusetts, defendant negligently drove a motor vehicle against plaintiff who was then crossing said highway.

5. As a result, plaintiff was thrown down and had her leg broken and was otherwise injured, was prevented from transacting her business, suffered great pain of body and mind, and incurred expenses for medical attention and hospitalization in the sum of $40,000.

WHEREFORE, plaintiff demands judgment against defendant in an amount in excess of $50,000 plus costs.*

(signed)
Attorney for plaintiff

*Note that in a complaint where there have been physical injuries, pain and suffering damages will be requested and it is generally unwise and not proper to ask for a specific dollar amount since the judge or jury will determine the degree of pain and suffering.
Based on Official Form 9.

**EXHIBIT 6.5**

## Form 4

COMPLAINT ON AN ACCOUNT

1. Allegation of jurisdiction.

2. Defendant owes plaintiff _____ dollars according to the account hereto annexed as Exhibit A.

Wherefore (etc. as in Form 3).

As amended Jan. 21, 1963, eff. July 1, 1963.

**EXHIBIT 6.6**
## Form 5

### COMPLAINT FOR GOODS SOLD AND DELIVERED

1. Allegation of jurisdiction.
2. Defendant owes plaintiff _____ dollars for goods sold and delivered by plaintiff to defendant between June 1, 1963 and December 1, 1963.
Wherefore (etc. as in Form 3).
As amended Jan. 21, 1963, eff. July 1, 1963.

**EXHIBIT 6.7**
## Form 6

### COMPLAINT FOR MONEY LENT

1. Allegation of jurisdiction.
2. Defendant owes plaintiff _____ dollars for money lent by plaintiff to defendant on June 1, 1963.
Wherefore (etc. as in Form 3).
As amended Jan. 21, 1963, eff. July 1, 1963.

**EXHIBIT 6.8**
## Form 7

### COMPLAINT FOR MONEY PAID BY MISTAKE

1. Allegation of jurisdiction.
2. Defendant owes plaintiff _____ dollars for money paid by plaintiff to defendant by mistake on June 1, 1963, under the following circumstances: [here state the circumstances with particularity—see Rule 9(b)].
Wherefore (etc. as in Form 3).
As amended Jan. 21, 1963, eff. July 1, 1963.

**EXHIBIT 6.9**

## Form 8

### COMPLAINT FOR MONEY HAD AND RECEIVED

1. Allegation of jurisdiction.
2. Defendant owes plaintiff _____ dollars for money had and received from one G. H. on June 1, 1963, to be paid by defendant to plaintiff.
Wherefore (etc. as in Form 3).
As amended Jan. 21, 1963, eff. July 1, 1963.

**EXHIBIT 6.10**

## Form 10

COMPLAINT FOR NEGLIGENCE WHERE PLAINTIFF IS UNABLE TO DE-TERMINE DEFINITELY WHETHER THE PERSON RESPONSIBLE IS C. D. OR E. F. OR WHETHER BOTH ARE RESPONSIBLE AND WHERE HIS EVI-DENCE MAY JUSTIFY A FINDING OF WILFULNESS OR OF RECKLESS-NESS OR OF NEGLIGENCE.

A. B., Plaintiff
    v.     }   *Complaint*
C. D. and E. F., Defendants

1. Allegation of jurisdiction.
2. On June 1, 1963, in a public highway called Boylston Street in Boston, Massachusetts, defendant C. D. or defendant E. F., or both defendants C. D. and E. F., wilfully or recklessly or negligently drove or caused to be driven a motor vehicle against plaintiff who was then crossing said highway.
3. As a result plaintiff was thrown down and had his leg broken and was otherwise injured, was prevented from transacting his business, suffered great pain of body and mind, and incurred expenses for medical attention and hospitalization in the sum of thirty thousand dollars.
Wherefore plaintiff demands judgment against C. D. or against E. F. or against both in the sum of _____ dollars and costs.
As amended Jan. 21, 1963, eff. July 1, 1963.

**EXHIBIT 6.11**

# Form 14

## COMPLAINT FOR NEGLIGENCE UNDER FEDERAL EMPLOYER'S LIABILITY ACT

1. Allegation of jurisdiction.

2. During all the times herein mentioned defendant owned and operated in interstate commerce a railroad which passed through a tunnel located at _____ and known as Tunnel No. _____.

3. On or about June 1, 1963, defendant was repairing and enlarging the tunnel in order to protect interstate trains and passengers and freight from injury and in order to make the tunnel more conveniently usable for interstate commerce.

4. In the course of thus repairing and enlarging the tunnel on said day defendant employed plaintiff as one of its workmen, and negligently put plaintiff to work in a portion of the tunnel which defendant had left unprotected and unsupported.

5. By reason of defendant's negligence in thus putting plaintiff to work in that portion of the tunnel, plaintiff was, while so working, pursuant to defendant's orders, struck and crushed by a rock, which fell from the unsupported portion of the tunnel, and was (here describe plaintiff's injuries).

6. Prior to these injuries, plaintiff was a strong, able-bodied man, capable of earning and actually earning _____ dollars per day. By these injuries he has been made incapable of any gainful activity, has suffered great physical and mental pain, and has incurred expense in the amount of _____ dollars for medicine, medical attendance, and hospitalization.

Wherefore plaintiff demands judgment against defendant in the sum of _____ dollars and costs.

a certification that the attorney has read the pleading, motion, or other paper; that to the best of the attorney's belief, knowledge, and information formed after reasonable inquiry it is well grounded in fact and is warranted by existing law or a good faith argument for the extension, modification, or reversal of existing law; and that it is not interposed for an improper purpose like delay, harassment, or needless increase in the cost of litigation. This serves to "verify" the pleading.

In addition, if an attorney is found to have violated rule 11 by signing a pleading that is not well-founded, the attorney may be subject to sanctions by the court. Accordingly, the paralegal and attorney should take great care in investigating the facts of a case underlying a pleading before the supervising attorney signs the pleading.

## 6. Demand for Jury Trial

The complaint can also contain a demand for a jury trial.[14] The demand for a jury trial can be made by an endorsement upon the complaint or by a separate instrument filed with the court. The demand for a jury trial is deemed waived if it is not requested in time.

## 7. General Pleading Comments

Each pleading is to be typed in paragraph form.[15] The paragraphs should be consecutively numbered, and, as far as practical, each paragraph should contain a single set of circumstances. A paragraph is referred to by the same number in all succeeding pleadings. For example, in an answer to a complaint, paragraph 1 of the complaint is answered in paragraph 1 of the answer. Statements in a different part of the same pleading, in another pleading, or in a motion may be referred to by **adoption by reference.** For example, a complaint might contain a paragraph that incorporates by reference certain allegations presented previously in the complaint by saying:[16]

> Paragraphs 1, 2, 3, and 11 are here realleged with the same force and effect as though said paragraphs were here set forth in full.

In the federal courts, a complaint involving more than one claim or cause or action is usually divided into **counts,** or causes of action.[17] Each count should be limited to a separate transaction or occurrence. For example, a complaint against one defendant may contain a count for product liability, a separate count for negligence, another for breach of express warranties, and finally a count for breach of implied warranties.

Although it is not required under the federal procedural rules, it is quite common for the first paragraph of a federal court complaint to be a preliminary statement informing the reader (especially the judge) of what the case is about. Therefore this paragraph can be an opportunity to describe your legal theory and the harm suffered by the plaintiff. Exhibit 6.12 is an example of a simple federal court complaint.

If documents are referred to in a pleading, they normally are attached as exhibits. Generally, exhibits are inserted after the body of the complaint and then the entire group of papers is bound with a backer, a heavy colored paper used as a cover for a pleading. Each exhibit should be lettered or numbered. The exhibits in a federal pleading are considered part of the pleading for all purposes.[18] Typically, a document that is attached as an exhibit is referred to as follows:

> On or about June 10, 1982, plaintiff and defendant entered into a written contract. A true and correct copy of said contract is attached hereto and made a part hereof as Exhibit "A."

---

[14] FRCP 38(b).
[15] FRCP 10(b).
[16] FRCP 10(c).
[17] FRCP 10(b).
[18] FRCP 10(c).

**EXHIBIT 6.12**

## Sample Federal Court Complaint

# IN THE UNITED STATES DISTRICT COURT FOR THE EASTERN DISTRICT OF PENNSYLVANIA

| | | |
|---|---|---|
| JOHN A. SMITH<br>1 Main Street<br>Elizabeth, NJ | : <br> : <br> : | |
| | : | |
| Plaintiff | : | |
| | : | |
| v. | : | Civil Action No. 92-100 |
| | : | |
| LEE G. JONES<br>100 First Street<br>Allentown, PA | : <br> : <br> : | |
| | : | |
| Defendant | : | JURY TRIAL DEMANDED |

COMPLAINT

### I. PRELIMINARY STATEMENT

1. Plaintiff seeks to recover money damages from the defendant for personal injuries suffered as a result of being struck by an automobile driven by the defendant.

### II. JURISDICTION

2. Jurisdiction of this Court is based on diversity of citizenship. The amount in controversy, exclusive of interest and costs, exceeds $50,000.00.

### III. PARTIES

3. Plaintiff, John A. Smith, is an adult individual who resides at 1 Main Street, Elizabeth, New Jersey.

4. Defendant, Lee G. Jones, is an adult individual who resides at 100 First Street, Allentown, Pennsylvania.

### IV. STATEMENT OF CLAIM

5. On or about March 5, 1992, in a public highway known as Linden Street in Allentown, Pennsylvania, defendant negligently drove a motor vehicle and struck the plaintiff who was then crossing said highway.

6. As a result of being stuck by defendant's automobile, plaintiff was thrown down and had his leg broken and was otherwise injured, was prevented from transacting his business, suffered great pain of body and mind, and incurred expenses for medical attention and hospitalization in the sum of Forty Thousand ($40,000.00) Dollars.

**EXHIBIT 6.12**

## Sample Federal Court Complaint (continued)

WHEREFORE, plaintiff demands judgment against the defendant in an amount in excess of $50,000 plus costs.

SCHMITT AND GONIFF

By:_____

M. Schmitt
1 North Fifth Street
Allentown, PA 18101
(215) 400-0000

Attorneys for plaintiff

---

Some states require that whenever a written contract or other document is a basis for the lawsuit it must be attached to the complaint as an exhibit. The Federal Rules of Civil Procedure do not so provide. It is considered good practice, however, to attach such a writing as an exhibit to the pleading.

### 8. Filing and Service of Process

Once the complaint has been prepared, the paralegal should then file the complaint. The complaint gets filed by taking it to the clerk of court's office in the United States District Courthouse, presenting the complaint to the appropriate clerk and paying the requisite filing fee. Pursuant to local rule, other forms may have to be completed and filed with the complaint.

In the United States District Court for the Eastern District of Pennsylvania, two forms must be completed and filed with the complaint: **designation form** and **civil cover sheet.** On the designation form counsel indicates the category of the cause of action so it can be assigned to the appropriate calendar. Two copies must be filed. The civil cover sheet allows the clerk of court to initiate a civil docket sheet. Only one copy must be filed.

On presentation of the complaint and supporting documents (if necessary) to the clerk, a civil action number is assigned. This number appears in the caption and is used on all subsequent pleadings. Also the case is assigned to a judge and the judge's initials are stamped at the top of the cover page. At the same time, the clerk opens a **docket sheet** with the corresponding number. The docket contains a precise history of the activity in a case. It will show what progress and proceedings occur during the course of the litigation. The docket sheet example in Exhibit 6.15 only shows that a complaint was filed, the fee for it paid, and marshal's service ordered and paid. As further things happen, for example, service of the complaint and filing of an answer, they will be added to the docket sheet.

Examples of the designation form, civil cover sheet, and a docket sheet are given in Exhibits 6.13 through 6.15.

**EXHIBIT 6.13**

## Designation Form

FOR THE EASTERN DISTRICT OF PENNSYLVANIA

DESIGNATION FORM to be used by counsel to indicate the category of the case for the purpose of assignment to appropriate calendar.

_____

Address of Plaintiff: _____

Post Office: _____ County: _____

Address of Defendant: _____

Post Office: _____ County: _____

Place of accident, incident, or transaction: _____

Post Office: _____ County: _____
(use reverse side for additional space)

_____

Does this case involve multidistrict litigation possibilities:    Yes ☐ No ☐

RELATED CASE IF ANY

Case Number: _____ Judge: _____ Date Terminated: _____

Civil cases are deemed related when yes is answered to any of the following questions:

1. Is this case related to property included in an earlier numbered suit pending or within one year previously terminated action in this court?    Yes ☐ No ☐

2. Does this case involve the same issue of fact or grow out of the same transaction as a prior suit pending or within one year previously terminated action in this court?    Yes ☐ No ☐

3. Does this case involve the validity or infringement of a patent already in suit or any earlier numbered case pending or within one year previously terminated action in this court?    Yes ☐ No ☐

**EXHIBIT 6.13**

## Designation Form (continued)

CIVIL: (Place (X) in <u>ONE CATEGORY ONLY</u>)

A. <u>Federal Question Cases:</u>
( ) Indemnity Contract, Marine
    Contract, and All Other
    Contracts
( ) FELA
( ) Jones Act—Personal Injury
( ) Antitrust
( ) Patent
( ) Labor-Management Relations
( ) Civil Rights
( ) Habeas Corpus
( ) Securities Act(s) Cases
( ) All Other Federal Question Cases
    (Please specify)

B. <u>Diversity Jurisdiction Cases:</u>
1. ( ) Insurance Contract and Other
     Contracts
2. ( ) Airplane Personal Injury
3. ( ) Assault; Defamation
4. ( ) Marine Personal Injury
5. ( ) Motor Vehicle Personal Injury
6. ( ) Other Personal Injury
     (Please specify)
7. ( ) Products Liability
8. ( ) All Other Diversity Cases
     (Please specify)

<u>ARBITRATION CERTIFICATION</u>

_____ , counsel of record do hereby certify pursuant to Local Civil Rule 8, Section 4(a)(2), that, to the best of my knowledge and belief, the damages recoverable in this civil action case exceed the sum of $75,000.00 exclusive of interest and cost.

DATE: _____          _____
                                     ATTORNEY-AT-LAW

_____

I certify that, to my knowledge, the within case is not related to any case now pending or within the year previously terminated action in this court except as noted above.

DATE: _____          _____
                                     ATTORNEY-AT-LAW

**EXHIBIT 6.14**

## Civil Cover Sheet

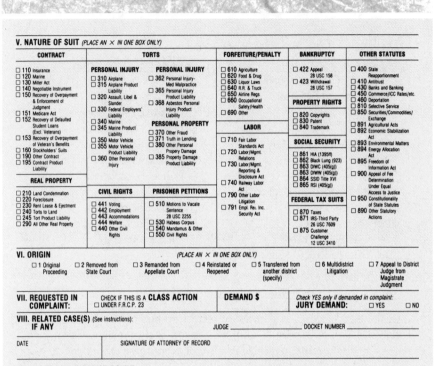

**V. NATURE OF SUIT** (PLACE AN × IN ONE BOX ONLY)

| CONTRACT | TORTS | | FORFEITURE/PENALTY | BANKRUPTCY | OTHER STATUTES |
|---|---|---|---|---|---|
| ☐ 110 Insurance | **PERSONAL INJURY** | **PERSONAL INJURY** | ☐ 610 Agriculture | ☐ 422 Appeal 28 USC 158 | ☐ 400 State Reapportionment |
| ☐ 120 Marine | ☐ 310 Airplane | ☐ 362 Personal Injury- Med Malpractice | ☐ 620 Food & Drug | ☐ 423 Withdrawal 28 USC 157 | ☐ 410 Antitrust |
| ☐ 130 Miller Act | ☐ 315 Airplane Product Liability | ☐ 365 Personal Injury Product Liability | ☐ 630 Liquor Laws | | ☐ 430 Banks and Banking |
| ☐ 140 Negotiable Instrument | ☐ 320 Assault, Libel & Slander | ☐ 368 Asbestos Personal Injury Product Liability | ☐ 640 R.R. & Truck | **PROPERTY RIGHTS** | ☐ 450 Commerce/ICC Rates/etc. |
| ☐ 150 Recovery of Overpayment & Enforcement of Judgment | ☐ 330 Federal Employers' Liability | | ☐ 650 Airline Regs | ☐ 820 Copyrights | ☐ 460 Deportation |
| ☐ 151 Medicare Act | ☐ 340 Marine | **PERSONAL PROPERTY** | ☐ 660 Occupational Safety/Health | ☐ 830 Patent | ☐ 810 Selective Service |
| ☐ 152 Recovery of Defaulted Student Loans (Excl. Veterans) | ☐ 345 Marine Product Liability | ☐ 370 Other Fraud | ☐ 690 Other | ☐ 840 Trademark | ☐ 850 Securities/Commodities/ Exchange |
| ☐ 153 Recovery of Overpayment of Veteran's Benefits | ☐ 350 Motor Vehicle | ☐ 371 Truth in Lending | **LABOR** | | ☐ 891 Agricultural Acts |
| ☐ 160 Stockholders' Suits | ☐ 355 Motor Vehicle Product Liability | ☐ 380 Other Personal Property Damage | ☐ 710 Fair Labor Standards Act | **SOCIAL SECURITY** | ☐ 892 Economic Stabilization Act |
| ☐ 190 Other Contract | ☐ 360 Other Personal Injury | ☐ 385 Property Damage Product Liability | ☐ 720 Labor/Mgmt. Relations | ☐ 861 HIA (1395ff) | ☐ 893 Environmental Matters |
| ☐ 195 Contract Product Liability | | | ☐ 730 Labor/Mgmt. Reporting & Disclosure Act | ☐ 862 Black Lung (923) | ☐ 894 Energy Allocation Act |
| **REAL PROPERTY** | **CIVIL RIGHTS** | **PRISONER PETITIONS** | ☐ 740 Railway Labor Act | ☐ 863 DIWC (405(g)) | ☐ 895 Freedom of Information Act |
| ☐ 210 Land Condemnation | ☐ 441 Voting | ☐ 510 Motions to Vacate Sentence 28 USC 2255 | ☐ 790 Other Labor Litigation | ☐ 863 DIWW (405(g)) | ☐ 900 Appeal of Fee Determination Under Equal Access to Justice |
| ☐ 220 Foreclosure | ☐ 442 Employment | | ☐ 791 Empl. Re. Inc. Security Act | ☐ 864 SSID Title XVI | |
| ☐ 230 Rent Lease & Ejectment | ☐ 443 Accommodations | ☐ 530 Habeas Corpus | | ☐ 865 RSI (405(g)) | ☐ 950 Constitutionality of State Statutes |
| ☐ 240 Torts to Land | ☐ 444 Welfare | ☐ 540 Mandamus & Other | | **FEDERAL TAX SUITS** | ☐ 890 Other Statutory Actions |
| ☐ 245 Tort Product Liability | ☐ 440 Other Civil Rights | ☐ 550 Civil Rights | | ☐ 870 Taxes | |
| ☐ 290 All Other Real Property | | | | ☐ 871 IRS-Third Party 26 USC 7609 | |
| | | | | ☐ 875 Customer Challenge 12 USC 3410 | |

**VI. ORIGIN**  (PLACE AN × IN ONE BOX ONLY)

☐ 1 Original Proceeding  ☐ 2 Removed from State Court  ☐ 3 Remanded from Appellate Court  ☐ 4 Reinstated or Reopened  ☐ 5 Transferred from another district (specify)  ☐ 6 Multidistrict Litigation  ☐ 7 Appeal to District Judge from Magistrate Judgment

**VII. REQUESTED IN COMPLAINT:**  CHECK IF THIS IS A **CLASS ACTION** ☐ UNDER F.R.C.P. 23  **DEMAND $**  Check YES only if demanded in complaint:  **JURY DEMAND:** ☐ YES  ☐ NO

**VIII. RELATED CASE(S) IF ANY** (See instructions):  JUDGE _____  DOCKET NUMBER _____

DATE _____  SIGNATURE OF ATTORNEY OF RECORD _____

**UNITED STATES DISTRICT COURT**

JS 44C
(Rev. 12/84)  **CIVIL COVER SHEET**

The JS-44 civil cover sheet and the information contained herein neither replace nor supplement the filing and service of pleadings or other papers as required by law, except as provided by local rules of court. This form, approved by the Judicial Conference of the United States in September 1974, is required for the use of the Clerk of Court for the purpose of initiating the civil docket sheet. (SEE INSTRUCTIONS ON THE REVERSE OF THE FORM.)

**I (a) PLAINTIFFS**  **DEFENDANTS**

**(b)** COUNTY OF RESIDENCE OF FIRST LISTED PLAINTIFF _____
(EXCEPT IN U.S. PLAINTIFF CASES)

COUNTY OF RESIDENCE OF FIRST LISTED DEFENDANT _____
(IN U.S. PLAINTIFF CASES ONLY)
NOTE: IN LAND CONDEMNATION CASES, USE THE LOCATION OF THE TRACT OF LAND INVOLVED

**(c)** ATTORNEYS (FIRM NAME, ADDRESS, AND TELEPHONE NUMBER)  ATTORNEYS (IF KNOWN)

**II. BASIS OF JURISDICTION** (PLACE AN × IN ONE BOX ONLY)

☐ 1 U.S. Government Plaintiff
☐ 2 U.S. Government Defendant
☐ 3 Federal Question (U.S. Government Not a Party)
☐ 4 Diversity (Indicate Citizenship of Parties in Item III)

**III. CITIZENSHIP OF PRINCIPAL PARTIES** (For Diversity Cases Only)  (PLACE AN × IN ONE BOX FOR PLAINTIFF AND ONE BOX FOR DEFENDANT)

| | PTF | DEF | | PTF | DEF |
|---|---|---|---|---|---|
| Citizen of This State | ☐ 1 | ☐ 1 | Incorporated or Principal Place of Business in This State | ☐ 4 | ☐ 4 |
| Citizen of Another State | ☐ 2 | ☐ 2 | Incorporated and Principal Place of Business in Another State | ☐ 5 | ☐ 5 |
| Citizen or Subject of a Foreign Country | ☐ 3 | ☐ 3 | Foreign Nation | ☐ 6 | ☐ 6 |

**IV. CAUSE OF ACTION** (CITE THE U.S. CIVIL STATUTE UNDER WHICH YOU ARE FILING AND WRITE A BRIEF STATEMENT OF CAUSE. DO NOT CITE JURISDICTIONAL STATUTES UNLESS DIVERSITY.)

## EXHIBIT 6.15
## Docket Sheet

CIVIL DOCKET
UNITED STATES DISTRICT COURT
D. C. Form No. 106A Rev.

Jury demand date:
4-6___

| TITLE OF CASE | ATTORNEYS |
|---|---|
| PERCY'S GALVINIZING COMPANY<br><br>vs.<br><br>BIG CHIP MINES, INC. | For plaintiff:<br><br>I. McMillan<br>1902 Tree Street<br>Scarborough Fair, Mass.<br><br>For defendant:<br><br>Walter Fremont<br>109 S. North Street<br>Brookings, Indiana |

| STATISTICAL RECORD | COSTS | | | DATE | NAME OR RECEIPT NO. | REC. | | DISB. | |
|---|---|---|---|---|---|---|---|---|---|
| | Clerk | 15 | 00 | 4–6–7 | #4875 | 15 | — | | |
| | | | | APR 7 | 1971 to<br>U.S. TREAS. | | | 15 | — |
| | Marshal | 5 | 00 | 4/15/74 | 58445<br>(APPEAL) | 5 | — | | |
| Basis of Action:<br>Anti-Trust | Docket fee | | | 4/16/74 | | | | 5 | — |
| | Witness fees | | | | | | | | |
| Action arose at: | Depositions: | | | | | | | | |

### Filing and Service of Process

After the complaint is filed, the clerk of court issues a summons and delivers it and the complaint to the federal marshal or to a person specifically appointed to make **service of process.** If marshal service is desired, the paralegal should prepare an instruction and process record for each defendant. This form is an order to the marshal to make service, and is also the record of when, where, and upon whom service was made. It is a preprinted form directly obtainable from the marshal's office. The marshal serves the summons and complaint together on the defendant(s).

See Exhibit 6.16 for an example of a summons and Exhibit 6.17 for an example of an instruction and process record.

**EXHIBIT 6.16**

## Summons

UNITED STATES DISTRICT COURT FOR THE
SOUTHERN DISTRICT OF NEW YORK

CIVIL ACTION, FILE NUMBER _____

A. B., Plaintiff
      v.      }    *Summons*
C. D., Defendant

*To the above-named defendant:*

    You are hereby summoned and required to serve upon _____ , plaintiff's attorney, whose address is _____ , an answer to the complaint which is herewith served upon you, within 20 days after service of this summons upon you, exclusive of the day of service. If you fail to do so, judgment by default will be taken against you for the relief demanded in the complaint.

_____

                                                *Clerk of Court*

[Seal of the U.S. District Court]

Dated: _____

There are two alternatives to having the complaint and summons served by the marshal's office. In lieu of service, counsel for the defendant(s) may accept service on behalf of their clients. Also, pursuant to FRCP 4(c), the court, upon motion of the plaintiff's attorney, may appoint a person (other than a marshal) to serve the summons and complaint. This motion is given to the court clerk when the complaint is filed. It is not uncommon that paralegals may be used and designated as these special process servers.

An example of a motion for special appointment to serve process and order appears in Exhibit 6.18.

The person serving the process shall make an affidavit of service setting forth the time, date, location, and manner of service on the defendant.[19] This form is called a return of service of summons and complaint (see Exhibit 6.19). It gets filed with the clerk of court.

The Federal Rules also authorize service of a summons and complaint by regular mail. The sender must send to the defendant(s) by first class mail, postage prepaid, a copy of the summons and complaint together with two copies of a notice and acknowledgment form and a postage prepaid return envelope

---

[19] FRCP 4(g).

## EXHIBIT 6.17

# Instruction and Process Record

**EXAMPLE—Instruction and Process Record**

| U.S. MARSHALS SERVICE INSTRUCTION AND PROCESS RECORD | INSTRUCTIONS: See "INSTRUCTIONS FOR SERVICE OF PROCESS BY THE U.S. MARSHAL," on the reverse of the last (No. 5) copy of this form. Please type or print legibly, insuring readability of all copies. Do not detach any copies. | |
|---|---|---|
| PLAINTIFF | | COURT NUMBER |
| DEFENDANT | | TYPE OF WRIT |

| | |
|---|---|
| SERVE | NAME OF INDIVIDUAL, COMPANY, CORPORATION, ETC., TO SERVE OR DESCRIPTION OF PROPERTY TO SEIZE OR CONDEMN |
| AT | ADDRESS (Street or RFD, Apartment No., City, State and ZIP Code) |

SEND NOTICE OF SERVICE COPY TO NAME AND ADDRESS BELOW:

Show number of this writ and total number of writs submitted, i.e., 1 of 1, 1 of 3, etc.     NO ___ OF ___   TOTAL

CHECK IF APPLICABLE:

☐ One copy for U. S. Attorney or designee and two copies for Attorney General of the U. S included.

SHOW IN THE SPACE BELOW AND TO THE LEFT ANY SPECIAL INSTRUCTIONS OR OTHER INFORMATION PERTINENT TO SERVING THE WRIT DESCRIBED ABOVE.

SPECIAL INSTRUCTIONS:

| NAME AND SIGNATURE OF ATTORNEY OR OTHER ORIGINATOR | TELEPHONE NUMBER | DATE |
|---|---|---|

**SPACE BELOW FOR USE OF U.S. MARSHAL ONLY - DO NOT WRITE BELOW THIS LINE**

| Show amount of deposit (or applicable code) and sign USM-285 for first writ only if more than one writ submitted. | DEPOSIT/CODE | DIST. OF ORIGIN | DISTRICT TO SERVE | LOCATION OF SUB-OFFICE OF DIST. TO SERVE |
|---|---|---|---|---|
| I acknowledge receipt for the total number of writs indicated and for the deposit (if applicable) shown. | SIGNATURE OF AUTHORIZED USMS DEPUTY OR CLERK | | DATE | |

☐ I hereby certify and return that I have personally served, have legal evidence of service, or have executed as shown in "REMARKS," the writ described on the individual, company, corporation, etc., at the address shown above or on the individual, company, corporation, etc., at the address inserted below.

☐ I hereby certify and return that, after diligent investigation, I am unable to locate the individual, company, corporation, etc., named above within this Judicial District.

| NAME AND TITLE OF INDIVIDUAL SERVED (If not shown above) | ☐ A person of suitable age and discretion then abiding in the defendant's usual place of abode |
|---|---|
| ADDRESS (Complete only if different than shown above) | FEE (If applicable) $     MILEAGE $ |
| DATE(S) OF ENDEAVOR (Use Remarks if necessary)   DATE OF SERVICE   TIME AM PM | SIGNATURE OF U. S. MARSHAL OR DEPUTY |

REMARKS

USM-285 (Ed. 7-1-70)                    1. CLERK OF THE COURT                    [B5939]

**EXHIBIT 6.18**

## Motion for Special Appointment to Serve Process

IN THE UNITED STATES DISTRICT COURT FOR THE EASTERN
DISTRICT OF PENNSYLVANIA

: CIVIL ACTION

:

: NO.

### MOTION FOR SPECIAL APPOINTMENT
### TO SERVE PROCESS

Pursuant to Rule 4(c), Federal Rules of Civil Procedure, _____ in the above-captioned civil action hereby move(s) this Court to specially appoint to _____ serve the _____ upon _____ in this action and represent(s) that:

1. Said person is or would be competent and not less than eighteen (18) years of age.

2. Said person is not and will not be a party to this action.

3. Granting the instant motion will effect substantial savings in (e.g., time, travel fees for the United States Marshal).

_____

Attorney for

### ORDER

AND NOW, to wit, this _____ day of _____ , 198  , it is ORDERED that _____ be and the same is hereby SPECIALLY APPOINTED to serve the _____ upon _____ in this action.

It is FURTHER ORDERED that proof of such service shall be made by affidavit in accordance with Rule 4(g), Federal Rules of Civil Procedure.

BY THE COURT:

_____

J.

United States District Court

addressed to the sender. If a copy of the acknowledgment and notice form are not received by the sender within twenty days, one of the previously mentioned methods of service must be employed. See the notice and acknowledgment for service by mail form (Exhibit 6.20) and the acknowledgment of receipt of summons and complaint form (Exhibit 6.21).

**EXHIBIT 6.19**

## Return of Service of Summons and Complaint

IN THE UNITED STATES DISTRICT COURT FOR THE EASTERN
DISTRICT OF PENNSYLVANIA

: CIVIL ACTION

:

: NO.

### RETURN OF SERVICE OF SUMMONS AND COMPLAINT

I hereby certify and return that on the _____ day of _____ ,
19 ___ at _____ m., I served this summons together with the complaint
herein as follows:

Name of Individual/Company/Corporation/etc., served:
Address where service was made:

I DECLARE UNDER PENALTY OF
PERJURY THAT THE FOREGOING
IS TRUE AND CORRECT.

By: _____
        Process Server

## B. Pennsylvania (State Court)

Unlike federal practice, a civil action in Pennsylvania may be commenced by
filing a praecipe (request) for a **writ of summons,** a complaint, or an agreement for an amicable action.[20] A writ of summons is a form that starts a lawsuit
by identifying the parties and specifying that the lawsuit is a civil action. As will
be noted later, the manner in which a civil action is commenced by the plaintiff

---

[20] See Rule 1007, Pennsylvania Rules of Civil Procedure (hereinafter referred to as Pa.R.C.P.). An
agreement for an amicable action is a "case stated" where the parties agree to facts, form, nature, and
amount of judgment; it is very rarely used. The Pennsylvania civil rules divide the procedural rules
according to actions at law. The most common forms of actions are assumpsit (contract claims) and
trespass (tort claims), both of which can be commenced by complaint or praecipe for a writ of
summons. Although there are several other forms of actions (i.e., replevin, mandamus, ejectment)
the comments in this chapter will focus on assumpsit and trespass. Civil actions in Pennsylvania
proceed in accordance with rules established for actions in assumpsit unless specific provision to the
contrary is made.

124

Chapter 6

**EXHIBIT 6.20**

# Form 18A—Notice and Acknowledgment
## for Service by Mail

UNITED STATES DISTRICT COURT
FOR THE SOUTHERN DISTRICT OF NEW YORK

Civil Action, File Number_____

A. B., Plaintiff,

v.

C. D., Defendant

} *Notice and Acknowledgment of
Receipt of Summons and Complaint*

NOTICE

To: (insert the name and address of the person to be served)

The enclosed summons and complaint are served pursuant to Rule 4(c)(2)(C)(ii) of the Federal Rules of Civil Procedure.

You must complete the acknowledgment part of this form and return one copy of the completed form to the sender within 20 days.

You must sign and date the acknowledgment. If you are served on behalf of a corporation, unincorporated association (including a partnership), or other entity, you must indicate under your signature your relationship to that entity. If you are served on behalf of another person and you are authorized to receive process, you must indicate under your signature your authority.

If you do not complete and return the form to the sender within 20 days, you (or the party on whose behalf you are being served) may be required to pay any expenses incurred in serving a summons and complaint in any other manner permitted by law.

If you do complete and return this form, you (or the party on whose behalf you are being served) must answer the complaint within 20 days. If you fail to do so, judgment by default will be taken against you for the relief demanded in the complaint.

I declare, under penalty of perjury, that this notice and acknowledgment of receipt of summons and complaint was mailed on (insert date).

................................................................
Signature

................................................................
Date of Signature

**EXHIBIT 6.21**

## Acknowledgment of Receipt of Summons and Complaint

### ACKNOWLEDGMENT OF RECEIPT OF SUMMONS AND COMPLAINT

I declare, under penalty of perjury, that I received a copy of the summons and of the complaint in the above-captioned manner at (insert address):

.....................................................
Signature

.....................................................
Relationship to Entity/Authority
to Receive Service of Process

.....................................................
Date of Signature

will have a direct impact on the possible courses of action a defendant can select. See Exhibit 6.22 for a copy of a praecipe for a writ of summons and Exhibit 6.23 for a form for a writ of summons.

Notice that other than providing the defendant with notice that he or she has been sued, a **summons** provides very little information. This means of commencing a civil action can be a valuable device for a plaintiff who does not have sufficient time to prepare a complaint (that is, preventing the expiration of a statute of limitation that provides a time limit in which civil actions may be filed).

Most civil actions are instituted by the plaintiff filing a complaint. Unlike federal practice, notice pleading is not permitted. Instead, the state court practice requires **fact pleading,** that is, the material facts on which the cause of action is based, set forth in concise and summary form, divided into consecutively numbered paragraphs, each containing only one material allegation.[21] The factual averments must be set forth with a degree of specificity.

Exhibit 6.24 is an example of a state court pleading (Pennsylvania) in a trespass (tort) case.

As you will note when comparing the federal court complaint with this state court complaint, the degree of factual specificity is far greater under the concept of fact pleading (state) than notice pleading (federal). In addition, unlike its federal counterpart, the Pennsylvania procedural rules require that pleadings containing averments of fact have to be verified either in the form and manner

---

[21] Pa.R.C.P. 1019(a), 1022.

**EXHIBIT 6.22**

## Praecipe for a Writ of Summons

### IN THE COURT OF COMMON PLEAS OF LEHIGH COUNTY, PENNSYLVANIA CIVIL DIVISION

Plaintiff(s) & Address(es):                    :
                                               :
                                               :
                                               :
                                               :
                                               :
                                               :    File No. _____
                        vs.                    :
                                               :    Civil Action -
Defendant(s) & Address(es):                    :
                                               :
                                               :
                                               :
                                               :
                                               :

### PRAECIPE FOR SUMMONS

TO THE PROTHONOTARY/CLERK OF SAID COURT:

   Issue summons in _____
in the above case.
   _____ Writ of summons shall be issued and forwarded to Attorney
Sheriff.

                              _____
                                         Signature of Attorney
                              _____
                              _____
                              _____
                              _____
                              _____
                              Name/Address/Telephone Number of Attorney

Date: _____  Supreme Court ID Number _____

* * * * *

**EXHIBIT 6.22**

## Praecipe for a Writ of Summons (continued)

SUMMONS IN CIVIL ACTION

TO: _____

YOU ARE NOTIFIED THAT THE ABOVE-NAMED PLAINTIFF(S) HAS/HAVE COMMENCED AN ACTION AGAINST YOU.

_____

Prothonotary/Clerk, Civil Division

Date: _____ by _____

Deputy

NOTE: USE AN ATTACHED SHEET FOR LENGTHY LIST OF LITIGANTS.
FILING PARTY IS TO COMPLETE BOTH PRAECIPE & WRIT TO EXPEDITE PROCESSING

as the affidavit attached to the example of the Pennsylvania court complaint in Exhibit 6.24 or in the following manner.[22]

> I verify that the statements made in this complaint are true and correct. I understand that false statements herein are made subject to the penalties of 18 Pa. C.S. §4904 relating to unsworn falsification to authorities.
>
> Date: _____        _____
>                            Plaintiff

In addition to the verification, another form must be attached to the complaint. This form is called a notice to defend (see Exhibit 6.25). Its form is mandatory and pursuant to local court rule, the notice may also be required to include another language translation (Spanish, for example). Its purpose is similar to that of a summons required in federal civil practice, that is, to give the defendant notice that he or she has been sued, and notice of when to file a responsive pleading (20 days). Unlike its federal counterpart, a notice to defend is more explicit in providing the defendant notice of what can happen if he or she does not respond to the plaintiff's complaint.

Once the complaint has been prepared, it is filed with the clerk of court's office in the county (or judicial district) in which the lawsuit will proceed.[23] Once the complaint has been filed, a true and correct copy of the complaint is

---

[22] The unsworn verification dispenses with the requirement of swearing on an oath before a notary public. See Pa.R.C.P. 1024.

[23] The Clerk of Court's Office—Civil is often called the Prothonotary's Office in Pennsylvania.

**EXHIBIT 6.23**

# Writ of Summons

Rule 1351 Form of Writ of Summons in Actions of Assumpsit and Trespass
The writs of summons in actions of assumpsit and trespass shall be
directed to the defendant and shall be substantially in the following form:
Commonwealth of Pennsylvania
County of _____

[Caption]

To ...........................................................................................

You are hereby notified that _____ , the plaintiff(s), has (have) commenced an action in _____ against you which you are required to defend or a default judgment may be entered against you.

(Name(s) of Plaintiffs(s))

FORM OF ACTION

Date ...........................................................................................

(Name of Prothonotary (Clerk))

By ...........................................................................................
(Deputy)

Seal of the Court

then delivered to the local sheriff's office for service upon the defendant.[24] This service must be made upon the defendant within thirty days of the filing of the complaint.[25] If not, the complaint must be reissued by the clerk of court's office in order to effectuate valid service.[26]

The sheriff then has the responsibility to serve the complaint upon the defendant and make and file a return of service.[27] The return usually sets forth the day, hour, and place of service and the name of the person to whom a copy of the complaint was handed and any other facts necessary for service. When unable to serve the defendant, the sheriff makes a return of "not found."

---

[24] Depending on local practice and custom, the copy of the complaint to be served is either automatically delivered to the sheriff by the clerk's office personnel or by the plaintiff's representative (paralegal, attorney, or secretary).

[25] Pa.R.C.P. 1009.

[26] Pa.R.C.P. 1010.

[27] Pa.R.C.P. 1013.

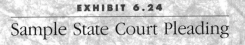

**EXHIBIT 6.24**

## Sample State Court Pleading

IN THE COURT OF COMMON PLEAS FOR LEHIGH COUNTY,
PENNSYLVANIA CIVIL DIVISION—LAW

| | |
|---|---|
| JOSEPH HUNT | : No. 92-C-243 |
| | : |
| Plaintiff | : |
| v. | : CIVIL ACTION |
| | : |
| JANE CARSON | : |
| | : |
| Defendant | : JURY TRIAL DEMANDED |

<u>COMPLAINT</u>

NOW COMES, JOSEPH HUNT, by his attorneys and files the within complaint:

1. Plaintiff is Joseph Hunt, an adult individual residing at 1 Main Street, Allentown, Lehigh County, Pennsylvania.

2. Defendant, Jane Carson, is an adult individual residing at R.D. #1, Macungie, Lehigh County, Pennsylvania.

3. At all times relevant to this complaint, defendant was the owner and operator of a 1982 BMW, Pennsylvania registration number BAD-100.

4. On or about March 5, 1992, at approximately 8:00 P.M., the plaintiff while crossing Linden Street, Allentown, was struck by defendant's vehicle causing him to suffer serious personal injury and damage by reason of the carelessness and negligence of the defendant.

5. The defendant, Jane Carson, was negligent in:

(a) operating her vehicle in a reckless manner under the circumstances;

(b) failing to keep her vehicle under proper control;

(c) failing to keep a proper lookout for pedestrians crossing the street;

(d) operating her vehicle at a speed too fast for conditions; and

(e) failing to use due care under the circumstances.

6. Solely by reason of the negligence of the defendant, plaintiff suffered a broken leg and severe lacerations to the face, shoulder, arms and legs, and great pain and suffering.

7. As a result of the negligence of the defendant and the injuries sustained by plaintiff, the plaintiff incurred expenses for medical care and hospitalization in the amount of $14,000.00.

8. As a result of the negligence of the defendant and the injuries sustained by plaintiff, the plaintiff was forced to miss 15 days of work and was unable to engage in his usual duties, pleasures, and recreations he had been accustomed and capable of engaging in prior to his injuries for a period of 10 weeks.

EXHIBIT 6.24

## Sample State Court Pleading (continued)

WHEREFORE, plaintiff demands judgment against the defendant in an amount in excess of Fourteen Thousand ($14,000) Dollars, plus costs.

CAHILL, RUBEN & DALY

By: _____

William Cahill
Attorney No. 11111*
Attorneys for Plaintiff
1 North Fifth Street
Allentown, PA
(215) 000-0000

---

AFFIDAVIT

COMMONWEALTH OF PENNSYLVANIA )
                                                          ) SS:
COUNTY OF LEHIGH                            )

JOHN HUNT, being duly sworn according to law, deposes and says that the facts contained in the foregoing complaint are true and correct to the best of his information, knowledge and belief.

_____
John Hunt

SWORN TO and subscribed
before me this                        day
of                                          1992

_____
Notary Public

My Commission Expires:

(SEAL)

*In Pennsylvania, there is a state registration system required for attorneys. Upon admission to the bar, each attorney is assigned a number. Many jurisdictions in Pennsylvania require attorneys to provide their attorney numbers after their name.

**EXHIBIT 6.25**

## Notice to Defend

IN THE COURT OF COMMON PLEAS OF LEHIGH COUNTY,
PENNSYLVANIA CIVIL DIVISION—LAW

```
                    )
                    )
                    )
                .   )  NO.
                    )
                    )  IN
                    )
                    )
                    )
```

<u>NOTICE</u>

YOU HAVE BEEN SUED IN COURT. IF YOU WISH TO DEFEND AGAINST THE CLAIMS SET FORTH IN THE FOLLOWING PAGES, YOU MUST TAKE ACTION WITHIN TWENTY (20) DAYS AFTER THIS COMPLAINT AND NOTICE ARE SERVED, BY ENTERING A WRITTEN APPEARANCE PERSONALLY OR BY ATTORNEY AND FILING IN WRITING WITH THE COURT YOUR DEFENSES OR OBJECTIONS TO THE CLAIMS SET FORTH AGAINST YOU. YOU ARE WARNED THAT IF YOU FAIL TO DO SO THE CASE MAY PROCEED WITHOUT YOU AND A JUDGMENT MAY BE ENTERED AGAINST YOU BY THE COURT WITHOUT FURTHER NOTICE FOR ANY MONEY CLAIMED IN THE COMPLAINT OF FOR ANY OTHER CLAIM OR RELIEF REQUESTED BY THE PLAINTIFF. YOU MAY LOSE MONEY OR PROPERTY OR OTHER RIGHTS IMPORTANT TO YOU.

YOU SHOULD TAKE THIS PAPER TO YOUR LAWYER AT ONCE. IF YOU DO NOT HAVE A LAWYER OR CANNOT AFFORD ONE, GO TO OR TELEPHONE THE OFFICE SET FORTH BELOW TO FIND OUT WHERE YOU CAN GET LEGAL HELP.

LEHIGH COUNTY BAR ASSOCIATION
LEGAL REFERRAL SERVICE
THIRD FLOOR-ROOM 304
OLD LEHIGH COUNTY COURTHOUSE
FIFTH AND HAMILTON STREETS
ALLENTOWN, PENNSYLVANIA 18105

PHONE: 215-820-3804

_____

ATTORNEY FOR

## III. DEFENDING THE CIVIL ACTION: SUBSEQUENT PLEADINGS, ANSWERS, AND MOTIONS

When a defendant is served with a complaint, he or she has a number of alternatives from which to choose. There may be some reason that the court should not proceed with the case that has no bearing on the intrinsic merits of the claim. For example, the defendant may wish to assert that the jurisdiction of the court is improper or that the plaintiff has selected an improper venue to begin the action. Another defense position is that the plaintiff has failed to state a claim on which relief may be granted.

If the defendant believes that the factual statement of the plaintiff's claim is incorrect, the defendant can challenge the truth of one or more of the factual allegations. This is done by denying the relevant allegations. Finally, even if the basic allegations of plaintiff's complaint are true, there may be additional matters that would relieve the defendant of liability, such as the running of the statute of limitations or other **affirmative defenses.** An affirmative defense is a fact that contradicts the plaintiff's right to recover or to seek the relief requested. Each of these possibilities is discussed below.

## A. Federal Court

Once a defendant has been served with a summons and a complaint he or she has twenty days in which to file a response. The defendant has the option either to file an **answer,** to file a **motion to dismiss** the lawsuit, or to join a third party to a lawsuit.[28] Other options available to the defendant, such as **cross-claims** and **counterclaims,** are also discussed below.

### 1. Motion to Dismiss

A motion to dismiss the lawsuit may be filed prior to the defendant's answer. FRCP 12(b) specifies certain defenses that may be made by motion prior to filing an answer to the complaint. They do not go to the merits of the plaintiff's case but, if successful, may result in the dismissal of the action.

The more common motions to dismiss under FRCP 12(b) are:

- ◆ lack of subject matter jurisdiction
- ◆ lack of personal jurisdiction
- ◆ improper venue
- ◆ improper service of process
- ◆ failure to state a claim on which relief may be granted
- ◆ failure to join an indispensable party

Motions themselves look like simple pleadings. Local rules may require that briefs be filed with or after the motion and also that the party making the motion give notice to all other parties. It is also common that facts necessary to support the motion are presented in the form of affidavits. Exhibit 6.26 is taken from the

---

[28] The defendant, pursuant to FRCP 14, may bring in a third party to the lawsuit who is or may be liable to him or her for all or part of the plaintiff's claim against the defendant.

**EXHIBIT 6.26**

# Motion to Dismiss, Presenting Defenses of Failure to State a Claim, of Lack of Service of Process, of Improper Venue, and of Lack of Jurisdiction under Rule 12(b) (Form 19 — Appendix of Forms)

IN THE UNITED STATES DISTRICT COURT FOR
THE DISTRICT OF COLUMBIA

MOTION TO DISMISS, PRESENTING DEFENSES OF FAILURE
TO STATE A CLAIM, OF LACK OF SERVICE OF PROCESS, OF
IMPROPER VENUE, AND OF LACK OF JURISDICTION UNDER RULE 12(b)

The defendant moves the court as follows:

1. To dismiss the action because the complaint fails to state a claim against defendant upon which relief can be granted.

2. To dismiss the action or in lieu thereof to quash the return of service of summons on the grounds (a) that the defendant is a corporation organized under the laws of [Delaware] and was not and is not subject to service of process within the [Southern District of New York,] and (b) that the defendant has not been properly served with process in this action, all of which more clearly appears in the affidavits of M. N. and X. Y. hereto annexed as Exhibit A and Exhibit B respectively.

3. To dismiss the action on the ground that it is in the wrong district because (a) the jurisdiction of this court is invoked solely on the ground that the action arises under the Constitution and laws of the United States and (b) the defendant is a corporation incorporated under the laws of the [State of Delaware] and is not licensed to do or doing business in the [Southern District of New York,] all of which more clearly appears in the affidavits of K. L. and V. W. hereto annexed as Exhibits C and D, respectively.

4. To dismiss the action on the ground that the court lacks jurisdiction because the amount actually in controversy is less than fifty thousand dollars exclusive of interest and costs.

Signed: _____
Attorney for Defendant.
Address: _____

Notice of Motion

To: _____
    Attorney for Plaintiff

Please take notice, that the undersigned will bring the above motion on for hearing before this Court at Room _____ , United States Court House, Foley Square, [City of New York,] on the _____ day of _____ , 199___ , at 10 o'clock in the forenoon of that day or as soon thereafter as counsel can be heard.

Signed: _____
Attorney for Defendant
Address: _____

(As amended Dec. 29, 1948, eff. Oct. 20, 1949; Apr. 17, 1961, eff. July 19,1961.)

Appendix of Forms (Form 19) and provides an example of the format for a motion to dismiss. Exhibit 6.27 provides an example of a motion to dismiss on grounds of lack of personal jurisdiction, improper venue, and improper service of process, while Exhibit 6.28 shows the supporting affidavit.

**EXHIBIT 6.27**

## Motion to Dismiss

IN THE UNITED STATES DISTRICT COURT FOR
THE DISTRICT OF COLUMBIA

THE CHICAGO HOUSING
AUTHORITY, on behalf of
itself and all others
similarly situated,
    Plaintiff,
      v.
A Company, B Company,
C Company, D Company, E Company,
F Company and G Company
    Defendants

CIVIL ACTION

NO. 69-1

MOTION OF DEFENDANT G COMPANY
TO DISMISS IN NO. 69-1

Defendant, G Company, moves the Court pursuant to Rule 12(b) of the Federal Rules of Civil Procedure to dismiss the action against it or, in lieu thereof, to quash the return of service of summons on it on the grounds of lack of personal jurisdiction, improper venue, and insufficient service of process for the reasons that defendant, G Company, is not an inhabitant of the District of Columbia, cannot be found in the District of Columbia, and does not transact business in the District of Columbia and the alleged claim does not arise in the District of Columbia. The affidavit of J. P. Stevens, President of G Company, is attached in support of this motion.

_____
Attorney for Defendant
G Company

EXHIBIT 6.28

# Affidavit

IN THE UNITED STATES DISTRICT COURT FOR
THE DISTRICT OF COLUMBIA

THE CHICAGO HOUSING
AUTHORITY, on behalf of
itself and all others
similarly situated,                          CIVIL ACTION
      Plaintiff
      v.                                   NO. 69-1
A COMPANY, et al.,
      Defendants

AFFIDAVIT OF J. P. STEVENS

STATE OF TEXAS
COUNTY OF GREGG } ss:

J. P. Stevens, being duly sworn according to law, deposes and says that he is President of G Company; that he makes this affidavit on its behalf having the authority so to do and that:

1. G Company is a corporation organized and existing under the laws of the State of Texas with its principal place of business on U.S. Highway 1 just outside the city limits of the city of Way-Cross, Texas.

2. The summons and complaint in the above-captioned action were served on G Company at its office in Way-Cross, Texas, by the United States Marshal for the Eastern District of Texas on January 4, 1969.

3. G Company has never sold any of its products, either directly or indirectly, to the plaintiff in the above-captioned action.

4. G Company is not registered, licensed, or certified or authorized to do business in the District of Columbia; it has never filed any tax returns with the District of Columbia; and it has never paid any taxes to the District of Columbia.

5. G Company has never leased or owned any real estate in the District of Columbia, has never had any office, factory, or warehouse, or other facility or place of business in the District of Columbia.

6. G Company has no bank account or other funds in the District of Columbia and owns no property, real or personal, in the District of Columbia.

7. G Company has never entered into any contracts in the District of Columbia for the sale of its products within or without the District of Columbia.

**EXHIBIT 6.28**

## Affidavit (continued)

8. G Company has no officers or employees located within the District of Columbia and has no officers or employees outside the District of Columbia who solicits orders for G Company's products with the District of Columbia.

9. All orders for G Company's products are solicited through independent manufacturers' agents. No manufacturer's agent has ever represented G Company in the District of Columbia and G Company has received no orders for its products emanating from the District of Columbia.

10. G Company has not shipped any merchandise into the District of Columbia, and no bids have been placed by G Company in the District of Columbia.

11. No employer of G Company has made any telephone calls into the District of Columbia for any business purpose.

12. G Company has never placed, authorized, paid for or shared in the payment for any advertisement of its products in newspapers, magazines or other publications, whether for general or trade circulation, which were published in the District of Columbia. G Company has placed advertisements in three trade publications published in Chicago, Illinois, which have been distributed in the District of Columbia.

13. G Company does not have any person in charge of or responsible for advertisement and promotion of its products in the District of Columbia.

_____

J. P. Stevens

Sworn to and subscribed before me this _____ day of _____ , 1969.

_____

Notary Public

My Commission Expires: _____ .

All motions (including motions to dismiss) must be on the proper size paper, which is 8½-by 11 inches. In addition they must contain the following:

- Caption: the requirements are similar to plaintiff's complaint (you can leave off parties' addresses). It is sufficient, in documents other than the complaint, to name only the first party on each side with an appropriate indication (et al.) of other parties.

- Number of copies: only the original is required to be filed.

- Serve a copy on all defendants.

- Certificate of service: every motion filed should be accompanied by a written statement as to the date and manner of service of the motion (and supporting documents, if applicable).

- Signature: every motion wherein a party is represented by an attorney must be signed by the attorney.

In many federal districts, local rules may require the moving party to submit the form of order, which if approved by the court would grant the relief sought by the motion. Even when local rules do not require the submission of a form of order, it is better practice to submit the order so that the moving party may suggest the precise language he or she wants in the order.

Exhibit 6.29 is an example of an order that might be submitted by G Company along with its motion (Exhibit 6.27).


## 2. Answer

The purpose of an answer is to give notice as to which allegations in the plaintiff's complaint the defendant will be contesting and to provide notice of any affirmative defenses the defendant is raising. In other words, an answer is a procedural device intended to clarify and limit the issues of dispute.

FRCP 8(b) provides that a party shall admit or deny the allegations made by the opponent and state in short, plain terms the defense to each claim asserted. Thus, in the federal courts, if a party disagrees with an allegation it is enough simply to say "denied" without any further explanation. During discovery the opponent will have the opportunity to learn the reason for the denial. For example, a denial might read:

From plaintiff's complaint:
3. The jurisdiction of this Court is founded on diversity of citizenship, pursuant to 28 U.S.C. §1332, and the amount in controversy exceeds fifty thousand dollars ($50,000) exclusive of interest and costs.

From defendant's answer:
3. Denied.

## EXHIBIT 6.29
# Order

IN THE UNITED STATES DISTRICT COURT
FOR THE DISTRICT OF COLUMBIA

THE CHICAGO HOUSING
AUTHORITY, on behalf of
itself and all others
similarly situated,
       Plaintiff,
         v.
A COMPANY, et al.,
       Defendants

CIVIL ACTION

NO. 69-1

ORDER

AND NOW, to wit, this _____ day of _____ , 1969, upon consideration of the motion of G Company to dismiss this action against it, it is hereby
ORDERED, that the complaint filed in this action against G Company is hereby dismissed.

_____
                                                      J.

FRCP 8(d) provides that any allegations that are not denied are deemed to be admitted. Normally, however, when an allegation is admitted, it is so stated. For example:

From plaintiff's complaint:
2. Defendant Smith Corporation is a Delaware corporation having its principal place of business in Terre Haute, Indiana.

From defendant's answer:
2. Admitted.

If a party is without knowledge or information sufficient to form a belief concerning the truth of an allegation, FRCP 8(b) allows the party to so state, and this is interpreted as a denial. Thus, if the plaintiff in paragraph 1 of its complaint says:

Plaintiff Compton Corporation is an Illinois Corporation having its principal place of business in Chicago, Illinois.

Then the defendant, in the answer, might say:

Defendant is without knowledge sufficient to form a belief as to the truth of the allegations contained in paragraph 1 of plaintiff's complaint and therefore denies same.

To aver lack of knowledge, a party should not only lack firsthand knowledge of the facts, but should also lack of information from which he or she may reasonably form a firm belief concerning the truth of the allegations. A party should not assert a lack of knowledge or information if the facts or data involved could easily be learned or are a matter of general knowledge in the community or a matter of public record. A denial within either of these contexts casts doubt on the good faith of the pleader. If knowledge or information cannot be ascertained within the time a party is given to answer with the expenditure of modest effort, a denial on the basis of lack of information or belief is proper. A defendant is not required to make an exhaustive or burdensome search in order to ascertain the truth or falsity of plaintiff's allegations.

The situation may arise in which some of the allegations in a particular paragraph of a pleading are acknowledged by the opponent but others are not. The pleader may specifically deny certain designated averments and admit others:

From plaintiff's complaint.

4. On or about December 12, 1991, plaintiff was a pedestrian on Main Street in the city of Rockville, Montana, at its intersection with Cherry Street when defendant negligently drove his motor vehicle causing it to strike plaintiff.

From defendant's answer:

4. Admitted that on or about December 12, 1991, plaintiff was a pedestrian at the location indicated in paragraph 4 of plaintiff's complaint. It is denied that defendant was negligently driving his motor vehicle or that it struck plaintiff.

In the federal system, the defendant may not only answer the allegations made in the complaint but may show other circumstances that deny or avoid the plaintiff's claim. This is done by pleading affirmative defenses. For example, if plaintiff sues to recover a debt, defendant may admit to owing the money but assert that the action is barred by the statute of limitations. FRCP 8(c) sets out a number of affirmative defenses that must be set forth as such if they are to be raised at all. These include assumption of the risk, contributory negligence, discharge in bankruptcy, failure of consideration, fraud, statute of limitations, payment, and any other matter constituting an avoidance or affirmative defense. Generally, failure to plead an affirmative defense results in its waiver, that is, being denied the right to assert it at a later time. Therefore, it is normal for defendants to plead a variety of affirmative defenses, even though they may not seem appropriate, to avoid any possibility of waiver.

Typically, affirmative defenses are set forth after the main body of the answer and are very brief. Also, it is quite common for affirmative defenses to be numbered consecutively from the last paragraph number in the answer and listed as first, second, third, and so on, affirmative defense.

Below is an example of how affirmative defenses are drafted in an answer:

First Affirmative Defense
The court lacks subject matter jurisdiction as the amount in controversy does not exceed $50,000, exclusive of interest and costs.

Second Affirmative Defense
Plaintiff's complaint fails to state a claim against the defendant for which relief may be granted.[29]

Third Affirmative Defense
Plaintiff was negligent and is therefore barred from recovery.

Fourth Affirmative Defense
Plaintiff assumed the risk of the injury, which he alleged he incurred.

No response is required to an affirmative defense. The allegations made in them are presumed to be denied by the plaintiff.

### 3. Counterclaims and Cross-Claims

A **counterclaim** is a claim that the defendant in a lawsuit has against the plaintiff. **Cross-claim** refers to a claim that a party has against a coparty (for example, by a defendant against a codefendant, or by a plaintiff against a co-plaintiff) arising out of the same transaction or occurrence that is the subject matter of the original action or counterclaim. For example, assume A sues B and C claiming they were both at fault in an intersectional collision injuring A, the driver of a third car. B or C may answer that complaint and also assert a counterclaim against A, alleging that A was at fault. B could also cross-claim against C saying that C was solely responsible and if B is found liable to A, C must reimburse B for all or part of the amount paid over to A.

FRCP 13 governs counterclaims and cross-claims. It is broad enough to allow for the resolution of virtually all controversies between the parties in a single action.

*a. Compulsory Counterclaims.* A counterclaim may be either **compulsory** or **permissive.** FRCP 13(a) provides that, with a few stated exceptions, all claims that arise out of the same transaction or occurrence, which is the basis of a claim by the opposing party, must be asserted as counterclaims; such claims are called compulsory counterclaims. If a party fails to assert a compulsory counterclaim, it is barred from commencing a new lawsuit at some later date based on such a claim. The compulsory counterclaim rule furthers the policy of discouraging multiple litigation based on the same transaction or occurrence. For example, if seller sues buyer for not paying for goods sold and buyer has a claim that the goods were defective and that buyer thereby incurred damages, the claim for defective goods must be asserted as a counterclaim against the seller in seller's action. If not, buyer will not be able to make such a claim anytime in the future.

In view of the nature of a compulsory counterclaim, no independent grounds for federal jurisdiction are required. Since the rule requires that the claim be presented or barred, it would be unfair to the defendant to prevent the assertion of a counterclaim because of jurisdictional problems. Thus, in the prior example, if the case is based on diversity and seller's claim is more than $50,000, the buyer's counterclaim does not have to meet the minimum jurisdictional amount of $50,000.

---

[29] Note that the same matters that may be raised in a motion to dismiss may also be raised as affirmative defenses.

***b. Permissive Counterclaims.***   Under FRCP 13(b) a party may assert as a counterclaim any claim it has against the opposing party. The policy behind FRCP 13(b) is to encourage parties to assert all independent and unrelated claims against an opposing party in one action to avoid the costs of multiple suits. If, as a result of the liberal policy of allowing unrelated counterclaims, the action becomes unmanageable, the court may exercise its discretion under FRCP 13(i) and order separate trials for the claims. For example, P sues D in federal court, based on diversity, for injuries sustained in an automobile collision. P and D do business together and D now counterclaims for money owed as a result of an alleged breach of contract by P. This counterclaim may be asserted even though it does not arise out of the same transaction or occurrence as P's original suit.

The rules relating to permissive counterclaims differ from the rules regarding compulsory counterclaims. Since a permissive counterclaim is unrelated to the original claim, it must be supported by an independent ground of federal jurisdiction. As with the original claim, jurisdiction may be based on a federal question or on diversity of citizenship, and the required jurisdictional amount is necessary for each permissive counterclaim. Thus, in the prior example, D could assert the counterclaim only if it was for an amount in excess of $50,000.

Because assertion of the permissive counterclaim is optional, the defendant will not be prevented from bringing a separate lawsuit on it at another time if it was not raised in the pending litigation.

***c. Cross-Claims.***   FRCP 13(g) permits assertion of any claim by one party against a coparty (for example, defendant against codefendant) when it has arisen out of the same transaction or occurrence that is the subject matter of the original action or a counterclaim to it. Like a compulsory counterclaim, no independent grounds for federal subject matter jurisdiction is required. The cross-claim provision is similar to the permissive counterclaim, however, in that the assertion of the claim is optional and it will not be barred from being brought in the future if not presented in the original action.

A cross-claim asserts that the person against whom the cross-claim was filed is, or may be, liable to the cross-claimant (the person filing the cross-claim) for all or part of the plaintiff's claim. For example, a cross-claim would be appropriate in a case arising out of a two-car collision when a passenger in one automobile sues both the driver of the car in which he or she was a passenger and the driver of the other car. In this case, the driver of the car in which the plaintiff was riding might cross-claim against the driver of the other car, asserting that the accident was caused by the other driver and that he or she has no liability to the passenger.

Exhibit 6.30 provides a summary and comparison of counterclaims and cross-claims, and Exhibit 6.31 is an example of an answer and counterclaim based on the Smith v. Jones complaint (see Exhibit 6.12).

When the defendant asserts a counterclaim in addition to the complaint and answer, the plaintiff must file a **reply** within twenty days of service of the counterclaim. When the defendant asserts a cross-claim, the codefendant must file a reply within twenty days of service of the cross-claim. The reply functions the same as an answer.

### 4. Third-Party Practice

**Third-party practice** (also known as **impleader**) refers to the procedure whereby a defendant brings in a third party to the lawsuit because the

**EXHIBIT 6.30**

## Summary and Comparison of Counterclaims and Cross-Claims

| | Factual Connection to Plaintiff's Claim | Subject-Matter Jurisdiction Required | Must Raise Claim or Lose It |
|---|---|---|---|
| Compulsory Counterclaim | YES | NO | YES |
| Permissive Counterclaim | NO | YES | NO |
| Cross-Claim | YES | NO | NO |

defendant claims that this third party is responsible (liable) to him or her for all or part of the plaintiff's claim against him or her. The original defendant becomes known as the third-party plaintiff and the new third party becomes known as the third-party defendant (also called additional defendant).

Third-party practice provides a mechanism in one action for disposing of multiple claims arising from a single set of facts. It makes it unnecessary for a defendant who has been found liable to a plaintiff to bring a separate action against a third party who may be liable to the defendant for part or all of the original claim of plaintiff. If the rights of all three parties involve a common factual setting, it is obviously more economical to combine the suits in one action. Such a combination eliminates duplication in presentation of evidence and increases the likelihood of consistent results.

Procedurally, the defendant files a third-party complaint and has a summons issued and serves both on the third-party defendant. The defendant who files a third-party complaint no later than ten days after filing the original answer can do so without seeking the court's permission. If the defendant waits beyond the ten-day period, he or she must seek and receive the court's permission.

Personal jurisdiction over a third-party defendant must be obtained by the court before it can adjudicate a third-party claim. The requirements of valid service of process and personal jurisdiction in a third-party action are the same as with any other type of litigation with the exception that, under FRCP 4(f), service on a third-party defendant is permitted anywhere within 100 miles of the courthouse, whether or not the place of service happens to be inside the forum state. Independent subject matter jurisdiction is not required to file a third-party complaint, however.

Third parties have the same options as plaintiffs and defendants in the original actions. The third-party defendant can assert defenses as provided in FRCP 12 and can assert counterclaims against the third-party plaintiff and cross-claims against other third-party defendants as provided in FRCP 13. The third-party defendant may also assert against the plaintiff any defenses that the original defendant (the third-party plaintiff) has to the plaintiff's claim (because if the original defendant is not liable, then the third-party defendant gets off, since the extent of his or her liability is for part or all of the plaintiff's claim against the

## EXHIBIT 6.31

# Sample Answer and Counterclaim

IN THE UNITED STATES DISTRICT COURT FOR THE EASTERN
DISTRICT OF PENNSYLVANIA

| | | |
|---|---|---|
| JOHN A. SMITH | : | |
| Plaintiff | : | CIVIL ACTION NO. 92-100 |
| | : | |
| v. | : | |
| | : | |
| LEE G. JONES | : | |
| Defendant | : | JURY TRIAL DEMANDED |

DEFENDANT'S ANSWER AND COUNTERCLAIM

1. Denied.
2. Denied.
3. Admitted.
4. Admitted.
5. Denied.
6. Denied.

FIRST AFFIRMATIVE DEFENSE

7. This court lacks subject matter jurisdiction as the amount in controversy does not exceed $50,000, exclusive of interest and costs.

SECOND AFFIRMATIVE DEFENSE

8. Plaintiff was negligent and is therefore barred from recovery:
WHEREFORE, defendant Lee G. Jones requests judgment in his behalf and against plaintiff on plaintiff's compliant.

DEFENDANT'S COUNTERCLAIM

9. On or about March 5, 1991, in a public highway known as Linden Street, Allentown, Pennsylvania, plaintiff negligently crossed a highway and struck defendant's vehicle.

10. As a result of plaintiff's carelessness, defendant's vehicle was damaged in the amount of $2,000.

WHEREFORE, defendant demands judgment against the plaintiff in the sum of $2,000, plus interest and costs.

CAHILL, RUBEN & DALY
By: _____
William Cahill
Attorney for Defendant

1 North Fifth Street
Allentown, PA 18101
(215) 000-0000

Note: This pleading is provided for illustration purposes only. The defense and counterclaim are not meant to be serious claims.

defendant).[30] Likewise, the third-party defendant may assert any claim against the plaintiff arising out of the transaction or occurrence that is the subject matter of the plaintiff's claim against the third-party plaintiff.

Obviously, third-party practice can become very complicated. In order to prevent undue complexity, FRCP 14 provides that any party may request the court to have the case broken down into several trials.

See Exhibit 6.32 for Official Forms 22-A (summons and complaint against third-party defendant) taken from the Appendix of Forms to the Federal Rules of Civil Procedure.

---

**EXHIBIT 6.32**

## Form 22-A. Summons and Complaint against Third-Party Defendant

UNITED STATES DISTRICT COURT FOR THE
SOUTHERN DISTRICT OF NEW YORK
Civil Action, File Number _____

A. B., Plaintiff,
  v.
C. D., Defendant and
Third-Party Plaintiff     Summons
  v.
E. F., Third-Party
  Defendant

To the above-named Third-Party Defendant:

You are hereby summoned and required to serve upon _____ plaintiff's attorney whose address is _____ and upon _____ , who is attorney for C. D., defendant and third-party plaintiff, and whose address is _____ , an answer to the third-party complaint which is herewith served upon you within 20 days after the service of this summons upon you exclusive of the day of service. If you fail to do so, judgment by default will be taken against you for the relief demanded in the third-party complaint. There is also served upon you herewith a copy of the complaint of the plaintiff which you may but are not required to answer.

_____
       Clerk of Court

[Seal of District Court]

Dated _____

---

[30] Under federal pleadings, the plaintiff has no direct claim against the third-party defendant. This is an important distinction from Pennsylvania civil procedure where any defendant can be fully liable for plaintiff's claims.

**EXHIBIT 6.32**

## Summons and Complaint against Third-Party Defendant (continued)

UNITED STATES DISTRICT COURT FOR THE
SOUTHERN DISTRICT OF NEW YORK

Civil Action, File Number _____

A. B., Plaintiff

v.

C. D., Defendant and
Third-Party Plaintiff        }        Third-Party Complaint

v.

E. F., Third-Party
Defendant

1. Plaintiff A. B. has filed against C. D. a complaint, a copy of which is hereto attached as "Exhibit A."

2. (Here state the grounds upon which C. D. is entitled to recover from E. F., all or part of what A. B. may recover from C. D. The statement should be framed as in an original complaint.)

Wherefore C. D. demands judgment against third-party defendant E. F. for all sums that may be adjudged against defendant C. D. in favor of plaintiff A. B.

Signed: _____

Attorney for C. D.,
Third-Party Plaintiff

Address: _____

Added Jan. 21, 1963, eff. July 1, 1963

Make appropriate change where C. D. is entitled to only partial recovery over against E. F.

## B. Pennsylvania Practice

Once served with a complaint, a defendant has two options: file an answer or file preliminary objections.[31] Preliminary objections are Pennsylvania's counterpart to a motion to dismiss and the other motions under FRCP 12. Their purpose is to challenge the plaintiff's cause of action or to attack some deficiency in the plaintiff's pleading. An answer also serves the same purpose as an answer in

---

[31] Pa.R.C.P. 1017. In addition, if the lawsuit was commenced by a writ of summons, the defendant can file a rule (demand) on the plaintiff to file a complaint within twenty days or have the lawsuit dismissed.

federal practice; that is, to define and limit the issues in dispute. The decision whether to file preliminary objections or an answer must be made relatively soon after service of the complaint, as both pleadings are required to be filed within twenty days after service of the complaint. However, if preliminary objections are filed, no answer is required until the preliminary objections are adjudicated.

In drafting an answer under this state's civil practice rules, some responses will be the same as in the federal court. An admission may be stated simply as "admitted." Similarly, when there is insufficient information to answer, the pleader will so state and deny as in federal court. The important area of denials is, however, drastically different in fact pleading. It is not enough to say "denied." In this state this may even act as an admission. Instead, the pleader must give the factual basis for the denial and affirmatively aver what did occur. For example, if a plaintiff pleads breach of contract and the defendant denies that the terms of the contract are correctly stated, the defendant must plead the correct terms of the contract. Another example of a specific denial would be the case in which the plaintiff avers that a fair and reasonable cost for repairs is a certain stated amount. To make a specific denial, the defendant must deny that the sum stated by the plaintiff was a fair and reasonable cost for the repairs and must allege the amount it claims to be a correct charge. If the pleader simply states "it is denied that" and then repeats word for word the averments of the opposing pleading, the denial is not specific enough.

### 1. Affirmative Defenses

All affirmative defenses must be raised after the answer to the complaint under the heading of "New Matter."[32] This is the Pennsylvania counterpart to affirmative defenses under FRCP 8(c). In addition, the defendant may allege under this heading any other material facts that are not merely denials of the averments of the complaint.

The defendant who pleads an affirmative defense under new matter must serve this pleading on the plaintiff with a notice to the plaintiff that he or she must respond to the new matter within twenty days of service or suffer a default judgment.[33] This notice is called a notice to plead.

### 2. Cross-Claims and Counterclaims

Under the heading of New Matter, in addition to raising affirmative defenses, the defendant may raise a cross-claim against one of the codefendants (if applicable) or may claim that one of the plaintiffs is alone liable to another plaintiff (if applicable), or is liable over to the defendant, or is jointly liable to or severally liable with the defendant on the cause of action set forth in the complaint.[34] This cross-claim may be pleaded at any time within sixty days after

---

[32] Pa.R.C.P. 1030.

[33] Pa.R.C.P. 1026, 1361. Also, a default judgment is a judgment without a hearing based on a party's failure to file a responsive pleading.

[34] Pa.R.C.P. 2252(d).

service of the complaint. Therefore, this cross-claim may be filed separately as a supplemental response.

A counterclaim in Pennsylvania is optional. Unlike the federal courts, no distinction is made between compulsory and permissive counterclaims. Like new matter, the counterclaim requires a reply within twenty days of service if it is endorsed with a proper notice to plead. In a counterclaim the defendant may:

> ... set forth in the answer under the heading 'Counterclaim' any cause of action or set off which he has against the plaintiff at the time of filing the answer (1) which arises from the same transaction or occurrence or series of transactions or occurrences from which the plaintiff's cause of action arose, or (2) which arises from contract or is quasi-contractual. [Rule 1031, Pa. R.C.P.]

New matter, cross-claims, or counterclaims should be alleged in separate paragraphs numbered consecutively after the last allegation contained in the complaint.

Exhibit 6.33 provides an example of an answer, new matter, and counterclaim.

### 3. Additional Defendants

A complaint to join an additional defendant may be filed within sixty days after service of the plaintiff's complaint to join any person not a party to the action who may be alone liable to the plaintiff or liable over to the defendant or jointly or severally liable with the defendant.[35] If a joinder is desired beyond the sixty-day period, permission of the court is necessary.[36]

One of the significant differences between Pennsylvania and federal court practice is that in Pennsylvania a third party may be joined who may alone be directly liable to the plaintiff. In federal court, third-party practice does not permit such a method of pleading direct liability. Instead, a plaintiff would have to amend his or her complaint to include a new codefendant or a defendant would seek to be indemnified if he or she was found liable to the plaintiff.

The complaint to join an additional defendant should be similar in form to a plaintiff's complaint. In addition, a copy of plaintiff's complaint must be attached to the third-party complaint and served on the additional defendant as well as on all prior parties to the action.

## IV. AMENDMENTS

Under the federal and Pennsylvania rules of civil procedure, the right of parties to amend (or change) their pleadings is liberally granted. Under FRCP 15(a), any pleading[37] may be amended once as a matter of course anytime before a re-

---

[35] See Pa.R.C.P. 2252, 2253.
[36] Pa.R.C.P. 2254.
[37] A complaint, answer, counterclaim, cross-claim, or third-party complaint may all be amended.

**EXHIBIT 6.33**

## Answer, New Matter, and Counterclaim

WE DO HEREBY CERTIFY
THAT THE WITHIN IS A
TRUE AND CORRECT COPY
OF THE ORIGINAL FILED
IN THIS ACTION.

_____
Attorney

TO: _____
YOU ARE HEREBY NOTIFIED
TO PLEAD TO THE ENCLOSED
ANSWER, NEW MATTER, AND
COUNTERCLAIM WITHIN TWENTY
(20) DAYS FROM SERVICE
HEREOF OR A DEFAULT JUDGMENT
WILL BE ENTERED AGAINST YOU.

_____
Attorney for Defendant

IN THE COURT OF COMMON PLEAS OF LEHIGH COUNTY,
PENNSYLVANIA CIVIL DIVISION—LAW

JOHN SMITH          )    No. 82-C-0000
    Plaintiff          )
    v.                 )
JIM JONES           )
    Defendant          )

ANSWER, NEW MATTER, AND COUNTERCLAIM

1. Admitted.

2. Admitted in part, denied in part. Defendant denies that he currently maintains a place of business at "Name of Street." The balance of the averment is admitted.

3. Admitted in part, denied in part. Defendant admits Exhibit A is the original proposal submitted to the plaintiff. Defendant denies that this writing evidences the final contract entered into between the parties and demands proof thereof at the time of trial. On the contrary, defendant avers there was a subsequent oral modification of said proposal as more fully set forth in defendant's new matter.

4. Admitted.

5. Admitted in part, denied in part. Defendant specifically denies plaintiff's payments to defendant were made based on defendant's assurances, and demands proof thereof at the time of trial. The balance of the averment is admitted.

6. Denied. Defendant specifically denies that the air conditioning system in question was insufficient to cool the plaintiff's premises and that it failed to function for the purpose for which it was contracted for and further demands strict proof thereof at the time of trial.

EXHIBIT 6.33

## Answer, New Matter, and Counterclaim (continued)

7. Denied. After reasonable investigation, the defendant is without sufficient information or knowledge as to form a belief as to the truth of this averment, and demands proof thereof at the time of trial. In addition, said averment is not in conformity with the rules of pleading and no answer is required.

8. Denied. Defendant specifically denies that the design and installation of the air conditioning system in question was either deficient in design or installed in an unworkmanlike manner and demands strict proof thereof at the time of trial.

9. Denied. After reasonable investigation the defendant is without sufficient information or knowledge as to form a belief as to the truth of this averment, and demands proof thereof at the time of trial.

WHEREFORE, defendant requests that plaintiff's complaint be dismissed.

### NEW MATTER

10. Defendant incorporates by reference his answers (Paragraphs 1-9) to plaintiff's complaint as if fully set forth herein.

11. Defendant avers that as a condition precedent to defendant's written proposal and subsequent final agreement, the plaintiff was to install insulation in his home in the following manner:
   a) install insulation in the ceiling between 3rd floor and roof;
   b) install insulation on the south wall of the house from the mid-dining room area to the back of the house; and
   c) install insulation in the whole west wall of the house.

12. Plaintiff failed to install the insulation as set forth in the preceding paragraph.

13. That subsequent to the submission of the written proposal marked Exhibit A and attached to plaintiff's complaint, plaintiff and defendant orally modified the proposal to reach the following agreement:
   a) Defendant furnished and installed the following:
      1 York model MCB 30-6B
      1 York model 306A
      1 York model 30YFIZ
      plus additional ductwork to accommodate the plaintiff's desire to move the blower unit to a different part of the plaintiff's basement;
   b) Plaintiff agreed to pay defendant an additional $200 for additional ductwork and labor.

14. The defendant avers that the design of the air conditioning system is satisfactory and adequate in accordance with the manufacturer's standards for a residential dwelling.

15. The defendant avers that all work performed to install the air conditioning system was done in a good workmanlike manner.

**EXHIBIT 6.33**

## Answer, New Matter, and Counterclaim (continued)

16. Defendant avers that he has fully performed his obligations under the contract as set forth in this new matter.

WHEREFORE, defendant requests that plaintiff's complaint be dismissed.

### COUNTERCLAIM

17. Defendant incorporates by reference his answers to plaintiff's complaint (Paragraphs 1-9) and his averments in his new matter (Paragraphs 10-16) as if fully set forth herein.

18. Defendant has fully performed all the work required of him pursuant to the contract between plaintiff and defendant.

19. That based on the contract between defendant and plaintiff, plaintiff owes a balance due to the defendant in the amount of $1,450.

20. That plaintiff refuses to pay the requested balance due and owing to the defendant.

WHEREFORE, defendant demands judgment against the plaintiff in the amount of $1,450 plus costs and interests.

FUNT, ROTHMAN & WEINSTEIN

By: _____

Mark I. Weinstein, Esquire
Attorney for Defendant
34 North Fifth St., Allentown, PA 18101
(215) 432-4552

### AFFIDAVIT

I verify that the statements made in this answer, new matter, and counterclaim are true and correct. I understand that false statements herein are made subject to the penalties of 18 Pa. C.S. § 4904, relating to unsworn falsification to authorities.

Date: _____          _____
                                                Defendant

Note: This example is given simply to provide a visual model of what this pleading involves. Therefore the complaint is not also being provided.

sponsive pleading is filed,[38] at any time within twenty days after service of the original pleading. Other amendments may be made only with the court's permission or by written consent of the adverse party. FRCP 15 assists in attaining

---

[38]For example, no reply to an answer is allowed in the federal courts.

the objective of the federal rules on pleadings—that they are only a means to proper presentation of the case and to assist a disposition on the merits.[39] Accordingly, only when an amendment is made in bad faith, is unduly delayed, would be prejudicial to a party, or is totally frivolous is the court likely to disallow it.

When filing an amended pleading it is better practice to resubmit the entire pleading rather than to simply file only the changed portion. It is a lot easier for both the judge and the attorneys to refer to one document instead of having to look back and forth between two separate ones.

After a pleading is amended, the opposing party must respond to the amended pleading by the later of (1) the time remaining for response to the original pleading or (2) ten days after service of the amended pleading.

If an amendment asserts a new claim that arises out of the "conduct, transaction, or occurrence" set forth in the original claim, the new claim "relates back" and is treated as if it had been asserted on the date of the original pleading for purposes of statutes of limitations. This treatment is based on the view that since the original pleadings fulfilled the notice requirement, a change in the technical form of the claim arising out of the particular conduct or transaction upon which the original pleading was based should not entitle a party to assert a statute of limitations defense. If a plaintiff attempts to assert an entirely new and different transaction or occurrence by an amendment to the original pleading, however, the new claim is subject to a statute of limitations defense.

## V. DEFAULT JUDGMENTS

After service of the complaint the defendant must respond or be subject to having a "default" entered. This means that the plaintiff has won without a trial. The allegations of the complaint are deemed to be true because they have not been contested. The plaintiff may, however, get only what has been requested in the complaint. There are two different types of default in the federal courts under FRCP 55. They are judgment entered by the clerk (55a) and judgment entered by the court (55b). Exhibit 6.34 is an example of a request for a default judgment. Included are the simple request itself and an affidavit to show the amount owing (with a statement to show how that amount was reached) and that it is proper to enter the default (that is, that the defendant is competent, has not paid the money due, has not responded to the action, and is not entitled to the defense of being in military service).

Because default has been entered against the defendant does not mean the defendant is totally without recourse. A default may be set aside by the court if good cause is shown. The party in default (it could be the plaintiff on a counterclaim) must show that there was some good reason why no response was made (for example, the attorney or party was ill and unable to attend to business) and that there is a valid defense to the action brought.

---

[39]This is similar to Pa.R.C.P. 1033. However, the actual procedure required to amend a pleading is different.

EXHIBIT 6.34

# Request for a Default Judgment

IN THE UNITED STATES DISTRICT COURT FOR THE
NORTHERN DISTRICT OF CALIFORNIA

CAMEO CORPORATION, Plaintiff ⎫
              v.           ⎬ CIVIL ACTION
PETERS CO., INC., Defendant ⎭ NO. 91-188

### REQUEST FOR DEFAULT JUDGMENT BY CLERK

TO THE CLERK OF THE UNITED STATES DISTRICT COURT FOR THE
NORTHERN DISTRICT OF CALIFORNIA:

Upon the affidavit attached hereto, you will please enter judgment by default against Peters Co., Inc., defendant in the above-entitled action, for Fifty-Eight Thousand Two Hundred Eighty Dollars ($58,280), interest at the rate of six per cent (6%), and costs.

_____
(Attorney)
Attorney for Plaintiff
(Address)

**Affidavit for Default Judgment**

IN THE UNITED STATES DISTRICT COURT FOR THE
NORTHERN DISTRICT OF CALIFORNIA

CAMEO CORPORATION, Plaintiff ⎫
              v.           ⎬ CIVIL ACTION
PETERS CO., INC., Defendant ⎭ NO. 91-188

### AFFIDAVIT FOR DEFAULT JUDGMENT

COMMONWEALTH OF PENNSYLVANIA ⎫
                               ⎬ ss
COUNTY OF PHILADELPHIA ⎭

(Name of attorney for plaintiff), being duly sworn, deposes and says that he is attorney for plaintiff in the above-entitled action; that the amount due plaintiff from defendant is Sixty-One Thousand Seven Hundred Seventy-Six Dollars and Eighty Cents ($61,776.80) as appears from the statement attached hereto: that the defendant is not an infant or incompetent person; that the default of the defendant has been entered for failure to appear in the action; that the amount shown by the statement is justly due and owing and that no part thereof has been paid; that the disbursements sought to be taxed have been made in this action or will necessarily be made or incurred therein; and that the defendant is not in the military service of the United States.

_____
(Attorney)

Sworn to and subscribed before me on this _____ day of _____ , 1992.
_____    My Commission Expires: _____

(Notary Public)

**EXHIBIT 6.34**

## Request for a Default Judgment (continued)

**Statement of Amount Due**

IN THE UNITED STATES DISTRICT COURT FOR THE
NORTHERN DISTRICT OF CALIFORNIA

CAMEO CORPORATION, Plaintiff ⎫   CIVIL ACTION
         v.          ⎬   NO. 91-188
PETERS CO., INC., Defendant ⎭

STATEMENT OF AMOUNT DUE

Amount of debt sued upon ........................................ $58,280.00
Interest on $58,280 to Feb. 1, 1992 ............................... $ 3,496.80
Total                                                              $61,776.80
Costs:                                                             $    18.48

**Judgment**

IN THE UNITED STATES DISTRICT COURT FOR THE
NORTHERN DISTRICT OF CALIFORNIA

CAMEO CORPORATION, Plaintiff ⎫   CIVIL ACTION
         v.          ⎬   NO. 91-188
PETERS CO., INC., Defendant ⎭

JUDGMENT

The defendant Peters Co., Inc. having failed to plead or otherwise defend in this action and its default having been entered,

NOW, upon application of the plaintiff and upon affidavit that defendant is indebted to plaintiff in the sum of $61,776.80, that defendant has
been defaulted for failure to appear, and that defendant is not an infant or
incompetent person, and is not in the military service of the United States,
it is hereby

ORDERED, ADJUDGED AND DECREED that plaintiff recover of defendant the sum of $61,776.80 with interest at the rate of six per cent (6%) per
annum from the 1st day of February, 1992, and costs in the sum of Eighteen
Dollars and Forty-Eight Cents ($18.48).

_____
Clerk

Dated: _____

In Pennsylvania, there can be no judgment by the prothonotary (clerk of court) unless the praecipe (request) for entry of default judgment includes a certification that a written notice was mailed to the defendant giving ten days' notice that a default judgment would be entered against him or her.[40] This ten-day notice is in addition to the twenty days the defendant had to respond to the complaint. The form for this notice is provided in Exhibit 6.35 in addition to the form for a praecipe for judgment.

---

**EXHIBIT 6.35**

# Notice of Default

IN THE COURT OF COMMON PLEAS, LEHIGH COUNTY, PENNSYLVANIA
CIVIL DIVISION

_____

_____     v.     _____

_____

TO:

DATE OF NOTICE: _____

<u>IMPORTANT NOTICE</u>

YOU ARE IN DEFAULT BECAUSE YOU HAVE FAILED TO TAKE ACTION REQUIRED OF YOU IN THIS CASE. UNLESS YOU ACT WITHIN TEN DAYS FROM THE DATE OF THIS NOTICE, A JUDGMENT MAY BE ENTERED AGAINST YOU WITHOUT A HEARING AND YOU MAY LOSE YOUR PROPERTY OR OTHER IMPORTANT RIGHTS. YOU SHOULD TAKE THIS NOTICE TO A LAWYER AT ONCE. IF YOU DO NOT HAVE A LAWYER OR CANNOT AFFORD ONE, GO TO OR TELEPHONE THE FOLLOWING OFFICE TO FIND OUT WHERE YOU CAN GET LEGAL HELP.

LEHIGH COUNTY BAR ASSOCIATION
LEGAL REFERRAL SERVICE
ROOM 304 OLD LEHIGH COUNTY COURTHOUSE
FIFTH AND HAMILTON STREETS
ALLENTOWN, PA 18105

TELEPHONE: 215-820-3804

_____

ATTORNEY FOR PLAINTIFF/DEFENDANT

_____

_____

---

[40]Pa.R.C.P. 237.1. No ten-day notice is needed either if an extension of time to respond has been previously agreed to in writing by the parties or if an extension of time has been previously granted by the court.

**EXHIBIT 6.35**

## Notice of Default (continued)

IN THE COURT OF COMMON PLEAS OF LEHIGH COUNTY, PENNSYLVANIA
CIVIL DIVISION

        :

        :

        :    File No. _____

        :

        :

        :

TO: CLERK OF COURTS—CIVIL DIVISION:

( ) Enter Judgment Non-Pros against above-named plaintiff(s)_____

_____

( ) Enter Judgment against above-named defendant(s)_____

_____

Clerk of Courts to assess damages as follows:

Debt . . . . . . . . . . . . . . . . . . . . . . . . . . . . . . . . . . . . . . . . . . . $_____

Interest from_____ $_____

Attorney's Commission  . . . . . . . . . . . . . . . . . . . . . . . . . . . . . $_____

                                             $_____

( ) PURSUANT TO RCP 237.1, I HEREBY CERTIFY THAT NOTICE TO FILE THIS PRAECIPE WAS MAILED/DELIVERED TO THE ABOVE-NAMED PLAINTIFF(S)/DEFENDANT(S) AND THE ATTORNEY OF RECORD (if applicable) ON _____ AND COPY/COPIES OF SAME IS/ARE ATTACHED HEREWITH.

( ) PURSUANT TO RULE 237 (NOTICE OF PRAECIPE FOR FINAL JUDGMENT OR DECREE), I HEREBY CERTIFY THAT A COPY OF THIS PRAECIPE HAS BEEN MAILED TO EACH OTHER PARTY WHO HAS APPEARED IN THE ACTION OR TO HIS ATTORNEY OF RECORD.

Allentown, Pennsylvania: _____, 19___ .

_____

Signature of Filing Party

_____

Type/Print Name of Filing Party

**EXHIBIT 6.35**

## Notice of Default (continued)

Term No._____

_____

_____

_____

vs.

_____

_____

_____

_____

PRAECIPE FOR JUDGMENT

_____

I do certify that the precise residence of the within-named Plaintiff is:

_____

_____

_____

Deft. is:_____

_____

_____

_____

_____

## VI. MOTION FOR JUDGMENT ON THE PLEADINGS AND MOTION FOR SUMMARY JUDGMENT

### A. Motion for Judgment on the Pleadings

After the complaint has been served, and the parties have filed their answers or replies, the pleadings stage of the case is usually considered closed. After the closing of the pleadings, under FRCP 12(c) a party may move for a judgment on the pleadings.[41] However, the party who chooses to file this motion must do so in a manner so as not to delay trial.

In ruling on this motion, a court must accept as true all the factual allegations of the opposing party and reject as false all allegations of the movant that

---

[41]Pa.R.C.P. 1034 is similar to FRCP 12(c).

have been denied. In other words, no factual matters outside the pleadings may be presented with this motion. As a result, this motion has traditionally been used in the following situations:

- When there is a substitute for FRCP 12(b) motion for failure to state a cause of action upon which relief may be granted.

- When there is failure to join an indispensable party [FRCP 12(h)(2)]. This refers to a party missing from the lawsuit who is necessary to afford complete relief or who has an interest in the outcome that could adversely affect the existing parties.

- When an affirmative defense (that is, statute of limitations) is apparent from the allegations in the pleadings.

## B. Motion for Summary Judgment

A motion for summary judgment is a procedural device by which one of the parties can seek a court determination concerning the merits of an issue, a claim or all of the issues and claims in a lawsuit without the necessity of a full trial.[42] This motion differs from a motion for judgment on the pleadings in that the party making the motion can introduce factual information that is outside the pleadings filed in the case (the court is not limited to the pleadings in making its decision).

The purposes of this motion are to avoid unnecessary trials and to simplify and streamline the process of adjudication. The grounds for obtaining a summary judgment are that there are "no genuine issues of material fact" and that the moving party is "entitled to a judgment as a matter of law.[43] If there are contested issues of fact, the motion will be denied. This motion is not to be used as a substitute for a trial on contested factual allegations.

The moving party usually sets forth new evidence (outside of the pleadings) in support of his or her motion using any of the following types of outside materials:

- affidavits

- depositions

- admissions

- answers to interrogatories

The party opposing the motion may not rely on the factual allegations in his or her pleadings but rather must affirmatively present his or her own evidence to show that a contested issue of fact genuinely exists.

The actual form of the motion is similar to other motions. The motion must state the grounds on which judgment is sought and is usually accompanied by

---

[42]See FRCP 56 and Pa.R.C.P. 1035.
[43]FRCP 56(c) and Pa.R.C.P. 1035(b).

a brief (or memorandum of law) in support of the motion and affidavits. It is not uncommon for parties to file cross-motions for summary judgment (each party files a motion for summary judgment); the court must resolve these motions prior to trial. Also, a court can decide only some of the issues raised in these motions and can leave the balance of the claims to be decided by a trial (this is called partial summary judgment).

Typically, a motion for summary judgment, like other motions made before trial, may be assembled for filing with the clerk of courts in the following order:

**1.** the proposed order

**2.** the motion itself, attaching affidavits or exhibits as necessary

**3.** the memorandum of law setting forth the legal authority for the motion

**4.** a request for oral argument, if desired

**5.** a certificate of service

A reply to the motion is assembled in the same manner except that the answer or response is substituted for the motion.

The following exhibits are examples of a sample motion for summary judgment and proposed order (Exhibit 6.36 and 6.37), a brief in support of motion for summary judgment (Exhibit 6.38), a brief in opposition to motion for summary judgment (Exhibit 6.39), and an order denying the motion for summary judgment (Exhibit 6.40).

---

**EXHIBIT 6.36**
## Proposed Order

IN THE UNITED STATES DISTRICT COURT
FOR THE SOUTHERN DISTRICT OF CALIFORNIA

HENRY GREENE,                           :
    Plaintiff,                      :
                                 : CIVIL ACTION
     v.                             :
                                   : NO. XX-XXXX
FEDERAL ELECTRIC               :
GOVERNMENT SERVICES,    :
    Defendant.                      _____

                                     ORDER
                                     _____

AND NOW, this _____ day of October, 1990, upon consideration of defendant's motion for summary judgment and plaintiff's response thereto, said motion is hereby GRANTED. Judgment will be entered for defendant and against plaintiff on all claims.

_____

                                                       J.

**EXHIBIT 6.37**

## Motion for Summary Judgment

IN THE UNITED STATES DISTRICT COURT
FOR THE SOUTHERN DISTRICT OF CALIFORNIA

| | | |
|---|---|---|
| HENRY GREENE, | : | |
| | : | |
| Plaintiff, | : | |
| | : | CIVIL ACTION |
| v. | : | |
| | : | NO. XX-XXXX |
| FEDERAL ELECTRIC | : | |
| GOVERNMENT SERVICES, | : | |
| | : | |
| Defendant. | : | |

---

### DEFENDANT'S MOTION FOR SUMMARY JUDGMENT

---

Defendant, Federal Electric Government Services ("FE"), hereby moves, pursuant to Rule 56 of the Federal Rules of Civil Procedure, for summary judgment. In support of this motion, defendant states as follows.

1. Plaintiff, Henry Greene, was employed, first by RCA and then by Federal Electric Government Services, as the Project Manager at the Westville Intensive Treatment Unit. (Plaintiff's Answer to Interrogatory No. 8, attached as Exhibit A.)

2. In early 1989, FE determined that it would leave the "corrections business" and that it therefore would not bid on contracts in Rhode Island, Cornwells Heights, and Westville. (Nadel Affidavit, Paragraph 3, attached as Exhibit B.)

3. FE's involvement in all three of these projects concluded on June 30, 1989, and each was taken over by a successor contractor who continued to employ many of the individuals previously employed on the projects. (Nadel Affidavit, Paragraph 4.)

4. Until June 30, 1989, Henry Greene was a Federal Electric employee whose benefits were covered by FE benefit plans, including the FE Layoff Benefit Plan (the "Plan"). (Plaintiff's Answer to Interrogatory No. 8; Affidavit of Myron Door, attached as Exhibit C.)

5. Section 9(a) of the Plan provides as follows:

The terms "plant closing" and "to close a plant" mean the announcement and carrying out of a plan to terminate and discontinue all Company operations at any plant, service shop or facility. Such terms do not refer to the termination and discontinuance of only part of the Company operations at any plant, service shop or other facility nor to

EXHIBIT 6.37

# Motion for Summary Judgment (continued)

the termination or discontinuance of all of its former operations coupled with the announced intention to commence there either larger or smaller operations. Any employees released by such latter changes will be considered as laid off employees and will be subject to provisions applicable to those on layoff. *Also, such terms do not refer to the transfer or sale of such operations to a successor employer who offers continued employment to Company employees. Company employees who are not offered continued employment by the Company or by the successor employer will be considered as laid off employees and will be subject to provisions applicable to those on layoff* (emphasis added). (Plan, attached as Exhibit to Door Affidavit.)

6. Pursuant to the terms of the Plan, plaintiff was informed that he would not be eligible for plant closing benefits under any circumstances and that he would not be eligible for layoff benefits if he was offered or accepted a position with the successor contractor at Westville. (Plaintiff's Answer to Interrogatory No. 4; Nadel Affidavit, Paragraph 10.)

7. Pursuant to these Plan provisions, plaintiff was informed, by letter of June 7, that he would be eligible for layoff benefits unless he was offered employment by the successor contractor. (June 7, 1989, letter, attached to Nadel Affidavit.)

8. The successor contractor at the Westville facility was Career Systems Development Corporation. (Plaintiff's Answer to Interrogatory No. 18.)

9. Plaintiff was offered and accepted employment by Career Systems Development Corporation, working for them from July 1, 1989, until October 6, 1989. (Plaintiff's Answers to Interrogatories Nos. 8 and 9.)

10. On March 7, 1990, plaintiff filed a complaint in the Court of Common Pleas of Dade County claiming layoff benefits (Count I) and plant closing benefits (Count II) pursuant to the Plan. (Complaint, attached as Exhibit D.)

11. Defendant removed the case to the United States District Court for the Southern District of California. Upon plaintiff's motion to remand, denied by the Court on July 12, 1990, the Court determined that plaintiff's claim was a claim for benefits pursuant to section 502(a)(1)(B) of ERISA, 29 U.S.C. § 1132(a)(1)(B). (Memorandum and Order, attached as Exhibit E.)

12. Plaintiff's claim for benefits was properly denied by defendant in that he was ineligible, under the terms of the Plan, for the benefits he claims.

WHEREFORE, summary judgment must be entered for defendant-

Respectfully submitted,

_____

ERIN HOFFNER
Attorneys for Defendant
Federal Electric
Government Services

Dated: October 4, 1990

**EXHIBIT 6.38**

## Memorandum of Law (Brief) in Support of Motion

IN THE UNITED STATES DISTRICT COURT
FOR THE SOUTHERN DISTRICT OF CALIFORNIA

| | | |
|---|---|---|
| HENRY GREENE, | : | |
| | : | |
| Plaintiff, | : | |
| | : | CIVIL ACTION |
| v. | : | |
| | : | NO. XX-XXXX |
| FEDERAL ELECTRIC | : | |
| GOVERNMENT SERVICES, | : | |
| | : | |
| Defendant. | : | |

---

MEMORANDUM IN SUPPORT OF
DEFENDANT'S MOTION FOR SUMMARY JUDGMENT

---

Plaintiff claims, in this case, to be entitled to benefits under the Federal Electric Layoff Benefit Plan for Exempt Employees (the "Plan"). The relevant facts are undisputed and establish that plaintiff was ineligible for benefits under the Plan. Summary judgment must therefore be entered for defendant.

Plaintiff was the Project Director at the Westville Intensive Treatment Unit when FE decided to divest itself of its corrections operations, including Westville. Greene was a FE employee and the terms of his severance were governed by the FE Layoff Benefit Plan (attached to the Affidavit of Myron Door, Exhibit C).[1] There were FE employees at the other sites affected by FE's decision and all were treated with regard to severance just as Greene was. (Nadel Affidavit, Paragraph 7.) Indeed, FE has consistently followed this same policy with respect to all similarly situated employees. (Nadel Affidavit, Paragraph 8.)

The Plan provides for plant closing benefits in the case of a plant closing and layoff benefits in the case of layoffs. Greene claims both in the present lawsuit, even though he could, at most, qualify for one or the other. It is plain that Greene is not entitled to plant closing benefits (Count II of his complaint) since the plant was not closed. Section 9(a) of the Plan states:

The terms "plant closing" and "to close a plant" mean the
announcement and carrying out of a plant to terminate and
discontinue all Company operations at any plant, service shop or

---

1. Aside from Greene, who was a FE employee, all of the remaining employees at Westville were employees of OMS, whose employment was governed by different plans. (Nadel Affidavit, Paragraph 5.)

**EXHIBIT 6.38**

# Memorandum of Law (Brief) in Support of Motion (continued)

facility. . . . [S]*uch terms do not refer to the transfer or sale of such operations to a successor employer who offers continued employment to Company employees.* Company employees who are not offered continued employment by the Company or by the successor employer will be considered as laid off employees and will be subject to provision applicable to those on layoff. (Emphasis added.)

It is undisputed that the Westville facility was transferred to a successor contractor who offered continued employment to Company employees. (Plaintiff's Answers to Interrogatories Nos. 8 and 18; Nadel Affidavit, Paragraphs 4 & 11.) Thus, "plant closing" benefits were not available. Indeed, the Plan is explicit that, if any benefits were available in these circumstances, they would have been layoff benefits.

Under the terms of the Plan, Greene would have been entitled to layoff benefits (which he claims in Count I of his complaint) if he had not been offered employment by the successor contractor. In answer to interrogatories, however, Greene has stated clearly that he *was* offered, indeed that he accepted, employment by the successor contractor at Westville.[2] It is therefore established that, in the language of the Plan, plaintiff was "offered continued employment . . . by the successor employer." For this reason, he was not entitled to layoff benefits. (Affidavit of Myron Door, Paragraph 6.)

Two further points, while not really relevant, confirm this conclusion. Plaintiff's answers to interrogatories state clearly and consistently that he was repeatedly *told* that he would not get any severance payment if he took the job with Career Systems.[3] Never does plaintiff even allege that anyone told him that he could take the job, as he did, and get the benefits anyway. It is therefore puzzling on what possible basis he could be claiming benefits under the Plan.

Second, all FE employees who were affected by this decision, and by other similar decisions, were treated the same way. Those who were not offered continued employment by the successor contractor were given layoff benefits; those who were offered such employment were not. This policy has been followed by FE consistently and without exception in all other similar circumstances. (Nadel Affidavit, Paragraphs 7 & 8.)

2. Interrogatory No. 18 asked plaintiff to "identify the contractor who succeeded Federal Electric Government Services in the operation of the Westville facility." Plaintiff's response was, "Career Systems Development Corporation." Interrogatory No. 8 asked plaintiff to identify each entity by which he was employed since January 1, 1988. His response indicated that he was employed by FE through June 30, 1989 and began work with Career Systems Development Corporation the next day, July 1, 1989, at an increased salary. (Exhibit A.)

3. Under the Plan, the question is not whether he took the job, but whether he was offered the job. This distinction is irrelevant here, however, since he did take the job.

**EXHIBIT 6.38**

## Memorandum of Law (Brief) in Support of Motion (continued)

The Supreme Court has recognized that a motion for summary judgment is "the principal tool by which factually insufficient claims or defenses [can] be isolated and prevented from going to trial with the attendant unwarranted consumption of public and private resources." Celotex Corp. v. Catrett, 477 U.S. 317, 327 (1986). If there is any case in which it is clear that there are no factual issues to be tried and that the undisputed facts require entry of judgment for defendant, this is the case.

For these reasons, defendant requests that the Court enter judgment for defendant on both of plaintiff's claims.

Respectfully submitted,

_____

ERIN HOFFNER
Attorneys for Defendant
Federal Electric
Government Services

Dated: October 4, 1990

---

**EXHIBIT 6.39**

## Brief in Opposition to Motion for Summary Judgment

IN THE UNITED STATES DISTRICT COURT
FOR THE SOUTHERN DISTRICT OF CALIFORNIA

| | | |
|---|---|---|
| HENRY GREENE | ) | |
| | ) | No. XX-XXXX |
| Plaintiff | ) | |
| | ) | |
| vs. | ) | CIVIL ACTION |
| | ) | |
| FEDERAL ELECTRIC | ) | |
| GOVERNMENT SERVICES, | ) | |
| | ) | |
| Defendant | ) | |

EXHIBIT 6.39

# Brief in Opposition to Motion for Summary Judgment
(continued)

## PLAINTIFF'S MEMORANDUM IN OPPOSITION TO DEFENDANT'S MOTION FOR SUMMARY JUDGMENT

In this action, plaintiff is seeking layoff and plant closing benefits from the defendant, Federal Electric Government Services. For the specific reasons cited below, plaintiff contends that defendant's motion for summary judgment must be denied for there exists genuine issues of fact to be determined and as a matter of law the defendant is not entitled to a judgment.

Plaintiff was the project director at the Westville Intensive Treatment Unit when the defendant decided not to attempt to renew its contract with the Commonwealth of Pennsylvania. Accordingly, Federal Electric Government Services decided to divest itself of its correction operations, which included this Westville site. At the time that Federal Electric Government Services decided to divest itself of the Westville operation, it totally discontinued its operation at the Westville facility. It did not transfer any assets to a successor company. It took back and/or pulled out everything that it owned. Accordingly, no transfer of assets took place with any new contractor with the Commonwealth of Pennsylvania to operate the Westville facility.

By definition as included in the defendant's brief and exhibit "C," the term plant closing means "the announcement and carrying out of a plan to terminate and discontinue all company operations at any plant, service shop or other facility." The plaintiff contends and the defendant concedes in its own documents filed in this case that Federal Electric Government Services voluntarily chose to terminate and discontinue all company operations at the Westville facility. Therefore, a plant closing as defined in the benefit plan took place.

Further, the defendant's attempt to rely on the language of what is not a plant closing is misplaced and inappropriate. The Benefit Plan states that "plant closing does not refer to the transfer or sale of such operations to a successor employer who offers continued employment to company employees." There is no proof of a transfer or sale of Federal Electric Government Services's operations at Westville to a successor employer. Federal Electric Government Services chose to shut down its entire operation at Westville. In fact when Federal Electric Government Services's contract with the State terminated, only the State's property remained. Nothing belonging to Federal Electric Government Services was either sold or transferred to a successor employer. Therefore, the question of plaintiff's hiring by a new contractor with the State is irrelevant because there was no transfer or sale of operations. Accordingly, by virtue of the defendant's own documents filed in this case, the plaintiff is entitled to plant closing benefits.

It is factually disputed by the plaintiff that the Westville facility was transferred by Federal Electric Government Services to a successor employer. Federal Electric Government Services contract with the Commonwealth of

**EXHIBIT 6.39**

# Brief in Opposition to Motion for Summary Judgment (continued)

Pennsylvania terminated as of June 30, 1989. There was no transfer of operations by Federal Electric Government Services. They removed themselves "lock, stock, and barrel." The assumption that Career Systems Development Corporation is a successor contractor is not borne out by the facts. Accordingly, whether in fact a contractor who obtained a contract with the Commonwealth of Pennsylvania to operate this facility after the termination of Federal Electric Government Services contract with the state hired the plaintiff or not is irrelevant. By operation of Federal Electric Government Services's own benefit plan, the plaintiff was clearly entitled to benefits. In any event, a factual controversy exists as to whether or not the Westville facility was transferred to a successor employer.

In addition to this argument, the plaintiff contends that he is entitled to layoff benefits. Attached to plaintiff's affidavit is a Summary of Benefit Plan, 1989, that was provided to him by the defendant, Federal Electric Government Services. This plan description constitutes a summary plan description as articulated in the Employee Retirement Income Security Act, 29 U.S.C. § 1021(a). Under Section 1022 of this Act, a summary plan description of any employee benefit plan "shall be written in a manner calculated to be understood by the average plan participant and shall be sufficiently accurate and comprehensive to reasonably apprise such participants and beneficiaries of the rights and obligations under the plan." On page 31 of defendant's summary plan description, the concept of layoff benefits is described as follows:

> If you are laid off, you may receive Layoff Benefits equal to the greater of: (a) four week's pay or (b) one week's pay for each full year of continuous service, plus ¼ week's pay for each additional three months of service. While you are on layoff, you will continue to receive Comprehensive Medical Benefits, life insurance and other benefits for up to 12 months.

It is undisputed that plaintiff's employment with the defendant Federal Electric Government Services was terminated by the defendant. This would seem to meet the definition of layoff. However, it is interesting to note what is not included in this definition. If the summary plan description is supposed to be accurate and descriptive of the actual plan, it is obvious that there is discrepancy between the summary plan description and the plan itself. Noticeably absent from the summary plan description is the concept of being hired by a subsequent employer. Since Federal Electric Government Services drew up the summary plan benefit one can only conclude that it was intended to deceive the plan participants. In essence what the plan gave in its summary form was taken away by detailed qualifying provisions in the plan itself. In Genter vs. Acme Scale & Supply Company, 776 F.2d 1180, 1186 (3rd Cir. 1985), the Court held that a summary plan

**EXHIBIT 6.39**

## Brief in Opposition to Motion for Summary Judgment (continued)

description must not mislead, misinform, or fail to inform the participant and beneficiaries of what is actually provided in the benefit plan. It is plaintiff's position that the summary plan prepared by Federal Electric Government Services misleads and misinforms. In addition, as stated in the affidavit of the plaintiff, the plaintiff received his comprehensive medical benefits for a continuous period of twelve months following the termination. Therefore, it appears that Federal Electric Government Services treated the plaintiff as eligible for these layoff benefits in accordance with the summary plan.

It is the plaintiff's position that if the summary plan description conflicts with the actual plan document, then the summary plan description will govern. This position is based upon the holdings in Edwards vs. State Farm Mutual Automobile Insurance Company, 851 F.2d 134 (6th Cir. 1988) and McKnight vs. Southern Life and Health Insurance Company, 758 F.2d 1266 (11th Cir. 1985). This is true in spite of an attempted disclaimer by the defendant (Hurd vs. Hutnik, 419 F. Supp. 630, 656-657 (D.N.J. 1976)). Therefore, based upon the language in the summary plan, plaintiff is entitled to either plant closing benefits or layoff benefits because all of the disqualifying provisions advanced by the defendant are not contained in the summary plan description.

In addition to the above, the plaintiff states in his affidavit that he was advised by Lisa Smith, an employee in the employees' relations department with Federal Electric Government Services that the actual Federal Electric Government Services benefit plan (which was unseen by the plaintiff and never given to the plaintiff), was similar to the RCA plan, which the plaintiff had seen and had access to in his office since it related to other employees within the same facility. Given the statement of Ms. Smith and given his reliance on the summary plan description, which is inaccurate in describing the plan, the plaintiff contends that he is justified in relying on the documents provided by the defendant in concluding that he was entitled to receive layoff benefits.

Lastly, plaintiff contends that the defendant's filing of a motion for summary judgment in the manner and time that it did may have prejudiced the rights of the plaintiff. Plaintiff originally scheduled a deposition of Lisa Smith, an employee of defendant, for October 4, 1990. This date was selected by prearranging the date with defendant's counsel. Included in the notice of deposition was a request for production of documents. A few days prior to the scheduled deposition, defendant's counsel contacted plaintiff's counsel requesting that the deposition be rescheduled. On October 4, 1990, the date of the scheduled deposition, the defendant filed its motion for summary judgment. The practical result of defendant's action is that plaintiff is forced to respond to this motion for summary judgment without the benefit of deposition or document production. The defendant obviously was aware of this practical result when it chose its course of action. Accordingly,

**EXHIBIT 6.39**

# Brief in Opposition to Motion for Summary Judgment (continued)

the plaintiff requests that either defendant's motion be denied or that plaintiff be allowed to supplement his opposition to defendant's motion based on any information acquired at the deposition now scheduled for October 18, 1990, before this Court adjudicates this motion for summary judgment.

Accordingly, and in light of the above, the plaintiff requests this Honorable Court to dismiss the defendant's motion for summary judgment.

Respectfully submitted:

_____

Mark I. Weinstein, Esquire
462 Walnut Street
Allentown, Pennsylvania 18102
(215) 432-4552

Attorney for Plaintiff

CERTIFICATE OF SERVICE

I, Mark I. Weinstein, Esquire, hereby certify that plaintiff's memorandum in opposition to defendant's motion for summary judgment and proposed order was served today by first class mail, postage prepaid to:

Dated: 10/17/90

IN THE UNITED STATES DISTRICT COURT
FOR THE SOUTHERN DISTRICT OF CALIFORNIA

| | | |
|---|---|---|
| HENRY GREENE, | ) | |
| | ) | |
| Plaintiff | ) | No. XX-XXXX |
| | ) | |
| vs. | ) | CIVIL ACTION |
| | ) | |
| FEDERAL ELECTRIC | ) | |
| GOVERNMENT SERVICES, | ) | |
| | ) | |
| Defendant | ) | |

ORDER

AND NOW, this _____ day of October, 1990, defendant's motion for summary judgment is hereby DENIED.

_____

U.S. District Court Judge

**EXHIBIT 6.40**

## Court Order

IN THE UNITED STATES DISTRICT COURT
FOR THE SOUTHERN DISTRICT OF CALIFORNIA

HENRY GREENE,

v.                                    CIVIL ACTION NO. XX-XXXX

FEDERAL ELECTRIC GOVERNMENT
SERVICES

### O R D E R

AND NOW, this 31st day of October, 1990, IT IS ORDERED that defendant's motion for summary judgment is DENIED without prejudice to raise similar issues before the arbitrators or, in the event of an appeal, before the court at the Rule 41(b) stage.

BY THE COURT:

_____

J.

## VII. Injunctions

In most of what has been covered so far, the plaintiff in a lawsuit has been trying to collect money damages from a defendant. However, money damages are not the only type of relief that is permissible in courts. An **injunction** is a remedy that is available only in cases in which there is a showing that irreparable injury will occur and where money damages would not be an adequate remedy.

An injunction is an order of a court requiring that an act be done or restraining an act. For example, if pickets are physically preventing shoppers from entering a store, an injunction might be issued by a court ordering the pickets to disperse, or perhaps to picket only at a certain distance away from the store. This would be an injunction restraining conduct. If a union strikes illegally, as for example public employees who are not permitted to strike, a court might order the strikers back to work. This is a mandatory injunction in that it compels positive action.

The question of whether an injunction should be granted is a matter of substantive law. The method by which one goes about getting an injunction is a procedural question.

The Federal Rules of Civil Procedure provide guidelines for the district courts' use of its equitable power in granting injunctions. The rules distinguish between temporary restraining orders (TROs), which are granted principally to preserve the rights of parties until a hearing can be held, and preliminary injunctions, which are granted to preserve the rights of parties until the final determination of the case. Ultimately, at the trial, a permanent injunction may be issued.

## A. Temporary Restraining Orders

A TRO may be granted when there is some emergency that requires immediate action by the court or some irreparable damage will be done to the party seeking the TRO. A TRO may be used to freeze all action, preserving the status quo until there can be some hearing on the matter. A request for a TRO, unlike most federal pleadings, must be made in a "verified" complaint. That is, the plaintiff must sign an affidavit attesting to the truth of the statements contained in the complaint.

Generally, a TRO may not last for more than ten days, unless the party against whom it is issued consents to an extension. Further, in order to have a TRO issued, the plaintiff has to post security in an amount fixed by the court to protect the defendant from loss sustained by reason of the grant of the TRO if the defendant is found to have been wrongfully enjoined. Security is normally a bond posted by an insurance company under terms that money is to be paid upon the order of the court. This protects the defendant from having to sue the plaintiff for damages sustained if the TRO is found not to have been a necessary form of relief for the plaintiff.

## B. Preliminary Injunctions

Unlike a TRO, which may be granted on an immediate basis without a hearing, a preliminary injunction only issues after both sides have had an opportunity to present evidence to the court. Thus the next normal step would be a preliminary injunction hearing. When a court issues a preliminary injunction, that remedy stays in effect until a full trial takes place or for a fixed period of time.

To avoid prolonging a case unduly FRCP 65(a)(2) allows the court to order the trial of the action on the merits to be advanced and consolidated with the hearing on the application for a preliminary injunction. Even if there is no consolidation, any evidence received at the preliminary injunction hearing that would be admissible at trial is considered part of the trial record and need not be repeated at trial.

Ultimately, a final decision is reached on the question of injunctive relief and the order of the court becomes binding on the parties for all time, or for the specific period of time that the injunction is to last.

## C. Special Procedural Requirements

A request by a plaintiff for a TRO or a preliminary injunction must be made in a document separate from the complaint. However, it is to be filed at the same time as the complaint. In addition, a proposed order specifying the action or ruling sought from the court and a statement of explanation and/or legal authority in support of the request for an injunction should accompany the complaint and motion for an injunction.

## VIII. Intervention and Class Actions

### A. Intervention

**Intervention** is the procedure whereby an interested party seeks either by right or permission to become a party (either a plaintiff or defendant) in a pending lawsuit for the purpose of presenting a claim or defense.[44] This procedure should be distinguished from the rules concerning joinder of persons[45] in that in joinder the existing parties are seeking the addition of the party to be joined or that the lawsuit should be dismissed for failure to join a party. In intervention, a third person seeks to be joined as a party to the lawsuit.

Intervention provides nonparties with a way of protecting their interests when a pending action may jeopardize that interest. For example, a creditor whose loan is in default would want to intervene in a suit brought by a third party against the debtor if the debtor did not have sufficient assets to pay the creditor and the third party in full. Intervention is available by motion made by the applicant or by stipulation (written agreement) of all the parties.

Intervention in the federal courts may be "by right" or "permissive." When an applicant claims an interest relating to the subject matter of the pending action and is so situated that the disposition of the action may, as a practical matter, impair the ability of the applicant to protect that interest, he or she has a right to intervene. A further requirement for intervention as of right is that the proposed intervenor must show that his or her interests are not being adequately represented by the existing parties to the lawsuit. If these requirements are met, the judge must allow the intervenor into the existing lawsuit.

Permissive intervention, on the other hand, is a discretionary matter. If an applicant's claim or defense has a common question of law or fact with the pending action, the trial judge may allow intervention when an appropriate motion is presented to the court, but is not required to do so. See Exhibits 6.41 and 6.42 for examples of a motion to intervene and an intervenor's answer.

### B. Class Actions

A **class action** is a procedural device that allows one or more persons to institute a lawsuit on behalf of themselves and other individuals who have been harmed in a similar way. The purpose of class actions is to allow someone with a relatively small claim, who would not be expected to sue separately, to benefit from a lawsuit brought by a representative of a large group of people. Similarly, the plaintiff may sue a defendant as a representative of a large group of potential defendants. Class actions can be very complex and very controversial.

---

[44]FRCP 24.
[45]FRCP 19.

**EXHIBIT 6.41**

## Motion to Intervene taken from Form 23 of the Appendix of Forms

MOTION TO INTERVENE AS A
DEFENDANT UNDER RULE 24
(Based upon the complaint, Form 16)

United States District Court for the
Southern District of New York
Civil Action, File Number _____

| | |
|---|---|
| A.B., plaintiff | ) |
| | ) |
| v. | ) Motion to intervene |
| | ) as a defendant |
| C.D., defendant | ) |
| E.F., applicant for | ) |
| intervention | ) |

E.F. moves for leave to intervene as a defendant in this action, in order to assert the defenses set forth in his proposed answer, of which a copy is hereto attached, on the ground that he is the manufacturer and vendor to the defendant, as well as to others, of the articles alleged in the complaint to be an infringement of plaintiff's patent, and as such has a defense to plaintiff's claim presenting both questions of law and of fact which are common to the main action.

Signed: _____
Attorney for E.F.,
Applicant for
Intervention

Address: _____

The goal of class actions is to avoid repetitious lawsuits with the prospect of inconsistent results. There are, however, four basic requirements that must be met before a lawsuit is allowed to proceed as a class action. These requirements are set out in FRCP 23(a):

(1) the class is so numerous that joinder of all members is impracticable,
(2) there are questions of law or fact common to the class,
(3) the claims or defenses of the representative parties are typical of the claims or defenses of the class, and
(4) the representative parties will fairly and adequately protect the interests of the class.

---

**EXHIBIT 6.42**

## Intervener's Answer taken from Form 23 of the Appendix of Forms

United States District Court for the
Southern District of New York
Civil Action, File Number _____

A.B., plaintiff                )
                         )
          v.            )  Intervener's Answer
                         )
C.D., defendant        )
E.F., intervener        )

### First Defense

Intervener admits the allegations stated in paragraphs 1 and 4 of the complaint; denies the allegations in paragraph 3, and denies the allegations in paragraph 2 in so far as they assert the legality of the issuance of the Letters Patent to plaintiff.

### Second Defense

Plaintiff is not the first inventor of the articles covered by the Letters Patent specified in his complaint, since articles substantially identical in character were previously patented in Letters Patent granted to intervener on January 5, 1920.

Signed: _____
           Attorney for E.F.,
           Intervener

Address: _____

---

In order for a class action to be certified as a proper class action, the moving party must establish that all the requirements of rule 23(a) are met and at least one of the alternatives of rule 23(b) is met. Collectively, these requirements are intended to establish that a class, in fact, exists and that there are sound reasons to believe that certain parties can legitimately represent other parties.

Rule 23(b) provides the following:

(b) Class Actions Maintainable. An action may be maintained as a class action if the prerequisites of subdivision (a) are satisfied, and in addition;

(1) the prosecution of separate actions by or against individual members of the class would create a risk of

(A) inconsistent or varying adjudications with respect to individual members of the class which would establish incompatible standards of conduct for the party opposing the class, or

(B) adjudications with respect to individual members of the class which would as a practical matter be dispositive of the interests of the other members not parties to the adjudications or substantially impair or impede their ability to protect their interests; or

(2) the party opposing the class has acted or refused to act on grounds generally applicable to the class, thereby making appropriate final injunctive relief or corresponding declaratory relief with respect to the class as a whole; or

(3) the court finds that the questions of law or fact common to the members of the class predominate over any questions affecting only individual members, and that a class action is superior to other available methods for the fair and efficient adjudication of the controversy. The matters pertinent to the findings include: (A) the interest of members of the class in individually controlling the prosecution or defense of separate actions; (B) the extent and nature of any litigation concerning the controversy already commenced by or against members of the class; (C) the desirability or undesirability of concentrating the litigation of the claims in the particular forum; (D) the difficulties likely to be encountered in the management of a class action.

## 1. Pleading Requirements

Many jurisdictions (either federal districts pursuant to local rule or states) require that there be a notation in the caption indicating that the action is a class action. An example would be: "Complaint—Class Action." In addition, within the complaint itself, there should be a separate heading entitled "Class Action Allegations" followed by separate averments alleging specific facts about the proposed class.

Rule 27 of the Local Rules of Civil Procedure for the United States District Court for the Eastern District of Pennsylvania provides a good model of precisely what has to be included in the allegations under the Class Action heading:

In any case sought to be maintained as a class action:

(a) The complaint shall bear next to its caption the legend, "Complaint—Class Action."

(b) The complaint shall contain under a separate heading, styled "Class Action Allegations:"

(1) A reference to the portion or portions of Rule 23, F.R.Civ. P., under which it is claimed that the suit is properly maintainable as a class action.

(2) Appropriate allegations thought to justify such claim, including, but not necessarily limited to:

A. the size (or approximate size) and definition of the alleged class,

B. the basis upon which the plaintiff (or plaintiffs) claims

    (i) to be an adequate representative of the class, or

    (ii) if the class is comprised of defendants, that those named as parties are adequate representatives of the class.

    C. the alleged questions of law and fact claimed to be common to the class, and

    D. in actions claimed to be maintainable as class actions under subdivision (b)(3) of Rule 23, F.R.Civ.P., allegations thought to support the findings required by that subdivision.

## 2. Determination of Class and Notice

FRCP 23(c)(1) requires that the court "as soon as practicable after the commencement of an action" determine whether it may be maintained as a class action. Many jurisdictions establish a time limit for making a motion for class certification.[46] The following is an example of a rule establishing such a time limit from the Local Rules of Civil Procedure [27(c)] for the United States District Court for the Eastern District of Pennsylvania:

> (c) Within ninety (90) days after the filing of a complaint in a class action, unless this period is extended on motion of good cause appearing, the plaintiff shall move for a determination under sub-division (c)(1) of Rule 23, F.R.Civ.P., as to whether the case is to be maintained as a class action.

If the court validates the class action, in most cases the court is required to direct to the class members the "best notice practicable under the circumstances."[47] Typically, notice will be given by mailing to all members of the class who can be identified and by publishing copies of the notices in several periodicals that are likely to be read by members of the class (for example, trade journals). Class members in the most common type of class actions are given the opportunity not to be bound by the action. This is known as "opting out." If the class member does not opt out, he or she will be bound by the result of the class action just as if he or she were a participant in it.

An example of a notice to class members and the form used to exclude oneself from the class are shown in Exhibits 6.43 and 6.44.

There are also special provisions for a final judgment in class action cases. In most class actions, the final judgment must describe those persons whom the court found to be members of the class.

If the class action is settled prior to judgment, as are a large number of class actions that have been filed in recent years, court approval is necessary. In

---

[46]In Pennsylvania, the time limit is thirty (30) days from the filing of the last required pleading. Pa.R.C.P. 1707(a).

[47]The responsibility for the mechanics of reproducing and addressing notices is usually placed on the representatives of the class.

EXHIBIT 6.43

# Notice of Pendency of Class Action

IN THE UNITED STATES DISTRICT COURT
FOR THE EASTERN DISTRICT OF PENNSYLVANIA

MARVIN GOULD, Executor
of the Estate of J. GOULD
ROGASNER,                CIVIL ACTION
    Plaintiff,

   v.

AMERICAN COMPANY,
NATIONAL, INC.,
LIFTON, INC., McCLING,      NO. 1000
INC. and REYNOLDS CO.,
    Defendants.

NOTICE OF PENDENCY
OF CLASS ACTION

To: All persons who were owners of record of the Common Stock of Mc-Cling, Inc. on May 13, 1971, except defendants:

You are hereby notified that plaintiff has filed a suit which is presently pending in the United States District Court for the Eastern District of Pennsylvania, alleging that the above-named defendants committed violations of state and federal law in connection with the merger of McCling, Inc. (hereinafter referred to as "McCling") into Reynolds Co. (hereinafter referred to as "Reynolds") on May 13, 1971. On behalf of itself and all others similarly situated, plaintiff, the present owner of 700 shares of McCling common stock, seeks to recover money damages for injuries sustained as a result of the alleged violations.

The complaint in substance alleges that:

(1) upon the merger of McCling into Reynolds, Reynolds agreed to pay certain defendants, namely American Company, National, Inc. and Lifton, Inc. fifty dollars ($50.00) cash for each share of McCling common stock, whereas all other shareholders were to receive for each share of McCling common stock one share of newly issued Reynolds, two dollars and twenty-five cents ($2.25) convertible preferred stock worth substantially less than fifty dollars ($50.00) per share;

(2) certain defendants breached their fiduciary duties to plaintiff and its class by sponsoring a merger resulting in such discriminatory treatment;

(3) the notice to shareholders issued on March 14, 1971, and the proxy statement issued on April 10, 1971, violated the Securities Exchange Act of 1934 in that they contain material misrepresentations and omitted facts essential to make them not misleading, thus failing to disclose the illegality of this treatment and the breaches of fiduciary duty.

**EXHIBIT 6.43**

## Notice of Pendency of Class Action (continued)

Defendants have denied any wrongdoing or any violation of the law.

On February 27, 1972, this Court directed that this case proceed as a class action on behalf of all owners of record, as of May 13, 1971, of McCling common stock other than defendants. The class includes those who exercised their appraisal rights pursuant to the merger. All such persons are herein referred to as the class.

Pursuant to Rule 23(c)(2) of the Federal Rules of Civil Procedure, NOTICE IS HEREBY GIVEN THAT:

1. The Court will exclude you from the class if you request exclusion in writing postmarked on or before June 5, 1972. Persons who request exclusion will not be entitled to share in the benefits of the judgment if it is favorable to plaintiff and will not be bound by the judgment if it is adverse to plaintiff. Requests for exclusion should be sent to the Clerk of the United States District Court for the Eastern District of Pennsylvania. A form and envelope for this purpose are enclosed.

2. If you do not request exclusion, you may, if you desire, enter an appearance through counsel of your own choosing. If you do not request exclusion and do not enter an appearance through counsel of your own choosing, your interest will be represented by plaintiffs through their counsel, and you will be bound by any judgment rendered in this action.

3. If you elect to participate in the class, you will be subject to the orders and notices with reference to the furnishing of statements or testimony and other matters relating to this case. You will be entitled to share pro rata, after deductions for attorneys' fees and disbursements, in any recovery in favor of the class or subclass of which you are ultimately determined to be a member.

4. Failure to return the enclosed form with the postmark earlier than June 5, 1972, automatically includes you in the class represented by plaintiff. You must notify the court in order to be excluded. All communications regarding this notice should be sent to the following address:

John J. Jones, Clerk
United States District Court for
   the Eastern District of Pennsylvania
9th & Chestnut Streets
Philadelphia, Pennsylvania 19107.

5. This court expresses no view as to the merit of this action.

**EXHIBIT 6.44**

## Request to Be Excluded from the Class of Plaintiffs

IN THE UNITED STATES DISTRICT COURT
FOR THE EASTERN DISTRICT OF PENNSYLVANIA

MARVIN GOULD, Executor
of the Estate of J. GOULD
ROGASNER,                                    CIVIL ACTION
    Plaintiff,

   v.

AMERICAN COMPANY,
NATIONAL, INC.,
LIFTON, INC., McCLING,               NO. 1000
INC. and REYNOLDS CO.,
    Defendants.

REQUEST TO BE EXCLUDED
FROM THE CLASS OF PLAINTIFFS

To: The Clerk of the United States District Court for the Eastern District of Pennsylvania.

    Please take notice that _____
                                          Name

_____ , hereby requests to be ex-
                Address
cluded from the class of plaintiffs herein.

addition, FRCP 23(e) requires that notice of the proposed dismissal of the action and the terms of the settlement be given to all members of the class in a manner directed by the court.

Whether there is a settlement or a favorable judgment, members of the class must submit claims to prove they are entitled to share in the proceeds of the lawsuit. Typically, the claim form will show the amount of damages that the class member maintains have been suffered. Claim forms are then reviewed and the proceeds distributed pro rata to the class members. The attorneys representing the class will receive a fee, which must be approved by the court, which comes out of the proceeds and is also borne, pro rata, by the various class members, if they win and if the attorneys have not been paid by their clients.

An example of a complaint for an injunction including a class action allegation is provided in Exhibit 6.45.

**EXHIBIT 6.45**

## Complaint for Injunction with Class Action Allegation

IN THE UNITED STATES DISTRICT COURT
FOR THE EASTERN DISTRICT OF PENNSYLVANIA

| | |
|---|---|
| FIFI LARUE, by her owner, next friend and natural guardian, MADYLYN LARUE | : |
| | : |
| | : |
| v. | : |
| | : |
| COMMONWEALTH OF PENNSYLVANIA and | : |
| HONORABLE MILTON SHAPP, Governor of the Commonwealth of Pennsylvania and | : |
| COUNTY OF BERKS and | : |
| CITY OF READING and | : |
| HONORABLE EUGENE SHIRK, Mayor of Reading and | : CIVIL ACTION NO. 74-90 |
| HONORABLE WARREN HESS, President Judge Court of Common Pleas of Berks County and | : |
| READING POLICE DEPARTMENT and | : |
| BERNARD J. DOBINSKY, CHIEF OF POLICE and | : |
| READING PARK DIRECTOR and | : |
| READING SOCIETY FOR THE PREVENTION OF CRUELTY TO ANIMALS and | : |
| OFFICER LENNARD SCHNABEL, Reading Police Department | : |

COMPLAINT

I. *Preliminary Statement*

1. This is an action contesting the validity on its face and as applied to the City of Reading, Pennsylvania, Ordinance #13, which provides:

**EXHIBIT 6.45**

# Complaint for Injunction with Class Action Allegation (continued)

"No dog in the City of Reading, its environs or any political subdivision thereof shall be permitted by its owner, master, caretaker or any agent or employee thereof to encroach upon the streets, sidewalks, public places or parks without being properly bound, restrained or otherwise tethered by a leash, chain or other suitable form of restraint. . . ."

II. *Cause of Action and Jurisdiction*

2. This action arises under §1 of the Civil Rights Act of 1871, 42 U.S.C. § 1983, and seeks declaratory and injunctive relief in addition to compensatory and punitive damages to vindicate and redress deprivations of rights, privileges, and immunities secured by the Constitution and laws of the United States and perpetrated by hereinafter named defendants under color of state law.

3. Jurisdiction is conferred on this Court by 28 U.S.C. §1343(3).

III. *The Parties*

4. Plaintiff is a natural person of the canine species and is a citizen and resident of the City of Reading, Commonwealth of Pennsylvania, and the United States of America.

5. Defendants, Commonwealth of Pennsylvania, County of Berks, and City of Reading are a state, county, and city respectively. The County of Berks is a political subdivision of the Commonwealth of Pennsylvania. The City of Reading is a political subdivision of the County of Berks.

6. Defendant, Milton J. Shapp, is Governor of Pennsylvania.

7. Defendant, Eugene Shirk, is the Mayor of Reading and is ultimately responsible for the enforcement of all city ordinances.

8. Defendant, Warren Hess, is the President Judge of the Court of Common Pleas of Berks County.

9. Defendant, Reading Police Department, is the municipal agency responsible for the enforcement of City of Reading Ordinance No. 13.

10. Defendant, Bernard J. Dobinsky, is the Chief of the Reading Police Department.

11. Defendant, Reading Park Director, is responsible for the enforcement of City of Reading Ordinance No. 13 in public parks and property.

12. Defendant, Reading Society for the Prevention of Cruelty to Animals, is also responsible for the enforcement of local Ordinance No. 13.

13. Defendant, Lennard Schnabel, is a police officer employed by the Reading Police Department.

EXHIBIT 6.45

# Complaint for Injunction with Class Action Allegation (continued)

*IV. The Class Action*

14. Plaintiff herein sues on her own behalf and on behalf of all others similarly situated, pursuant to rule 23 of the Federal Rules of Civil Procedure, the class consisting of all natural persons of the canine species who are subject to "leashing" statutes or ordinances throughout the United States and its territories, including all states and political subdivisions located therein.

15. The members of the class on behalf of which plaintiffs sue are too numerous to make joinder of all members practical. The questions of law and fact are common to the class and the named plaintiffs have claims typical of the class and will fairly and adequately protect the interest of the class.

16. The defendants have acted on grounds generally applicable to the class of which plaintiffs are members thereby making appropriate final injunctive relief with respect to the class as a whole. Questions of law and fact common to the members of the class predominate over questions affecting individual members. A class action will provide the best available method for a fair and efficient adjudication of the controversy.

*V. Three-Judge Court*

17. Insofar as this action challenges the statutes and ordinances pertaining to the leashing on a nationwide state by state basis, a three-judge court must be convened pursuant to 28 U.S.C. §§2281 and 2284.

*VI. Facts*

18. On or about February 28, 1974, at approximately 10:15 A.M. plaintiff was proceeding through City Parks, City of Reading, formerly known as Penn's Commons, on her morning constitution.

19. While in the company of her natural guardian, plaintiff was approached by Officer Schnabel, and her natural guardian was questioned as to the whereabouts of her leash.

20. Upon the failure and refusal of plaintiff's natural guardian to respond, plaintiff was taken into custody by Officer Schnabel in a surly manner and her outer garments were searched and thereafter removed.

21. Upon information and belief, plaintiff was transported by Officer Schnabel to the Reading Society for the Prevention of Cruelty to Animals pound.

22. Plaintiff's natural guardian attempted to visit her at the pound, but was denied access to her.

23. Plaintiff was released from custody on March 13, 1974, upon the receipt of $25.00 in fines and costs, and now alleges the following causes of action:

EXHIBIT 6.45

# Complaint for Injunction with Class Action Allegation (continued)

## COUNT I

24. Plaintiff incorporates allegations contained in ¶¶ 18-23 of the complaint.

25. The City of Reading Ordinance No. 13 and other like acts are unconstitutional on its face in that it deprives plaintiff and others similarly situated of freedom of speech and freedom of assembly in contravention of the First Amendment to the Constitution.

## COUNT II

26. Plaintiff incorporates the allegations contained in ¶¶ 18-23 of the complaint.

27. The City of Reading Ordinance No. 13 and other like are unconstitutional on their face in that they are overbroad to the extent they regulate activity protected by the First Amendment.

## COUNT III

28. Plaintiff incorporates the allegations contained in ¶¶ 18-23 of the complaint.

29. Officer Schnabel arrested plaintiff and conducted a search and seizure of her person pursuant to City of Reading Local Ordinance No. 13 without probable cause in violation of the Fourth Amendment of the Constitution.

## COUNT IV

30. Plaintiff realleges the allegations contained in ¶¶ 18-23 of the complaint.

31. Plaintiff was held in custody without a speedy and public trial and was not informed of the nature and cause of her accusations in violation of the Sixth Amendment of the Constitution.

## COUNT V

32. Plaintiff incorporated the allegations contained in ¶¶ 18-23 of the complaint.

33. Plaintiff was denied a trial by an impartial jury of her peers in violation of the Sixth Amendment to the Constitution.

## COUNT VI

34. Plaintiff incorporates the allegations contained in ¶¶ 18-23 of the complaint.

35. Plaintiff was not afforded counsel to assist in her defense in violation of the Sixth Amendment of the Constitution.

## COUNT VII

36. Plaintiff incorporates the allegations contained in ¶¶ 18-23 of the complaint.

37. Plaintiff was not afforded the right to confront her accusers, to wit, Officer Schnabel, in contravention of the Sixth Amendment of the Constitution.

EXHIBIT 6.45
## Complaint for Injunction with Class Action Allegation (continued)

### COUNT VIII

38. Plaintiff incorporates the allegations contained in ¶¶ 18-23 the complaint.

39. Plaintiff was denied bail and subjected to cruel and unusual punishment during her incarceration at the Reading S.P.C.A. in contravention of the Eighth Amendment in that her cell was contaminated with fleas, excrement, bones, and other dehumanizing matter.

### COUNT IX

40. Plaintiff incorporates the allegations contained in ¶¶ 18-23 of the complaint.

41. Plaintiff was deprived of her liberty without notice or a prior hearing in contravention of the Due Process Clause of the Fourteenth Amendment of the Constitution.

### COUNT X

42. Plaintiff incorporates the allegations contained in ¶¶ 18-23 of the complaint.

43. City of Reading Ordinance No. 13 creates two inherently suspect classes, one of the human species and one of the canine species, discriminating against the latter absent a compelling state interest in contravention of the Equal Protection Clause of the Fourteenth Amendment to the Constitution.

WHEREFORE, plaintiff demands that the Court accord the following relief:

1. issue a temporary restraining order, enjoining enforcement of City of Reading Local Ordinance No. 13,

2. convene a three-judge court pursuant to 28 U.S.C. §2281, §2284,

3. certify that this action may be maintained as a class action,

4. issue a preliminary and permanent injunction, restraining the enforcement of City of Reading Local Ordinance No. 13,

5. issue a declaratory judgment, declaring City of Reading Local Ordinance No. 13 unconstitutional,

6. award plaintiff and her class compensatory and punitive damages in the amount of $3,000,000.

7. award such other relief as the Court deems just and proper.

Mark I. Weinstein, Esquire
Attorney for Plaintiff
462 Walnut St.
Allentown, PA 18102
(215) 432-4552

## IX. SUMMARY

The purposes of pleadings are to set out a party's position with respect to a lawsuit and to control how and when a case proceeds through the various stages of litigation. Pleadings are intended to show the real dispute between parties involved in litigation.

In the federal courts a lawsuit is started by filing a complaint and serving it on the defendant with a summons. The complaint consists of a caption, jurisdictional statement, statement of the claim, demand for judgment, and the signature of plaintiff's attorney. The complaint can also contain a demand for jury trial.

Once the complaint has been served on the defendant, the defendant will file an answer or, where appropriate, a motion to dismiss. In addition, the defendant can file a counterclaim against the plaintiff, cross-claim against a codefendant, and/or a third-party claim against a party not originally joined by the plaintiff. Each party responding to a counterclaim, cross-claim, or third-party claim can file a reply/answer or where appropriate, a motion to dismiss. Under the federal rules, all pleadings are based on the concept of notice pleading.

Pennsylvania differs from the federal rules in that the concept of pleading is based in fact pleading not notice pleading. Fact pleading requires a larger quantum of information than notice pleading. In addition, a civil action in Pennsylvania can be started by a writ of summons prior to filing a complaint. The rules differ with respect to the names of some pleadings and with respect to the optional nature of the counterclaims, but to a significant degree, they provide the same menu of responses available under the federal system.

Other issues of pleadings discussed in this chapter are amendments and default judgments. Amendments allow a party to change a previously articulated claim or defense or to add a new party(s). Default judgments occur when a party fails to respond to a pleading, resulting in a win without a trial. Accordingly, from a defense standpoint, great care should be taken to avoid a default judgment.

Various pretrial motions typically occur in civil litigation in addition to motions to dismiss. Most importantly is a motion for summary judgment. It allows a party to use information acquired outside of the pleadings either from discovery documents or affidavits to show that no genuine facts are in dispute and the party filing the motion is correct as to the law. In essence the motion dispenses with the requirement of a trial if there is no factual controversy to be determined.

Pleadings are also used in situations involving intervention and class actions. Intervention is where a party who was not originally part of a lawsuit seeks to join the lawsuit voluntarily. Class actions are designed to handle situations where a group of individuals have been harmed by a defendant or group of defendants in a similar fashion. The intent of class action suits is to prevent the costly and time-consuming litigation of multiple lawsuits involving the same issues with the potential of inconsistent results.

## X. Key Terms

Adoption by
  reference

Affirmative defenses

Answer

Caption

Civil cover sheet

Class-action

Complaint

Compulsory
  counterclaim

Counterclaim

Counts

Cross-claim

Demand for judgment

Designation form

Docket sheet

Fact pleading

Impleader

Injunction

Intervention

Motion to dismiss

Notice pleading

Permissive
  counterclaim

Pleading

Pretrial motion

Reply

Service of Process

Signature of attorney

Statement of claim

Statement of
  jurisdiction

Summons

Third-party practice

Writ of summons

## XI. Questions

1. What is the difference between a pleading and a pretrial motion?
2. Under the FRCP, what pleading is used to institute a lawsuit? How about in Pennsylvania?
3. Under the FRCP, name the typical elements of a complaint.
4. What is meant by a "count" under the FRCP?
5. What options are available to a defendant in responding to a complaint under the FRCP?
6. What is the difference between notice pleading and fact pleading?
7. What is the purpose of an answer?
8. Compare and contrast compulsory with permissive counterclaim under the FRCP.
9. Compare and contrast counterclaims under the FRCP with Pennsylvania.
10. What is a cross-claim? How is it different from a counterclaim?
11. How is an impleader different from intervention?
12. What is a default judgment?
13. Compare and contrast a motion to dismiss and a motion for judgment on the pleadings. How do both differ from a motion for summary judgment?
14. Name and explain the three types of injunctions under the FRCP.

# CHAPTER 7

# DISCOVERY

## I. INTRODUCTION

The focus of this chapter is to expand on the discussion of case preparation outlined in chapter 4. Chapter 4 explores fact investigation from the perspective of obtaining information on an informal basis; this chapter focuses on the formal discovery devices used in civil litigation. The next chapter discusses what to do with the information obtained through either the informal fact investigation or the formal discovery process.

Courts and legislatures have created various pretrial devices that enable each party to "discover" certain information concerning the factual and legal position of the opposite party on the issues in dispute. Thus, the purposes of discovery are:

- ◆ To narrow the factual and legal issues by ascertaining the bases of the plaintiff's complaint and the bases of the defendant's defenses to the complaint.

- ◆ To preserve testimony (evidence) of witnesses who are unable to testify at the trial.

- ◆ To eliminate the element of surprise in litigation, thereby facilitating and encouraging settlements of litigation prior to trial.

- ◆ To prepare factual data that will support a motion for summary judgment.

Most lawsuits where discovery is used will be based on one or more of these purposes.

The general process of discovery is implemented through five devices:

1. *Written interrogatories.* **Interrogatories** are written questions prepared by one party and directed to another party for answer under oath.

2. *Requests for production of Documents, Things, and Inspections.* **Requests for production of documents, things, and inspections** are written requests by one party asking another party to the lawsuit to deliver certain written materials or objects for inspection and study.

3. *Requests for admissions.* **Requests for admission** are written requests by one party asking another party to acknowledge the truth of certain facts or the authenticity of certain materials.

4. *Depositions.* **Depositions** are formal interviews under oath in the presence of a court reporter at which a party or witness (the "deponent") is asked questions and is expected to provide oral answers. In most cases the deponent does not know what questions will be asked; the questions can be submitted either in writing or orally.

5. *Physical and mental examinations.* An adverse party may require a **physical or mental examination** by an impartial doctor when the physical or mental condition of a person is at issue in a lawsuit.

While the meaning and scope of each of the above discovery devices will be examined in this chapter, our focus will be on the operation of discovery devices in civil lawsuits in federal courts governed by the Federal Rules of Civil Procedure. Comparable discovery devices exist in state court proceedings as well.

With the exception of physical and mental examinations, which are used primarily in personal injury, paternity, and civil commitment cases, the discovery devices are available for use in most civil cases. Moreover, these devices are complementary rather than mutually exclusive, and the federal rules specifically provide that, subject to the provisions relating to protective orders, "frequency of use of these methods is not limited."[1]

Discovery devices may be divided into two broad categories: (1) preliminary pretrial discovery, consisting of interrogatories, requests for production of documents, requests for admissions, and physical and mental examinations; and (2) depositions. The first category of devices may be directed only at parties[2] to the lawsuit and are used primarily to narrow the issues, to obtain precise factual data, to establish facts that are not in serious dispute, and, most significantly, to learn the identity of witnesses and to obtain copies of relevant documentary evidence. In major cases, the preliminary pretrial devices are commonly used as a prelude to oral depositions.

Depositions are the primary discovery device that may be used for non-parties as well as parties. Moreover, depositions provide the only opportunity to observe the demeanor and responsiveness of key witnesses while responding to questions.

FRCP 26(b)(1) establishes the general parameters of all discovery within the federal court system. Because of its importance, the language of this rule cannot be emphasized enough:

> Parties may obtain discovery regarding any matter, not privileged, which is relevant to the subject matter involved in the pending action, whether it relates to the claim or defense of the party seeking discovery or to the claim or defense of any other party, including the existence, description, nature, custody, condition and location of any books, documents or other tangible things and the identity and location of persons having knowledge of any discoverable matter. It is not ground for objection that the information sought will be inadmissible at the trial if the information sought appears reasonably calculated to lead to the discovery of admissible evidence.

Thus, either one of two prerequisites must be satisfied in order to engage in discovery. Either the discovery must be relevant to the subject matter involved in the litigation or it must appear reasonably calculated to lead to the discovery of admissible evidence. Discovery that meets one of the above two tests may not be challenged on the ground that the specific information sought by the party seeking discovery will not be admissible at trial.

For example, during discovery it may be possible to learn what transpired in a conversation between a witness and some third person even though during the trial testimony on this point would be objectionable as being hearsay.[3] Because this information is relevant and/or also may lead to admissible evidence (as by calling in the third party as a witness) it will be discoverable, although perhaps not admissible itself.

---

[1]FRCP 26(a).
[2]Physical and mental examinations may also be directed at persons under the control of parties.
[3]Hearsay is a rule of evidence. It has been defined as an out-of-court statement being offered in court for the truth of the matter asserted in the out-of-court statement. See Rule 801 of the Federal Rules of Evidence.

The fundamental test is whether the information sought is "relevant to the subject matter involved in the pending action." This is an extremely flexible standard. "Relevant" is a term that has been given a very broad definition. The definition of "relevant" in the Federal Rules of Evidence is illustrative:

> "Relevant evidence" means evidence having any tendency to make the existence of any fact that is of consequence to the determination of the action more probable or less probable than it would be without the evidence.

Prior to beginning discovery, it is essential to formulate a **discovery plan** appropriate to the unique circumstances of a given lawsuit. This process involves a thoughtful evaluation of the purposes of discovery, a knowledge of the available discovery devices, and consideration of the following factors:

- the nature of the information sought

- cost or expense to client of using a particular discovery device

- the person from whom information is sought

- the amount of time available for obtaining the information

- the local federal procedural rules concerning the amount of discovery, and the enforcement practices if judicial intervention is required

- an evaluation of your opponent

In other words, the paralegal under the guidance of the supervising attorney should identify the goals of the lawsuit and design and implement a discovery strategy that is consistent with those goals. Keep in mind that the discovery process is a unique procedure in the American legal system. In civil cases, it is designed to allow you a maximum opportunity to find out all about your opponent's case.

Before turning to a discussion on the actual discovery devices commonly available, further elaboration on the factors articulated in the preceding paragraph is necessary.

**1.** *Nature of information sought.* Generally, information sought may be characterized as either being documents, things or objects, and/or live testimony. Depending on what information you are seeking, certain discovery devices may either be required or be more advantageous than other devices. For instance, if the information sought is a document from a party, a request to produce the document would be appropriate. However, if the document sought is not from a party, a motion to produce would be unavailable and inappropriate. Instead a "records" deposition would be the only available method. A records deposition is a form of discovery whereby someone (a nonparty) is requested through the use of the court's subpoena power to produce certain documents, things, or information. More information on depositions is provided later in this chapter.

**2.** *Cost to client.* Some discovery devices are more expensive to use than others. For example, oral depositions are relatively expensive in that they include stenographic transcription costs, attorney's fees for attendance at deposition, and possible witness fees. This process is more expensive than preparing interrogatories and reviewing the answers. Therefore if your client is concerned about expending large sums of money during the litigation process (as most clients are), this factor must be taken into account when deciding which form of discovery should be used.

3. *Person from whom the information is sought.* As was mentioned previously, certain discovery devices may be directed only to parties while others may be directed to nonparties. For example, interrogatories may be directed only to parties. They cannot be sent to nonparties. However, written depositions may be directed to nonparties and may accomplish the same desired result as interrogatories. Written depositions are similar to interrogatories as they are both written questions submitted to someone for responses under oath. Also, oral depositions may be directed to nonparties.

4. *Time available.* Time available is an important factor in selecting or choosing a particular form of discovery. For example, information can usually be obtained from a person in a much speedier fashion in an oral deposition than through the use of a set of interrogatories. Interrogatories take time to answer and as a result, most procedural rules allow thirty days in which to respond. Since many court systems impose deadlines on the time in which to complete discovery, this factor may become critical in the determination of which form of discovery is the most appropriate.

5. *Local procedural rules.* Courts may impose limits on the amount of discovery a party may use. For example, it is not uncommon to have limits imposed on the amount of interrogatories that may be submitted by one party to another party.[4] Also some courts may look more favorably upon requests to conduct depositions by nonstenographic means (for example, audiotape or videotape) than others. In addition, courts may limit the timing of depositions.

Finally, the discovery enforcement practice of a court is an important factor to consider. For example, judicial intervention in the discovery process may be easier to obtain in one jurisdiction than another. In some jurisdictions it is possible to contact a judge by conference telephone call in the middle of an oral deposition to rule on a particular objection or on a particular problem that has arisen. In other jurisdictions, this procedure may be unavailable and a formal motion must be submitted to the court for a ruling that could take several weeks to be resolved.

6. *Evaluation of your opponent (opposing party's attorney).* This factor is really a summary of several subfactors: competency, cooperation, resources available, and an opponent's discovery plan. In assessing an opponent, always remember that an opponent is going to formulate his or her own discovery strategy. As a result, when developing a plan, the litigation team must attempt to account for the resources available to an opponent (for example, the opponent may force the litigation team to spend more money through the use of oral depositions). Also an opponent's attitude towards discovery (for example, being cooperative) may allow the paralegal to obtain information in an easier and less expensive fashion (interrogatories and document production) because

---

[4]Some judges in the U.S. District Court for the Eastern District of Pennsylvania limit the number of interrogatories to fifteen. The party who requires more interrogatories must seek the permission of the judge before he or she can submit additional interrogatories.

the paralegal might not have to worry about completeness of answers and enforcement.

An opponent's discovery schedule may either conflict or coincide with that of the paralegal or supervising lawyer. This is another factor that the litigation team should evaluate when choosing which discovery device to use.

Finally, an assessment of an opponent's competence is a critical factor not only during discovery, but throughout the entire litigation process. Although few generalizations can be made, competence generally impacts on the amount and completeness of the information one can expect to receive voluntarily.

In addition to an evaluation of the purposes of discovery and the factors described above, discovery planning should also include consideration of how to sequence discovery. Under FRCP 26(d) parties may use the provided discovery devices in any sequence they desire. As a result, there is no one way of sequencing discovery. However, it is quite common to begin the discovery process with interrogatories (to identify witnesses and documents) and re-quests for production of documents and then, depending on the information received, to engage in oral depositions and to submit requests for admissions. The advantage of this sequence is that by the time a party conducts an oral deposition of a key witness, he or she already has had an opportunity to review valuable information about the case. Also, in order to submit a meaningful request for admissions, a party should have already obtained information and accumulated documents to be verified and authenticated by the admissions.

Of course, this common sequence should be, and often is, modified to meet the particular needs of your case. For example, a witness (nonparty) in poor health or about to leave the court's jurisdiction may warrant the immediate taking of oral deposition. Likewise, it may be useful to depose a witness (nonparty) or a party early in the case before an opponent has time to establish his or her position.

In preparing the discovery plan, one final factor must be taken into account. As the discovery process begins and information is provided, the litigation team should re-evaluate the original discovery plan. As the litigation progresses through the discovery phase, there may be changes in the original facts and potential theories. Therefore, modifications in the discovery plan will occur, and the litigation team should be flexible enough to make the necessary changes when formulating a revised discovery strategy.

## II. Types of Discovery Devices

This part of the chapter will describe the various types of discovery devices available in the civil litigation process, using the federal procedural rules as the model. The federal rules concerning discovery have been adopted in whole or in part by many states. However, a paralegal should check the specific discovery rules governing a specific lawsuit since they may be different than the rules described in this chapter.

### A. Interrogatories

FRCP 33(a), which governs the use of interrogatories in the federal system, provides that "any party may serve upon any other party written interrogatories to be answered by the party served. . . ." Thus, only a plaintiff, defendant, or additional third parties may be required to answer interrogatories.

## 1. Procedure under the Federal Rules

The original copy of the interrogatories must be filed with the clerk of court and copies served upon all parties to the litigation. Even if the interrogatories are directed to only one of several defendants, service must be made on all parties to the lawsuit. Service of interrogatories may be effected either in person or by mail upon the party's counsel of record if there is one, or upon the party directly, if there is no attorney of record. When copies of interrogatories are sent to an opponent, a simple cover letter is normally used to accomplish service. For example:

[Letterhead]
Date

Name and Address

Re: Glockenspiel Industries v. Quizzlemitt

Dear Gentlemen:

Enclosed herewith is a copy of defendant's interrogatories to plaintiff, the original of which was filed with the court today.

Very truly yours,

(Name of Defendant's Attorney)

Generally, under the federal rules, interrogatories may be served (1) upon the plaintiff at any time after the complaint is filed and (2) upon the defendant at the time of service of the complaint and summons or thereafter.

The party served with interrogatories must answer or object to each question separately within thirty days (forty-five days if interrogatories are served with the complaint), unless a party requests and the court allows a shorter or longer time. All answers must be signed by the party answering. Objections to interrogatories must be signed by counsel for the party objecting.

Interrogatories addressed to an individual must be answered personally by the individual. Interrogatories directed to a corporation, partnership, or association must be answered by an officer or agent, who must furnish enough information to answer the questions based on information available to the corporation, partnership, or association, even if not within the personal knowledge of the person answering.

In lieu of a formal answer to an interrogatory, the party answering may make available business records for examination if (1) the answer may be derived from the business records produced and (2) it is no more difficult for the party who asked the interrogatory to get the information out of the business records than it would be for the party who is answering.

## 2. Use of Interrogatories

Interrogatories are particularly useful in preliminary discovery for the following purposes:

  ◆ Obtaining identity of key witnesses or persons with knowledge

  ◆ Identifying relevant documentary evidence, and the custodians of the records

  ◆ Obtaining precise dates or figures, which may not be remembered by a witness on oral examination

  ◆ Ascertaining facts relied upon by a party (for example, the sources relied upon to support an allegedly libelous statement)

  ◆ Determining the specific amount of damages the plaintiff claims has been sustained

  ◆ Obtaining information concerning letters, notes, or other written materials a party or witness has written, signed, and/or read

  ◆ Determining positions of the parties on various issues in the case

  ◆ Learning the identity of expert witnesses, the substance of the expert's opinions, and the grounds for those opinions

Certain advantages and disadvantages are associated with the use of interrogatories. The advantages are: (1) they are a relatively inexpensive discovery device (the time spent in preparation is the major expense); (2) they can be used at any time prior to trial beginning with the service of the complaint and summons; and (3) they are a relatively straightforward device to prepare. The disadvantages are: (1) they do not permit spontaneous responses (often leading to self-serving and less than satisfactory responses); and (2) they can be directed only to parties.

By proper use of interrogatories, parties may learn a great deal about their opponent's case. The plaintiff will primarily be looking for information to prove his or her case. The defendant will want to find flaws in the plaintiff's case and also facts that will limit damages in the event that the plaintiff wins at the trial.

Discovery by way of interrogatories is not intended as an exclusive device. Rather, the various discovery devices should be used together to gain the most information possible. It is easy to get carried away and use interrogatories for purposes for which they are clearly unsuited. For example, it serves little function to use an interrogatory to attempt to elicit the substance of the conversation during a meeting when such information is better obtained from documents relating or referring to the meeting and from oral depositions of the participants therein. Interrogatories should be used merely to learn that a meeting took place.

### 3. Role of the Paralegal

The paralegal, under the supervision of a lawyer, is often given the job of preparing and/or answering interrogatories. To prepare a set of interrogatories that will produce meaningful information the paralegal must analyze the case carefully. This requires deciding (1) what information is needed to get further discovery (such as names and addresses of witnesses, identification of documents), (2) what information is needed regarding the liability aspect of the case, (3) if representing a defendant, what information is needed on damages, and

(4) what background information is needed on the opponent that will allow an evaluation of the opponent's truthfulness and usefulness as a potential witness.

In order to determine what questions to ask in interrogatories the paralegal must know all the facts already gathered in the case and also the law applicable to the case. An analysis of the law will indicate what facts must be proven in order to win, to establish damages, to mitigate damages, or to increase damages. The supervising attorney should provide the analysis of the law to assist the paralegal in preparing the interrogatories.

Only after determining the information needed in the case should the paralegal turn to forms of interrogatories to aid in drafting the questions. There are numerous form books of interrogatories and the office may have indexed sets of interrogatories used in other cases.

After drafting the questions, the paralegal should review each one to see if it could be answered truthfully and still give little or no information. If this can be done, the paralegal will have to either redraft or expand the interrogatory. You shouldn't let the opponent off easily by posing interrogatories that can be answered properly without giving any assistance in the proof of the case. The interrogatories should force the adversary to provide the needed information.

### 4. Drafting Techniques

A set of interrogatories has two main components. The first is the introductory part, which contains a preface, instructions, and definitions. The second part contains the questions. Although the introductory part is not required, it is generally considered good practice (so as to avoid any claims of confusion by your opponent) to include a preface and to use at least some instructions and definitions.

A preface usually explains the basis for the interrogatories and the time limit in which a response is to be filed. For example:

> Defendant requests that the plaintiff answer the following interrogatories in writing pursuant to rule 33 of the Federal Rules of Civil Procedure and that the answers be served on the defendant within thirty (30) days after service of these interrogatories.

Instructions can be included in the introduction to inform the responding party how to respond in certain situations. For example, an instruction could provide for the production of a document in lieu of a written response to an interrogatory (with a reference to rule 33[c]).

It is standard practice to preface a set of interrogatories with definitions that clearly delineate for the answering party the scope of interrogatories. For example, since one of the functions of interrogatories is to determine the existence, location, and custodian of documents, it is important to define what is meant by the word "document." That word might be defined as follows in an opening paragraph of the interrogatories:

> any written, recorded, or graphic matter however produced or reproduced, including but not limited to correspondence, telegrams, other written communications, contracts, agreements, notes, memoranda, analyses, projections, studies, work papers, diaries, calendars, lists, catalogues, and minutes of meetings.

Since documents may no longer be in possession of the answering party, it is important to ascertain the present custodians of relevant documents. This can be accomplished by defining the words "identify" and "identity" as follows:

"Identify" or "identity" when used in reference to a document means to state the date and author, type of document (for example, letter, memorandum, chart) or some other means of identifying it, and its present location or custodian.

Another way of locating the document may be expressed the following way:

Any reference to documentary material refers to documents that any of the defendants may have delivered to a third party, including but not limited to government officials or agencies.

Further, since names of persons given in answer to an interrogatory may not be sufficient to locate that person, it is common in an introductory paragraph to ask the opponent the following:

"Identify" when used in reference to a person means to state the person's full name, home and business address, and position held with his or her employer.

Exhibit 7.1 is provided as an aid in helping to construct the actual interrogatories.

Exhibit 7.2 provides an example of a set of interrogatories. (A word of caution: this set of interrogatories is merely for demonstrative purposes. It is not intended to be a model of a comprehensive set of interrogatories.)

---

**EXHIBIT 7.1**

## Interrogatory Drafting Techniques

Drafting Techniques

A. Reduce a clause or lengthy phrase to one word or a concise phrase. Try to reduce all the species of something to the basic genus. Do not ask:

Please state the color, number of wheels, size of windows, and texture of the bumpers of Defendant's self-propelled vehicular motor machine.

Rather, ask:

Please describe in detail Defendant's car.

B. The previous suggestion may not produce the specifications or exact details you want, so another suggestion is to: include related words and subtopics in one question. Try to detail the several species of a common genus. Ask:

Please describe Plaintiff's hair including but not limited to the color, style, approximate length of sideburns, and color of the roots.

**EXHIBIT 7.1**

## Interrogatory Drafting Techniques (continued)

C. Avoid multiple questions seeking multiple answers. Do not ask:

State the names of the setter, swingperson, follower, chalker, and scorer of the Faculty Skittlepool Team.

Rather, ask singular questions which require multiple answers:

State the name of all members of the Faculty Skittlepool Team.

D. Employ questions that seek only one possible response from a list of alternative suggested answers. Ask:

State whether Plaintiff is a direct descendent of an Australopithecus robustus, a Dryopithecus africanus, or a homo habilis.

E. One effective drafting technique particularly suitable for interrogatories is the "ladder" or "branching" approach. A broad question is asked, usually answerable by one or two or more answers, and then followed by specific questions relating to one or more of the possible responses. For example:

State whether Defendant is a corporation or a partnership. If a corporation, identify the members of the Board of Directors. If a partnership, identify all the partners.

There are occasions when such drafting techniques may waste an interrogatory. A branching interrogatory may be phrased to receive a yes or no response followed by specific questions. But you may know, or be fairly certain, whether the response will be yes or no, and you will be able to save an interrogatory. For example, a pleading may reveal that a defendant is a corporation. Rather than drafting "State whether defendant is a corporation," and then drafting follow-up questions, merely ask the follow-up question:

State the date and state of defendant's incorporation and its principal place of business.

Poorly drafted interrogatories inevitably produce poor responses on the principle that if you ask a foolish question you should expect, and will receive, a foolish answer. You can avoid this phenomenon by playing the devil's advocate role after drafting your interrogatories and:

1. Consider whether any question can be redrafted in a simpler, less complex fashion.

2. Ask yourself how the answer to that interrogatory will provide you with information helpful to the case.

3. Decide whether some questions can be eliminated or consolidated.

4. Consider ways the responses to your questions could be fudged and then attempt to redraft the question to eliminate the fudge.

Source: Reprinted with permission from Roger S. Haydock, Clinical Director, William Mitchell College of Law. Adapted from R. Haydock and D. Herr, *Discovery Practice*, 1982, pp. 286, 292–295.

**EXHIBIT 7.2**

# Interrogatories

IN THE UNITED STATES DISTRICT COURT
FOR THE EASTERN DISTRICT OF PENNSYLVANIA

JOHN A. SMITH                :

    Plaintiff            :

                      :

    v.                   :      CIVIL ACTION NO. 82–100

                      :

LEE G. JONES             :

    Defendant         :

## DEFENDANT'S INTERROGATORIES TO PLAINTIFF

Defendant requests that the plaintiff, John A. Smith, answer the following interrogatories under oath and in writing pursuant to rule 33 of the Federal Rules of Civil Procedure and that the answers be served upon the defendant within thirty (30) days after service of these interrogatories.

## DEFINITIONS

The terms set forth below are defined as follows:

A. "Document"—any written, recorded, or graphic matter however produced or reproduced, including but not limited to correspondence, telegrams, other written communications, contracts, agreements, notes, memoranda, analyses, projections, studies, work papers, diaries, calendars, lists, catalogues, and minutes of meetings.

B. "Identify" or "Identity"—when used in reference to an individual person means to state his or her full name, home address, telephone number, and the name of such person's present employer, place of employment, and job title, if any. When used in reference to a document means to state the date and author, type of document (for example, letter, memorandum, chart) or some other means of identifying it, and its present location or custodian.

## INSTRUCTIONS

C. Each interrogatory shall be answered separately and as completely as possible. The fact that investigation is continuing or that discovery is not complete is not an excuse for failure to answer each interrogatory as fully as possible. If you are unable to answer an interrogatory after you have attempted to obtain the information, answer to the extent possible.

D. A question that seeks information contained in or information about or identification of any documents may be answered by providing a copy of such document for inspection and copying or by furnishing a copy of such document without a request for production.

**EXHIBIT 7.2**

# Interrogatories (continued)

## INTERROGATORIES

1. Please state the following for the plaintiff:
   a) your age
   b) your occupation and place of employment
   c) your education
   d) your marital status
   e) your length of service in your present employment position
   f) your previous occupational experience

2. Since the date of the accident set forth in the complaint, has plaintiff engaged in one or more gainful occupations? If so, state:
   a) The names and addresses of his employers and the dates between which he worked for each such employer; and
   b) The nature of the work in each such occupation and the wage or salary received by him in each such occupation.

3. a) State the total amounts earned by plaintiff in each full year for the preceding five years and the total amounts earned by plaintiff in the present calendar year up until the date of the answer to this interrogatory.
   b) State the sources (by names and addresses) and amounts of all income received by plaintiff from gainful employment during these periods from each employer.

4. Has plaintiff been absent from work at any time or times since the date of the accident set forth in the complaint? If so, state:
   a) The dates of all absences from work and the reasons therefor; and
   b) Plaintiff's rates of pay on the dates of such absences, whether plaintiff received pay for the dates of absences, and, if so, for what reason.

5. State whether plaintiff has been unable to perform satisfactorily any of the duties required of him in any of his employments since the date of the accident set forth in the complaint, indicating with particularity what duties he was unable to perform and the names and addresses of all persons having knowledge of such facts, including plaintiff's supervisors and employer at the time of such incapacities.

6. Have you or has anyone acting in your behalf obtained from any person or persons any report, statement, memorandum, or testimony concerning the accident involved in this cause of action?

7. If so, what is the name and last known address and present whereabouts, if known, of each such person?

8. If so, when, where, and by whom was each such report, statement, memorandum, or testimony obtained or made?

9. If so, where is each located?

EXHIBIT 7.2

# Interrogatories (continued)

10. What is the name and last known address and present whereabouts, if known, of each person whom you or anyone acting in your behalf knows or believes to have witnessed said accident?

11. What is the name, last known address, and present whereabouts, if known, of each person whom you or anyone acting in your behalf know or believe to have any relevant knowledge of the conditions at the scene of the accident existing prior to, at, or immediately after the same?

12. Exactly where did this accident occur, stated in feet from specific landmarks?

13. Have you or any representative of yours at any time received any medical reports or X-ray reports from any hospitals or physicians reporting on the injuries sustained in the accident upon which this action is based? If so, state when, where, and from whom you or any representative of yours received any such reports; indicating the nature thereof (medical report, hospital report, and so on), and state the name and address of the person in possession or custody thereof.
State the names of the plaintiff's doctors, if any, who attended plaintiff, the dates and places of such treatment, and the nature of the treatment.

14. State whether any photographs were taken of the site of the alleged occurrence. If yes, state:
    a) The subject matter of said photographs;
    b) The date and time of day said photographs were taken;
    c) The name, address, and job classification of the person taking same, and the name and address of his employer if not in your employ; and
    d) The name, address, and job classification of the person having custody of the photographs.

15. State whether the plaintiff was interviewed in connection with the alleged accident and/or injury and, if yes, state:
    a) The place or places where said interviews occurred;
    b) The names, residential addresses, and job classifications of persons interviewing him and the name and address of their respective employers, if not in your employ;
    c) The dates and the time of day thereof;
    d) Whether any recording or memorandum were made and, in the event of the latter, the date or dates thereof;
    e) Whether a signed statement was obtained; and
    f) The name, address and job classification of the person having custody of the recording or memoranda.

16. State whether the defendant was interviewed in connection with the alleged accident and/or injury and, if yes, state:
    a) The place or places where said interviews occurred;
    b) The names, residential addresses, and job classifications of persons interviewing him and the name and address of their respective employers, if not in your employ;

EXHIBIT 7.2

# Interrogatories (continued)

   c) The dates and the time of day thereof;

   d) Whether any recording or memorandum were made and, in the event of the latter, the date or dates thereof;

   e) Whether a signed statement was obtained; and

   f) The name, address and job classification of the person having custody of the recording or memoranda.

17. Did plaintiff ever suffer any injuries, sickness, disease, or abnormality of any kind prior to the accident alleged in this action involving any part or function of the body claimed in this suit to have been injured?

18. If so, when? What was the said injury, sickness, disease, or abnormality?

19. Was plaintiff ever examined or treated for any injuries, sickness, disease, or abnormality prior to the accident alleged in this action involving any part or function of the body claimed in this suit to have been injured?

20. If so, when, where, and by whom?

21. What specific expenses were incurred by plaintiff as a result of this accident?

22. Exactly what total wage loss did you sustain as a result of this accident?

23. Exactly how do you compute the sum?

24. Have you been known by any name other than that in which this action is brought at any time since the date of the accident involved in this action?

Respectfully Submitted:
CAHILL, RUBEN, & DALY

Dated:        By:_____
WILLIAM CAHILL
Attorney for Defendant
Address
_____   Telephone Number

---

## CERTIFICATION OF SERVICE

I hereby certify that I served the foregoing interrogatories on the plaintiff by mailing a copy to his attorney by first class mail on the date below.

Date:_____

William Cahill
Attorney for Defendant

### 5. Answering Interrogatories

Only when absolutely necessary should interrogatories be answered without the client coming into the office and reviewing the questions with the attorney or paralegal. The alternative would be to prepare a proposed answer and mail it to the client with a copy of the interrogatories for the client to review. However, by being with the client you may identify corrections in the facts you have gathered, new facts, or additional information the client has gathered but forgotten to tell the attorney.

It is essential to be thoroughly familiar with the case when the client comes in to answer interrogatories. Clients sometimes forget the essential facts, and a review of the paralegal's notes of earlier statements serves to refresh their memories.

In preparing answers to interrogatories, which is generally a much easier job than formulating them, questions should be answered as concisely as possible. You are required only to answer the question that has been asked, not the question that should have been asked. In answering questions it is permissible to refer to documents that should be attached (in photocopy form) to the answers.

If a question is objectionable and you are not going to answer it, you may simply state "objected to" and give the reason for the objection. It will then fall upon the party propounding the interrogatories to compel that they be answered. (See section on Objections to Interrogatories, Production of Documents, and Admissions, later in chapter, for more information on objections.)

It is not necessary to repeat the particular interrogatory before giving the answer to it, although this is sometimes done in cases with extensive interrogatories to facilitate their review. Some states require that the propounder of the interrogatories leave enough space to fill in the answer or that the answering party restate the question before the answer.

## B. Requests for Production of Documents, Things, and Inspections

Requests for production, which are governed by FRCP 34, is the common generic name for written requests seeking formal permission to

- ◆ copy relevant documents

- ◆ test tangible things, such as machines

- ◆ enter onto land to inspect, survey, photograph, or the like

The purpose of this procedure is to make documents and objects in the possession of one party available to another. Like interrogatories, requests for production may be directed only to parties.

### 1. Procedure under the Federal Rules

FRCP 34 establishes the same filing and service requirements for requests for production as are required for interrogatories. The thirty (or forty-five) day period provided for answers or objections to interrogatories also applies to requests for production. Requests for production must (1) set forth the items to be inspected or tested specifically, or by category, and describe them "with reasonable particularity," and (2) specify a "reasonable time, place, and manner" of making inspection, performing testing, or entering the land. The party upon whom a request is served must state that inspection or testing will be permitted, or must state the basis for any objections to the requests.

## 2. Scope of Requests for Production under the Federal Rules

Requests for production are limited to documents, things, and land "which are in the possession, custody or control of the party upon whom the request is served." Thus, documents that are not within a party's control need not be produced or identified in response to a request under FRCP 34. Therefore, before making requests for production, documents should be discovered through the use of interrogatories.

Anything that contains written, printed, or recorded information is discoverable. This also includes computerized information. In addition, tangible objects and land can be inspected, tested, measured, and photographed.

## 3. Preparation of Requests for Production

Requests for production can be divided into three separate sections: (a) definitions and time periods covered, (b) a designation of individual items or categories of documents to be inspected or tested, and (c) specification of a time, place, and manner for making the inspection.

*a. Definitions and Time Periods.* Definitions and time periods pinpoint what documents are being sought, and for what period. Time periods and definitions may be mechanically included in separate sections of the beginning of the request, as in the case of definitions for interrogatories, or by defining each term parenthetically or in a footnote as it appears in the request, and by specifying the time periods, where they differ, for each category sought.

In order to prepare those sections devoted to time periods and definitions, it is necessary for a paralegal to be familiar with the manner in which records are kept in the industry in question (for example, the use of computers for storage of important information), and what important documents are likely to exist. This information may be gained by reading trade journals or through discussions with the client. The definitions of "documents" should always include electronic data compilations and, where possible, include a precise definition fitted to industry practices. FRCP 34(a) clearly extends to such data and permits the moving party to require the respondent to "translate" such data into usable form through use of his or her electronic devices. In most instances, this will oblige the respondent to supply a computer printout.

Because of the greater need for precision in this area, please note that the definition of document is more detailed than in the example used in the discussion of interrogatories. An example of a definition of "documents" is provided below:

"Documents" means, without limitation, the following items, whether printed, recorded, reproduced, or written by hand: all writings of any kind, including the originals and all nonidentical copies, whether different from the originals by reason of any notation made on such copies or otherwise, including without limitation, correspondence, memoranda, notes, diaries, statistics, letters, telegrams, minutes, contracts, reports, studies, checks, statements, receipts, returns, summaries, pamphlets, books, interoffice and intra-office communications, notations of any sort of conversations, telephone calls, meetings, or other communications, bulletins, printed matter, computer printouts, teletypes, telefax, invoices, worksheets, all drafts, alterations, modifications, repealings, changes, and amendments of any of the foregoing, graphic or oral records or representations of any kind (including, without limitation, photographs, charts, graphs, microfiche, microfilm, videotapes, recordings, motion pictures), and any electronic, mechanical, or electric records or representations of any kind (including, without limitation, tapes, cassettes, discs, recordings, and computer memories).

*b. Designation of Items or Categories of Documents.*  The core of any request for production is included in the designation section, which specifies either individual items or categories of documents to be produced. Rule 34(b) requires such designation to be done "with reasonable particularity," and the vast bulk of all objections to requests are that the categories called for are "vague," "overbroad," "imprecise," or would require a "burdensome" effort to produce, since they cover "thousands of pages" or "hundreds of file drawers." Therefore, the key to a successful request is as great an amount of precision as is possible under the circumstances. In some cases, designation of specific individual items or precise categories will be possible and should be adopted. The use of interrogatories first can often be quite helpful in obtaining the necessary precision required to identify the individual items or precise categories.

*c. Time, Place, and Manner of Inspection.*  A date thirty days after service of the request for production at the offices of opposing counsel is usually specified. Sometimes, however, copies of the requested documents are instead delivered to the requesting counsel's office, when only a small number of documents exists. Otherwise, the original documents are usually inspected.

### 4. Uses of Requests for Production of Documents

A witness may intentionally or inadvertently omit information. However, if a document contains the information, it will be more reliable than an unfriendly witness. Therefore, all relevant documentary evidence should be secured before proceeding to oral depositions, as documents may provide a basis for challenging inconsistent positions taken by a deponent. In addition, securing an opponent's records will help identify key witnesses and indicate which elements of liability are fairly clear and which must be pursued further through other discovery devices.

*a. Requests for Production by Plaintiffs.*  To employ requests for production of documents to the best advantage of a plaintiff, it is helpful, after establishing the elements of liability in the particular case (and gaining background knowledge of industry practices, where appropriate), to compile an analytical list of categories of documents corresponding to each element of liability. Each such category should be included in the requests for production. The documents produced can again be reviewed against the various elements of liability to see which elements are fairly clear, which must be pursued further in discovery, and who should be deposed.

**b. Requests for Production by Defendants.**   Defendants will usually focus on the questions of whether the plaintiff was injured or sustained a loss and, if so, to what extent the existence of affirmative defenses may be available. Some of the types of documentation that should be sought by defendants are as follows:

- all documents that are in plaintiff's possession, custody, or control that form the basis for a particular allegation of the complaint (for example, an alleged conspiracy);

- all written communications from individuals advising the plaintiff as to the amount of plaintiff's damages;

- all proofs of purchase (invoices, for example) and books of record indicating dates of transactions and terms of sale including price;

- all internal memoranda, notes, or other documentation indicating company policy on purchases of articles in question, and resale of such items;

- all documentation supporting plaintiff's claimed damage figure, and sources relied upon to compute such figure;

- in a contract case, memoranda of meetings, drafts of agreement, internal memoranda discussing the negotiations, and correspondence to third parties discussing the alleged contract and its status.

### 5. Uses of Testing and Entry onto Land Provisions of FRCP 34

While less frequently used, the testing and entry onto land provisions of FRCP 34 are occasionally helpful. For example, in a personal injury case, testing the machines that injured the plaintiff may indicate the cause of a malfunction. Where the quality of goods is at issue, as in a breach of warranty case, testing the machines on which the item is produced may indicate that products of a higher quality are obtainable.

The entry provisions of FRCP 34 authorize photographs and sampling. They may be used in personal injury cases as well as in property cases. For example, the plaintiff may investigate the scene of an accident (a machine shop, for example) and take photographs.

An example of a request for production of documents is provided in Exhibit 7.3.

## C. Requests for Admissions

Requests for admissions, which are governed by FRCP 36, are written requests asking a party to a lawsuit to confirm that specified matters are true, or that designated documents are accurate and genuine copies. Facts admitted are deemed conclusively established for purposes of the lawsuit. The objective of this discovery device is to define and limit the matters in controversy between the parties.

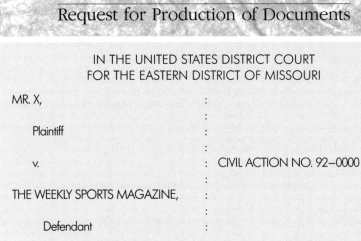

**EXHIBIT 7.3**

## Request for Production of Documents

IN THE UNITED STATES DISTRICT COURT
FOR THE EASTERN DISTRICT OF MISSOURI

| | | |
|---|---|---|
| MR. X, | : | |
| | : | |
| Plaintiff | : | |
| | : | |
| | : | |
| v. | : | CIVIL ACTION NO. 92–0000 |
| | : | |
| THE WEEKLY SPORTS MAGAZINE, | : | |
| | : | |
| Defendant | : | |

DEFENDANT'S REQUEST FOR PRODUCTION OF DOCUMENTS

Defendant hereby requests plaintiff, pursuant to rule 34 of the Federal Rules of Civil Procedure, to respond within thirty (30) days to the following requests:

### DEFINITIONS

A.  "Document" means, without limitation, the following items, whether printed, recorded, reproduced, or written by hand: all writings of any kind, including the originals and all nonidentical copies, whether different from the originals by reason of any notation made on such copies or otherwise, including, without limitation, correspondence, memoranda, notes, diaries, statistics, letters, telegrams, minutes, contracts, reports, studies, checks, statements, receipts, returns, summaries, pamphlets, books, interoffice and intra-office communications, notations of any sort of conversations, telephone calls, meetings, or other communications, bulletins, printed matter, computer printouts, teletypes, telefax, invoices, worksheets, all drafts, alterations, modifications, changes, and amendments of any of the foregoing, graphic or oral records or representations of any kind (including, without limitation, photographs, charts, graphs, microfiche, microfilm, videotapes, recordings, motion pictures), and any electronic, mechanical, or electric records or representations of any kind (including, without limitation, tapes, cassettes, discs, recordings, and computer memories).

B.  "Reports" shall include every written communication from a physician, medical practitioner, or any other person engaged in diagnosing and treating illness or injury, or from the agent of any such person, containing information respecting the medical history, condition, diagnosis and/or prognosis of the person examined.

**EXHIBIT 7.3**

# Request for Production of Documents (continued)

C. "Medical Examination," as used herein, shall include any interview, observation, physical or mental examination, and any other scientific or medical technique or practice designed to obtain information respecting the medical history, condition, diagnosis, and/or prognosis of the person examined.

## INSTRUCTIONS

A. Defendant's request includes all documents in the possession, custody, or control of the plaintiff. If your response to any request herein is that the documents are not in your possession, custody, or control, explain in detail the unsuccessful efforts made to locate the documents.

B. If your response to any request herein is that the documents are not in your possession, custody, or control, identify who has possession, custody, or control of the documents and where they are located.

C. State the date each document was written and a descriptive title of each produced document.

## REQUEST FOR PRODUCTION OF DOCUMENTS

A. That plaintiff produce and permit defendant to inspect and to copy each of the following documents:
   1) All of plaintiff's federal income tax returns for the years 1987 through 1991;
   2) All scrapbooks of plaintiff's sports activities, in plaintiff's possession or under his control, made or kept at any time by plaintiff, by any member of his family, by any fan club of plaintiff, or by any other person, including the scrapbook made by plaintiff for his son in 1991;
   3) All documentation of any type relating or referring to any damages alleged to have been suffered by plaintiff as a result of the publication complained of in this action, including, without limitation, all correspondence from and to any psychiatrist or doctor of medicine relating to plaintiff and all reports of medical examinations of plaintiff;
   4) All programs, pamphlets, or yearbooks issued by (x, y, or z) or by any other professional basketball team in which plaintiff's picture appears;
   5) All papers relating to the bankruptcy petition filed by plaintiff in Chicago, Illinois, in 1990, and
   6) All letters or other documents in plaintiff's possession or under his control received, sent, made, or read by plaintiff, or by any member of his family, referring or relating to the story and picture of plaintiff printed in the April 1992 issue of *The Weekly Sports Magazine*.

These requests shall continue in force for all documents described above until after the completion of the trial in this case.

## Request for Production of Documents (continued)

Defendant will inspect and make copies of such documents at the offices of (Defense Counsel name and address), on Monday, September 21, 1992, or at any other place or date, at the mutual convenience of counsel for plaintiff and defendant.

_____
Name and Address of Attorney for Defendant

Dated: August 20, 1992.

_____
### CERTIFICATION OF SERVICE

I hereby certify that I served the foregoing request for production of documents on plaintiff by mailing a copy to his attorney by first class mail on the date below.

Date: _____         _____
                                                                Attorney

### 1. Procedure under the Federal Rules.

Requests for admission must either (1) set forth statements or opinions and request that their truth be admitted or (2) attach copies of documents and request that their genuineness be conceded. Each matter or document must be set forth separately. The party served must file a written answer or objection within thirty days (or within such longer time as the court may allow). The answer must either admit the parts that are true and deny other matters specifically or set forth in detail reasons why the answering party is not able to truthfully admit or deny the matter. If no answer or objection is filed, the matter is deemed to have been admitted.

### 2. Uses of Requests for Admissions

Requests for admissions are most often used to eliminate or narrow issues of fact or law that are essential to one's case, but are not seriously in dispute, as, for example, the authority of certain corporate officers to execute an agreement on behalf of the corporation. In addition, requests for admissions provide a convenient way of establishing for use at trial the genuineness and authenticity of documents turned up during discovery, and the truth of formal matters not justifying an oral deposition. (Genuineness of documents means that a document actually is what it purports to be or is what the proponent claims it is.)

There are three general types of requests for admission:

◆ requests to admit the truth of certain facts

◆ requests to admit the truth of certain opinions of fact, or of the application of law to fact

◆ requests to admit the genuineness of certain documents

Mechanically, each fact, opinion, or admission must be set forth separately. To avoid objections, list each fact or opinion in a clear, precise, and short statement. To obtain an admission that a given document is genuine, the document should be described by (1) type (letter, for example), (2) title, if any, (3) number of pages, (4) date, (5) sender, and (6) addressee, and a copy of the document should be attached to the request. It is usually advisable when requesting an admission that a given document is genuine to also request an admission that such document was sent or received on or about the date thereon and, if prepared by the party served, that he or she was authorized to prepare it and that it was prepared in the regular course of his or her duties.

Examples of the three types of requests for admission follow:

*Facts*
That each of the following statements is true:
Defendant, XYZ Corporation, has, since 1958, been a member of the Inter-Industry Trade Association.

*Opinions*
That each of the following statements is true:
Each of the individuals who prepared the documents attached hereto was authorized to prepare such document, and prepared it in the regular course of his or her duties.

*Documents*
That each of the following documents, exhibited with this request, is genuine:
A two-page memorandum entitled "Policies for Complying with Federal Anti-trust Laws," dated May 1, 1991, sent by Samuel Smith, President of Defendant, to Messrs. Jones, Clark, Evans, Brown and Williams, all vice-presidents of the defendant.

Requests for admission may be used at two different stages of the litigation for different purposes. In the preliminary stages, admission should be sought of those facts or opinions not expected to be seriously in issue. In addition, admissions of the genuineness of certain documents produced in response to a request for production may be sought by a request for admission in the early stages of the litigation.

In the later stages of the litigation, requests for admission serve the purpose of preparing the case for trial and narrowing the issues in controversy. At this point, it is advisable for a paralegal first to check the documents produced against the oral depositions to see which documents that may be used at trial have not yet been authenticated. Requests for admissions are also valuable tools in resolving evidentiary issues regarding documents before trial (for example, documents are authentic, copies are admissible, and documents are either non-hearsay or fall within an exception to the hearsay rule). Also, at this stage in the case, requests should be sought of so-called opinion matters. Typically, these are mixed law and fact issues, which proper requests may eliminate as legal issues in dispute at the trial of the case. For example, in a case in which control of the premises on which an accident occurred is an issue, a request to admit that one of the defendants was then occupying the premises might be used. In a contract case, a request to admit that a purchase took place at a certain date and that the defendant delivered certain goods could be filed.

Provided in Exhibit 7.4 is Form 25, Appendix of Forms of the Federal Rules of Civil Procedure, which covers requests for admissions.

### 3. Responding to Requests for Admissions

Generally, a responding party has several options available depending on the nature of the particular request:

♦ admit

♦ deny

♦ qualify the answer

♦ object or move for a protective order

♦ not respond to request

If a party chooses not to respond, the proposed admission is usually deemed admitted. A party admits the request by responding in the affirmative. A party can deny a request only when in good faith the request cannot honestly be admitted. A party can attempt to qualify a response by providing a reason(s) why either

---

EXHIBIT 7.4

## Form 25, Request for Admission under Rule 36

Plaintiff A. B. requests defendant C. D. within _____ days after service of this request to make the following admissions for the purpose of this action only and subject to all pertinent objections to admissibility which may be interposed at the trial:

1. That each of the following documents, exhibited with this request, is genuine.

(Here list the documents and describe each document.)

2. That each of the following statements is true.

(Here list the statements.)

Signed: _____

Attorney for Plaintiff

Address:_____

As amended Dec. 27, 1946, eff. March 19, 1948.

admission or denial cannot be stated. Last, a party can object to a particular request and/or move for a protective order (see the Resisting Discovery section later in this chapter).

A response is usually prepared like an answer to interrogatories. However, it may be helpful to also include the original requests with the responses for purposes of clarity. The response must be signed by the attorney or the party and be served on all the parties to the lawsuit.

An example of how to draft a response to a request for admissions is provided in Exhibit 7.5.

## D. Depositions

Depositions are the only discovery device available to obtain information from nonparties. They are intended to elicit information regarding a person's knowledge of the contested factual issues. Depositions upon oral examination also provide a means before trial of observing the appearance and demeanor of a witness and watching his or her responses to adversary cross-examination. Depositions are conducted under oath, cross-examination is permitted, and the record is transcribed by an official court reporter. They are usually conducted in the office of the counsel for the party taking the deposition, although they are sometimes taken in a room in the courthouse, or in a party's office, where a view of the premises might be helpful (for example, in a personal injury case where unsafe conditions are alleged to have caused an accident). Neither judge nor jury is present at a deposition; only the parties, the witnesses, and their attorneys normally attend.

---

**EXHIBIT 7.5**

## Response to a Request for Admissions

[Caption]

DEFENDANT'S RESPONSE TO PLAINTIFF'S REQUEST FOR ADMISSIONS

1. Defendant denies the genuineness of the document described in paragraph 1 of the Plaintiff's Requests for Admissions.

2. Defendant cannot admit or deny the truth of the statement in paragraph 2 of the Plaintiff's Requests for Admissions because after reasonable inquiry, the information known to him is insufficient to enable him to admit or deny.

3. Admitted.

Dated: _____    _____

                          Attorney's name and address

## 1. Procedure under the Federal Rules

Under the federal rules, depositions may be conducted either upon oral examination (FRCP 30) or upon written questions (FRCP 31).

***a. Depositions upon Oral Examination.***   This most common type of deposition is a simulation of what will go on at trial except there is no judge or jury. A court reporter will be present to transcribe the deposition. (More information will be provided later in this chapter on the different stenographic formats used in depositions.) Examination follows the rules for direct and cross-examination at trial, and counsel for the deponent may object to questions and direct the witness not to answer. There are very few rules governing what actually occurs during an oral deposition. In actuality, this form of deposition depends on the interaction (cooperative or hostile) and attitudes of the attorneys involved.

***b. Depositions upon Written Questions.***   This device provided by FRCP 31 is seldom used. It combines the quality of interrogatories with those of oral depositions, and may be used against a nonparty to establish basic facts such as dates or places of meetings that could be established by interrogatories if a party had the relevant information. The examination is conducted by the court reporter, who reads the questions, and records the deponent's oral answers verbatim. The major difference between oral and written depositions is that in written depositions the questions are written in advance of the actual deposition (the questions are submitted in advance). This results in a loss of spontaneity in obtaining and following up witness responses. The major difference between written depositions and interrogatories is that interrogatories can be directed only to a party; written depositions can be directed to nonparties.

## 2. Uses of Depositions

Depositions are the most versatile discovery device because they permit the lawyers for a party to

- observe the demeanor of a party or important witness under cross-examination;

- test the recollection of a party or important witness in response to unexpected questions;

- commit a party or important witness to a specific version of the facts and prevent surprises during trial;

- identify witnesses known to the deponent;

- authenticate documents produced in response to a request for production and establish them as business records or party admissions;

- question a nonparty employee of a corporate party or require such witness to produce documents (neither of which can be done by any other discovery device, since all other discovery devices are limited to parties);

- accomplish the same objectives as are achievable through the use of interrogatories;

- preserve testimony if the witness is unavailable at the time of trial due to death, illness, or location beyond the jurisdiction of the court.

### 3. Use of Information Acquired through Discovery and Other Forms of Fact Investigation in Preparation for Oral Depositions

Before any oral depositions, the attorney and paralegal should review all answers to previous interrogatories, documents produced (pursuant to a request for production), and any other information obtained that is germane to the lawsuit. This review is for the following purposes:

- identifying persons whose oral depositions should be taken;

- identifying general areas of questioning to be pursued at oral depositions;

- preparing specific questions for individual deponents;

- defending the deposition.

*a. Identifying Persons Whose Oral Depositions Must Be Taken.* To determine who should be deposed, the litigation team should review answers to interrogatories to ascertain the identity of the individuals conceded to be key witnesses by the opposing party. The term "key witnesses" is used here to describe witnesses with knowledge of important transactions or who have possession of relevant documents.

In most cases, the attorney and paralegal should take the depositions of nonparties with relevant documents prior to the oral depositions of parties to make sure that all relevant documentation has been reviewed prior to the scheduling of the major oral deposition.

After reviewing any answers to interrogatories, the litigation team should review all documents produced to ascertain independently who the key individuals are and to catch any inadvertent or deliberate omissions of individuals with relevant information. Typically, interoffice memoranda will indicate who has been assigned responsibility for a given transaction, and with whom such individual has corresponded, both within and outside the organization, with respect to such transaction. Finally, they should check all admissions to ascertain whether individuals with some relevant information possess knowledge in more than just one area. New information may be obtained during the course of the deposition that may indicate the identity of other witnesses who have knowledge of the facts in the lawsuit. These new witnesses should also then be deposed.

*b. Identifying General Areas of Questioning to Be Pursued at Oral Depositions.* After the persons to be deposed have been identified, the attorney and paralegal should prepare an analysis of the general areas of questioning to be pursued at the oral depositions on the basis of information obtained from documents, admissions, and answers to interrogatories. They should correlate all answers to interrogatories and requests for admissions with the various elements of liability and/or damage in order to identify those aspects of liability or damage that are either conceded or that cannot be seriously disputed in light of the answers to interrogatories. This process will eliminate unnecessary areas of questioning.

Next, they must review the documents that have been produced and prepare lists of significant documents both by subject matter, by elements of liability, and by author or addressee. By so correlating evidence already discovered, the litigation team can distinguish elements of liability clearly established by admissions or by statements in the documents from those elements that they must vigorously pursue in oral depositions. The author–addressee list will also indicate which individuals have knowledge of both the elements of liability and the documents. The team should prepare the subject matter list by arranging the documents under headings corresponding to elements of liability or damage with descriptions of type (letter), title, author, addressee, date, and a short summary of each document's contents. After preparing these lists, they should write a short memorandum summarizing the information obtained on each of the relevant elements needed to establish (or disprove) liability and damages. (More information on preparing these lists, digests, and summaries is provided in the next chapter.)

Finally, in preparation for an oral deposition, the litigation team must review all documents to be referred to during the deposition for any reference to documents not produced through the discovery process thus far. Any unproduced documents should be requested before the examination if possible.

### c. Preparing Specific Questions for Individual Deponents.
After reviewing the summary, list, and key documents, the attorney and paralegal can prepare first drafts of questions for particular deponents (or at least a detailed checklist of those specific areas to be pursued with a given deponent) and lists of documents that must be authenticated or questioned. Questions may be divided into two general groupings: personal background information regarding the deponent, and information regarding "transactional" events (the relevant facts in controversy).

The background questions asked at the beginning of the deposition cover the present position and responsibilities of the deponent and his or her business and educational background. The purpose of these questions is to discover whether the deponent is an expert on the matters in question, and to what extent he or she should be personally familiar with the facts. Such questions should elicit the entire professional history of the deponent both within the adverse party's organization and outside it, test the general knowledge of the organization, and reveal any possible conflicts of interest in other positions currently held outside the organization. The identities of key subordinates or aides and the identity of the person to whom the deponent reports should be probed.

The transactional questions focus upon the facts in dispute in the litigation. As a general rule, clarity of examination dictates a chronological approach, although many lawyers prefer to ask selected important questions out of order to catch the witness off guard, and perhaps secure a helpful statement.

If relevant documents have been produced prior to the deposition, examination may proceed in either of two ways. If the document supports the examining party's position, it is best to show it to the deponent, ask if the deponent prepared (or received) it on or about the date appearing thereon and whether it represents an accurate account of the facts discussed, and mark it as an exhibit after it is authenticated.

If, on the other hand, the document is unclear or harmful to the examining attorney's case, it is best to examine the deponent without reference to it, to test independent recollection, and perhaps secure a better version of the facts than the document reflects. Although the deponent's attorney may want to refer to such a document and get the deponent to admit its correctness, direct testimony by the deponent may help to impeach the document.

If no documents on a particular point have been introduced, questioning should proceed by asking the witness questions about key events. For example, if there was a meeting to discuss the point, the deponent should be asked when it was held, who attended, whether a certain subject was discussed, whether he or she recalls any record being made, and whether it was the practice within the organization to keep records of such meetings.

***d. "Defending" the Deposition (Preparing the Deponent).*** When a client or "friendly" nonparty is deposed, it is crucial that the answers given by such deponent be consistent with the client's legal and factual positions in the lawsuit and not be otherwise harmful. In order to help prepare a person for a deposition, the litigation team will use the same process of preparing lists and summaries of documents and authors and relating the documents to different elements in the case as described in the preceding pages. The key to a successful deposition of the client or a friendly witness (often referred to as a successful "defense of the deposition") is familiarity with the documents relating to the witness who is to be deposed and the areas in which the witness has information. The lawyer or paralegal should meet with the deponent before the deposition to review documents and to review anticipated questions. The deponent must review all relevant documents that have been supplied to the opponent to refresh his or her recollection. Where multiple depositions of clients or friendly witnesses are being taken, separate interviews for each deponent are advisable to make sure a thorough job is done with each one.

### 4. Arranging the Deposition

If, as a paralegal, you are charged with setting up depositions you must do the following.

***a. Reserve a Time and Place.*** Set up a convenient date and time after consultation with the lawyer and client, if the client wishes to attend or is the deponent. If the deposition is to take place in the lawyer's office, as in most cases, reserve a conference room. If the deposition will take place out of town, it is helpful to have a cooperating attorney in the other city at whose office the deposition may take place. Alternatively, courtrooms may often be reserved in the federal courts by arrangements well in advance with the clerk of court. As a matter of courtesy, you should contact other attorneys and/or their paralegals in the case to try to arrange a time and place for the deposition that is convenient for everyone. Once tentative arrangements have been made and agreed upon, you should prepare and send out the deposition notice.

*b. Arrange for a Court Reporter (Stenographer) or Other Means of Recording the Deposition.*   Most federal courts maintain a list of official court reporters, usually with offices in the federal courthouse, or other approved reporters. One of these reporters must attend to record the witnesses' testimony if a stenographic record is required. Arrange for a reporter to transcribe the deposition as soon as the date has been selected.

In addition to the traditional use of a stenographer to record the testimony, the federal rules also allow for testimony at a deposition to be recorded by other than stenographic means. This may be done either by written agreement of the parties or by court order and allows for a tape recording to be made of the deposition. The manner of recording the deposition, the manner of preserving the deposition, and the manner of filing the deposition are usually specified either by written agreement or by court order. Once the recording has been made, a party may have a stenographic transcript made at personal expense. The obvious advantage to this method of taking a deposition is to minimize the cost.

Videotaping depositions in lieu of or in addition to a stenographic recording is becoming increasingly more popular. This method is beneficial in situations in which the deponent will not be present at the trial to testify and one of the parties is trying to preserve his or her testimony as part of the evidence to be introduced at trial. Commercial services are available for taking this kind of deposition. In addition, the district court might provide a videotape studio free of charge. Counsel simply has to supply the necessary videotape. Check with the local clerk's office to see if a similar provision is made in your locality.

Finally, pursuant to written agreement of the parties or by court order, a deposition may be taken by telephone. Again, some means of transcribing the conversation needs to be specified.

*c. Notice of Depositions, Subpoenas.*   In order to take an oral deposition of any person, it is necessary to notify not only the party or person whose oral deposition will be taken but all other parties as well. FRCP 30(b)(1) sets forth the elements of a notice of oral depositions:

> A party desiring to take the deposition of any person upon oral examination shall give reasonable notice in writing to every other party to the action. The notice shall state the time and place for taking the deposition and the name and address of each person to be examined, if known, and if the name is not known, a general description sufficient to identify him or the particular class or group to which he belongs. If a subpoena duces tecum is to be served on the person to be examined, the designation of the materials to be produced as set forth in the subpoena shall be attached to or included in the notice.[5]

In the case of a party to the lawsuit, notice of the deposition is sufficient to compel the attendance of a party, or an officer, director, or managing agent of a party, at the deposition pursuant to sanctions established by FRCP 37(b).

An example of a notice of deposition for the deposition of a party to the lawsuit is shown in Exhibit 7.6.

---

[5]A subpoena is an order from the court requiring a person to attend a proceeding as a witness. A subpoena duces tecum requires that the witness also bring along certain documents or other things.

**EXHIBIT 7.6**

## Notice of Oral Depositions

[Caption]

PLAINTIFF'S NOTICE OF ORAL DEPOSITIONS

TO: (LIST OF NAMES AND ADDRESSES OF DEFENDANTS' COUNSEL)

PLEASE TAKE NOTICE that plaintiff in the above-captioned action will take the oral deposition of (name) pursuant to the Federal Rules of Civil Procedure, on January 21, 1992, at 10:00 A.M. in the offices of Feesch, Foote & O'Rourke, 1000 The Glip Building, Wallingford, West Virginia.

_____

Name and Address of Plaintiff's Counsel

Dated:

In order to take the deposition of a nonparty or a minor employee of a party, a **subpoena** is necessary to ensure attendance. Under FRCP 45(d), the clerk of the district court for the district in which the deposition is to be taken is authorized to issue subpoenas upon proof that parties to the lawsuit have been served with notice of the deposition. Normally, this is done by the presentation to the clerk of a certified copy of a notice of deposition; the clerk will then issue the subpoena in blank. The subpoena should be filled out and personally served on the deponent. This may be done by any adult (over eighteen years of age) and it is normal to have a paralegal or messenger make the service. There are also agencies that specialize in serving subpoenas. They might be used if service is either difficult or dangerous.

Service of the subpoena is sufficient to compel the deponent's personal appearance. The subpoena must be accompanied, however, by a check for attendance fees (an amount set by statute as a witness fee), plus mileage.

If the deponent has, or may have, relevant documents, a list of the documents that are required to be brought to the deposition should be inserted in the blank spaces provided on the subpoena, or on a "rider" attached to the subpoena. An example of a **subpoena duces tecum** is given in Exhibit 7.7.

Exhibit 7.8 is an example of a notice of deposition by designation as part of a notice to certain named individuals.

### 5. Oral Deposition Procedure

*a. Stipulations.* The taking of an oral deposition is accompanied by several requirements: the court reporter before whom the oral deposition is taken must seal (that is, apply a notary seal), certify, and file the oral deposition;

**EXHIBIT 7.7**

# Subpoena Duces Tecum

DEPOSITION SUBPOENA TO TESTIFY OR PRODUCE DOCUMENTS OR THINGS

UNITED STATES DISTRICT COURT
FOR THE EASTERN DISTRICT OF PENNSYLVANIA
CIVIL ACTION FILE NO.

[Caption]

TO: [Name of Deponent], M.D.
  [Address]
 Philadelphia, Pennsylvania

 YOU ARE COMMANDED to appear at [office address of counsel] in the city of _____ on the 22nd day of December, 1991, at 10:00 o'clock A.M. to testify on behalf of defendant at the taking of a deposition in the above entitled action pending in the United States District Court for the Eastern District of Pennsylvania and bring with you all documents described on the attached rider, which are within your possession, custody, or control.

Dated December 15, 1991.

_____  _____

Attorney for Defendant      Clerk

_____  By _____

Address           Deputy Clerk

## RETURN ON SERVICE

Received this subpoena at _____ on _____ and on _____ at _____ served it on the within named _____ by delivering a copy to h ___ and tendering to h ___ the fee for one day's attendance and the mileage allowed by law.

1. Strike the words "and bring with you" unless the subpoena is to require the production of documents of tangible things, in which case the documents and things should be designated in the blank space provided for that purpose.

2. Fees and mileage must not be tendered to the witness upon service of a subpoena issued in behalf of the United States or an officer or agency thereof. 28 USC 1825.

Note—Affidavit required only if service is made by a person other than a United States Marshal or his deputy.

Dated:

        _____

_____, 19___      By_____

**EXHIBIT 7.7**

# Subpoena Duces Tecum (continued)

Service Fees

    Travel         _____   \$_____

    Services     _____

                              _____

    Total          _____   \$_____

Subscribed and sworn to before me, on _____ this _____ day of _____ , 19 \_\_

                                                _____

**Rider to Subpoena Duces Tecum**

### DIRECTED TO [NAME OF DEPONENT]

All files, books and records, and any other documents referring or relating to [name], plaintiff herein, including any and all reports of medical examinations of plaintiff.

As used herein, "documents" includes any written, printed, typed, or graphic matter of any kind of nature however produced or reproduced, and all mechanical and electronic sound recordings or transcripts thereof, however produced or reproduced.

As used herein, "reports" includes every written communication from a physician, medical practitioner, or any other person engaged in diagnosing and treating illness or injury, or from the agent of any such person, containing information respecting the medical history, condition, diagnosis, and/or prognosis of the person examined.

As used herein, "medical examinations" includes any interview, observation, physical or mental examination, and any other scientific or medical technique or practice designed to obtain information respecting the medical history, condition, diagnosis, and or prognosis of the person examined.

In those cases where a party does not know who to notice for an oral deposition FRCP 30(b)(6) provides:

"A party may in his notice name as the deponent a public or private corporation or a partnership or association or governmental agency and designate with reasonable particularity the matters on which examination is requested. The organization so named shall designate one or more officers, directors, or managing agents, or other persons who consent to testify on its behalf and may set forth, for each person designated, the matters on which he will testify. The persons so designated shall testify as to matters known or reasonably available to the organization. This subdivision (b)(6) does not preclude taking a deposition by any other procedure authorized in these rules.

**EXHIBIT 7.8**

## Notice of Deposition

[Caption]

PLAINTIFF'S FIRST NOTICE OF ORAL DEPOSITIONS

TO: (Name & Address of Attorney)

PLEASE TAKE NOTICE that plaintiff in the above-captioned action will take the following oral depositions, pursuant to the Federal Rules of Civil Procedure, in the offices of (name & address of attorney taking oral deposition) at 10:00 A.M. on the dates set forth below:

MILTON I. BARON                                        November 16, 1991

JACK B. PENTA                                          November 17, 1991

Pursuant to Rule 30(b)(6) of the Federal Rules of Civil Procedure, plaintiff will take the oral deposition of the United States Postal Service with regard to its statutes, rules, and regulations in the offices of (name & address of attorney taking oral deposition) at 10:00 A.M. on November 23.

Pursuant to Rule 30(b)(6) of the Federal Rules of Civil Procedure, plaintiff will take the oral deposition of the United States Civil Service Commission with regard to its statutes, rules, and regulations in the offices of (name & address of attorney taking oral depositions) at 10:00 A.M. on November 24, 1991.

_____

Name and Address of Attorney

Dates:

and the deponent must read and sign the transcript of the oral deposition. This is done after the deposition has been transcribed by the court reporter.

By stipulation, these requirements may be waived either in whole or in part. For example, counsel may stipulate that sealing, certification, and filing of the oral deposition are waived. In most cases, reading and signing will not be waived. The most common form of stipulation is as follows:

It is hereby stipulated and agreed by and between the attorneys for the respective parties hereto that the sealing, filing, and certification of the transcript of the within examination be, and the same are, waived; and the said transcript may be signed and sworn to before any Notary Public with the same force and effect as if before an officer of this court.

This stipulation would be agreed to orally by deponent's counsel and the examining attorney and would be recorded by the stenographer. The waiver of any or all requirements does not prevent the oral deposition from being used at trial.

In addition, attorneys commonly agree to waive all objections to questions during the course of the deposition except as to objections to the form of a question. All other objections are reserved until the time of trial (relevant, hearsay, and so on).

**b. Exhibits and Documents.**   During the course of a deposition it is common for the examining attorney to refer to various documents and papers in order to ascertain the validity of the documents and papers and ask questions that relate to them. FRCP 30(f)(1) establishes a procedure for identifying "documents and things." They are to be marked by the court reporter (designations of "P" for plaintiff and "D" for defendant are usually used followed by the number of the exhibit identified) and attached to the transcript of the deposition. If, however, the party producing the document does not attach the original to the transcript, copies are to be supplied to all parties instead.

## E. Physical and Mental Examinations

The discovery device of compulsory physical and mental examinations ordered by the court, unlike the discovery devices previously discussed, is relatively limited in its availability and usefulness. In most cases in which the results are relevant to a claim or defense, parties will stipulate (agree) to medical examinations. If there is no stipulation, the compulsory examination is made available only when (1) "the mental or physical condition (including the blood group)" of a party, or a person in a party's custody or legal control, is "in controversy" and (2) the moving party demonstrates that there is "good cause" for ordering such an examination.

In practice, the availability of the device is usually limited to personal injury or paternity cases, although no provision of FRCP 35 limits it. As discussed below, meeting the "in controversy" and "good cause" requirements presents no problem in a personal injury case (and related types of cases) but is almost impossible in other type cases.

These dual limitations upon the availability of medical examinations are actually closely related requirements in practice. Thus it is usually conceded that "good cause" for a compulsory examination has been established where the party to be examined has placed his or her physical or mental condition "in controversy" in the allegations of the complaint or other pleadings. For example, a "good cause" will be demonstrated for a compulsory examination when the plaintiff in a personal injury action alleges mental or physical injuries.

The party requesting the examination can designate or select the doctor to conduct the examination. Potentially, the role of the paralegal in this situation is to select a physician (although this is usually done by the lawyer), to contact the physician's office, and to make the necessary arrangements for the actual examination if there is no agreement between the parties. See Exhibit 7.9 for an example of a motion for a compulsory examination.

## F. Limitation as to the Use of Discovery

Despite the wide latitude permitted parties engaged in the process of discovery, there are exceptions and limitations based on the subject matter of discovery.

# Motion for Compulsory Examination

[Caption]

## MOTION FOR COMPULSORY PHYSICAL EXAMINATION OF PLAINTIFF

Defendant, [name], hereby moves this court for entry of an order requiring plaintiff, [name], to submit to a physical examination to determine the nature and extent, if any, of his injuries resulting from the accident which forms the basis for the instant suit. In support of this motion, defendant alleges as follows:

1. Plaintiff initiated this action on August 2, 1991, alleging that he suffered permanent paralysis of the right arm and leg as a result of an automobile collision between his car and that of defendant, and further alleging that said accident was caused by defendant's negligence in operation of his vehicle.

2. Defendant has denied any negligence, and in addition has disputed that plaintiff suffered any injuries as a result of the aforesaid collision. There is thus a controversy between the parties as to plaintiff's actual physical condition.

3. Defendant's investigation has revealed that plaintiff has been continuously employed, at the same level and pay since the time of the aforesaid collision, at the same job with [name of company].

4. Plaintiff has refused to submit to a physical examination; and, unless such an examination is ordered, the exact nature of plaintiff's physical condition, which forms the essential basis for the present suit, cannot be determined prior to trial, and defendant will thus not be able to present an intelligent defense at trial.

5. Defendant submits that the court should enter an order compelling plaintiff to appear before Doctor [name], at 10:00 A.M., November 2, 1992, at [address] for a complete physical examination, including X-rays of plaintiff's right arm and leg, and such other standard medical tests as Doctor [name], in his professional judgment, shall deem necessary and appropriate to ascertain the nature and extent, if any, of the injuries suffered by plaintiff. Defendant will bear the costs and expenses of such examination.

_____

(Attorney for Defendant)

Dated:

## 1. Privileged Matters

The first and most important limitation to the scope of discovery is found in the words "not privileged" in FRCP 26(b)(1). If the communication is **privileged,** the subject matter of the communication may not be learned by discovery.

The most common form of privilege is the attorney–client privilege, which prohibits any third party from obtaining information about the subject matters discussed between an attorney and client. The purpose of the privilege is to instill confidence in clients that they are free to discuss legal problems with their lawyers. There is no absolute right for a court, government official, or private person to require the lawyer or the client to disclose the content of the discussions. One of the few exceptions to the attorney–client privilege in which discovery is permitted is when the assertion of the attorney–client privilege would perpetrate, or assist in the perpetration of, a fraud on the court or the commission of a crime. For example, an attorney is not permitted to assert a privilege relating to communications with a client in which advice is given to the client of ways to illegally evade the payment of income taxes because such evasion constitutes a crime.

While the attorney–client privilege prevents disclosure of the subject matter of certain communications, it may not be asserted to prevent the disclosure of the fact that an attorney–client communication occurred. Thus, a party seeking discovery is entitled to ascertain whether a communication between an attorney and client occurred and, if so, the form of the communication (letter or oral discussion) and its date. The privilege may be claimed only to avoid the disclosure of the subject matter of the communication.

In a case in which multiple parties are represented by different counsel, only the attorney and client involved in the communication may assert the privilege. Assume that there are three defendants in a case, X, Y, and Z, represented by attorneys XX, YY, and ZZ, respectively. Neither Y and Z nor YY and ZZ, their counsel, have a right to assert the attorney–client privilege to prevent the disclosure of the subject matter of communication between X and XX. If X (the person protected by the privilege) and XX have no objection to disclosing the subject matter of a privileged communication, the privilege may be relinquished and no one else may object to such answer. Finally, the attorney–client privilege is waived (that is, it may not be asserted) when the communication between an attorney and client occurs in the presence of a third party unrelated to the client. (Such waiver does not occur if employees of the attorney (paralegal, secretary, and so on) are present during the communication as the scope of this privilege includes them.) In such situations, the court will normally conduct an in camera (confidential) inspection of the communications, documents, or other tangible things in order to determine whether the attorney–client privilege was properly asserted to prevent the requested discovery. (If the "client" is a corporation, all the corporate officers are considered the "client" and the presence of more than one corporate officer at the time of an attorney–client communication does not constitute a waiver of the privilege.)

Other generally accepted privileges include physician/patient, clergy/congregant, husband/wife, accountant/client, and therapist/patient. The law of privilege may, however, vary significantly from state to state.

## 2. Insurance Agreements

Under FRCP 26(b)(2), it is expressly permissible for a party to obtain discovery of the "existence and contents of any insurance agreement under which any person carrying on an insurance business may be liable to satisfy part or all of a judgment which may be entered in the action or to indemnify or reimburse for payments made to satisfy the judgment." (State rules of procedure are often unclear on this point and the states differ widely on whether such discovery is permissible.) In many cases, particularly those involving personal injury, knowledge regarding the existence or nonexistence of insurance and the amount of such insurance will facilitate pretrial settlements. If the plaintiff is able to learn that the policy limit on the insurance that will ultimately pay any judgment is only $10,000, this may lead the plaintiff to accept a settlement figure at or near that amount rather than go to trial and win a larger verdict that the defendant will not be able to pay personally. In any case, once information about an insurance policy is discovered, it may not be introduced at trial as this might prejudice the jury.

Below is an example of an interrogatory about the defendant's insurance coverage:

State whether defendant (name) is covered by any liability insurance policy. If so, state:

(a) The name of the insurance carrier of the defendant.

(b) The limits of the policy.

(c) Whether the insurance carrier is handling or participating in the defense of this lawsuit.

(d) If the answer to subparagraph (c) is affirmative, describe the contractual basis for such handling or participating.

## 3. Trial Preparation Materials

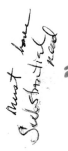

FRCP 26(b)(3) regulates discovery regarding materials "prepared in anticipation of litigation or for trial." Under that rule, discovery of trial preparation materials is allowed "only upon a showing that the party seeking discovery has substantial need of the materials in the preparation of his case and that he is unable without undue hardship to obtain the substantial equivalent of the materials by other means."

For example, assume there has been a bus accident. Shortly after the incident the bus company takes statements of all passengers and witnesses, expecting that many of the passengers will sue. An action is commenced by a passenger and before that passenger's attorney begins investigating the case, a very important witness dies. Later, during discovery the passenger seeks to have a copy of that witness's statement produced. The request will be allowed because the passenger cannot obtain the information any other way (the witness is dead) and the statement may be critical to the passenger's lawsuit, perhaps by indicating negligence on the part of the bus company. Therefore, despite the fact that the statement was taken in anticipation of litigation, it will be discoverable. If no good cause could be shown why the statement was necessary (as, for example, if the witness were still alive) then it could not be "discovered."

### 4. Attorney's Work Products

Under FRCP 26(b)(3) materials prepared by an attorney prior to trial, or **attorney's work products**, are not discoverable when such materials contain the mental impressions, conclusions, opinions, or legal theories of the attorney. This is not a question of the attorney–client privilege, because such materials may be the result of contact by the attorney with outsiders or simply the result of the attorney's own thinking. Thus, for example, two attorneys working on a case may exchange letters or memoranda setting out tactics to be used or commenting on evidence expected to surface at the trial. Such communications fit into the attorney's work product rule and could be kept out of the hands of opposing parties even when requested in discovery proceedings.

### 5. Experts

Experts may be retained during litigation either to testify at the trial or to give advice to the lawyer in preparing for trial. With respect to a testifying expert, under FRCP 26(b)(4) interrogatories addressed to the opposing party may be used to learn the subject matter, substance of the facts and opinions to which an expert is expected to testify, and a summary of the grounds for each such opinion. Only interrogatories may be used, however. It is not permissible to take the deposition of an expert who the opponent expects to call as a witness at the trial without receiving special permission from the court.

As to experts who have been specially retained by the adverse party for advice in preparation for trial, but who are not expected to be called as witnesses at trial, no discovery is allowed except under extraordinary circumstances. However, you may be able to get the identity of nontestifying experts.

Exhibit 7.10 shows a sample set of interrogatories regarding expert witnesses who are expected to testify at trial.

### 6. Timing of Discovery

Normally, general discovery regarding all aspects of the litigation is available to any party from the commencement of the litigation. Under certain circumstances, however, general discovery may be postponed until other preliminary proceedings such as motions to dismiss or motions to transfer to another district are completed. In these cases discovery will be allowed only on those areas that are the subject of the pending motions until the motions are decided by the court. For example, if a motion to dismiss for lack of personal jurisdiction is filed, discovery will be allowed only on such things as the method of service of process, domicile of the defendant, and so on. Once that motion is decided, and the case is not dismissed, full discovery will proceed.

## III. Resisting Discovery

The availability of the discovery devices outlined in the preceding section does not mean that their use is unlimited or never subject to objection. In general, there are two methods by which to oppose the propriety of discovery: applica-

**EXHIBIT 7.10**

## Interrogatories (Expert Witnesses)

[Caption]

DEFENDANT'S INTERROGATORIES TO PLAINTIFF

1. (a) Identify each expert witness you intend to call at trial;

    (b) As to each such expert, state the subject matter on which the expert is expected to testify;

    (c) As to each such expert, state in detail the substance of the facts to which the expert is expected to testify;

    (d) As to each such expert, state in detail the opinions to which the expert is expected to testify;

    (e) As to each such expert, state in detail a summary of the grounds for the opinions referred to in your answer to interrogatory No. 1(d);

    (f) As to each such expert, identify each document sent from you, your representatives, or your attorneys, to the expert;

    (g) As to each such expert, identify each document to you, your representatives, or your attorneys, from the expert; and

    (h) As to each such expert, state in detail the qualifications of said expert, listing the schools attended, including years of attendance and degrees received, experience in particular fields, including names and addresses of employers with inclusive years of employment, and a list of all publications authored by said expert, including the title of work, the name of the periodical or book in which it was printed, and the date of its printing.

_____

(Name and Address of Counsel)

Dates

---

tion for a protective order and objections to interrogatories, requests for production of documents, requests for admission, and deposition questions.

## A. Protective Orders

**Protective orders,** which are governed by FRCP 26(c) and are substantially similar under most state rules, apply largely to discovery through deposition, although they are not so limited. FRCP 26(c) provides that protective orders may be issued by the court "to protect a party or person from annoyance, embarrassment, oppression, or undue burden or expense . . ." upon a showing of good cause.

It might be helpful to give examples of reasons that would justify a specific protective order, relating the reasons to the types of orders set forth in rule 26(c):

1. If the information sought is irrelevant to the case and not reasonably calculated to lead to the discovery of admissible evidence, a court could issue an "order that the discovery not be had." Suppose, for example, defendant asked for the deposition of plaintiff's boyfriend in a suit brought for breach of contract that in no way related to the boyfriend. Plaintiff would maintain that taking the deposition was irrelevant and not reasonably calculated to lead to the discovery of admissible evidence to the case.

2. If the deposition is to be held at a location that is distant and inconvenient to the deponent, a court could issue an order that "the discovery may be had only on specified terms and conditions" and a time and place would be designated.

3. If a party suing the U.S. Government seeks to depose a high government official named as a party to the lawsuit, a court may require that "discovery may be had only by a method of discovery other than that selected by the party seeking discovery" and order that only written interrogatories may be submitted to the government official.

4. If the examining party has spent a large amount of time on irrelevant matters in prior depositions, or if there is a serious question of subject matter or personal jurisdiction, the court may issue an order "that certain matters not be inquired into, or that the scope of the discovery be limited to certain matters."

5. If personal matters will be explored in a deposition, the court may issue an order that "discovery be conducted with no one present except persons designated by the court" or "that a deposition after being sealed be opened only by order of the court."

6. If trade secrets or other confidential information are involved, the court may issue an order "that a trade secret or other confidential research, development or commercial information not be disclosed or be disclosed only in a designated way."

7. If customer lists or accounts are involved, the court may issue an order that "the parties simultaneously file specified documents or information enclosed in sealed envelopes to be opened as directed by the court."

Exhibit 7.11 provides an example of a motion for protective order.

## B. Termination or Limitation Orders for Depositions

FRCP 30(d) protects deponents once a deposition has been started from bad faith examinations and unreasonable actions of the attorney taking the deposition. If it is shown that the attorney taking the deposition is trying to annoy, embarrass, or oppress the deponent, the court may order that the deposition stop or limit the scope and manner of taking the deposition.

If the attorney representing the deponent objects to the manner in which the deposition is being taken for one of the above reasons, the deposition may be suspended so that the appropriate motion may be filed with the court. Often the objection is simply noted for the record and the deposition continues.

**EXHIBIT 7.11**

## Motion for Protective Order

[Caption]

### MOTION FOR PROTECTIVE ORDER AND STAY OF PROCEEDINGS

Defendant, R. Publishing Co., by its attorneys, hereby moves this Honorable Court to enter a protective order staying the depositions noticed by plaintiffs herein, or granting such other relief as may be appropriate, as set forth below. In support of this motion, defendant alleges as follows:

1. Plaintiffs, by a "Notice of Taking Depositions" dated November 3, 1991, noticed the depositions of Richard Smith and Alan Brown, the authors of a book entitled *Doctors' Journal*, which was published by defendant.

2. In response to the complaint herein, defendant moved for summary judgment on October 30, 1991, four days before the instant notice of taking depositions was filed, on the grounds that the suit was barred by the statute of limitations, and also that the suit was barred by the doctrine of New York Times Company v. Sullivan, 376 U.S. 254 (1964), since plaintiffs were both "public officer" and "public figures" within the holding of that and subsequent decisions.

3. Defendant's motion for summary judgment is presently scheduled to be argued before the court on February 1, 1992. Defendant believes that its motion for summary judgment is sufficient to terminate this action, without any further discovery.

4. Permitting discovery to go forward without first ruling on defendant's motion for summary judgment will have a chilling effect upon defendant's right of free speech under the First and Fourteenth Amendments to the United States Constitution.

WHEREFORE, defendant respectfully requests this Honorable Court to enter an order ruling that all depositions noticed by plaintiffs be stayed pending decision on defendant's motion for summary judgment. In the alternative, defendant respectfully requests this Honorable Court to enter on order limiting the said depositions to those matters raised by defendant's motion for summary judgment.

_____

(Name and Address of Attorney)

Leaving the deposition is a measure of last resort. This is done simply by walking out of the deposition after explaining the reason for doing so.

The provisions of FRCP 26(c) apply to the termination or limitation of a deposition and so any motion that might be made prior to the deposition may also be made while it is in progress.

## C. Award of Expenses

FRCP 37(a)(4) provides that if a motion under FRCP 26(c) or 30(d) is granted and the court finds that the conduct of the attorney taking or requesting the deposition was not substantially justified, the court may award reasonable expenses, including attorney's fees, incurred by the moving party in making the motion for protective order, termination, or limitation. On the other hand, if the motion under FRCP 26(c) or 30(d) is denied and the court finds that making the motion was not substantially justified, the court may award reasonable expenses, including attorney's fees, incurred by the party taking the deposition in opposing the motion.

## D. Objections to Interrogatories, Production of Documents, and Admissions

### 1. Nature of Objections

**Objections** to discovery are normally based on one or more of the following grounds.

- The information sought is irrelevant to the lawsuit and is not reasonably calculated to lead to the discovery of admissible evidence. Thus, in the answer to the interrogatory, the answering party might respond as follows:

This interrogatory is objected to because it calls for information that is irrelevant to the subject matter of this action and that cannot reasonably lead to the discovery of evidence that would be admissible with respect to any issue raised in this action.

- The information sought is privileged or constitutes a lawyer's "work product." The following is an example of a response to an interrogatory based on the attorney–client privilege and other grounds:

This interrogatory is objected to for the following reasons:
1. It calls for information that is irrelevant to the subject matter of this action and not reasonably calculated to lead to the discovery of admissible evidence.
2. It calls for information protected from disclosure by the attorney–client privilege.
3. It calls for information prepared by counsel in preparation for trial.

- The information sought would require a burdensome effort to produce, and is harassing and vexing.

- The information sought is too broad, too vague, too extensive, or too general.

- The timing of the interrogatories is inappropriate because: (1) Motions to dismiss have been filed. The correct form of an objection to interrogatories on this ground is as follows:

Defendant (name) objects to plaintiff's interrogatories, Set No. 1, in their entirety because of the pendency of the motion of defendant (name) to dismiss under rule 12 of the Federal Rules of Civil Procedure for lack of jurisdiction over the subject matter, lack of jurisdiction over the person, improper venue, and insufficiency of process and service or process.

♦ (2) A motion to transfer under 28 U.S.C.A. § 1404(a) for the convenience of parties and witnesses and in the interest of justice has been filed. The form of objection to interrogatories on this ground is as follows:

Defendant (name) objects to plaintiff's interrogatories, Set No. 1, in their entirety because of the pendency of the motion of defendant (name) to transfer this action to the United States District Court for the Central District of California, pursuant to 28 U.S.C.A. § 1404(a).

### 2. Effect of Filing Objections

Objections defer the obligation of the party from whom discovery is sought to answer only those specific questions or requests contained in interrogatories, requests for production of documents, and requests for admissions to which actual objections are raised. All other questions and requests must be answered or satisfied in a timely fashion.

### 3. Conciliatory Conference between Parties to Compromise Objections

In most federal district courts, either as a result of local rule or local custom, after a party has filed objections to discovery, counsel for both parties will confer in an attempt to resolve their disagreements without seeking judicial intervention. It is customary for these conferences to become bartering sessions in which counsel give and take in an effort to avoid judicial intervention.

### 4. Judicial Resolution of Objections

In most federal district courts, judicial resolution of objections to discovery must be preceded by a certification by counsel that they attempted in good faith to resolve their disagreements. Generally, the burden to seek judicial resolution is on the party seeking discovery. Once the court becomes involved in disagreements between parties regarding discovery, **sanctions** (penalties imposed by the court) may be imposed on either party.

## E. Supplementation of Discovery Responses

FRCP 26(e) provides that, as a general rule, the responding party is under no duty to supplement the response to discovery. There are exceptions to this, however. If a party has forwarded to the adversary (for example, in answers to interrogatories) the identity of persons expected to be called as experts or those with knowledge of facts, and later learns of other persons, the burden is on the responding party to supplement the initial response. Further, if it is learned that an answer was incorrect when given there is also a duty to supplement.

In order to negate all possibility of inaccurate or incomplete responses to discovery, however, the parties should take advantage of FRCP 26(e)(3) and, either by order of court or by agreement, impose a duty on each other to provide all information that they become aware of after initial discovery responses. Such an approach should eliminate, or at least minimize, the possibility of trial surprise.

## IV. SANCTIONS

### A. Motion for Order Compelling Discovery

As discussed previously, the discovery process is designed to proceed with a minimum of judicial interference in order to encourage the parties to resolve their discovery disagreements without seeking judicial sanctions, which can be imposed when a party unjustifiably fails to respond to discovery.

FRCP 37(a)(2) provides a mechanism for compelling discovery when a party has failed to answer a question propounded during an oral deposition taken pursuant to FRCP 30, failed to answer an interrogatory submitted pursuant to FRCP 33, or failed to produce a document for inspection and copying pursuant to a FRCP 34 request. "An evasive or incomplete answer is to be treated as a failure to answer" under FRCP 37(a)(3). The party requesting discovery may apply for an order from the court compelling discovery. This is done by a **motion to compel,** filed with the court where the litigation is pending. See Exhibit 7.12 for an example of a motion to compel answers to interrogatories, where the defendant has neither answered nor objected to the interrogatories propounded within the thirty days allowed by the federal rules. (Note the different sections of FRCP 37 referred to in the motion, which provide for the various sanctions requested.)

Exhibit 7.13 is an example of a motion to compel someone to answer a question asked during the course of an oral deposition. (Note that it is not unusual to make a single motion relating to more than one deponent.)

### B. Failure to Comply with Order

In those rare instances when a court order compelling discovery is disobeyed, FRCP 37(b) provides a variety of sanctions. For example, a witness at a deposition may be held in contempt of court for continued failure to answer. An order of contempt is a serious sanction in that it may ultimately result in the imprisonment of the uncooperative deponent. In "contempt" a person intentionally obstructs a court's work or willfully disobeys a judge's order. The imprisonment is designed to make the disobeying witness comply with the order to respond.

Sanctions may take other forms: presuming the truth of what the inquiring party is trying to prove by the discovery (as in a request for admissions); not allowing the disobeying party to oppose a particular claim; prohibiting the introduction of certain matters at the trial; striking out parts of pleadings; or even dismissing an action or giving a judgment by default. In any of these, expenses, including attorney's fees, may be awarded to the party who is justified in seeking the discovery.

Thus, failure to comply with an order compelling discovery may often mean that the disobeying party will lose the lawsuit. This is only fair in view of the

**EXHIBIT 7.12**

# Motion to Compel Answers to Interrogatories

[Caption]

PLAINTIFF'S MOTION TO COMPEL ANSWERS TO HIS INTERROGATO-
RIES AND TO IMPOSE SANCTIONS ON DEFENDANTS FOR THEIR FAIL-
URE TO ANSWER HIS INTERROGATORIES

---

AND NOW, this 5th day of March, 1992, plaintiff (name), by his attorneys, respectfully moves this Court, as follows:

1. Under Rule 37(a)(2):
   (a) To compel defendants to answer plaintiff's interrogatories in their
       entirety no later than April 30, 1992; and
   (b) To require defendants to pay to plaintiff the reasonable expenses, in-
       cluding attorney's fees, incurred in obtaining the relief requested herein.

2. Under Rule 37(b)(2):
   (a) To preclude defendants from asserting any objections to plaintiff's
       interrogatories;
   (b) To treat as a contempt of court the failure of any defendant to
       answer plaintiff's interrogatories by April 30, 1992;
   (c) To decide all contested issues of fact embraced by plaintiff's inter-
       rogatories in favor of plaintiff;
   (d) To strike all of defendants' defenses and to preclude defendants
       from introducing any evidence in support thereof;
   (e) To enter a judgment by default on the issue of liability in favor of
       plaintiff and against defendants under Counts I, II, and III of plain-
       tiff's complaint; and
   (f) To require defendants to pay to plaintiff the reasonable expenses,
       including attorney's fees, incurred in obtaining the relief requested
       herein.

3. Under Rule 37(d):
   (a) To preclude defendants from asserting any objections to plaintiff's
       interrogatories;
   (b) To treat as a contempt of court the failure of any defendant to
       answer plaintiff's interrogatories by April 30, 1992;
   (c) To decide all contested issues of fact embraced by plaintiff's inter-
       rogatories in favor of plaintiff;
   (d) To strike all of defendants' defenses and to preclude defendants
       from introducing any evidence in support thereof;
   (e) To enter a judgment by default on the issue of liability in favor of
       plaintiff and against defendants under Counts I, II, and III of plain-
       tiff's complaint; and
   (f) To require defendants to pay to plaintiff the reasonable expense,
       including attorney's fees, incurred in obtaining the relief requested
       herein.

---

Name and Address of Plaintiff's Counsel

---

**EXHIBIT 7.13**

---

## Motion to Compel Answer During Depositions

---

[Caption]

PLAINTIFF'S MOTION UNDER RULE 37(a)(2) TO COMPEL A PARTY DE-PONENT AND A NON-PARTY DEPONENT TO ANSWER QUESTIONS PROPOUNDED DURING THEIR RESPECTIVE ORAL DEPOSITIONS

---

AND NOW, this 5th day of March, 1992: plaintiff, by his attorneys, respectfully moves this Court, as follows:

1. Under Rule 37(a)(2), to compel Sam Johnson, an officer of defendant Detective Agency, Inc., to answer the following questions that were propounded during his oral deposition of January 7, 1992:

(List Questions)

2. Under Rule 37(a)(2), to compel Jim Clark, a nonparty deponent, to answer the following questions that were propounded during his oral deposition of January 8, 1992.

(List Questions)

---

Name and Address of Plaintiff's Counsel

---

intent of the liberal discovery rules in the federal courts. Only by such freedom to obtain information through discovery does the notice pleading philosophy of the federal rules work. For the party who tries to circumvent the purpose of the federal rules there is small chance of reaping the benefits of a judgment by the court in his or her favor.

## V. SUMMARY

The process of discovery typically begins after a lawsuit is filed. It is a critical stage of litigation during which the script for the trial is usually written.

The scope of discovery allows a party to go after relevant information and/or information that is likely to lead to the discovery of admissible evidence. The major limitations on scope are privileged matters, attorney work product, and trial preparation materials. These limitations were created or preserved in order to uphold important policies systemic to our legal system such as the sanctity of attorney–client privilege.

Written interrogatories, oral depositions, depositions upon written questions, requests for production of documents, things, and inspections, requests for admissions, and physical and mental examinations are all discovery devices. They can be used in any sequence that makes sense, and they are supplemental to each other; using one device does not foreclose the ability to use another device.

Interrogatories are written questions submitted by one party to another to be answered in writing under oath. Requests for production of documents and things and inspections are written requests by one party to another to make available certain written materials or objects for inspection, photocopying, or study. Depositions are formal interviews under oath in the presence of a court reporter. They can either be oral depositions or depositions upon written questions. Requests for admissions are written requests to a party to acknowledge the truth of certain facts or the authenticity of certain materials. And an adverse party may require a physical or mental examination by an impartial doctor when the physical or mental condition of a party is at issue.

A party who wishes to resist a discovery request can employ one of two procedural strategies: object to a discovery request, or file a motion for a protective order. Discovery is usually resisted if it is outside of the scope permitted, the information is privileged, or the amount of discovery is out of proportion to the size of the lawsuit.

Enforcing a discovery request is a three step process. First the parties attempt to informally reconcile their own differences. The second step involves filing a motion to compel a party to respond to a discovery request and obtaining a court order. The third step involves requesting further sanctions from a court if a party ignores a court order compelling discovery. Typical sanctions involve attorneys fees and costs, contempt, dismissal of a lawsuit, striking defenses, or imposing a default judgment.

---

## VI. KEY TERMS

Attorney's Work
    Products
Depositions
Discovery Plan
Motion to Compel
Objections
Physical and Mental
    Examinations
Privileged Matters

Protective Orders
Requests for
    Admissions
Requests for
    Production of
    Documents and
    Things and
    Inspections

Sanctions
Subpoena (duces
    tecum)
Trial Preparation
    Materials
Written
    Interrogatories

## VII. QUESTIONS

1. Under the FRCP, what is the scope of discovery?
2. What is the only discovery device that can be used to obtain information from a nonparty?
3. Compare and contrast interrogatories with a deposition upon written questions.

4. What methods can be used to obtain documents from a party?
5. Which discovery device is not really a true discovery tool, and why?
6. What steps can be taken to force a party to respond to interrogatories?
7. What happens if a party does not respond to a set of requests for admissions?
8. What are the advantages and disadvantages of using an oral deposition as a discovery device?
9. Under the FRCP, what two methods of resisting discovery are generally used and how do they differ from one another?
10. Define the component parts typically found in the introductory part of a set of interrogatories or a set of requests for production of documents.

# DISCOVERY SUPPORT SYSTEMS

## I. Introduction

We have now reached the point in the civil litigation process where we need to address the question of what to do with all the information we have amassed through discovery or otherwise. The paralegal can play a significant role in setting up a **discovery support system** to organize information.

A discovery support system is a relatively new concept in the legal profession. It is a system designed to organize the mass of documents and information gathered during the course of discovery to aid in the preparation of a case for trial. Implicit in this system of organization are the concepts of document labeling and analysis, document storage and retrieval, and document production. These systems can be either manual or computer-assisted. Although the actual design of a discovery support system is directly related to the particular needs of a lawsuit, some elements are common to most systems. Since paralegals are used extensively in this area of civil litigation, especially in major or complex litigation, an understanding of these basic elements of a discovery support system design is necessary.[1]

Some basic requirements and specific uses of a discovery support system are as follows:[2]

**1.** maintaining a record of information either gathered from or given to other parties to the litigation;

**2.** preparing digests, summaries, and/or indexes of the information acquired;

**3.** preparing files for each witness including documents, exhibits and depositions (which are cross-referenced), and outlines of direct examination and/or cross examination;

**4.** preparing exhibit lists and chronologies for use at trial; and

**5.** preparing records of meetings, phone calls, and time records.

In addition to the above, the system of organization should also include at least a pleadings file, a correspondence file, a legal research file, and an exhibit file. A pleadings file contains all the original pleadings bound together in chronological order with an index page in front of the file describing the documents contained in the file (this file is also referred to as the "pleadings bible"). A correspondence file contains all the correspondence in the case arranged in chronological order. A legal research file should be based on the issue researched with an index in front of the file describing each issue and the documents (memo of law, brief, and so on) drafted on each issue. An exhibit file contains the exhibits intended to be used at trial arranged in the order in which they will be used. It also has an index at the front of the file listing describing each exhibit.

---

[1]The complexity of a lawsuit is usually dependent on the number of parties, the number of documents, the location of parties and documents, and the number of issues involved.

[2]Susan Strauss, *Advanced Discovery*, Vol. II, Massachusetts Law Reform Institute (1981): pp. 123–124.

## II. Manual Document Control and Retrieval

### A. Controlling Documents

The minimum goals of document organization are as follows:

- to keep track of every document so it can be located again

- to aid in recognizing the significance of any document

- to aid in recognizing the relationship of one document or event to another

The standard ways of organizing documents include by document number (the control file), by chronology (showing sequence of events), by individual witnesses, by key event ("the meeting of March 23"), by issue in the case, or as referenced in a pretrial order or statement. (Information on pretrial orders is provided in chapter 9.) In any case with numerous documents (1,000 or more) the main document files should always be kept by document number, and their subfiles should have copies of documents. The paralegal should have complete control of the documents and should always keep a complete set in numerical order.

The cardinal rule for document control is that every page of every document should be numbered in some logical manner. The immediate goals of a numbering system are accountability and general classification. Accountability is achieved by numbering each document. Numbering can be done manually or by an automatic cycling stamping machine. Where there is a significant number of documents, the automatic stamping machine, which automatically increases numbers by one after stamping a page, is the better solution.

Depending upon the number of digits and letters available, the classification system can be quite detailed. If the stamping machine will number up to 999,999, assign a series of numbers within that range for documents produced by plaintiff(s), defendant(s), and third party(ies). For example, plaintiff's documents may be assigned 100,000 to 199,999; defendant "A" assigned 200,000 to 299,999; defendant "B" assigned 300,000 to 399,999; and so forth. Obviously, this example assumes a large number of documents. If there are fewer documents the numbering system can be adjusted downward.

If the stamping machine includes a combination of letters and numbers, you can have a more detailed classification in the numbering system. For example, a machine with two letter spaces and six number spaces (AA000000) could be programmed to identify the source of the document, the time of production, and the case in which produced (if more than one is pending). It is not critical to include large amounts of control information on the document as long as separate indices are maintained that provide such information (the source of the document, the reason for producing the document, the case(s) in which produced, and the number produced). See Exhibit 8.1 for an example.

An example of a document production sheet that tracks every file that has been produced to the opponents and the subsequent history of its use is provided in Exhibit 8.2.

Once the documents are received and numbered, a master file or control set of documents should be established. This file consists of a complete set of the numbered documents. A physical inventory by file drawer (and if necessary

**EXHIBIT 8.1**

# Document Control

Record of Series of Documents

| Source | Number Assigned |
|---|---|
| Plaintiff | 100,000 to 199,999 |
| Defendant | 200,000 to 299,999 |
| Company "X" | 300,000 to 350,000 |
| Mr. "Y" | 350,001 to 399,999 |

Record of Documents Produced

| Party | Request | Date of Production | Documents Produced |
|---|---|---|---|
| Plaintiff | Defendant's 1st document request | 2/12/92 | 100,000 to 135,521 |
| Defendant | Plaintiff's 1st document request | 2/10/92 | 200,000 to 225,432 |
| | Plaintiff's 2nd document request | 3/14/92 | 225,433 to 281,719 |
| Company "X" | Plaintiff's subpoena | 4/17/92 | 300,000 to 313,411 |
| Mr. "Y" | Defendant's subpoena | 5/03/92 | 350,001 to 350,197 |

**EXHIBIT 8.2**

# Document Production Sheet

| FILE NO. | DESCRIPTION | PRODUCE? REQ.# | DATE PROD. | COPIES MADE | CONFID. PAGES | DATE TO PLFF. |
|---|---|---|---|---|---|---|
| | | | | | | |

room) location should be prepared. This control set should not be used for working purposes. Those documents should be photocopied. Once duplicated, they will constitute the working files that are available for use and sign out. The reason for this duplication process is to minimize the risk of losing documents that are looked at regularly.

With respect to preparation of document indices, a chronological receipt file should be prepared for documents received from the client, indicating the type, source, and date the documents were received. For example:

Correspondence file from purchasing manager rec'd 4/92.

After documents have been produced in discovery, the following information can be added:

Produced to plaintiff in response to 2nd document request on 8/28/92. Doc Nos. 205,031 - 205,075.

Any numbered document should be included in an index prepared numerically—the index should include the document number, date of document, author, addressee, subject, and a coding notation. A suggested index format follows:

Index of Documents

Coded   Document   #   Type   of   Document   Subject   Author   Address   Date

Include within the index a notation as to whether the document has been coded as part of the retrieval system (manual or computerized). This assists in the control of critical documents.

It is entirely possible that whole categories of documents will not be of major interest. In such instances, you may decide in the interest of time and economy not to index each document, but instead to index these documents by category. For example:

Company "X" cancelled checks from 1982. Doc Nos. 313,452 - 317,453.

This method provides some record for an index so that if these documents become more relevant at a later date you can prepare a more specific index.

You should also prepare a chronological document index. This can be accomplished from the document number index. The chronological index provides the easiest method to locate a particular document within the inventory.

## B. Organizing Documents

Although the paralegal may carefully provide for the accountability and actual organization of all documents, this mass of documents will be essentially useless unless some rational manner of organizing and retrieving information is devised. Described below are some helpful ways of organizing information.

### 1. The Subject Matter Index

The subject matter index is probably the most useful, for it enables the paralegal to organize the documents by subject matter issues in the case. In order to prepare such an index, however, it is necessary to code each relevant document as to the subject matter issue(s) that it concerns. The subject of coding is discussed below.

## 2. Witness Indices

Witness indices organize documents according to the witness or potential witness who authored or received them. Such indices are useful in preparing for depositions of those individuals and for both preparing a witness and pinpointing the testimony of an opponent's witness at time of trial. An attorney can obviate answers such as "I can't remember" by producing a document prepared by the witness concerning the subject on which there is no present memory.

# C. Coding Documents for Retrieval

After one or more additional indices have been prepared, it is usual to rearrange all documents according to the indices. This may be done (and usually is done in smaller cases) by duplicating however many additional copies of the document are necessary for rearranging according to the number and type of indices prepared. In large cases, however, this can be expensive, time consuming, and physically impractical, in that there may be insufficient storage space for these duplicate sets of documents. Greater flexibility is provided through a system of document summarization/coding that reduces the bulk of and thereby increases the flexibility of the document management system. The issue book file and the index card file are two standard coding systems.

## 1. The Index Card File

The index card file system involves creating a document surrogate for each relevant document by placing various bibliographic data from the document onto an index card (3 by 5 or 5 by 8), together with a summary of the contents, a coding of the document by subject matter, and, in some instances, an evaluation of the importance of the document. After this information is recorded on the card, the card can be duplicated and arranged in whatever number of files (subject matter, witness, and so on) is desired.

## 2. The Issue Book File

The issue book file system involves using either a document surrogate, that is, a coding sheet for a particular document with the bibliographic information and other coding and evaluations described above for the index card, or a copy of the document itself, including its coding and evaluation. The coding sheet has more space on which to include additional bibliographic information or summarizations than a file card does, but the two document surrogates are quite similar otherwise. If you are coding the documents, remember never to code an original document.

Some or all of the following items would be included in any document surrogate:

- ◆ document number

- ◆ type of document (letter, memo)

- ◆ date of document

- ◆ number of pages
- ◆ name(s) of author(s)
- ◆ name(s) of addressee(s)
- ◆ names of individuals receiving copies (cc) or blind copies (bcc)
- ◆ subject matter (code or narrative description)
- ◆ handwritten notes or marginalia
- ◆ document privileged
- ◆ document confidential
- ◆ document produced in discovery
- ◆ document used as deposition exhibit
- ◆ importance of document
- ◆ name of coder and date of coding

An example of a document coding sheet is provided in Exhibit 8.3.

**EXHIBIT 8.3**

## Document Coding Sheet

Analyst _____ Date _____ Addendum Pages_____

| File | | Type | Document Date |
|------|------|------|---------------|
| ☐☐☐☐☐☐ | | ☐☐☐ | ☐☐ ☐☐ ☐☐ |
| Plff/Deft Common | # | (EDPA) | ☐ German |
| ☐☐☐☐☐☐ | — | ☐☐☐ | ☐ Handwritten Notes |
| Plff/Deft Common | # | (MD) | ☐ Illegible |
| ☐☐☐☐☐☐ | — | ☐☐☐ | ☐ Underlining |
| Phila/Balt Common | # | | ☐ Draft |
| ☐☐☐☐☐☐ | — | ☐☐☐ | ☐ Pages Missing |
| | | | ☐ Confidential |

TITLE:_____ ☐

    Name                Organization

TO:_____

_____

_____ ☐

FROM:_____

_____

_____ ☐

**EXHIBIT 8.3**

## Document Coding Sheet (continued)

CC:_____

PERSONS/DEALERS/COMPANIES
MENTIONED:_____

DOCUMENTS
REFERENCED:_____

EVENTS
REFERENCED:_____

CONTENT:_____

CROSS REFERENCES:_____

## C. Preparing Documents for Review by Opposing Party[3]

In order to avoid confusion, a record needs to be made concerning which documents are going to be produced with respect to each document request. There are different methods of approaching this task. One method involves reviewing all the documents to determine whether a document falls within the category of a requested item. If the document does fall within a requested category, it should be noted on a master file and separated into an itemized

---

[3]The materials in this section are adapted from materials prepared by Mary Dickerson for the Paralegal institute.

compilation of documents listed under a specific document request number. If it does not fall within a requested category, it should be separated from the documents that are to be produced and noted on a master document file.

Another method of approaching this task is to rely on the index files made from coding the files. The advantage of this method is that it saves time by alleviating the necessity of reviewing each document a subsequent time. The disadvantage is that the paralegal must rely solely on the accuracy of the document coding. A suggestion would be to review those items to be produced in order to ensure accuracy.

If a response to a specific request contains several documents, one method of memorializing the review process would be to produce a record such as that shown in Exhibit 8.4 below.

The attorney would review both the document request and the proposed response before any document is actually produced. The attorney would also review whether possible objections to the production of certain documents exist, such as privilege, and whether the documents are responsive to the request. Again, a record needs to be made indicating whether a document is objectionable, the basis of the objection, and whether it is not subject to production. See Exhibit 8.5 for an example.

Based on these compilations, the litigation team will have records of all the documents received from the client, those documents which have been produced for inspection, and those documents that have not been produced and the reasons therefore. As a reminder, those documents that are not going to be produced for inspection should be kept in a separate area from the documents to be inspected. This prevents the accidental revelation of documents that are not subject to inspection.

Sometimes a document may contain information that is partially objectionable. If the document is to be produced, care should be taken to hide or "mask" the portion of the document that is objectionable. Typically, if a copy of the document is to be produced, or if the original is altered to mask a portion, it must be noted as such.

During the actual inspection process, the paralegal may have the task of monitoring the inspection. The paralegal should be careful that only the agreed

---

**EXHIBIT 8.4**

## Record of Review: Compilation of Documents to Be Produced Pursuant to a Document Request

Request Number 10 — All Documents
Pertaining to Engineer's Reports on Testing Metal Integrety of Widget

1–15
27
35–50
73–75

**EXHIBIT 8.5**

## Document Review—
## Listing of Documents Not Produced

| Doc. No. | Source | Location | Reason for Nonproduction |
|---|---|---|---|
|  |  |  |  |

upon documents are inspected by the reviewers, that no documents are either altered or removed from the inspection area without authorization, and that a record is made of all documents that are photocopied.

## III. COMPUTER-ASSISTED DOCUMENT CONTROL AND RETRIEVAL

The computer technology explosion of the last twenty years has produced phenomenal advancement in the use of computers in document control and retrieval (litigation support systems). Although almost every large firm in the country has its own in-house computer to perform word processing and administrative functions such as billing and work in progress, the use of computers in litigation support is still growing; however it is the wave of the future. Improvements in the cost structure of such systems coupled with the benefits this support system brings to the management of a complex case means that paralegals will soon be seeing and using this type of document control, analysis, and retrieval system in the litigation of both complex cases and not-so-complex cases.

Because computer technology is subject to such rapid advancement and change, it is far beyond the scope of this book to evaluate the various programming techniques available in the area of litigation support. However, it is appropriate to discuss in general terms the advantages of computer-assisted litigation support, the factors used to determine when it is appropriate, and the factors that determine what type of system to use.

### A. Advantages of Computer-Assisted Litigation Support

Visualize the computer as merely an electronic set of the card index files discussed above. Instead of attorneys and paralegals having to physically sort those cards to discover a particular document or documents, the computer performs the search electronically and advises the searcher of the results. This offers the following advantages:

- Accuracy. The machine will be unerringly accurate in its search. If the information exists in the database and the proper search has been initiated, the desired result will be achieved.

- Thoroughness. The computer will do completely that which it is instructed to do. All data will be searched and nothing can be inadvertently (or intentionally) overlooked.

- Speed. The computer will perform its operation at a speed thousands of times faster than an individual can.

- Cost effectiveness. The computer may well be a cheaper (as well as faster) way to obtain information. In some cases, the computer may be the only feasible way to store and retrieve information.

- Access. The computer may provide a convenient means of access to the stored information from more than one computer terminal either in the same office or in different offices in distant cities.

- Additional information. The computer may be able to compile new information, charts, and statistics based on an analysis of the stored documents and programmed information.

## B. Determining the Appropriateness of a Computer-Assisted Litigation Support System

When is it appropriate to use computer-assisted litigation support? There is no simple answer. All the factors considered at the commencement of the litigation are again relevant to this determination, including the following:

- Number of documents. There is no cutoff point. Computer vendors suggest that computer-assisted litigation support is called for when the relevant documents exceed 5,000, and that such support may be appropriate for as few as 1,000 relevant documents if you already own a computer.

- Type of documents. Is the information readily converted to computer input and storage, or are there large numbers of blueprints or drawings? Similarly, if there will be computer-stored evidence produced in discovery, use of a computer will facilitate the employment of that evidence in your case preparation.

- Anticipated discovery schedule. A heavy deposition schedule over an extended period with large numbers of documents virtually mandates the use of computer-assisted litigation support because there will not be sufficient time to gather necessary materials for deposition preparation through a manual retrieval system. However, a light deposition schedule, even where there are large numbers of documents, may well permit use of a manual system.

- The litigation team. What are the feelings of the attorneys and paralegals on the case towards computer-assisted litigation support? Do they work in such a manner to facilitate this use, or would it be inconsistent with their working style? A computerized support system requires both detailed planning and active supervision by the attorneys and paralegals. If they are unable or unwilling to do both, the system probably won't be worth the money that will be spent on it.

♦ Geographical aspects of case. If attorneys or paralegals from several different locations (intrafirm or other firms or client) are involved, computer access is easily administered. Physical files would have to be duplicated for each location or at least multiple indices distributed for a manual system approach in these circumstances.

♦ Complexity of litigation. This refers to the complexity of the issues of the case, the amount in controversy, the importance of the case, and the perceived chances (or desire) for settlement.

## C. Deciding What Type of System to Use

Assuming that your firm has determined to employ some form of computer-assisted litigation support, you must make several decisions before a program can be activated. Specifically, you must determine the sophistication of the system (off-line or on-line), the source of the computer system (firm, client, or vendor), and the knowledge of the user.

### 1. Off-line vs. On-line Systems

The distinction between off-line and on-line (or shared-logic) systems is that with the off-line system limited information from the document can be captured, and that information is then entered on a small disk that can be sorted various ways to produce the various indices applicable to the information. The disk is thereafter removed from the machine so that the machine is free to perform other functions. If you want to use the machine, you must remove its present disk and insert the program disk before adding to it. This type of assistance is usually limited to the sorting and preparation of lists, for example, authors alphabetically arranged, recipients alphabetically arranged, subjects alphabetically arranged, and chronological arrangements.

This computer-generated off-line system is really a more accurate, more complete, more easily reorganized, and more reliable equivalent to the manual card index files. The benefit of this system is that most law firms have a computer that can perform these limited functions so it can be justified for as few as 500 to 1,000 relevant documents.

The on-line system, on the other hand, permits more information from the document to be captured (up to enriched full text) and more manipulations of the captured information. The information is stored on-line, that is, the user has instant access to the information through a computer terminal. Here the computer performs the visual inspections of lists that the user would otherwise examine if using a manual or off-line computer system and the computer provides the answer to the user.

For large, complex litigation, only the on-line system offers a feasible solution for the computer-assisted organization of your documents.

### 2. Designing the System

Because the computer-assisted litigation support system is only as good as its design and management, it is important that the litigation team seek outside expertise unless this expertise is available within the firm or through the client. Although the assistance of a vendor can add appreciably to the cost of the system, there is no alternative when you want a cost-effective system and you lack any other source of expertise.

The most important part of the program is its design. This is determined by the litigation team, specifically the case attorneys. This decision cannot be delegated to outside experts or even to the legal assistants familiar with the system. However, the value of outside or in-house experts (and legal assistants will be looked to for such in-house expertise) is in suggesting the myriad issues that must be considered in the design of the system. The type of documents that you will be dealing with and what you want to be able to do with those documents will control the system that is designed for your case. How do you intend to handle deposition transcripts? How will the system accommodate documents used as deposition exhibits? How should the system be designed to facilitate trial preparation? How can the system be used at the time of trial? All these issues must be addressed and resolved in the design.

The system designer must determine what information about the document should be entered into the computer and whether that information should be loaded in coded form or in full text. The designer must also decide whether to include (and at what time) an abstract or summary of the document prepared by an attorney or legal assistant.

*a. Full-Text Input.* Significant disadvantages of full-text input are the storage costs within the system for enhanced amounts of information (as opposed to a coded document) and the possible loss of any work-product protection of the system from discovery by your adversaries. Full-text coding requires no early analysis of documents in terms of the case outline.

*b. Coded Input.* The disadvantage of the coded input approach is the amount of time and training required at the beginning of the system's implementation. Documents to be coded must be carefully reviewed by personnel trained in the facts and issues of the case. This has the benefit, however, of forcing some initial discipline into the case preparation and further results in a work-product system that is likely to be protected from discovery.

*c. Abstracts or Summaries.* Whatever coding system is used, you will often want to include abstracts or summaries of the most critical documents. This need is best accommodated by including within the program a mechanism for "enriching" the text of the document later in the case with such information. Remember, it is rare that you will be able to identify your important documents at the start of the case.

### 3. Determining What Information Should Be Coded and Who Will Perform the Coding

The coding operation is the heart, and bottleneck, of the operation. This is the time-consuming, often boring, yet significant part of the operation. It is critical that the coding be done accurately by well-trained personnel, and with quality control checks in the system.

Although the specific information to be coded is determined in your design of the system, that information is generally some or all of the following items:

- document number
- document date
- document author
- document recipients
- type of document
- source of document
- key words from document text (dates, locations, persons or places mentioned)
- subject codes from your case outline
- importance of document
- deposition exhibit
- coder
- when coded
- document privileged or confidential
- document produced in discovery

There are two series of coding steps, which are (or can be) performed by different people. Administrative staff (document clerks or secretaries) can code the bibliographic and source data. This is known as objective coding. Coding by case outline and by importance of the document is performed by legal assistants (and perhaps attorneys) or vendor technical staff. This is known as subjective coding. One or a combination of the following sources of coders can be used:

**1.** The law firm can do the coding if it has sufficient internal capacity for the task. Particularly for the subjective coding, it is desirable for educational purposes to have people who are assigned to the case perform this task.

**2.** The client can dc the coding, although this is usually practical only if the client is a major corporation. The benefit here is that the client will be familiar with the area of litigation and will not require extensive training before coding.

**3.** Vendor support is an alternative if in-house and client assets are insufficient for the coding task. Though it increases the cost of the operation, this option may be attractive precisely because it does not tie up large numbers of firm or client people for extended times.

### 4. Data Entry, Storage, and Update

Once the coding operation is complete, the information must be converted into machine-readable form by keying the information into the computer, which will store the information in its main file and also store key words in its electronic card index. Information can then be added to the individual document record, or more documents can be added.

### 5. Choosing a Computer System

You generally have three choices when deciding whose computer system to use: the client's, the law firm's, or a vendor's.

*a. Client.*    This is likely the least expensive alternative, assuming there is spare capacity. Several questions must be answered. Does the client have a litigation support software package, or is there one available in the market for the client's computer? What is the experience of the client's computer staff with litigation support programs?

Two important issues for which satisfactory answers must be obtained in advance are the availability of time for and the priority of your program in the client's system. Be sure that your use is not restricted to certain inconvenient hours and that you will be able to use the system when you may need it most, as for example in deposition preparation.

*b. Law Firm.*    Not too many firms have computer capacity sufficient for this purpose, but if yours does, this can be the best arrangement for you and the client. The expense will be less than for a vendor-supplied operation, and there should be no problem with either priority or availability.

*c. Vendor.*    Vendors are in the business of providing this service, so they have the organization, people, software, and computers to provide you support. You will pay for that assistance, but with the increase of vendors providing these services, competitive shopping can be very advantageous. Experienced vendors are also in a position to get your system operative in the quickest time.

## IV. Digests of Oral Depositions

When a person's deposition is taken it is recorded and transcribed in typewritten form and is then available for review by counsel. Transcripts of depositions are brought to the trial to be used for one or more of the following three purposes:

**1.** To attack the credibility of a witness whose answers at trial differ from the answers during an oral deposition.

**2.** To introduce into evidence the content of the deposition where the deponent cannot be called as a live witness at trial because of death, being more than 100 miles from the place of trial, illness, or advanced age.[4]

**3.** To establish facts affirmatively through the use of all or a portion of the deposition of an adverse party.

As part of the ongoing case evaluation and preparation processes, the paralegal is often confronted with the problem of what is to be done with the information gained in depositions. After receiving the deposition transcript, the paralegal must integrate this information into a discovery support system (either manual or computer-assisted).

---

[4]FRCP 32(a)(3).

Oral deposition testimony is made manageable by digesting it, that is, by selecting only the testimony relevant to the claims and defenses advanced by the parties in the pending litigation and putting it into concise, shorthand form. The digest may be reviewed quickly both in preparing for trial and also at the trial itself to aid the attorney in examining a witness.

In order to digest an oral deposition, it is of critical importance that the paralegal preparing the digest understand the legal theories underlying the claims and defenses and the kind of factual evidence used to prove or disprove such claims and defenses. It is also helpful to be familiar with the strengths and weaknesses of the testimony of prospective witnesses for all the parties. With such understandings the paralegal will be able to evaluate the information.

After determining which form of digest to use (forms are provided later in this chapter) the paralegal must integrate the digest and/or the actual deposition into the discovery support system. If the paralegal is using a manual system, he or she must number, code, index, and store the digests, summaries, and the deposition itself so that this valuable information can be retrieved. In a computer-assisted program that has the capability of full-text input, the deposition is captured in machine-readable form by the deposition reporter. This process, known as computer-aided transcription (CAT), permits prompt loading of deposition information that can be processed for use either in preparing for additional depositions or at trial. This kind of programming facilitates the preparation of outlines of witness testimony and is invaluable for witness impeachment purposes based on prior inconsistent statements and testimony.

Although the following discussion focuses on depositions, much of this information is equally applicable to preparing digests for answers to interrogatories, documents, medical examinations, and answers to requests for admission.

## A. Digests by Deponents

A **digest by deponent** is a digest of the oral deposition of a particular person that simply sets forth by page number of the transcript of the deposition the relevant testimony of such person. This is the most important type of digest since it serves as the synopsis of the entire deposition. The deponent digests of witnesses will normally be used to prepare the other types of digests. They are usually prepared immediately after the transcripts of depositions are received from the court reporter. The idea behind deponent digests is to make it easy for someone reviewing the case to have quick access to what a witness has testified without having to read the entire deposition.

Typically, a deponent digest eliminates very little of what a witness has said but transcribes the questions and answers of the deposition into short statements. Full sentences are not used. Thus, for example, the following excerpt from a deposition

> Question: In which direction was your car headed immediately prior to the collision?
> Answer: I believe my car was going north just before the accident.

might be condensed in a digest as follows: "page 8: Headed north prior to collision."

The use of page numbers allows the person reviewing the digest to ascertain the full statement made by the witness. If a deponent's testimony was repetitive, all page numbers where the same statement was made will be indicated. At trial, when a deposition is referred to, the examining attorney will have to point out the exact question and answer, and perhaps read them, in order to properly present any contradiction by the witness or to refresh the memory of the witness.

Normally, the only things omitted from the deponent digest are discussions between attorneys that do not bear on the propriety of questions. Thus, if counsel discuss the fact that notice of the deposition may or may not have been given properly, this would not appear in the digest. It simply has nothing to do with the witness's testimony. Frequently, to avoid paying large bills for court reporters, counsel will have such nonessential discussions "off the record." That is, the reporter is directed not to record such conversations and will not do so as long as all attorneys agree.

## B. Digests by Subject Matter

In those cases in which several depositions have been taken and many exhibits have been referred to in the depositions, it may be useful to create a digest of all deposition testimony dealing with a particular subject matter or a particular exhibit. For example, in a motor vehicle collision case, different witnesses will probably tell the story of how the collision occurred in varying manners. By grouping together what each witness has said at a deposition on certain important topics, the conflicts become obvious. This type of digesting then serves as a ready tool in preparing for trial. It shows the attorney what to expect in testimony from the several witnesses at trial.

**Subject matter digests** should include a table of contents divided into the relevant issues in the case. It is helpful to use index cards for the various statements of the several witnesses. These may be arranged by subject matter. Always indicate which witness made the statement you are using in the digest.

Frequently, subject matter digests are prepared from the several deponent digests. In relatively short depositions, however, it may be just as easy to prepare the subject matter digest directly.

Exhibit 8.6 provides an example of a subject matter digest based on three depositions of people involved in an automobile accident. For brevity's sake, their depositions are not provided. However, as background, Samuel Hall and Phyllis Hall are the plaintiffs in this tort suit for personal injuries and property damage. Richard Jumble is the driver of the other vehicle in the accident and there is a question of whether Jumble was on company business when he was involved in the accident. The defendant in the case is Jumble's employer, Aimes Electric Company. This example is given to provide a visual model of what a subject matter digest consists of.

## C. Chronological Digests

In some cases, a lawyer will prefer to have the depositions of one or more deponents digested in such a manner as to create a **chronological** history of the relevant events. To do this, the digester must first prepare deponent digests and then arrange and integrate the entries in all the deponent digests in chronological order. This is a relatively simple undertaking when you have the deponent digests to work with.

**EXHIBIT 8.6**

# Subject Matter Digest

[Caption]

TABLE OF CONTENTS

**EXHIBIT 8.6**

# Subject Matter Digest (continued)

### 1. PERSONAL HISTORY

Page

*Samuel Hall*

| | |
|---|---|
| 2 | Born: May 28, 1938; Aimes |
| 2 | Schooling: went through the Aimes Public School system up to 11th grade at South Aimes High School. Left school 1955 |
| 2 | Service: joined in 1955 |
| 2 | Wife: Phyllis Hall |
| 2 | Type of marriage—common law |
| 2 | Children: Kenneth— 10 years |
| |         Phyllis— 7 years |
| |         Pamela— 6 years |
| 2 | Occupation: Service Manager at Flit Brothers |
| |         State Inspector of Cars at Flits |
| 2 | Employer: Flit Brothers |
| |         total length of time with Flit: 11 years |
| |         length of time at the store: 5 years |
| |         store: 69th and Walnut |
| 2 | Immediate Supervisor: Mr. Staley, Store Manager |
| | Home Address: |
| 1 |         former: 3219 Winter Street |
| 1 |         length: 3 or 4 years |
| 1 |         present: 5359 Hazel Street, Wynfield |
| 1 |         length: 3 years |

*Phyllis Hall*

| | |
|---|---|
| 10 | Employer: Mulehouse Packaging Co. |
| 10 | Occupation: meat packer |
| 10 | Out of work due to accident: about 3 months |
| 10 | Salary at that period: $113.60 |
| 10 | Laid off work due to lack of work: April 6 |
| 10 | Salary at that time: $127.60 |

*Richard David Jumble*

| | |
|---|---|
| 1 | Age: 27 years |
| 1-2 | Married: yes, and is living with his wife |
| 1 | Address: 422K Knowles Avenue |
| 2 | Occupation: he is a draftsman, and works in the field |
| 2 | Employer: Aimes Electric Co. |
| 6 | Length of employment: 6 years, and is still employed |
| 6 | Does not wear glasses |

(NOTE that there was only one volume for the depositions of Mr. and Mrs. Hall, thus page numbers for Mrs. Hall do not begin with the number 1.)

EXHIBIT 8.6

# Subject Matter Digest (continued)

### 2. ACCIDENT

|   |     |                          |
|---|-----|--------------------------|
|   | A.  | *Year*                   |
| 2 | SH: | November 21, 1992        |
| 2 | J:  | Saturday, Nov. 21, 1992  |
|   | B.  | *Time*                   |
| 2 | SH: | 10:00 o'clock            |
|   | C.  | *Vehicle*                |

*1. owner*
- 2    SH: Samuel Hall
- 2    J: Aimes Electric Co.

*2. type*
- 2    SH: 1985 Chevrolet Caprice
- 2    J: 1989 Ford Escort

*3. condition prior to accident*
- 8    SH: car was in good shape, there was no problem with the brakes or tires. It had a state inspection sticker that Hall had put on himself.

|   |     |                              |
|---|-----|------------------------------|
|   | D.  | *Weather*                    |
| 8 | SH: | "nice, dry"                  |
| 5 | J:  | "Ideal, clear dry day"       |
|   | E.  | *Passengers*                 |
| 3 | SH: | Had only his wife with him   |
| 9 | PH: | she was in the right front seat |
|   | F.  | *Road Conditions*            |
| 8 | SH: | the road was pretty level    |
|   | G.  | *Driving Stipulations*       |
| 5 | J:  | the car was driven strictly on company time and he does not know where it was parked |
|   | H.  | *Purpose of Trip*            |
| 3 | SH: | was coming home, which was 8 or 10 miles from accident. |

He was on his way to a funeral at 20th and Oak at the Chaw Funeral Home

He had to be there at 10:30, when they were leaving for the cemetery.

The funeral was for his first cousin, John Chaplin

The funeral parlor was about 7 or 8 blocks from the intersection of Dupont and Oak St.

EXHIBIT 8.6

## Subject Matter Digest (continued)

| | | |
|---|---|---|
| 2 | J: | had just come from a job at 12th and Pine, Aimes |
| | | He was on company business |
| | | He was going out covering a construction and was going into the office |
| | | Office is located at intersection of Oak and Dupont where the accident occurred |
| | I. | *Traffic Conditions* |
| 3 | SH: | "pretty fair" |
| 3 | J: | remembers no cars in front of him on Oak Street going west, nor on Dupont Ave. going north. The only car on Dupont coming south was the plaintiff |
| | J. | *Street Patterns and Parking* |
| 3 | SH: | Dupont is about 40 feet wide and is two way |
| | | Traffic goes north and south, one lane each |
| | | There is parking on both sides, but doesn't know if it is permitted or not |
| | | On the morning of the accident, there were cars parked on both sides of the street |
| 2 | J: | Oak and Dupont intersection is approx. an 80 or 85 degree angle street |
| | | Oak goes east and west and does not cross Dupont. Oak and Dupont intersect, and Dupont runs north and south. It is an "L" intersection |
| | | The intersection is about 40 feet wide |
| | | There are two driving lanes on Dupont, one each way |
| | | There is parking on both sides |
| | | On the morning of the accident, there were cars solidly parked on both sides |
| | K. | *Occurrence of Accident* |
| | | 1. *Proceeding* |
| 3-4 | SH: | was in right hand lane proceeding down Dupont Ave., next to curb. There was a distance between the right side of car and edge of parked cars of about 2 or 3 feet. |
| | | The distance between left side of car and center of road was about 2 or 3 feet. |
| | | He came off Slip Street and around onto Dupont |
| | | There are about 6 blocks from Slip to Oak |
| | | He does not recall what street is north of Oak on Dupont |
| | | There are no lights on Dupont and it is straight through |
| | | He was going about 30 mph as he went south on Dupont |

EXHIBIT 8.6
## Subject Matter Digest (continued)

| | | |
|---|---|---|
| 3 | J: | was proceeding west on Oak St. |
| | | He made a righthand turn north on Dupont at intersection into the northbound lane |
| | | The entrance to the company yard is about 200 or 250 feet north of Oak St. |
| | | *2. Descriptions of how it happened* |
| 4 | SH: | was coming down Dupont. There were oncoming cars passing him |
| | | Suddenly he saw a car beginning to make a turn, when the plaintiff was about 25 feet from him |
| | | The car was coming on the other lane facing plaintiff |
| | | The car started to make a turn to get into the parking area on the plaintiff's side of street |
| | | Car cut in front of plaintiff and turned into him |
| | | When car turned it crossed the center line of st. into plaintiff's lane |
| | | At that point the plaintiff was about 25 feet away |
| | | Plaintiff did not see car stop in northbound lane before it made its left turn. |
| | | Plaintiff had been traveling at a distance 2 or 3 feet from center line, and continued straight so impact of car was about in the same position |
| | | After impact, car went another 2 or 3 feet and turned toward parking area at right |
| | | When plaintiff's car came to rest, it was still in southbound lane. |
| | | Jumble's car was still straddling center line. |
| 9 | PH: | does not really remember what happened in accident, except seeing other car turning to lot across their lane. Does not know how far it got, where their car was, or where Aimes Electric Co. was at that point. |
| 3-4,6 | J: | was proceeding north on Dupont |
| | | he had signal on to make left turn into company yard |
| | | he was in front of entrance when he noticed an oncoming car, which was about 100 feet away |
| | | He saw the Hall car 3 or 4 blocks up Dupont |
| | | From that point he moved about 200 or 250 feet north and the Hall car was coming in his direction about 50 mph |
| | | The Hall car did not seem to change its speed before it was 100 feet away from him. |

EXHIBIT 8.6

## Subject Matter Digest (continued)

The car was going in a straight line until he applied his brakes about 100 feet from Jumble

there were no other cars going either north or south

After noticing the oncoming car for the first time as it was about 100 feet away, Jumble stopped to allow it to go past.

The intersection is dangerous as the entrance to lot is only about 10 feet wide.

At about 30/40 feet the other driver tried to correct the skid that began about 60 feet, but the car continued to come directly at J.

J. started to put the car in reverse, realized it was a foolish effort, and put brake on

J's car was stopped 15 or 30 seconds from time he saw other car to time he tried to put it in reverse.

Car was stopped at point of impact

Car was stopped facing directly north with wheels cut west in anticipation of making turn

Car was in his own lane on east of midline, about 1 foot

Car did not turn its wheels any time before accident

Car traveled about 2 or 3 feet south from time he stopped to time of accident while in reverse

Car moved about 2 or 3 feet as a result of impact

Hall car was traveling about 50 mph before; at time of accident, it was traveling about 20 mph

3. *Signals*

| | | |
|---|---|---|
| 4 | SH: | Jumble did not have his signals on |
| 3 | J: | Had signal on to make right turn on Oak and put it on to make left turn into company yard. |

4. *Seatbelts*

| | | |
|---|---|---|
| 9 | PH: | she was not wearing one, and didn't think her husband was either |

5. *Effort to avoid accident*

| | | |
|---|---|---|
| 5 | SH: | applied his brake before impact |
| 3 | J: | tried to put car in reverse |

6. *Speed at impact*

| | | |
|---|---|---|
| 5 | SH: | was running 30 when he hit; probably dropped to 20 with brakes |
| 3 | J: | was stopped at time of impact; had put it in reverse but was no longer moving. |

EXHIBIT 8.6

## Subject Matter Digest (continued)

| | | |
|---|---|---|
| | | 7. *Point of impact* |
| 5 | SH: | point of impact was in southbound lane about 2 feet from center. |
| | | his car hit on the left front fender, center part of hood, bumper, and radiator. Jumble's car hit on the right, right fender across the whole front. |
| 4 | J: | said the car was in his lane east of the midline. the exact front of his car and Hall's hit |
| | | 8. *Skidmarks* |
| 6 | SH: | did not look for any marks |
| | | did not notice any marks when he went back for the car |
| 6 | J: | there were skidmarks |
| | | approximately 68 feet in length |
| | | 30 feet of them were in a straight southerly direction. |
| | | About 30 feet from the beginning of the skidmark they began to come in his direction, southeast. |
| 6-7 | J: | Marks were measured by Jumble about 10:30 AM after accident |
| | | He used a linen cloth tape, 100' tape |
| | | There was no one else from the Elec. Com. with him |
| | | He pointed out skidmarks to police |
| | | Marks ended 4 feet in northbound lane—his lane |
| | | He knew they were Hall's marks because: there were no other marks in area and these came from point he saw car beginning to skid straight to point of impact. |
| | | 9. *Actions of plaintiff and defendant* |
| 6 | SH: | Had no conversation with Mr. Jumble. |
| | | Did not discuss accident with police in front of Jumble |
| 5 | J: | Had no conversation with the Halls |
| | L | *Police* |
| 6 | SH: | They arrived about 15 minutes after accident and the cars had not been moved |
| | | He described what had happened and told them the same thing he is telling in deposition. |
| 5 | J: | Police arrived but he made no statements to police |
| | | He just gave them the license and owner's card |
| | | He pointed out skidmarks to police |
| | M. | *Witnesses* |
| 6 | SH: | none other than his wife and no one bothered to come on the scene other than to look |
| 5 | J: | does not know of any other witness than himself and Halls. |

EXHIBIT 8.6
# Subject Matter Digest (continued)

| 5 | J: | Thompkins is the shop foreman for maintenance, he did not see the accident but was somewhere behind a wall and came out at the sound of the screeching<br>He was on the scene before they were out of their cars. |
|---|---|---|
| | N. | *Cars* |
| 7 | SH: | checked damage sometime soon after accident while cars were in same position.<br>The car could not be driven right away but a couple of fellows bent his fender out from the wheel and someone pushed him in back across the street to the east side of Dupont.<br>He returned later about 5:00 that evening.<br>Car has not been repaired other than pulling fender and sticking steel wool in radiator to stop water from leaking<br>Radiator was running hot. He just drives the car himself. |
| 5 | J: | has not been driving car since accident |
| | O. | *Injuries* |
| 9 | SH: | hurt his back but received no medication and it healed in month |
| 9 | PH: | hurt her head when it hit the windshield visor. Hit her knee, jarred her foot. Had lower back pain, neck and top of shoulder pain, and bruised her head.<br>Was out of work for 3 months. |
| 10-11 | | Went in to work once on Dec. 29 and became dizzy and had headaches and was sent home by her supervisor, Joe Wold.<br>The last time she received medical treatment was Feb. 15, 1992<br>At that time she was discharged by her doctor, Dr. Sulman<br>She is not fully recovered but still has headaches and her foot swells about two or three times weekly. This usually happens when she drives or because of a certain type of shoes.<br>She takes medication for her headaches—Anacin and Darvon.<br>She has no prescription.<br>She is now laid off from work for lack of work |
| | P. | *Claim* |
| 7,8,9 | SH: | property damage = an estimate from Scottie's Garage for total of $4,660.40, dated Dec. 10, 1992.<br>Estimate was on the car. Claim is for $15,000.00<br>Includes a claim for pain and suffering, but not for lost time for Mr. Hall. |

# 260 Chapter 8

## D. Special-Use Digests or Indices

It may be necessary to use more than one type of deposition digest in a case. It may also be necessary to develop special-purpose indices. The type of index is limited only by the imagination of the attorney and paralegal. For example, a digest may be prepared for cross-examination of a particular witness by developing questions for cross-examination and expected answers from an analysis of the depositions. Such a digest would not be by subject matter or chronological; instead it would be designed to impeach the witness. Similarly, an index may be developed for cross-examining more than one witness in order to point out conflicts between the testimony of the several witnesses.

## V. SUMMARY

This chapter focuses on the issue of organizing the material gathered during the case preparation process. A discovery support system is designed to organize the documents and other information gathered during discovery to aid in the preparation of a case for trial. If information cannot be easily found, it will inhibit the trial preparation process. Critical to any organizing system are the concepts of document labeling and analysis, document storage and retrieval, and document production. These systems can be either manual or computer-assisted.

One of the tasks commonly performed by a litigation paralegal is the task of digesting discovery materials. These digests can be organized by the name of a deposition witness or party, by subject matter, or by chronology. Deponent digests highlight the relevant testimony of the person being deposed. Subject matter digests involve reviewing all depositions with a certain subject matter in mind and comparing each deponent's testimony with respect to the subject matter. Chronological digests are used to create a chronological history of relevant events.

## VI. KEY TERMS

Discovery support system
Documental control and retrieval

Document coding
Deponent digest

Subject matter digest
Chronological digest

## VII. QUESTIONS

1. What is meant by a digest of an oral deposition, and what are the most common forms of digests?
2. Name and explain the two most common methods used to organize document information.
3. What are the goals of a numbering system used in document control?
4. What is the difference between an off-line and on-line computer system?

# CHAPTER 9

# PREPARATION FOR TRIAL

## I. INTRODUCTION

While chapter 8 covers part of the process of preparing for trial, this chapter focuses on those procedures and devices commonly used to get a lawsuit ready for trial once the discovery process has been completed. We will examine the process by which an attorney and paralegal begin to select information and documents for presentation at the trial.

Up to this point in the book, much of the information concerns the process of gathering information. Now the focus will shift to a process of selecting information from all the data amassed as part of the case preparation process and to a process of organizing the selected information into a form that is useful during a trial. Once again, the paralegal plays an important role in this process. Typically a paralegal will organize trial exhibits, help prepare a trial notebook, help prepare a final pretrial order, organize and meet with witnesses, subpoena witnesses, and prepare jury instructions.

## II. THE PROCESS OF ORGANIZING FOR TRIAL

### A. Final Review before Trial

Before beginning the process of assembling information needed for trial, it is important to make sure that the attorney and paralegal have all the information necessary to successfully litigate their case. This process ensures that they have enough information or facts to establish the elements of their claim or defense.

First, they should organize the information into essential elements (facts) and how they intend to prove each element (source). The elements of the case should be taken from the pleadings or from the proposed jury instructions concerning the issues in the case. (More information on jury instructions will be provided later in this chapter and also in chapter 10.) This process is sometimes referred to as preparing a **proof chart.** It can be organized in the following fashion:

| essential facts | method or source of proof |
|---|---|
|  |  |

This process ensures that the litigation can establish a claim or defense sufficient to allow a jury to decide the case (also referred to as establishing a **prima facie** case). If there are any major gaps, you may have to do further discovery to establish these missing facts or you risk that upon motion of the opposing counsel at trial and the end of the presentation of your case the judge will decide that the case should not be decided by a jury but rather should be dismissed for insufficient evidence. These motions are commonly referred to as motions to dismiss, motion for involuntary nonsuit, or motion for directed verdict and are discussed in more detail in chapter 10.

Once this proof chart process is complete the litigation team should concentrate on the order of presentation of the case. This process encompasses a thoughtful analysis of what witnesses will be called to testify, the sequencing or order of witnesses, exhibits to be introduced into evidence at the trial, and what witnesses will be necessary to introduce each exhibit into evidence (commonly referred to as "laying a foundation" for each exhibit). Once each witness has been selected and sequenced, an outline of testimony for each witness should be prepared that encompasses the content of what each witness will present as testimony. The order or sequence of eliciting the detail of a witness's testimony should also be prepared. The order of calling witnesses to testify is very important. Some jurors are more likely to be influenced by what they have heard first and last, so it might be advisable for the litigation team to lead off and end with their strongest witnesses. Other jurors might be influenced by a presentation of witnesses that is based on chronological order. With respect to opposing witnesses who will be cross-examined at trial, a list of points to be made (including vulnerable points aimed to discredit the witness) should also be prepared. All prior statements and any inconsistencies should be digested from the discovery and included in the outline for cross-examination.

## B. Final Pretrial Order

Most federal district courts now require that all counsel enter into a **final pretrial order** after completion of discovery and prior to trial. The purpose of this order is to synthesize the issues and expected proof in a lawsuit into a simple blueprint for trial, making it easier for a judge to review the case just before trial at a pretrial conference. Local rules often require that opposing counsel meet and jointly prepare a single pretrial order or confer with each other about the contents of each attorney's own pretrial order. This has the effect of prompting settlement of cases, which is always encouraged by the courts.

Provided in Exhibit 9.1 is an excerpt of Rule 21 of the Local Rules of Civil Procedure of the U. S. District Court for the Eastern District of Pennsylvania—an example of a prescribed format for a pretrial order.

## C. Preparation of Exhibits

Documents and visual aids (photographs, charts, diagrams, models, and so on) must be organized prior to the trial if you intend to introduce them at the trial. These exhibits should be organized chronologically, based on the order in which they will be used at trial and according to what witness will be needed to either substantiate, authenticate, demonstrate, or explain the exhibit. Therefore, the paralegal should prepare two different kinds of charts with respect to exhibits: (1) a list of exhibits that includes a description of the exhibit and what witness will be used with the exhibit; and (2) a chart for each exhibit with a notation as to the identification number of the exhibit (for example, Plaintiff #1) and whether it was admitted into evidence or excluded. Another method commonly used is to combine both charts into a single master list as long as the above-designated categories are included.

## D. Methods of Organizing for Trial

Lawyers and paralegals commonly use two different methods to systematically organize for the actual trial—the **file folder method** and the **trial notebook** method.

EXHIBIT 9.1
# Pretrial Order

(d) Final Preparation for Trial.

1. Minimum requirements. In every case, counsel shall, before the commencement of trial:
   (a) Mark and exchange all exhibits to be offered in evidence during case in chief. Authenticity of all exhibits will be deemed established unless written objection is filed (either in a pretrial memorandum or by motion) at least five (5) days before trial.
   (b) Exchange lists of witnesses. No witness not listed may be called during case in chief. Requests during trial for offers of proof will not ordinarily be entertained with respect to listed witnesses; counsel are expected to clarify any uncertainties concerning the substance of proposed testimony in advance of trial, by conferring with opposing counsel.

2. Final Pretrial Order. If the case is unusually complex, or if the pretrial memoranda are inadequate, or if the judge determines that the circumstances of the litigation make it desirable to do so, the judge may require the parties to prepare and submit for approval a Final Pretrial Order. When a Final Pretrial Order is required, the following provisions shall apply:
   (a) Instructions for Preparation of Proposed Final Pretrial Order. The proposed pretrial order shall consist of one document signed by all counsel, reflecting the efforts of all counsel. It is the obligation of plaintiff's counsel to initiate the procedures for its preparation, and to assemble, and to submit the proposed pretrial order to the judge.

   Counsel may find it advantageous to prepare the proposed pretrial order jointly in one conference, or each attorney may prepare his section which will then be circulated with other counsel for review and approval. No explicit directions covering the mechanics of preparation are included in these instructions. However, after each counsel has submitted his respective proposed pretrial order suggestions to other counsel, all counsel *must* have a conference to attempt to reconcile any matters on which there is a disagreement. Counsel are expected to make a diligent effort to prepare a proposed pretrial order in which will be noted all of the issues on which the parties are in agreement and all of those issues on which they disagree. The proposed pretrial order shall be submitted by counsel for the plaintiff at chambers at least three days prior to the scheduled final pretrial conference, unless another date is specified by the judge.

   The proposed pretrial order, if accepted by the judge, will become a final pretrial order and shall govern the conduct of the trial and shall supersede all prior pleadings in the case. Amendments will be allowed only in exceptional circumstances to prevent manifest injustice.

   After the proposed pretrial order, the case will be considered ready for trial.

**EXHIBIT 9.1**

## Pretrial Order (continued)

(b) Form of Proposed Pretrial Order. The proposed pretrial order shall be in the following form:

(CAPTION)

(1) Jurisdiction. A statement as to the nature of the action and the basis on which the jurisdiction of the court is invoked.

(2) Facts. A comprehensive written stipulation of all uncontested facts in such form that it can be read to the jury as the first evidence at trial.

(A) These facts should include all matters capable of ascertainment, such as ownership, agency, dimensions, physical characteristics, weather conditions, road surfaces, etc. Approximations and estimates which are satisfactory to counsel will be accepted by the judge.

(B) No facts should be denied unless opposing counsel expects to present contrary evidence on the point at trial, or genuinely challenges the fact on credibility grounds.

(C) The facts relating to liability and to damages are to be separately stated.

(D) The parties shall reach agreement on uncontested facts even though relevancy is disputed; if such facts are ruled admissible, they need not be proved.

(E) The parties shall also set forth their respective statements as to the facts which are in dispute, separating those referring to liability from those referring to damages.

(3) Damages or Other Relief. A statement of damages claimed or relief sought.

(A) A party seeking damages shall list each item claimed under a separate descriptive heading (personal injury, wrongful death, survival, loss of profits, loss of wages, deprivation of civil rights, false imprisonment, libel, slander, property damage, pain, suffering, past and future medical expense, balance due under a contract, performance due under a contract, interest, etc.), shall provide a detailed description of each item, and state the amount of damages claimed.

(B) A party seeking relief other than damages shall list under separate paragraphs the exact form of relief sought with precise designations of the persons, parties, places, and things expected to be included in any order providing relief.

(4) Legal Issues. In separate paragraphs, each disputed legal issue that must be decided and the principal constitutional, statutory, regulatory, and decisional authorities relied upon.

EXHIBIT 9.1

## Pretrial Order (continued)

(5) Witnesses. Under separate headings, and under separate headings for liability and damages, the names and addresses of all witnesses whom the plaintiff, defendant, and third-parties actually intend to call at trial, during their respective case in chief.

(A) Witnesses shall be listed in the order they will be called. Each witness shall be identified and there shall be a brief statement of the evidence which the witness will give.

(B) A detailed summary of the qualifications of each expert witness shall be submitted. This summary shall be in such form that it can be read to the jury when the expert takes the stand to testify.

(C) Only those witnesses listed will be permitted to testify at trial, except to prevent manifest injustice.

(6) Exhibits. A schedule of all exhibits to be offered in evidence at trial, together with a statement of those agreed to be admissible and the grounds for objection to any not so agreed upon.

(A) The exhibits shall be serially numbered, and be physically marked before trial in accordance with the schedule.

(B) Where testimony is expected to be offered as to geographical location, building, structure, waterway, highway, road, walkway, or parcel of real estate, plaintiff shall furnish an exhibit in such form that it can be used in the courtroom as an aid to oral testimony.

  (i) Except in those cases where the issues require the use of exact scale, the exhibit may be a simple single-line hand-drawn sketch.

  (ii) In most instances, it will not be necessary that the exhibit be to scale or contain other than reasonably accurate features of the geographical characteristics involved.

  (iii) If of adequate size and clarity, this exhibit may be an existing drawing, plan or blueprint.

(C) Except for unusual circumstances, it is expected that the authenticity or genuineness of all exhibits, including nondocumentary items, documents, photographs and data from business records from sources other than parties to the litigation, will routinely be stipulated to and will be received in evidence if relevant. Counsel likewise are expected to agree upon the use of accurate extracts from or summaries of such records. Life expectancy tables, actuarial tables, and other similar statistical and tabular data routinely used in litigation in the Federal Courts should also normally be stipulated.

(D) At trial, counsel shall furnish a copy of each exhibit to the judge, if the judge so requests.

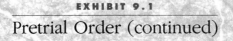

**EXHIBIT 9.1**

## Pretrial Order (continued)

(7) Legal Issues and Pleadings. Special comments regarding the legal issues or any amendments to the pleadings not otherwise set forth.

(8) Trial Time. An estimate of the number of trial days required, separately stated for liability and damages.

(9) Discovery Evidence and Trial Depositions. Each discovery item and trial deposition to be offered into evidence.

(A) Where the videotape or deposition of a witness is to be offered in evidence, counsel shall review it so that there can be eliminated irrelevancies, side comments, resolved objections, and other matters not necessary for consideration by the trier of fact. Counsel shall designate by page the specific portions of deposition testimony and by number of interrogatories which shall be offered in evidence at the trial.

(B) Depositions and interrogatories to be used for cross-examination or impeachment need not be listed or purged.

Source: Rule 21, Local Rules of Civil Procedure of the U.S. District Court for the Eastern District of Pennsylvania.

The file folder method is a very popular method of organizing for a trial. In chapter 4, it was noted that once a file is opened in a law office it is broken down into various subfiles. Those subfiles are correspondence, documents and reports, legal research, discovery, and a running narrative of contacts with clients, witnesses, and opposing counsel with applicable time records. The file folder method of preparation involves reorganizing those subfiles into the following new subfiles that can be used at trial:

* witnesses (including outlines of testimony)

* exhibits

* summaries/digests of discovery materials

* trial memorandum (a written memo outlining the legal authority for anticipated evidentiary issues that might arise during trial)

Although this method may be acceptable in relatively simple cases, it can become too cumbersome and sloppy at trial if the attorney has to search through the files to find a key outline, document, or case citation in the various subfiles.

The trial notebook method is becoming increasingly more popular because it is much easier to use in more complex litigation. A trial notebook's basic organization revolves around witnesses and trial procedure. Therefore its compilation requires a systematic analysis of the order of presenting witnesses and exhibits and the procedural steps involved in a civil jury (or nonjury) trial. The trial notebook is a three-ring binder usually divided into the following categories:

- pleadings
- voir dire questions for jury and jury selection chart
- opening statement
- witnesses
- exhibits
- closing statement
- jury instructions
- trial memorandum (brief)

A brief discussion follows on the information that is usually included in each of these categories. A more detailed discussion concerning jury selection, opening and closing statements, and submission of jury instructions is provided in chapter 10.

### 1. Pleadings

It is helpful to place a copy of all the pleadings in the trial notebook. In addition, the paralegal should prepare a set of **marked pleadings.**" This set of pleadings is usually based on the plaintiff's complaint or any counterclaims whereby a notation is marked in a column next to an allegation indicating whether the allegation is admitted, specifically denied, denied without knowledge, or admitted in part, denied in part. This may be helpful if the attorney needs to determine and/or show the trial judge exactly what issues are in dispute based on the pleadings.

### 2. Voir Dire Questions for Jury and a Jury Selection Chart

Since the first procedure in a jury trial is the process of selecting a jury, it is useful to have a section in the notebook that contains specific questions to be asked prospective jurors. In addition, sketching a seating chart to represent the jury box can be helpful in identifying and retaining the names of the individual jurors. It is helpful to note their names, ages, occupations, and any other information that may be useful (education, marital status, spouse's occupation, and so on).

### 3. Opening Statement

Although an opening statement should never be read to a jury, it can be helpful to have an outline that articulates the theme of the case and the major points to be covered.

### 4. Witnesses

The witness section of the notebook should include a list of the order of presenting witnesses. In addition, for each witness the notebook should list the following:

- addresses (home and work)
- phone numbers (home and work)
- notation of subpoena service
- an outline of direct examination and/or cross-examination
- exhibits to be introduced through the witness
- cross-references to discovery digests (deposition excerpts)
- anticipated evidentiary problems with legal authority

It is helpful to have copies of exhibits so they can be noted in more than one section of the trial notebook. For instance, an exhibit may be used in connection with several witnesses.

### 5. Exhibits

Include all the exhibits intended to be used in the trial and arrange them in chronological order, as explained in chapter 8.

### 6. Closing Statement

Like the opening statement, the closing statement should be outlined by the major points to be covered.

### 7. Jury Instructions

**Jury instructions** are given to the jury by the judge before the jury begins its deliberation of the case. These are the court's instructions as to the legal principles governing the case. Unless the instructions are routine and/or mandatory under state procedure, attorneys normally submit a set of proposed jury instructions to the judge either before trial, at the commencement of trial, or shortly after the testimony is closed (but prior to final summation) depending on local practice and procedure.[1]

There are form books that are very helpful in this area—for example, federal and state pattern jury instruction books. In addition, some states have adopted mandatory jury instructions, that is, the state courts must use certain instructions prepared and adopted by the state courts on various legal issues. Exhibit 9.2 is an example of a jury instruction from Missouri concerning an improper turn as evidence of negligence in an automobile accident.

---

[1]See FRCP 51.

**EXHIBIT 9.2**

## Sample Jury Instruction

17.17 [1978 Revision] Verdict Directing — Per se Negligence — Improper Turn

Your verdict must be for plaintiff if you believe:

First, defendant in approaching the intersection intending to turn left failed to drive his automobile in the portion of the right half of the roadway nearest the center line, and

Second, as a direct result of such conduct, plaintiff sustained damage.

*[unless you believe plaintiff is not entitled to recover by reason of Instruction Number _____ (here insert number of affirmative defense instruction)].

In the section of your notebook on jury instructions, include your requested instructions (one to a page). Once you receive your opponent's requested instructions insert them in this section too. If the court issues its own instructions, place them in this section also. At the bottom of your proposed jury instructions note whether your instructions were accepted, rejected, or modified.

### 8. Trial Memorandum

This section commonly includes both questions of law that may arise during the trial and the legal authority to support your position with respect to each anticipated issue. If a pretrial order has been submitted in the case, it too should be included in a separate section in the trial notebook.

In nonjury trials, it is common to submit requests for findings of fact and conclusions of law in lieu of jury instructions. Although they are not required under the federal rules, local court rules and various state court rules often require that counsel submit these requests at the start of the trial or shortly after the trial has been concluded. The requests should identify the parties, set forth the relevant facts in sufficient detail with references to exhibits where possible, and state conclusions of law that address the relevant legal issues. Both your requests and your opponent's requests should be included in a separate section of the trial notebook. Preparing these findings in advance can serve as a handy guide for the proof (evidence) the attorney needs to present at trial.

It should be obvious by now that the trial notebook is not only a useful tool for finding information and for reference during the actual trial but that the process of organizing it also ensures that preparation for trial will be accomplished in a systematic fashion.

## E. Preparation of Witnesses

In the final process of preparing for trial, the paralegal should contact all the witnesses the supervising attorney is planning to call to testify at the trial. Individual appointments should be arranged shortly before the trial, whenever possible, for the witness to meet with the attorney who is going to examine him or her during the trial. Prior to the meeting with this witness, the paralegal and attorney should discuss the major points that will be covered during the witness's testimony. Based on this discussion, the paralegal should prepare an outline of the examination of the witness. This outline should include all the points that the witness will be examined on and should be sequenced in a logical and/or chronological fashion.

If a witness has been deposed or has answered interrogatories, the paralegal should make sure that the witness has an opportunity to review these discovery documents prior to the witness interview/prep session. This will avoid the possibility of a failing memory and will save valuable time in preparing the witness.

Although the trial attorney will usually conduct the witness preparatory session, it is not uncommon for the paralegal to sit in on these sessions and take a participatory role. For most witnesses, the attorney will try to familiarize the witness with trial procedure. Then the attorney will go through a "mock" direct examination of the witness by asking questions in the same order that they will be asked at trial. After this rehearsal of direct examination, the attorney will usually explain the process of cross-examination and will role-play anticipated questions to be asked the witness by opposing counsel. In addition to this concept of role-playing direct and cross-examination, the attorney or paralegal may instruct the witness how to answer certain trick questions (truthfully, of course) and how to dress for trial. Never forget to explain to a witness where and when she or he is to appear in court.

For the expert witness who has some prior experience as a witness, an outline of direct examination is also prepared in advance to meeting with the witness. Relevant discovery documents and/or the witness's opinion letter should also be reviewed by the witness in advance of this preparatory session, if at all possible. The paralegal should make sure that the outline for direct examination includes information to qualify the witness as an expert as well as information to elicit the opinion of the expert. If the expert is going to use exhibits, models, diagrams, or charts, have these exhibits ready for the review session.

## F. Subpoena of Witnesses

In addition to arranging for witness preparatory sessions, preparing outlines for testimony, and participating in these preparatory sessions, the paralegal will be responsible for preparing subpoenas for witnesses and oftentimes for serving the subpoena on the witnesses.

It is considered good practice to subpoena all witnesses (willing and unwilling) whose testimony is important to the client's case at trial. Make sure each witness subpoenaed receives the appropriate witness fee and mileage, if applicable. It is better to take the precaution of issuing subpoenas than to be faced with the reality of starting a trial with a missing witness. If the witness is to bring certain records to the trial, make sure to note these records on the subpoena.

Once the subpoena has been prepared, it must be served. The task of providing for the service of subpoenas is often given to paralegals. Paralegals

will either serve the subpoenas themselves or make sure that an adult messenger or professional process-server serves the subpoena. In addition to making
the proper notation in the trial notebook reflecting that the witness has been
subpoenaed, the paralegal should make sure that an affidavit of service for the
subpoena is prepared and filed with the appropriate clerk of court's office. The
subpoena is often given to a friendly witness at the preparatory session.

## II. Summary

This chapter focuses on getting a lawsuit ready for trial once the discovery
process is complete. It is essentially a process of assembling the information
needed for trial.

As part of the final review before trial, the litigation team should prepare a
proof chart. This chart organizes information into essential elements (facts) and
method of proving elements (source). In addition, the litigators should determine the order in which they will present their case, and they should organize
their documents and visual aids.

Many courts require the litigation team to prepare and submit a final pretrial order. This provides the parties and the court with a blueprint for trial.

The litigation team must also organize for the actual trial. The two most
common organization methods are the file folder method and the trial notebook
method. Typically the information is organized around the following categories:
pleadings, jury selection, opening statement, witnesses, exhibits, closing statement, jury instructions, and trial memorandum.

The paralegal should contact all witnesses that the litigation team intends to
call to testify, and should issue and serve a subpoena to the witnesses.

## III. Key Terms

| | | |
|---|---|---|
| File folder | Marked pleadings | Proof chart |
| Final pretrial order | Prima facie | Trial notebook |
| Jury instructions | | |

## IV. Questions

1. What is a proof chart?
2. What is the purpose of a final pretrial order?
3. What are the two common methods used to organize for trial? What are the advantages and disadvantages of each method?
4. What is the purpose of a trial memorandum?
5. Why should a witness be subpoenaed to testify at trial?
6. What kinds of exhibit charts should a paralegal prepare in anticipation of trial?

# CHAPTER 10

# TRIAL

## I. INTRODUCTION

Throughout this book, the crescendo has been building to the ultimate goal: trial. Right? Absolutely not. The reality is that less than 25 percent of all the civil cases filed in this country ever reach the trial stage. Typically cases are settled either by compromise and voluntary dismissal, or by judgment prior to trial such as by default judgment, judgment on the pleadings, and summary judgments. (Settlements will be discussed in chapter 12.) However, because one never knows whether a particular lawsuit will be resolved without the necessity of trial, attorneys and paralegals should always prepare their cases as if there were going to be a trial.

The purpose of any trial is to determine the facts that are in dispute between the parties. If the facts were not disputed it would not be necessary to have a trial. Instead, lawyers would submit briefs pertaining to the legal points in dispute without the necessity of calling witnesses to testify. As discussed previously (see chapter 6 on pleadings) such situations do arise when only the law is at issue and no material facts are in dispute. In those situations, judicial resolutions of the cases are made by a motion for judgment on the pleadings or by a motion for summary judgment. In most cases, however, facts are in dispute. The purpose of trial is to make a determination as to the facts and only then to apply the applicable law to the facts that have been proved in the court trial.

Trials may take place before a judge alone or before a judge and jury. In a trial before a judge only, the judge acts as both the finder of fact and the determiner of applicable law. When a jury hears a case, the jury serves as the finder of fact and then applies the law relevant to the case as explained by the trial judge.

Trials before a judge without a jury are much simpler than jury trials. There always seems to be more drama in a case in front of a jury than when a judge alone renders the decision. Since judges understand the law and the tactics of attorneys, trials without juries proceed more quickly than jury trials. Rarely are impassioned pleas made to a judge. This is something saved for the jury.

A variety of things determine whether a case is to be heard by a judge alone or by a judge and jury. In some types of cases, like equity or matrimonial cases, the parties have no right to a trial by jury. Backlogs for jury trials may be longer than for nonjury trials in many areas (particularly in state courts) and this may influence the decision of whether to demand a jury trial or not. Furthermore, lawyers like to have juries in certain types of cases (for example, the plaintiff's lawyer in a personal injury case usually wants a jury, hoping to evoke the jury's sympathy for the injured party) but not in others. For example, a very complicated, technical case, such as a lengthy antitrust case, may never be understood by a jury and might result in no resolution at all. The decision whether or not to have a jury is made by the litigation team with the advice and consent of the client.

This chapter concentrates mainly on jury trials. Because jury trials are more complicated than nonjury trials, it is essential to understand the basic components of the more complex process before conceptualizing the more streamlined process. When appropriate, the distinctions between jury and nonjury trials will be pointed out.

The paralegal can play a significant role during the trial proceeding. Although the paralegal's role is predominately supportive during the trial, the tasks he or she performs can be invaluable to the attorney actively engaged in the trial process. The paralegal performs the following tasks during trial:

- coordinates the appearance of witnesses;

- assists in the preparation of all files and documents to be taken to court;

- controls the flow of and handles documents and exhibits during trial (especially true during the trial of a complex case involving hundreds or thousands of exhibits);

- assists in performing legal research on issues arising during trial;

- takes notes on the testimony of all witnesses.

In addition to these tasks, the paralegal should observe as much as possible of what is going on in the courtroom. While an attorney is actively involved in the actual trial process, things can occur in the courtroom that may be either behind the attorney or outside the scope of his or her vision. Since the attorney is usually concentrating on what is occurring at the counsel tables, the judge's bench, the witness stand, and the jury box, the paralegal's observations can be invaluable to an attorney who might otherwise have missed something of significance (for example, the demeanor of a key witness sitting in the audience, jury reactions, or opposing counsel's reactions).

This chapter is organized on the basis of the usual chronology of a trial:

1. conference with trial judge

2. selection of the jury

3. opening statement

4. presentation of plaintiff's case

5. presentation of defendant's case

6. presentation of additional defendant or third party's case, if any

7. rebuttal witnesses

8. closing argument by counsel

9. court's jury instructions

10. jury deliberation and verdict

Other than the conference with the judge, these phases or steps are all part of the process commonly referred to as a trial.

## II. CONFERENCE WITH THE TRIAL JUDGE

When a case is called for trial it is common for the judge to call counsel for all parties to his or her chambers for a conference. At this time the judge will review the pretrial order (if applicable) or will ask each lawyer for his or her version of the facts and law most favorable to the client's position. If there are any procedural or evidentiary questions raised by the pretrial order, they will also be discussed. The major purposes of this conference are to explore the final possibility of settlement and to lay down ground rules for conducting the trial.

Settlements are favored by judges because they save time. Litigants are also served by settlements because the risks of an unfavorable decision at trial are avoided. Some judges, especially when the case is to go to a trial by jury, make recommendations to the respective counsel about the dollar amount for which the case should be settled. Therefore counsel are usually required to come to the conference with authority from their clients to settle.

The following is an example of a local court rule concerning this final pretrial conference:

> 3. Final Pretrial Conference. A final pretrial conference will ordinarily be held shortly before trial. It shall be attended by trial counsel, who must be either authorized and empowered to make binding decisions concerning settlement, or able to obtain such authority by telephone in the course of the conference. In addition to exploring the final positions of the parties regarding settlement, the court will consider at the conference some or all of the following:
>
> The simplification of the issues, the necessity or desirability of amendments to the pleadings, the separation of issues, the desirability of an impartial medical examination, the limitation of the number of expert witnesses, the probable length of the trial, the desirability of trial briefs, evidentiary questions, the submission of points for charge, and such other matters as may aid in the trial or other disposition of the action.[1]

It is also appropriate at this conference for counsel to make a **motion in limine.** This is a motion whereby the litigants attempt to obtain an advance ruling by the judge on an anticipated evidentiary issue that may arise during trial. The reasons for making such a motion are: (1) to attempt to eliminate objectionable evidence that may be highly prejudicial if heard by a jury prior to an objection; and/or (2) to help litigants make strategy decision prior to trial. The motion can be made by either the party who plans to introduce the questionable evidence or the party who plans to oppose it.

In a nonjury case, it is common for the judge to require that the litigants submit requests for findings of fact and conclusions of law at this final conference. For example, under Local Civil Rule 21(d)(4)(c) in the U.S. District Court for the Eastern District of Pennsylvania, counsel are required to submit these requests in duplicate to the judge's chambers at the start of the trial or as the judge otherwise directs.

## III. TRIAL

## A. Selection of the Jury

When a case is to be tried by a jury, the first step in the trial is the selection of the jury. The precise procedure for selecting a jury varies from court to court and

---

[1]Local Rule 21(d)(3) of U.S. District Court for the Eastern District of Pennsylvania.

even from judge to judge within the same court. Typically, panels of prospective jurors (adult citizens residing within the jurisdiction of the court) are drawn at random from voting lists and/or driver license lists. The goal of selecting prospective jurors randomly from these lists is that the jury that is ultimately chosen will represent a fair cross-section of the community. Then, from such panels, the clerk of the trial court draws the names of whatever number of jurors is required to try the case.

Traditionally, a jury was composed of twelve jurors and two or more alternates (substitutes who sit in the jury box, hear the case, and are available to replace any regular juror who becomes incapacitated at any time before the jury begins its deliberation to reach a verdict). Recently, however, pursuant to FRCP 48, many courts have been using smaller juries, consisting of perhaps eight jurors, in an effort to reduce the cost, in both time and money, of a jury trial.

In order to select an unbiased jury, provision is made in all court systems for examination of prospective jurors and for challenges to jurors deemed objectionable. A **challenge** is an objection to a particular juror and a request that the person not be allowed to sit on the jury.

### 1. Voir Dire

In order for counsel to be able to exercise the privileges of challenge, they must be able to learn something about the prospective jurors. This is done through a method called **voir dire,** a French term meaning "to speak the truth," which has come to mean a preliminary examination to determine the competency and fitness of a prospective juror.

Before any of the oral voir dire begins, counsel are either given or must retrieve from the clerk's office jury questionnaires that have been filled out for each juror. Retrieving questionnaires is usually a function of the paralegal. While the precise information revealed in these forms varies from court to court, they generally contain basic information on the background of each juror such as name, address, number of years of residency at that address, marital status, number of children, occupation and employer, names and occupations of immediate family members, and whether they were ever a party to a lawsuit. After counsel has reviewed the juror questionnaire, the voir dire examination begins.

The exact procedure by which voir dire is conducted varies greatly. In some jurisdictions, it is the judge, rather than the attorneys, who conducts the voir dire. Sometimes in these situations the attorneys can submit suggested questions to the judge, in which case the judge can determine whether to ask the questions to the prospective jurors. If the attorneys are asking the questions, they may do so with or without the judge present, depending on the jurisdiction. If the judge is not actually present during the questioning, then he or she must be available if he or she is needed. If one lawyer believes the opponent is going too far in voir dire, application to the court will be made for a ruling limiting the scope of the voir dire.

Assuming that the lawyers are conducting the questioning, plaintiff's counsel rises, introduces all counsel and litigants, and very briefly describes the type of lawsuit the jury will be called upon to decide. A series of questions is then asked of the jury panel. The jurors are requested to respond to any questions posed to them. Do they know the lawyers? Do they know the litigants? Have they been involved in a lawsuit of this type before?

The voir dire permits an attorney to decide if a particular juror will be beneficial or harmful. For example, in a personal injury action in which the plaintiff is a five-year-old girl hurt in an automobile accident, the lawyer for plaintiff might be interested in retaining parents with small children on the jury. Plaintiff's counsel would also be interested in removing from the jury anyone who works for an automobile insurance company. Trial counsel should not be obvious with their questions, for fear of offending jurors who are not excluded.

After plaintiff's counsel has completed his or her voir dire, defense counsel is then given a turn to probe the jurors. The defense attorney will ask similar questions.

Voir dire can disclose antipathy between lawyer and prospective juror. We have all experienced the situation in which something about a person's manner or speech offends us. It is the lawyer's job to be alert to any such feelings.

Another frequent use of the voir dire is to educate the prospective jury about the case to be tried. It is an introduction to the case at hand and the legal and social issues that the case involves. In other words, it is an opportunity for counsel to sell his or her case.

The role of the paralegal during voir dire can be to prepare a chart showing the prospective jurors' assigned seats in the jury box. As each juror is questioned the paralegal can record the answers so that the attorney can review this information when exercising his or her jury challenges. In addition, the paralegal, as an observer, is in a good position to make suggestions to the lawyer on which prospective jurors to challenge.

### 2. Exercising the Jury Challenges

Each lawyer has a list of all prospective jurors called in one panel. Challenges are made by counsel striking off from the list the names of the jurors whom they wish to eliminate from the jury.

There are two types of challenges: **"peremptory"** and **"for cause."** Counsel will first try to exercise the challenges for cause. These challenges are based on the fact that a prospective juror has exhibited some bias or prejudice or has a physical problem that would prevent him or her from giving the case a fair hearing (some infirmity). For example, if a panel member knows one of the litigants personally, that person should not sit as a juror in the case because the personal relationship might influence the decision reached as a juror.

If counsel believes bias is present to warrant a challenge for cause, opposing counsel's agreement is sought. If opposing counsel disagrees, both will appear before the trial judge for a decision. Thus the opportunity exists for some compromise and give and take between opposing counsel in deciding who shall be stricken for cause. If counsel do not agree, the trial judge will have to determine whether the voir dire has revealed that a particular juror will be impartial or biased.

Once the challenges for cause have been resolved, the lawyers will exercise their peremptory challenges. In the case of a peremptory challenge, no reason need be given for rejecting a prospective juror. However, in order to prevent abuse of this special right, the number of such challenges is limited by statute —

generally to a small number (perhaps four). The criteria used to eliminate jurors by peremptory challenge are a matter of individual preference based on the nature of the case and the experience of the particular lawyer.

When counsel have concluded their challenges and a sufficient number of jurors remain, the clerk of the court will excuse those who have been stricken and assign the remaining jurors and alternates their respective positions in the jury box.

At the completion of voir dire, the clerk of the court will administer an oath to the jury. This oath is to follow the law as it is presented to the jury by the judge. Once the jury has been sworn in and seated, the next phase of the trial begins.

## B. Opening Statement

Upon selection of jurors and administration of the oath, the judge will enter the courtroom and assume his or her position on the bench. Counsel will then have the right to make an **opening statement.** The opening statement affords each counsel a chance to narrate a version of the facts and preview the evidence that will be submitted in support of such facts. The statement is critical because it permits the jurors to be told the whole story at one time rather than waiting for a piecemeal version to be told in trial. Studies have shown that in 80 percent of cases at trial, jurors would have returned the same verdict immediately after the opening statement as the verdict they return after all the evidence has been presented.[2]

Plaintiff's counsel goes first. Then defense counsel follows with a summary of the defense. Defense counsel may defer the opening statement until just before the defendant's case is presented. When declining to make an opening statement at the outset, defense counsel should make it clear to the jury that he or she is merely postponing the presentation of the statement, which has already been prepared. This way the jury does not get the impression that defense counsel is not prepared.

Counsel use this opportunity to emphasize the themes of their cases to the jury. The opening statement, like the first act of a three-act play, must evoke the jurors' interest in the plaintiff's or defendant's case. Counsel may also explain their trial plans. For example, if they plan to produce a great many witnesses, they should explain this so that the jury does not become confused or, perhaps worse, bored. Counsel will also tell the jury what proof to expect during the trial. If the defense is strong, its substance should be treated fairly so as not to lead the jurors to later conclude that they were misled in the opening statement. Some attorneys rehearse an opening statement before a nonlawyer friend. If, at the end of the opening statement, the friend believes he or she has been told an interesting short story, the purpose of the opening statement will have been accomplished.

The opening statement is normally made with sincerity and conviction, but in a friendly fashion. Rarely will plaintiff's counsel speak loudly or pound the table at this juncture; such theatrics are usually reserved for the closing argu-

---

[2]H. Kalven and H. Zeisel, *The American Jury* (Chicago, University of Chicago Press); J. Jeans, *Trial Advocacy* (St. Paul, West Publishing Co., 1975), p. 199.

ment at the end of the trial. A good opening statement will not, however, oversell the case about to be presented. A promise to the jury to prove an allegation that is not fulfilled may come back to haunt counsel in the opponent's closing statements. Thus, a plaintiff's attorney who promises the jury he or she will produce something had better keep that promise or defense counsel may use that failure to raise doubts about the plaintiff's case generally. The paralegal can play an important role in the preparation of opening statements. In addition to suggesting and collaborating on the theme and language to be used by the attorney, the paralegal can help the attorney rehearse the presentation.

## C. Presenting the Plaintiff's Case

After all the parties' counsel have had an opportunity to present opening statements, the plaintiff's counsel will proceed with the actual presentation of witnesses and evidence. The goal of plaintiff's counsel is to introduce enough evidence to allow the case to be decided by the jury and to have the jury decide the case in his or her client's favor. The plaintiff's attorney must present a "prima facie" case, in other words enough evidence to permit a jury to consider the case. This is based on the elements of proof necessary to establish liability on the part of the defendant(s). In addition to providing this bare minimum of evidence necessary to allow a jury to decide a case, the plaintiff wants to convince the jury to render a decision in his or her favor. This concept of persuading a jury is called the burden of persuasion.

Before the first witness for the plaintiff is called to the witness stand, the judge or counsel may begin by reading into evidence (reciting for the stenographic record of the proceedings and for the jury's consideration) the uncontested facts. These become evidence that the jury may consider just as if a live witness had stated the facts in testimony and the jury believed them.

Admissions by the party's opponent may also be read into the record. One source of admissions is the pleadings. Suppose in paragraph 5 of the complaint in an automobile accident case the plaintiff had pleaded: "On September 15, 1992, the defendant was operating a green 1992 Chevrolet north on Main Street." If, in response to that, the defendant pleaded "Admitted," that admission in the pleadings may be read into evidence by counsel for plaintiff.

Other sources of admissions are those contained in answers to requests for admissions made during the discovery proceedings as well as the admissions contained in answers to interrogatories and at depositions. To qualify as an admission, the facts must be admitted as such and not subject to reservations or qualifications.

If the parties have been able to agree on some of the facts and these have been reduced to a stipulation of facts in the pretrial order, such facts will also be read into evidence or reduced to a written statement that may be made part of the record as a document.

Depositions of unavailable witnesses may also be read into the record of the trial. A convenient procedure for reading the deposition into evidence is to have a paralegal, another attorney, or some other adult take the witness stand (with the court's prior permission) and play the role of the deponent while the lawyer reads the questions to him or her. If the deposition was videotaped, the videotape can be presented to the jury at this time or at a later time.

Counsel may, however, elect to read some portions of admissions or stipulated facts into the record at a later stage of the case, rather than at the inception of the case, in order that the particular facts will fit better into the picture counsel is attempting to paint in the jury's mind. (Note the use of the singular—the attempt is to paint one picture in the collective mind of the jury.)

Once all the desired stipulations and admissions have been read into evidence, the plaintiff's attorney calls his or her first witness to testify on the witness stand. This begins the process of examination of witnesses.

**1. Direct Examination**

The initial examination of a witness by the counsel calling the person to the stand (a proponent of the witness) is called **direct examination.** The main purpose of direct examination is to elicit facts that the witness knows and to do so in such a manner that the jury understands and believes what the witness is saying—in other words, to present the case in the most favorable light to the judge or jury. Direct examination is the process by which the plaintiff or proponent calls witnesses to testify who will help establish the merits of his or her claim. Witnesses may be called for various purposes:

♦ to establish facts based on their own recollection of an event;

♦ to establish the authenticity and/or admissibility of exhibits or documents;

♦ to provide information based on a specific expertise beyond the scope of ordinary people (expert witnesses).

One of the basic rules of evidence for conducting direct examination is that leading questions are generally not permitted. Leading questions are questions that suggest the desired response. An example is "Isn't it true that the defendant hit his sister?" The reason for this prohibition is that the witness on direct examination is most probably friendly or favorable to the plaintiff; as a result, the witness will probably follow the lead, rather than give his or her own accurate statement. This rule does have some exceptions.

In addition to calling witnesses who will provide favorable testimony to the plaintiff on direct examination, plaintiffs counsel may call adverse parties (that is, the defendant or the officers, directors, or agents of the defendant) as witnesses. Not only can a plaintiff call an adverse party to the witness stand, but plaintiffs counsel can ask the adverse party leading questions. Since this witness is often hostile to the attorney conducting the examination, the law permits the use of leading questions similar to the examination that occurs on cross-examination.

One of the principles upon which most trial lawyers agree is that witnesses should not be called on direct examination unless their testimony has been discussed in advance (adverse parties are excluded from this principle). This preparation should be done by the attorney or the paralegal before trial. In addition, based on the outline prepared by the paralegal on the direct examination of each witness, at trial the paralegal can check off each element of the outline as it has been covered by the attorney during direct examination. This ensures that all the points planned to be covered are in fact covered. Before the attorney conducting direct examination finishes the examination, he or she should consult with the assisting paralegal to make sure that no topics covered in the outline have been missed.

### 2. Cross-Examination

When the plaintiff's attorney has completed the questions on direct examination, the defendant's attorney **cross-examines** the witness. The main purposes of cross-examination are to persuade the jury that the witness is not worth believing and to try to use the witness to support some element of the cross-examiner's case. Another way of proving that the witness is not worthy of belief is impeaching the credibility or discrediting the witness.

In most jurisdictions and in the federal court system the scope of cross-examination is limited to the subject matter of the direct examination and to matters concerning the credibility of the witness. In some jurisdictions cross-examination may be more wide ranging and limited only to matters relevant to the issues in the trial.

Cross-examination is opposing counsel's chance to weaken or destroy direct testimony. Since the credibility of a witness is essential in a trial, when the testimony of a witness is discredited or shown to be unreliable, it can have an important impact on the jury. A witness may be impeached or discredited by demonstrating bias or prejudice by showing a prior inconsistent statement, by showing faulty memory or perception, or by showing a conviction of a serious crime or a crime involving dishonesty.

Unless the witness is a surprise witness, cross-examination is never begun without preparation. A substantial amount of preparation is absolutely essential for effective cross-examination. The deposition and interrogatories that were obtained and digested during pretrial discovery are used at trial to expose prior statements that are inconsistent with testimony at trial.

If the witness on direct examination testifies in a manner inconsistent with an earlier deposition, questions will be asked on cross-examination to elicit the fact that the earlier statement was, in fact, made. The earlier, inconsistent statement is then read to the jury. If the witness admits to making the earlier statement, it is sufficient to go no further and leave the impact of the inconsistency with the jury. Asking the witness to explain the inconsistency will only permit a fast-thinking witness to do so. To heighten the impact of the inconsistency, it is often the practice to ask the witness to repeat the statement made on direct examination and, after conveying a sense of certainty by repeating the statement, read aloud the prior inconsistent statement.

Cross-examination may not expose the witness as a liar but only mistaken. He or she may not have really had the opportunity to observe the facts. You may recall the movie *Twelve Angry Men,* in which an elderly man claimed to be an eyewitness to a murder. In the jury room one of the jurors, also an elderly man, remembered that although the witness did not wear glasses at trial, there were pinch marks on either side of the bridge of his nose. The ability of the witness to observe was thus questioned. This dramatic revelation is normal for Hollywood but in practice would be picked up immediately on cross-examination. The ability of a witness to hear or see, as well as a witness's ability to remember, are usual areas of cross-examination.

Another use of cross-examination is to produce facts that tend to show the witness is biased or prejudiced. If the witness has a personal interest in the outcome of the case this interest may be disclosed on cross-examination. Often, a situation that may lead to bias is uncovered in discovery. Counsel will then merely ask, Isn't it true you are employed by the plaintiff's father?" It is not necessary to go any further to leave a question mark surrounding this witness in the minds of the jurors.

The key to successful cross-examination is that the attorney conducting the examination must control the responses of the witness. The technique most commonly employed is the use of leading questions, which is permissible on cross-examination. These types of questions permit the witness to answer only in a "yes" or "no" fashion. By controlling the potential response to a question, the skilled cross-examiner avoids the pitfall by providing witnesses with an opportunity to explain their way out of whatever point the cross-examiner is trying to make to the jury. In addition to framing leading questions, the attorney's pace and rhythm helps limit the witness's response.

### 3. Redirect Examination

After a witness has been cross-examined, the party who originally called that witness has the right to **redirect examination.** The purpose of redirect is to rehabilitate the impeached witness by explaining damaging testimony produced on cross-examination or to clarify a point that became muddled during cross-examination. In other words, the purpose is to bolster the witness's testimony and establish the witness as being a trustworthy person. Normally, redirect examination is limited to matters that have been probed on cross-examination. Whether or not to call a witness on redirect is a matter of judgment. If counsel is certain that the witness's direct testimony has been impeached, there is no choice but to rehabilitate the witness. If counsel is unsure, sometimes it is best not to conduct redirect examination, thus indicating to the jury that the cross-examination is not considered to have been harmful.

### 4. Further Presentation of Witnesses

After plaintiff's first witness has completed direct examination, cross-examination, and redirect examination, the plaintiff's attorney will call his or her next witness. The same process of examination is repeated. This process of calling witnesses to testify and then examining those witnesses in the sequence described above continues until the plaintiff's lawyer has called enough witnesses to prove plaintiff's claim. At that time, the plaintiff's counsel will announce to the court that he or she does not plan to call any further witnesses, and "rests" his or her case. This procedure indicates that plaintiff's counsel feels enough evidence has been produced to submit the case to the jury for decision.

### 5. Exhibits

The production of exhibits is often the only way or the best way of proving a fact. For example, in the simple motor vehicle case, a photograph of the automobile after the accident is helpful, if there are conflicting versions, to show how the accident occurred or to demonstrate the damage done to the vehicle.

In a complex case, the number of exhibits may run into the hundreds. Good preparation requires that each exhibit be marked prior to trial and a brief outline clipped to each advising how that exhibit would be produced and who is needed for its production. The work of gathering, arranging, and labeling exhibits may be another part of the paralegal's job in helping the attorney prior to and at the trial.

In some instances the parties will have stipulated that the document is authentic—that it is what the proponent (party offering the document) claims it is. If, however, there has been no such agreement, the exhibit must be authenticated. If the photograph of the vehicles after the accident is introduced it is necessary to satisfy the judge *before* the photograph may be shown to the jury that the photograph is what it purports to be. It may be necessary, therefore, to produce the photographer to testify when he or she took the photograph and that the photograph is the one he or she took. In practice, this is easy, since professional photographers in accident cases date and initial photographs when printed.

Bookkeeping entries showing credits and debits will be introduced by having the bookkeeper, who probably does not remember the specific transaction, identify his or her own handwriting and testify to the practice followed in making the entries, to prove that they were made in the ordinary course of business and not in anticipation of the trial.

Note that in these examples the witnesses themselves may not have any recollection of ultimate facts. The photographer is not asked how the accident happened and the bookkeeper is not asked if he or she remembers the specific transaction. Each is merely asked to authenticate the exhibit so that it may be shown to the jury.

Many trial courts follow a standard procedure for introducing exhibits. The photograph or the document is handed to the court clerk and marked for identification with a letter indicating if it is plaintiff's or defendant's exhibit and with a number (P-1, D-5, and so on). It is then shown to opposing counsel and to the judge. It is next handed to the witness, who is asked to identify the exhibit, and finally to the jury. At the end of the presentation of each party's case, its exhibits are introduced into evidence by motion and, if admitted, are taken by the jury into the jury room at the close of trial.

It is, of course, critical that the witnesses necessary to authenticate exhibits be available. Otherwise the exhibit will not be accepted by the court and the jury will not be permitted to see it. This is but another example of the importance of taking care of matters fully even though they may seem mundane. Paralegals may have to do the "leg work" of finding witnesses and making sure they appear in court at the time their testimony is necessary.

Many judges require that all exhibits be premarked for identification. This can be included in the joint final pretrial order if one is required. If premarking is not included in such an order, it is good practice to meet with the court reporter in advance of trial and have all exhibits premarked for identification. The court reporter should have his or her own list of exhibits.

During trial it is important for the paralegal to keep track of which documents have been *introduced* into evidence. At the close of the client's case, the paralegal should make sure that all exhibits marked for identification have been admitted into evidence. An exhibit chart is the best way to ensure that the documents have been introduced. If an exhibit has been marked but not moved (and received) into evidence, the paralegal should advise trial counsel, who can then move the admission of all such exhibits, if appropriate.

### 6. Motion for Directed Verdict

After the plaintiff has rested, the defendant has the opportunity to test the sufficiency of the evidence presented by the plaintiff. The procedure for testing the strength of plaintiff's case is by an oral **motion for a directed verdict.** Another name for this type of procedure is a motion for a compulsory nonsuit (Pennsylvania). If the plaintiff has failed to introduce factual evidence to support all the elements of proof necessary to establish liability against the defendant(s), the judge will grant the motion and direct that judgment be entered against the plaintiff. This judgment has the effect of dismissing the plaintiff's claim and of preventing the jury from deciding the case (the case is over). If the motion is denied, the defense will then proceed to put their case before the jury.

## D. Presenting the Defendant's Case

Defense counsel will present the defendant's case subject to the same rules of evidence and examination that governed the presentation of the plaintiff's case, except that the roles are reversed. Defense counsel now feels the restraint of direct examination while plaintiff's counsel has the freedom of cross-examination.

Substantial preparation by defense counsel and paralegal is essential for direct examination. An outline of testimony, catalog of exhibits, and memoranda of law on expected objections to the evidence intended to be produced are a must. The defendant's version of the facts must be presented.

Defense counsel is not concerned, however, with producing a prima facie case since the defense is not subject to a motion for directed verdict. However, if the defendant is asserting a counterclaim, he or she must be concerned with proving a prima facie case with respect to the counterclaim. Failure to do so may result in a directed verdict against the defendant with respect to the counterclaim. Once the plaintiff rests, the burden of producing evidence shifts to the defendant. This burden may be met by introducing testimony relating toward disproving the plaintiff's case or toward supporting the defendant's affirmative defenses. After offering all the evidence he or she wishes to present, defendants counsel announces to the court that no further witnesses will testify on defendant's behalf and he or she rests his or her case.

## E. Rebuttal Evidence

After the defendant has rested, the plaintiff is permitted to put on additional evidence. This is known as **rebuttal.** Rebuttal is restricted to evidence that is in contradiction to the defendant's evidence. If the evidence is not relevant as rebuttal evidence, but just some extra ammunition the plaintiff was saving, the judge will exclude it, if properly objected to by the defendant's counsel.

The plaintiff's counsel is supposed to present all evidence that will be necessary to prove the claim made at the same time—in the original presentation of the case. The same procedure concerning examination of witnesses is followed as before: direct examination, cross-examination, and redirect examination.

## F. Motion for Directed Verdict at the Close of All the Evidence

A motion for a directed verdict may be made by either party after all the evidence has been presented by the parties. When such a motion is made, the judge must decide whether to permit the jury to decide the case. If the judge concludes that no reasonable person could find in favor of one of the parties, the judge will enter a directed verdict in favor of the other party. Such motions are not often granted. If the motion is denied, the case proceeds to the jury for decision. If the motion is granted, the case is decided in favor of the party making the motion and the case never reaches the jury for decision.

## G. Burden of Proof

The **burden of proof** is the standard that the factfinder is to apply to a set of facts in determining how to reach a verdict. Burden of proof is really a composite of two burdens: the burden of producing evidence and the burden of persuasion. For purposes of this chapter burden of proof means burden of persuasion.

In a civil case, in order for the plaintiff to prevail, "a preponderance of the evidence" must be shown, making it more likely that the plaintiff's version of the facts is correct than is the defendant's version of the facts. The applicable burden of proof is always covered by the trial judge in the charge to the jury. In a civil case the jurors will often be asked to imagine a set of scales with the defendant's evidence piled on one side and the plaintiff's evidence on the other. If the scale is in perfect equilibrium or if the defendant's scale tips lower than the plaintiff's, plaintiff may not recover since the burden of proof has not been satisfied. If plaintiff's tray of evidence is heavier than defendant's so that it tips lower, no matter how slightly, plaintiff is entitled to recover.

In practice, the test is far more complex. For example, the fact that plaintiff produced more witnesses than defendant does not satisfy the burden of proof. The credibility of each witness must be assessed, including the witness's opportunity to observe what happened, the interest or bias in testifying, the reliability of recollection, the inconsistencies shown on cross-examination, explanations on redirect, and the witness's general appearance and demeanor.

There is another burden of proof standard that is applied to a civil case. Although the traditional measure is a preponderance of the evidence, in fraud cases, for example, it is common to see the standard framed in terms of clear and convincing evidence. This is a harder standard to meet than a preponderance of evidence standard as the factfinder must be more than just convinced of the truth of the evidence presented.

## H. Closing Argument

After the close of the evidence, each counsel has the opportunity to "close" to the jury in a jury trial or to the judge in a nonjury case. **Closing argument** consists of a summation of the evidence and an attempt to persuade the factfinder as to the correctness of counsel's case. In jury trials this is the time when counsel try to be most persuasive by making long but coherent and logical arguments.

First, counsel will advise the jurors that it is their recollection of the facts that is critical, not counsels'. Attorneys are, however, permitted to cover the evidence from notes and attack the weak points of the opponent's case. It is legitimate to comment freely upon the credibility of witnesses, their bias, prejudice, lack of opportunity to observe, and their demeanor. Trial counsel have perhaps more freedom to give an opinion in closing argument than at any other time, restricted only by good taste and the evidence already produced. It is, however, improper for counsel in closing to go beyond the facts presented in the trial. A violation of this rule may result in a mistrial as well as sanctions from the judge.

The paralegal is essential to an effective closing argument. No matter how pervasive the pretrial discovery, there will always be surprises at trial. The paralegal who has been at counsel table keeping a running account of all testimony is in an excellent position to assist in the preparation of closing argument. Jurors are impressed by the accurate restatement of critical testimony by counsel during closing argument. Often the recollection of a word or phrase such as "I think," "maybe," or "perhaps" is critical to the credibility of an important witness and hence vital to the case. It is impossible for trial counsel to keep a running account of testimony; thus the accuracy of the trial assistant is crucial. Notes should be kept by the paralegal for all the essential testimony given by each witness. Paraphrasing will usually be sufficient except when comment is made by a witness on a very important point. Then it is best to get down the exact words of the witness.

The entire trial is recorded stenographically by the court reporter. Normally, transcripts of the notes of testimony of a trial are made only if and when an appeal is taken. In some cases, however, lawyers will arrange for daily transcription of the notes of testimony. This service is very expensive and is rarely requested. The advantage of having such transcripts for purposes of both cross-examining witnesses and preparing closing arguments may justify the expense in some cases.

An effective closing argument must be well organized. Trial counsel should discuss the theory of the case, how the evidence does or does not support that theory, and which witnesses and exhibits should be considered persuasive. Counsel will explain the burden of proof and may make some reference to the applicable law if, and only if, it is certain that the trial judge will agree in the instructions to the jury.

In most jurisdictions, plaintiff's counsel, having the burden of proof, closes first to the jury followed by defense counsel. There follows a chance for a brief rebuttal. Counsel's involvement with the jury is now over, and the jurors are given the opportunity to criticize the performances.

The trial judge who has not requested jury instructions at the beginning of the trial will make sure that the parties have submitted their requests prior to the start of closing argument. In cases in which the law is in dispute, the jury instructions (or points for charge) submitted by each party will necessarily differ and the judge must decide which points are correct. In most instances a ruling on contested points may be expected prior to closing argument. In others, the ruling is after closing. In the latter event, the trial lawyers risk the embarrassment of making a reference to the law only to find that the judge has selected a different interpretation of the law to present to the jury.

## I. Points for Charge

After the closing arguments, the case is submitted to the jury under instructions (or a "charge") by the court. The charge includes a statement of the law to be applied, which was furnished to the court by counsel in written **points for charge.**

Points for charge include: (1) statements of law and (2) requests for findings of fact. The judge's charge to the jurors consists of a review of the facts, not binding upon them, and a statement of the applicable law, which is absolutely binding upon them. Legal principles included in the charge are drafted by trial counsel and submitted to the court for approval.

In addition to statements of law, points for charge include requests for findings of fact or law. For example, in an intersectional motor vehicle collision, a typical request for finding might be the following:

> If you find that the defendant entered the intersection without observing traffic to his right or to his left then you must find that he was negligent.

Requests for findings are, therefore, as varied as the factual situation presented. They serve an extremely important purpose in focusing the jurors' attention on critical facts. Requests for findings and points for charge also force the jury to approach their decision-making process with logic by requiring them to think in cause and effect relationships.

## J. The Charge and the Deliberation

Throughout the trial, the judge will have been taking thorough notes of the testimony and ruling on objections to the submission of evidence.

After closing argument and upon receipt of the points for charge, the judge will usually recess to prepare the charge to the jury. The charge consists of the judge's review of the evidence, an explanation of the burden of proof, a statement of the applicable law, and a statement of those requests for findings that have been approved. Even in a simple negligence case the charge usually takes at least forty-five minutes. In a complex antitrust case the charge may last for several days. Upon completion of the charge, the judge will ask trial counsel whether they have any objections to the charge. (Counsel may disagree with a part of the charge.) To preserve their rights on appeal, counsel must object to the failure to include a point or the submission of a point they dispute. The method of exception is merely to advise the court of the exception that the court reporter will note in the transcript. Examples of the points for charge submitted by both counsel and the actual charge of the court in litigation concerning a contract for the construction of a building and whether the builder was entitled to final payment are found in Exhibits 10.1, 10.2, and 10.3.

EXHIBIT 10.1

# Plaintiff's Points for Charge

IN THE UNITED STATES DISTRICT COURT FOR
THE DISTRICT OF VERMONT

LABILE, INC.
   vs.           Civil Action No. 91-76
SPRING MANOR, INC.

PLAINTIFF'S POINTS FOR CHARGE

The Court is requested to charge the jury, on behalf of the plaintiff, as follows:

1. The job of a building contractor constructing a building pursuant to plans and specifications prepared by an architect engaged by the owner is to construct the building substantially in accordance with the plans and specifications prepared by the architect.

2. Where a builder builds pursuant to plans and specifications prepared by an architect engaged by the owner, the builder, here the plaintiff, assumes no responsibility for the design of the building.

3. If you should find that the plaintiff substantially completed the construction of the nursing home here involved in accordance with the plans and specifications prepared by the architect and if you should find, further, that the architect issued a final certificate for payment, the plaintiff was entitled to payment in full of the entire unpaid balance from the defendant within sixty days after substantial completion of the work.

4. The architect has testified that in his opinion plaintiff had substantially completed the work in accordance with his plans and specifications by September 25, 1990, and that he issued on that date a final certificate for payment. Your attention is called to the provisions of Article 10.5(a) of the Special Conditions of the contract which provides: "The decisions of the architect shall be final."

5. Where a contract provides that the work shall be done to the satisfaction, approval or acceptance of an architect, the architect is thereby constituted sole arbiter between the parties and the parties are bound by his decision unless there be proof of fraud, collusion or caprice.

6. There has been no proof of fraud, collusion or caprice in this case.

7. With respect to any question of faulty materials or defective workmanship, your attention is directed to Article 10.2(a) of the Special Conditions, which provides that the plaintiff is required to repair or replace only work determined by the architect to be faulty or defective within one year from the date of substantial completion of the project.

8. Even if you should find that the architect did determine that there was some defective or faulty work requiring repair by the contractor, any breach of that provision of the contract would not relieve the defendant from paying to plaintiff the unpaid balance under the contract.

EXHIBIT 10.1

## Plaintiff's Points for Charge (continued)

9. There was some testimony submitted on behalf of the defendant relating to compliance with the regulations of the Township of Springfield. The issuance of the certificate of occupancy is prima facie evidence that all regulations of the Township of Springfield have been complied with.

10. The contract provides that the plaintiff shall be deemed to have complied with the regulations of the Township of Springfield when the construction has been approved by the Township authorities having jurisdiction. The Township authority having jurisdiction is the authority which issues certificates of occupancy and you will recall that the defendant's own witness testified that the certificate of occupancy has been issued and is now free of any condition.

11. The certification by the Bureau of Aging of the Department of Welfare of the State of Vermont is prima facie evidence of compliance with applicable regulations of the State of Vermont as they pertain to the construction of nursing homes.

12. The contract provides that the plaintiff shall be deemed to have complied with the regulations of the State of Vermont when the construction has been approved by the State authorities having jurisdiction. The State authority having jurisdiction over nursing homes is the Bureau of Aging of the Department of Welfare and the defendant's own witnesses admitted issuance of proper certification by the Bureau of Aging.

13. The architect is the owner's representative during construction and until final payment has been made and Mr. Stillee as architect had authority to act on behalf of the defendant and to issue instructions to the plaintiff.

14. There has been testimony that included in the plaintiff's claim of $32,822.13 is a claim of $29,313.63 of changes and extras. Except for a change order in the amount of $175.00 relating to electrical receptacles, the remaining changes and extras were approved by the architect orally according to the testimony of both the architect and Mr. Labile. Further, this testimony is unrebutted and uncontroverted. In addition, the architect stated that he knew of the changes and extras being done at or about the time that the work was done. You are directed that under these circumstances, if you find either that the architect orally approved the changes and extras or knew of the changes and extras at or about the time the work was done, the defendant must pay for all of these changes.

15. In addition to the additions and deductions as covered by the claim for changes and extras, the contract provided that the defendant shall pay to plaintiff for the performance of the work, the actual cost of labor, services and material together with an additional sum of $32,000 but in no event a sum, exclusive of changes and extras, in excess of $665,000. Accordingly, if you find that the actual cost of labor, services and material incurred by the plaintiff, exclusive of the changes and extras, total $633,000 or more, then the plaintiff is entitled to payments totalling $665,000 under the

**EXHIBIT 10.1**

# Plaintiff's Points for Charge (continued)

contract plus the amount you find the plaintiff is entitled to receive by reason of the approved changes and extras.

16. Article 5.1 of the contract defines "actual cost" as follows:
    (a) In the event of a subcontract, the total sums paid by contractor to subcontractor for the performance of said subcontract pursuant to a written contract.
    (b) In the event that the labor is supplied by contractor, then the wages and salaries of all workers who actually performed services for the premises and any sums paid by contractor for their account, whether for insurance, social security, welfare or pension plan.
    (c) The actual cost to contractor of all material, supplies and equipment delivered to project and used pursuant to plans and specifications, and where the funds are made available to contractor in time to earn any discounts on materials purchased, the same shall be deducted.

17. Under the definition of "actual cost" the cost to the plaintiff of the equipment rentals delivered to the project and issued pursuant to the plans and specifications are a proper item to be included in actual cost.

18. The contract provides that the cost of furnishing a performance bond in order to guarantee performance under the contract is at the cost of the defendant and is includable within the sums to which the plaintiff is entitled to recover.

19. If you find:
    (a) that the plaintiff substantially completed the construction of the nursing home here involved in accordance with the plans and specifications prepared by the architect and in accordance with the contract, and
    (b) that the architect issued a final certificate of payment in the amount of $74,313.63 on September 25, 1990, and
    (c) the defendant has paid only a total of $45,000 against the amount shown in the final certificate of payment of $74,313.63, and
    (d) the plaintiff has incurred actual costs as defined under the contract of at least $633,000, and
    (e) the charges and extras totaling $32,822.13 were approved by the architect,

    then you are entitled to return a verdict in favor of the plaintiff and against the defendant in the amount of $29,313.63 and you should add to that amount, or any lesser amount you may award plaintiff, interest at 6% from November 25, 1990, to the present.

Respectfully submitted,

_____

H. Riddle Park
Attorney for Plaintiff

**EXHIBIT 10.2**

## Defendant's Points for Charge

IN THE UNITED STATES DISTRICT COURT FOR
THE DISTRICT OF VERMONT

LABILE, INC.
v.                          } Civil Action No. 91-76
SPRING MANOR, INC.

DEFENDANT'S POINTS FOR CHARGE

The learned Judge is requested to charge the jury, on behalf of the defendant, as follows:

1. Under all the evidence, your verdict shall be in favor of the defendant.

2. The claim of the plaintiff is for a balance due under an agreement which provided that for the performance of the work, subject to additions and deductions by change order, the plaintiff was to receive the actual cost of labor, services and material, plus the sum of $32,000, but the total was not to be more than $665,000.

3. Article 5 of the agreement defined what the parties agreed as "actual cost" and this related to three categories:
   (a) Where the work was delegated to a subcontractor: It would be the total sums paid to the subcontractor for the performance of the said subcontract pursuant to a written contract, but this price must be shown to be fair and reasonable and not exceed fair market value.
   (b) Where (the) labor is supplied by the plaintiff: In this instance, the amounts would be the wages and salaries of all workers who actually performed services for the project, including sums paid by the plaintiff for their account for insurance, social security, welfare or pension plan. It does not include supervisory or executive services.
   (c) Materials, supplies and equipment delivered to the project and used pursuant to plans and specifications: These must be used pursuant to the plans and specifications and reduced by any discounts which are made payable by reason of the plaintiff receiving the funds in time to obtain the same. Here again, the charges must be fair and reasonable and not exceed fair market value.
   (d) Please note that the reference to equipment is confined to such items as heating, plumbing, ventilating, air conditioning equipment and the like which are used pursuant to the plans and specifications, and incorporated in the project.
   (e) This does not include the cost for tools, appliances and equipment which the plaintiff must have in order to perform the construction of the nursing home as such items are part of the plaintiff's overhead in the same way as salaries for executive or administrative officers, interest charges, general office expenses, taxes, other than those related to the wages and salaries of the workers.

**EXHIBIT 10.2**

## Defendant's Points for Charge (continued)

4. (a) In considering whether the plaintiff substantially performed the building contract, you must consider the character of what is complained of and determine whether the plaintiff performed the contract in good faith.

(b) Good faith is present if you find the plaintiff faithfully and honestly performed its contract in all material and substantial particulars, and in that event the plaintiff is entitled to be paid if the omissions or defects are technical, inadvertent or unimportant and for such items the defendant is entitled to a credit.

(c) However, if you find there was a willful or obstinate refusal to fulfill the entire contract and the omissions are substantial and material, then the plaintiff cannot recover for any amount and your verdict must be for the defendant.

(d) I charge you that the omission to fulfill the requirements for heating, air conditioning, painting, drainage, blacktopping, parking area illumination, curbing, sidewalk paving, windows, a substitution of inferior equipment, the township regulations and the like are material phases of the contract.

(e) If you find the allowance for the cost of completing the unfinished and incompleted work exceeds any balance due under the contract, then you may find for the defendant in the amount of the difference, or if you find the plaintiff is not entitled to any amount then your verdict for the defendant shall be for the full amount required to complete the contract.

5. In the building contract herein, the plaintiff was obliged to perform in a good and workmanlike manner, in keeping with the plans and specifications, the regulations of Springfield Township, Dulct County and the State of Vermont excepting as they were changed in accordance with the contract terms, and where a phase of the work is not specifically covered by the foregoing or a change order, the law implies that the plaintiff will nevertheless construct the building in question in a reasonable and professional manner so that when it is completed it should be reasonably fit for the purposes intended, even though the parties did not specifically designate certain phases of the work to be done.

6. Because of the nature of the building to be erected for use as a nursing home, the Township of Springfield participated in the agreement between the owner and the plaintiff to the extent that the agreement provided that plaintiff was to comply with the regulations of Springfield Township during the course of construction and its compliance would be evidenced by approval from the Township. Attached to the building agreement was Exhibit "A" which set forth some of the requirements of the Township with which the plaintiff had to comply.

**EXHIBIT 10.2**

## Defendant's Points for Charge (continued)

7. (a) Some of the requirements of the Township which the plaintiff had to fulfill are all parking, loading, access and service areas shall be paved with concrete or blacktop and adequately illuminated at night.

   (b) The buildings, grounds, structures, open spaces, yards, access-ways, entrances, exits, off-street parking facilities, buffer strips, plantings, lawns, trees, landscaping, storm and sanitary sewer drainage structures and facilities, except those installations, the maintenance of which is assumed by the Township, curb and side-walks and screening, shall be faithfully prepared, upkept, maintained and/or replaced.

8. (a) It is clear from the contract provisions that the parking, loading, access and service areas were to be adequately illuminated at night. If you find that this was not performed, the defendant is entitled to a credit or payment equal to the fair and reasonable market value for having this work done.

   (b) You may also consider whether the omission to do this work, if it has occurred, was willful or stubborn refusal on the part of the plaintiff.

9. If you find that paving of the said areas with blacktop was not done in a reasonable and professional manner and when completed reasonably fit for the purpose intended, then you may give defendant credit or payment for the reasonable market value of correcting these omissions.

10. Because of the unique character of the building which was to be used as a nursing home, landscaping and storm sewer drainage were of more than ordinary importance, particularly in light of the uneven topography of the land upon which the nursing home was to be constructed.

11. I charge you that it was the obligation of the plaintiff to do those things by means of grading, landscaping or storm sewer drainage facilities to ensure that the completed project would be free from the vicissitudes of unwanted flow of water and accumulations, and if the plaintiff, as a result of its work, did not obtain a satisfactory result, plaintiff became obligated to pay the defendant the reasonable market cost of correcting any deficient condition.

Respectfully submitted,

_____

Michael O'Michael
Attorney for Defendant

**EXHIBIT 10.3**

## Charge of Court

### CHARGE OF THE COURT

CATO, J.

Members of the jury, this is what is known as a contract action. The plaintiff, the one who is bringing this suit, is suing the defendant for compensation to recover damages for an alleged breach of contract which they maintain happened in this particular case.

Now the object of the Court's charge is to give you the law of the case and to assist you as much as we possibly can in finding the true facts in the case. You should decide this case upon the facts as you find them from the witness stand, from the evidence produced from the witness stand, and the law as we give it to you. You must not decide it upon the basis of the facts or the law of some case you may have heard about in your own past experience. You and you alone are to determine the facts in this case.

It is your recollection of the testimony which is to guide you in reaching a conclusion. Your recollection is controlling, regardless of what may have been said to you by the attorneys or the parties involved, and regardless of my recollection of the facts or what I may say in regard thereto. It is your sworn duty as jurors to determine the facts, and then to apply them to the law in the case.

Now let me point out to you please that the experience in our courts and in ordinary life is that in situations such as exist in this case parties and their witnesses usually disagree as to the facts. This is no indication that they are not trying to be truthful. Human nature is such that it just works that way.

Now there is a conflict in the testimony produced in this case, and it is your sole duty to reconcile the conflicting statements and decide which is accurate and which in your judgment reflects the true picture in the case. That of course means that you are to pass upon the credibility of all the persons who have testified and decide wherein the truth lies.

A credible witness is one who is honestly trying to tell the truth, without taint or favor, and who convinces you of his or her integrity and inspires you with confidence. In passing upon the credibility of the witnesses you must consider their respective interests in favor of one side or the other, whether they are disinterested, whether they answered their questions in a straightforward, candid and honest manner; or whether they were evasive, lacking in candor, or indicated by their attitude that they were not telling the whole truth. All of these things you must consider in arriving at a fair, true and just verdict in accordance with your oaths as jurors. The number of witnesses on one side or the other has nothing to do with which witnesses you should believe.

As I indicated to you, this is an action for breach of contract in which the plaintiff seeks to recover the full amount of the contract price for the work done by him in the construction of a nursing home for the defendant. The

EXHIBIT 10.3
## Charge of Court (continued)

plaintiff claims that he has substantially performed his end of the bargain, that the work was completed in a good and professional manner, and the defendant is obligated to pay the balance due on the agreed contract price.

The defendant has a different view of the matter. He avers that the plaintiff did not fulfill the obligations of the written agreement, that the work was not completed with fidelity to the plans, specifications and understanding of the parties. The defendant's theory is, first, that the plaintiff deliberately and willfully breached the agreement or, in the alternative, secondly, that if his breach was unintentional it resulted in important changes in the structure which he contracted for and did not complete. His contention is that the contract was not substantially performed, and the changes being major in scope constituted a sufficient breach of the agreement to relieve him of all liability.

There is a third alternative to the defendant's position, and that is that if the jury concludes that there were minor changes only the defendant is entitled to a set-off of the balance due under the contract, such a set-off being what it will cost the defendant to correct the alterations or the mistakes.

You must first comprehend, members of the jury, what is meant by the term substantial compliance or substantial performance of a contract. The law is that where a party acting honestly and intending to fulfill his contract performs it substantially, but fails to some comparatively unimportant particulars, the other party will not be permitted to enjoy the fruits of such imperfect performance without paying compensation according to the contract, receiving a credit for any loss for inconveniences suffered. Of course the indulgence is not to be so stretched as to cover fraud, gross negligence or obstinate and willful refusal to fulfill the whole engagement. In this respect, whether the breach, if such there was, was willful or merely inadvertent is extremely important.

The plaintiff, having invoked the doctrine here, has the duty of presenting a case in which there has been no willful omission or departure from the terms of his contract. If there was no substantial performance, then there can be no recovery.

Now the test of substantial performance depends upon the character of the changes or alterations complained of, whether they materially affected the completed structure and were in good faith honestly intended to fulfill the contract. It is for you, the members of the jury, to say whether these departures, if there were any, were material, and whether the contractor was acting in good faith.

In discovering whether there was substantial compliance these are some of the things which you should consider:

One, the extent to which the defendant will obtain the substantial benefit which he was reasonably entitled to anticipate under his contract;

EXHIBIT 10.3

## Charge of Court (continued)

Two, the extent to which the defendant may be adequately compensated in the way of a set-off for lack of complete performance, if such there was;

Three, the extent to which the plaintiff has already performed;

Four, whether the plaintiff willfully neglected to perform, or whether he innocently failed to perform.

Now all of this can be distilled into these basic things. If there was substantial performance, the plaintiff is entitled to recover the balance due, less an allowance for the cost of completing the work, provided the failure of performance was not willful. If there were minor alterations or changes in the contract requirements, the plaintiff may recover the full amount due him less what it would cost the defendant reasonably to put the property in the condition contemplated by the contract terms. Your verdict in such case would be for the plaintiff for the contract price less what it would cost to put the property into the condition contemplated. If there was no substantial performance, your verdict would be for the defendant. If the plaintiff willfully and intentionally breached the agreement by not complying with the contract terms, he may not recover.

Now the plaintiff contends that the defendant requested that certain alterations and additions be made to the structure under construction, and that he acceded to such requests and did the work directed by the architect. For this reason he is asking compensation at the hands of the defendant for the additional labor and material cost, plus a reasonable profit for the extra work involved. The defendant denies that he requested the plaintiff to do anything outside of the contract requirements, and relies upon the fact that there are no written change orders for these changes as extras.

Members of the jury, if during the process of construction the plaintiff made changes in the construction which were not contained in the original plans and specifications, and if such changes were made at the request of the defendant or the defendant's architect, under the law the defendant would be liable for the reasonable cost, and a reasonable profit to the plaintiff, unless of course there is sufficient evidence that the parties agreed to a different result.

Notwithstanding there was a written contract in this case, the parties were always free to make further contracts which altered or changed the conditions specified in the writing. The question is, did they make such further contracts? The plaintiff says that the defendant did from time to time through the architect request that this extra work be done, and that he agreed to do it and did do it. If this extra work was not included in the written document, and if the parties agreed that it be done, then even though no specified price was agreed upon, a contract for the doing of the work was entered into and the plaintiff could recover for the reasonable value of the accomplished result, including a reasonable profit.

**EXHIBIT 10.3**

## Charge of Court (continued)

It has been maintained by the defendant that the written contract specified that there was to be no extra work or extra charges unless agreed upon in writing by the parties. Notwithstanding this and notwithstanding the previously expressed intention of the parties in the writing, the parties were still free to modify the original agreement by a subsequent verbal contract.

Now a contract means that the parties have a meeting of the minds; that is, that one party agreed to do a certain thing and the other party agreed to pay for it, either in performance or in some other way. Thus if the plaintiff orally agreed to make changes or alterations in the contract terms or the structure encompassed therein, and the defendant specifically or implicitly agreed to pay for such changes or alterations or extra work and materials, a full and legal contract was made which bound both parties, even though the original written contract stipulated against such an oral contract.

The oral contract if made would change the written one only in the particulars encompassed by the oral arrangement, and would not affect the remaining portions of the writing. But if the work done and the materials furnished were required in the original contract, there would be no consideration to support the oral agreement, and it would not be binding on the defendant. One does not suffer a detriment sufficient to constitute consideration for an oral contract if the detriment suffered was something he or she was already bound by the court to do.

Members of the jury, in making the determination whether there was an oral contract for extra work in this case, although the writing could not preclude the making of such oral agreement, you may still consider the provisions in the written agreement which stipulates against oral agreements for extras. You may not consider the writing as a proscription against oral contracts of that nature, but you may consider it in determining whether such an oral contract was made. The writing might be considered by you as some evidence of the intentions of the parties at the time, but it must not be construed as a prohibition against the making of such subsequent oral agreements.

Now where a party seeks to establish a change in a written contract, that party has the burden of proof. The plaintiff has that burden here. He must establish the oral contract by evidence which is convincing to you not to an absolute certainty or beyond a reasonable doubt, but sufficient in quantity and quality to establish the existence of the agreement and its terms.

The acts of the parties, their conduct, and the circumstances and relations existing between them are all elements to be given due consideration in determining both the existence and terms of such an agreement. The mere suggestion or possibility of a contract arising from transactions between the parties would not be enough. There must be evidence authorizing more than a conjecture or guess.

EXHIBIT 10.3

# Charge of Court (continued)

Members of the jury, the job of a building contractor constructing a building pursuant to plans and specifications prepared by an architect engaged by the owner is to construct the building substantially in accordance with the plans and specifications prepared by the architect.

Where a builder builds pursuant to plans and specifications prepared by an architect engaged by the owner, the builder, here the plaintiff, assumes no responsibility for the design of the building.

If you should find that the plaintiff substantially completed the construction of the nursing home here involved in accordance with the plans and specifications prepared by the architect, and if you should find further that the architect issued a final certificate for payment, the plaintiff would be entitled to payment in full of the entire unpaid balance from the defendant within sixty days after substantial completion of the work.

The architect in this case has testified, and you will be required to recall his exact testimony, that in his opinion the plaintiff had substantially completed the work in accordance with his plans and specifications by September 25, 1990, and that he issued on that date a final certificate for payment. Your attention is called to the provisions of Article 10.5(a) of the Special Conditions of the contract which provides that the decisions of the architect shall be final.

Where a contract provides that the work shall be done to the satisfaction, approval or acceptance of an architect, the architect is thereby constituted sole arbiter between the parties, and the parties are bound by his decision unless there be fraud, collusion or caprice.

There has been no proof of fraud, collusion or caprice in this case.

With respect to any question of faulty materials or defective workmanship, your attention is directed to Article 10.2(a) of the Special Conditions, which provides that the plaintiff is required to repair or replace only work determined by the architect to be faulty or defective within one year from the date of substantial completion of the project.

Even if you should find that the architect did determine that there was some defective or faulty work requiring repair by the contractor, any breach of that provision of the contract would not relieve the defendant from paying to plaintiff the unpaid balance under the contract.

There was some testimony submitted on behalf of the defendant relating to compliance with the regulations of the Township of Springfield. The issuance of the certificate of occupancy is prima facie evidence that all regulations of the Township of Springfield have been complied with.

The contract in this case provides that the plaintiff shall be deemed to have complied with the regulations of the Township of Springfield when the construction has been approved by the Township authorities having jurisdiction. The Township authority having jurisdiction is the authority which issues certificates of occupancy, and you will recall that the defendant's own witness testified that the certificate of occupancy had been issued and is now free of any condition.

**EXHIBIT 10.3**

# Charge of Court (continued)

The certification by the Bureau of Aging of the Department of Welfare of the State of Vermont is also prima facie evidence of compliance with applicable regulations of the State of Vermont as they pertain to the construction of nursing homes.

The contract here provides that the plaintiff shall be deemed to have complied with the regulations of the State of Vermont when the construction has been approved by the State authorities having jurisdiction. The State authority having jurisdiction over nursing homes is the Bureau of Aging of the Department of Welfare, and the defendant's own witnesses admitted issuance of proper certification by the Bureau of Aging. You will recall Mr. Gallo testified to that extent yesterday.

The architect is the owner's representative during construction and until final payment has been made, and Mr. Stillee as architect had authority to act on behalf of the defendant and to issue instructions to the plaintiff.

Members of the jury, there has been testimony that included in the plaintiff's claim of $32,822.13 is a claim of $29,313.63 of changes and extras. Except for a change order in the amount of $175 relating to electrical receptacles, the remaining changes and extras were approved by the architect orally, according to the testimony of both the architect and Mr. Labile. Further, this testimony is unrebutted and uncontroverted. In addition, the architect stated that he knew of the changes and extras being done at or about the time that the work was done. You are directed that under these circumstances, if you find either that the architect orally approved the changes and extras or knew of the changes and extras at or about the time the work was done, the defendant must pay for all of those changes.

In addition to the additions and deductions as covered by the claim for changes and extras, the contract provided that the defendant shall pay the plaintiff for the performance of the work, the actual cost of labor, services and material together with an additional sum of $32,000, but in no event a sum, exclusive of changes and extras, in excess of $665,000. Accordingly, if you find that the actual cost of labor, services and material incurred by the plaintiff, exclusive of the changes and extras, total $633,000 or more, then the plaintiff is entitled to payments totalling $665,000 under the contract plus the amount you find the plaintiff is entitled to receive by reason of the approved changes and extras.

Now Article 5.1 of the contract defines actual cost as follows:

"(a) In the event of a subcontract, the total sums paid by contractor to subcontractor for the performance of said subcontract pursuant to a written contract.

"(b) In the event that the labor is supplied by contractor, then the wages and salaries of all workers who actually performed services for the premises and any sums paid by contractor for their account, whether for insurance, social security, welfare or pension plan.

## EXHIBIT 10.3
# Charge of Court (continued)

"(c) The actual cost to contractor of all material, supplies and equipment delivered to project and used pursuant to plans and specifications, and where the funds are made available to contractor in time to earn any discounts on materials purchased the same shall be deducted."

Under the definition of actual cost, the cost of the equipment rentals delivered to the project and issued pursuant to the plans and specifications are a proper item to be included in actual cost.

The contract provides that the cost of furnishing a performance bond in order to guarantee performance under the contract is at the cost of the defendant and is includable within the sums to which the plaintiff is entitled to recovery.

Members of the jury, if you find that the plaintiff substantially completed the construction of the nursing home here involved in accordance with the plans and specifications prepared by the architect and in accordance with the contract, and that the architect issued a final certificate of payment in the amount of $74,313.63 on September 25, 1990, and that the defendant has paid only a total of $45,000 against the amount shown in the final certificate of payment of $74,313.63, and that the plaintiff has incurred actual costs as defined under the contract of at least $633,000, and the changes and extras totalling $32,822.13 were approved by the architect, then you would be entitled to return a verdict in favor of the plaintiff and against the defendant in the amount of $29,313.63; and if you do, you may add to that amount, or any lesser amount that you might find for the plaintiff, interest at the rate of 6% from November 25, 1990, to the present time.

The claim of the plaintiff here is for a balance due under an agreement which provided that for the performance of the work, subject to additions and deductions by change order, the plaintiff was to receive the actual cost of labor, services and materials plus the sum of $32,000, but the actual cost was not to be more than $665,000. In considering whether the plaintiff substantially performed the building contract, you must consider the character of what is complained of and determine whether the plaintiff performed the contract in good faith. Now good faith is present if you find the plaintiff faithfully and honestly performed its contract in all material and substantial particulars; and in that event the plaintiff is entitled to be paid if the omissions or defects are technical, inadvertent or unimportant, and for such items the defendant is entitled to a credit. However, if you find there was a willful or obstinate refusal to fulfill the entire contract, and the omissions are substantial and material, then the plaintiff cannot recover for any amount, and your verdict must be for the defendant.

Members of the jury, I charge you that the omission to fulfill the requirements for heating, air conditioning, painting, drainage, blacktopping, parking area illumination, curbing, sidewalk paving, windows, a substitution of inferior equipment, the Township regulations and the like are material phases of the contract if you so find.

**EXHIBIT 10.3**

## Charge of Court (continued)

If you find the allowance for the cost of completing the unfinished and incompleted work exceeds any balance due under the contract, as I have heretofore indicated to you, then you may find a verdict for the defendant in the amount of the difference. Or if you find the plaintiff is not entitled to any amount then your verdict for the defendant shall be for the full amount required to complete the contract.

In the building contract in this case the plaintiff was obliged to perform in a good and professional manner, in keeping with the plans and specifications, the regulations of Springfield Township, Dulcet County and the State of Vermont, excepting as they were changed in accordance with the contract terms. And where a phase of the work is not specifically covered by the foregoing or a change order, the law implies that the plaintiff will nevertheless construct the building in question in a reasonable and professional manner so that when it is completed it should be reasonably fit for the purposes intended, even though the parties did not specifically designate certain phases of the work to be done. Because of the nature of the building to be erected for use as a nursing home, the Township of Springfield participated in the agreement between the owner and the plaintiff to the extent that the agreement provided that the plaintiff was to comply with the regulations of Springfield Township during the course of construction, and its compliance would be evidenced by approval from the Township. Attached to the building agreement was Exhibit A, which set forth some of the requirements of the Township with which the plaintiff had to comply.

Some of the requirements of the Township which the plaintiff had to fulfill are all parking, loading, access and service areas shall be paved with concrete or blacktop and adequately illuminated at night. The buildings, grounds, structures, open spaces, yards, accessways, entrances, exits, off-street parking facilities, buffer strips, plantings, lawns, trees, landscaping, storm and sanitary sewer drainage structures and facilities, except those installations, the maintenance of which is assumed by the Township, curb and sidewalks and screening, shall be faithfully prepared, upkept, maintained and/or replaced.

It is clear from the contract provisions that the parking, loading, access and service areas were to be adequately illuminated at night. If you find that this was not performed, the defendant is entitled to a credit or a payment equal to the fair and reasonable market value for having this work done.

You may also consider whether the omission to do this work, if it occurred, was willful or stubborn refusal on the part of the plaintiff.

If you find that paving of the said areas with blacktop was not done in a reasonable and professional manner, and when completed reasonably fit for the purpose intended, then you may give defendant credit or payment for the reasonable market value of correcting these omissions.

**EXHIBIT 10.3**

## Charge of Court (continued)

Gentlemen, are there any exceptions or corrections to the court's charge? If so I will hear them at side Bar.*

[Side Bar conference, reported as follows:]

MR. PARK: I have none, Your Honor.

THE COURT: Let me make one statement on the record before we entertain your applications. I read all of the plaintiff's points and defendant's points to the jury which I approved without giving their number. The ones that I did not read are deemed to be refused, with an exception to the party whose point I did not read. With that understanding you may make your objections.

MR. O'MICHAEL: I only have a few. In the first place I think it might be pointed out to this jury that the architect's authority is circumscribed by the specific terms of the General Conditions, and that is that Article I think 12.12, or whatever it is; and that the architect as the agent of the owner must perform strictly within the terms of that limitation.

The other thing is, Your Honor referred to architect's certificate as a final certificate.

THE COURT: No, I did not say final; I said he said it was a final certificate.

MR. O'MICHAEL: I think it might be pointed out that the certificate specifically provides that its issuance, payment and acceptance are without prejudice to any rights of the owner or contractor under their contract.

THE COURT: I think that has been pointed out to them at least three or four times during the course of this trial by reference.

MR. O'MICHAEL: Excepting now, in other words, I think what you have done here, I think unwittingly, is to give them the impression that the fact that the architect issued the certificate is sort of conclusive. It is not the conclusive certificate. If you just clear that up—

THE COURT: I indicated to the jury that the architect termed it a certificate of completion, indicating to them that they have to find that.

MR. O'MICHAEL: Don't you think it would be rounded out to—

THE COURT: I think if I refer to it now I would be emphasizing it in your favor, and I think in the context in which it now appears it is a matter for their determination.

MR. O'MICHAEL: You see, what you have said to them does not call attention to the fact that it is not a conclusive or an unequivocal certificate. And also that certificate is not signed by Labile, which requires a certification that the work was performed. I am just talking about the certificate.

THE COURT: You went into great depth when you cross-examined the architect along those lines.

*Not within the hearing of the jury.

**EXHIBIT 10.3**

## Charge of Court (continued)

MR. O'MICHAEL: True, but I am talking now about in your charge having referred to it in one capacity, I thought you would round it out or you might say to them that when they examine the certificate they should look at it carefully.

THE COURT: I think that my reference to it was an impartial reference and it did not favor either the plaintiff or the defendant, and it was just calling it like it really is, indicating it was the architect's characterization of it as a certificate of completion, not mine or yours or the plaintiff's. I am satisfied with it. I will grant you an exception.

MR. O'MICHAEL: All right.

Now the reference to the certificate of occupancy you say is prima facie evidence, but don't you think you ought to extend that and make them understand the word—prima facie to them may be just a word—that this does not prevent them from considering whether or not the work was actually completed.

THE COURT: I think I covered—

MR. O'MICHAEL: I think your charge was excellent in most respects. I will repeat, but leaving it just hang there as prima facie evidence without explaining to the jury that this does not mean that they cannot consider whether in fact the work was fully completed, because as a matter of fact the work was not fully completed in several respects.

THE COURT: I think I did that for you when I affirmed your point for charge which enumerated everything but the dust on the window sills.

MR. O'MICHAEL: If these people were Latin scholars I would not suggest it, but I don't think they know what prima facie means. To them prima facie is an overpowering word.

THE COURT: Nowadays they know it. When you and I went to law school they didn't know it, but now they know it.

MR. O'MICHAEL: You did say at the beginning that contract was in accordance with the plans and specifications; when you read from my points, you did say plans and specifications and all the other things there. There is a contradiction in that respect.

THE COURT: No. It is adequately covered within the four corners of the charge.

MR. O'MICHAEL: Now the rental equipment if Your Honor please, I gave you a case which is directly on point.

THE COURT: I don't so find.

MR. O'MICHAEL: And the contract itself says that it has to be used pursuant to the plans and specifications. There is nothing in the plans and specifications that requires rental equipment.

THE COURT: I think a reasonable and logical reading of the plans and specifications would lead to the conclusion that rental equipment as used on this particular job was contemplated by the parties. That is the position I am taking. I will grant you an exception.

EXHIBIT 10.3

## Charge of Court (continued)

MR. O'MICHAEL: The last thing is, you referred to it as a final certificate of payment. It is not a final certificate of payment.

THE COURT: If I did, I read it from your points for charge.

MR. O'MICHAEL: I never called it a final certificate of payment. It is not a final certificate of payment. It is not headed that way, nor does it—

MR. PARK: I think Your Honor charged, if you find that it was a final certificate of payment. I think it is part of my last point.

MR. O'MICHAEL: When it came over to me—

THE COURT: You weren't writing fast enough. I prefaced it with if you find.

MR. O'MICHAEL: Okay.

THE COURT: I am going to read this additional notation to the jury, that the architect's authority is circumscribed in the general conditions of the contract, and the architect or agent of the owner must perform within the terms of that limitation.

MR. O'MICHAEL: That requires his authority to be in writing from the owner.

MR. PARK: I would object to that, because as between the building and the owner I believe that the law is that the builder can rely on instructions he receives from the architect.

THE COURT: Yes, but that is not the question; the question is the authority of the architect, and he is asking that I indicate to the jury that the authority of the architect is circumscribed in the general conditions of the contract, and the architect as agent of the owner must perform within the terms of that limitation.

MR. O'MICHAEL: And they provide that his instructions must be in writing.

MR. PARK: Your Honor will grant me an exception as to that?

THE COURT: Yes, I will grant you an exception.

[End of side Bar conference.]

THE COURT: Members of the jury, in addition to the law which I have given you in regard to this particular case, I would like to remind you that the architect's authority in this case is circumscribed in the general conditions of the contract, and the architect as the agent of the owner must perform his duties within the terms of that limitation, as they are outlined in the contract.

Members of the jury, you may now retire subject to further instructions that I will give you; and when you do, you are to go over the evidence carefully and find the true facts based on your mature, honest, sincere and fair consideration, free from bias or prejudice against anyone connected with this case. Apply those facts to the law as I have given it to you, and render what you believe to be a just and proper verdict in this case, which verdict must be concurred in by all of you unanimously.

## K. The Verdict

Upon completion of the charge, the jury retires to the jury room to begin its deliberations. The jury decision is called the **verdict.** There are two types of verdicts: special and general.[3] The general verdict is the most familiar as it describes who wins and in what amount. In addition, a general verdict may be accompanied by answers to interrogatories upon one or more issues of fact submitted by the court, the decision of which is necessary to a verdict. In this context, interrogatories are special questions submitted by the court to the jury for its deliberation. They are not the same as interrogatories used in the discovery procedure. For example, the jury may be asked to answer a question similar to the following in a case in which there were more than two defendants:

> Was the defendant X guilty of negligence which proximately contributed to the injury of the plaintiff?

A special verdict is one in which the court may require a jury to return a decision in the form of a special written finding upon each issue of fact that was submitted by the court. When the jury reaches a verdict the trial has come to an end.

## IV. Summary

Before a trial begins it is common to have a final conference with the trial judge to review the upcoming trial and to explore the possibility of settlement. Assuming the case does not settle at this juncture, it proceeds to trial. If the parties have requested a jury trial, the first step will be to select a jury. The method for examining prospective jurors is called voir dire. Based on this process, the trial lawyers can attempt to prevent prospective jurors from sitting on the jury by challenging them. There are two types of challenges: peremptory (no cause) and cause. Once the jury has been selected, they are sworn in and assigned seats.

Next the trial lawyers give their opening statements. Each party's attorney tells the jury about the merits of his or her case and what the jurors can expect during the trial. Upon completion of this phase, the plaintiff's counsel begins the presentation of witnesses and evidence.

When a witness is called to the witness box the attorney begins direct examination. After direct examination, the witness can be cross-examined by counsel for the defendant. The purpose of cross-examination is typically to discredit the witness. After cross-examination, the plaintiff's attorney can put the witness through redirect examination, which is intended to rehabilitate a witness's credibility.

The plaintiff's counsel continues to call witnesses until he or she has sufficiently presented the case. The plaintiff then "rests," and the defendant takes over. The defendant's counsel follows the same procedure as plaintiff's counsel in calling witnesses and presenting evidence to support his or her position. Each witness goes through direct examination, cross-examination, and redirect examination when appropriate.

---

[3]FCRP 49.

Once the parties have completed their presentation of evidence, the attorneys for each party present their closing arguments. The purpose of closing arguments is to highlight the strengths and weaknesses of each party's position based on the evidence presented at trial.

At the conclusion of the arguments, the trial judge will give the jurors instructions to guide them in their deliberation process. This charge to the jury includes a statement of the law to be applied. Armed with the judge's instructions or charge, the jury "retires" to deliberate a decision. Once the jury agrees upon its decision, it renders a verdict to the court.

---

## V. KEY TERMS

Burden of proof
Challenge for cause
Closing argument
Cross-examination
Direct examination
Jury challenge

Motion for directed
  verdict
Motion in limine
Opening statement
Peremptory challenge

Points for charge
Rebuttal
Redirect examination
Verdict
Voir dire

## VI. QUESTIONS

1. What are the main tasks a paralegal performs during trial?
2. What is "voir dire"?
3. What are the two types of jury challenges and how do they differ?
4. What is direct examination?
5. What is cross-examination?
6. What is a motion for a directed verdict?
7. What is a burden of proof?
8. What is a jury verdict?
9. What are the basic purposes of a conference with the trial judge before the trial actually begins?
10. Compare and contrast direct examination with redirect examination.

# CHAPTER 11

# POST-TRIAL PROCEEDINGS AND ENFORCEMENT OF JUDGMENTS

## I. INTRODUCTION

It is inevitable that once the jury has reached its verdict, at least one of the parties to a lawsuit has to lose. Sometimes both parties to a lawsuit are dissatisfied with the jury's verdict (for example, when a party is awarded damages he or she considers too low). This chapter initially focuses on the losing party. Specifically, we will explore the procedural mechanisms available to the party dissatisfied with the jury's verdict. These mechanisms are: motion for judgment notwithstanding the verdict, motion for a new trial, and appeal.

In addition, we will focus on the party who has received a favorable jury verdict that results in a judgment, and we will examine the procedure of enforcing a judgment (that is, collecting money from the losing party).

It will become obvious during this chapter that trial does not always resolve a dispute between the parties. When considering the processes of postverdict motions, appeals, and enforcement of judgments, paralegals should understand and accept the fact that the jury verdict can be viewed as only the end of a phase of the process of civil litigation, not the end of the case. Post-trial proceedings and enforcement of judgments can be both timeconsuming and expensive. It can also be frustrating to the winners and losers because many of the procedures covered here can act to hinder the potential goals of a lawsuit (finality of decision and compensation for injury).

The paralegal can perform the following tasks during the post-trial proceedings and enforcement of judgments:

- preparing and drafting postverdict motions

- legal research concerning the issues raised in the motions

- assisting in obtaining bonds to stay a judgment

- preparing bill of costs

- preparing notice of appeal

- coordinating and assisting in ordering the transcript and transmitting record on appeal

- assisting in preparation of brief on appeal

- assisting in locating assets

- preparing execution documents

## II. POSTVERDICT MOTIONS

Under the Federal Rules of Civil Procedure, there are two postverdict motions that can be used by a party dissatisfied with a jury's verdict to set aside that verdict. They are a motion for judgment notwithstanding the verdict and a motion for a new trial. Although under the federal rules these motions can be filed together, they are different with respect to both procedure and utilization; each will be explored separately in the following paragraphs. However both methods provide a way for the trial judge (sitting alone or with two additional trial-level judges) to review the case for possible errors.

# A. Motion for Judgment Notwithstanding the Verdict

The purpose of a **motion for judgment notwithstanding the verdict** (n.o.v.) is to request the judge to set aside the jury verdict and enter judgment in favor of the party making the motion. The grounds for this motion are that the verdict is unreasonable and unsupportable in light of the evidence presented during the trial. Procedurally, in order to make this motion, two criteria must be met under the federal procedural rules:[1]

**1.** The party filing the motion must have moved for a directed verdict at the close of all the evidence, and the motion was denied.

**2.** The motion must be filed within ten days after judgment has been rendered pursuant to the jury verdict.

This motion requests the same thing that a directed verdict requests earlier in the lawsuit. However, given the advantage of knowing the jury's verdict, the judge, in a motion for judgment n.o.v., must determine whether the particular decision of the jury is reasonable. N.o.v. is the Latin abbreviation for non obstante veredicto, which means notwithstanding the verdict. It is common to see this motion with its Latin abbreviation. Prior to the jury's verdict, in a motion for a directed verdict, the judge must determine what a reasonable jury would decide if given the opportunity.

If the judge determines that there was evidence to support the jury's verdict and the verdict was reasonable, the judge must deny the motion. If the motion is granted, the verdict is set aside and judgment is entered as the judge directs. Exhibit 11.1 is an example of a motion for judgment notwithstanding the verdict.

In addition to filing the actual motion, it is customary to submit a proposed order granting the relief sought by the motion and a brief or memorandum of law setting forth the legal authority relied upon in support of the motion. (These suggested submissions are also applicable to a motion for new trial.)

# B. Motion for a New Trial

A motion for judgment n.o.v. and a **motion for a new trial** are usually filed together in the form of a request for alternative relief. A motion for a new trial may be granted (instead of judgment n.o.v.) in cases in which, although a judge believed the jury's verdict to be incorrect, entry of judgment n.o.v. (which would reverse the jury's decision) would be inappropriate. Errors of a serious nature during the course of the trial that make it possible or likely that the jury (or judge) did not decide the case fairly are also reasons for granting a motion for a new trial. A motion for a new trial may also test the sufficiency of the evidence or attack the amount of the verdict.

A motion for a new trial usually must be made within the same ten-day time period as a motion for judgment notwithstanding the verdict. Unlike the motion for judgment n.o.v., no prior motions are required to have been made during the

---

[1]FRCP 50(b).

**EXHIBIT 11.1**

## Motion for Judgment N.O.V.

IN THE UNITED STATES DISTRICT COURT FOR THE
NORTHERN DISTRICT OF CALIFORNIA

Johnson, Inc.

    v.

Office Products, Inc.

} Civil Action No. 92-1969

DEFENDANT'S MOTION FOR JUDGMENT N.O.V.

AND NOW, to wit, this 3rd day of December, 1992, the defendant moves the court to have all the evidence taken upon the trial duly certified and filed so as to become part of the record and for judgment in favor of the defendant non obstante veredicto upon the whole record.

/s/

_____

Evelyn Good
Attorney for Defendant

trial. However, objections should have been made during the trial to any errors or evidentiary rulings of a serious nature that occurred during the course of the trial.

When preparing this motion, the attorney or paralegal must list all the reasons he or she feels would entitle the client to a new trial. Because most clients are financially unable to have each day's testimony transcribed by a court reporter on a daily basis, the litigators must rely on their notes taken during the trial. Once again, the paralegal's role in taking accurate notes of the testimony and other proceedings during trial can pay positive dividends as an aid in preparing a motion for new trial.

After the litigation team has had an opportunity to study the stenographic record of the trial, additional grounds of error may be discovered that may then be assigned in support of the motion for a new trial. Therefore, it is common practice always to state general grounds as reason for the new trial in addition to any specific ones. It is also common practice to state as grounds for the motion "such other grounds as may be discovered after the notes of testimony are transcribed." This latter practice may be permitted only upon specific authorization by the court or by the local rules of procedure. Exhibit 11.2 provides an example of a motion for new trial.

Unlike the motion for judgment notwithstanding the verdict, the effect of granting a motion for new trial is not the final disposition of the case. When a party is successful in this motion and the motion is granted, the moving party is entitled to a new trial by another jury.

EXHIBIT 11.2

# Motion for New Trial

## IN THE UNITED STATES DISTRICT COURT FOR THE NORTHERN DISTRICT OF CALIFORNIA

Johnson Inc.

v.

Office Products, Inc.

} Civil Action No. 91-1969

### MOTION FOR NEW TRIAL

AND NOW, to wit, this 3rd day of December, 1992, comes Evelyn Good, Esquire, attorney for the defendant in the above entitled case, and moves the court for a new trial.

In support of said motion, the following reasons are set forth, to be supplemented by additional reasons, which will appear from examination of the transcript of the record.

1. The verdict was against the evidence.
2. The verdict was against the weight of the evidence.
3. The verdict was against the law.
4. The verdict was against the charge of the court.

The learned trial judge erred:

5. In sustaining the plaintiff's objections to the admission of testimony of the witnesses:

Sylvia G. Forest
Derrick Bates
Carmen Velasquez

6. In instructing the jury upon the return of its verdict that they were required to find interest as an additional item of damage.

7. In failing to instruct the jury to return its verdict on the defendant's counterclaim.

/s/

_____

Evelyn Good
Attorney for Defendant

## III. THE PROCESS OF JUDGMENT AND TAXATION OF COSTS

If the case has been tried by a jury, the jury's verdict will generally be entered as a **judgment** of the court immediately after the close of the trial. The judge will make an order that judgment be entered in favor of the plaintiff in the amount of the verdict (if there are money damages) or in favor of the defendant and dismiss the complaint (if the plaintiff has failed to prove the case). A similar procedure would be used with respect to any cross-claims or counterclaims. Typically the judgment is a formal document prepared either by the winning attorney (with the assistance of his or her paralegal) or by the judge. It is filed with the clerk of court's office and entered on the civil docket sheet showing the entry of the judgment and the date.[2]

In the absence of postverdict motions, the judgment will usually follow the verdict of the jury. If postverdict motions are filed, judgment is still entered after the verdict. However, if the postverdict motions are successful, judgment will be either directed in favor of the moving party (modifying the earlier judgment) or removed because of an order granting a new trial.

If the case was tried without a jury, after the conclusion of the trial the judge will normally take the matter under advisement before making a decision. This may take a relatively long period of time as the judge may want to review the proceedings (through a transcript of the notes of testimony and exhibits presented at trial) and also may ask the opposing attorneys to prepare briefs showing why each is entitled to a decision in favor of his or her client. When this review is complete, the judge will give notice of the decision. As with jury trials, the judge will then issue an order for judgment based on the decision.

### A. Costs

Part of the process of judgment is the **taxation of costs.** Under Rule 54(d) of the Federal Rules of Civil Procedure costs are allowed to the prevailing party unless the court otherwise directs. The purpose of this taxation of costs is to help the winner defray some of the expenses incurred as a result of having to litigate a matter and to make the losing party pay for these expenses.

The following may be taxed as costs in federal civil litigation:

- fees of the clerk and marshal
- fees of the court reporter for all or any part of the stenographic transcript necessarily obtained for use in the case
- fees and disbursements for printing (briefs, for example)
- fees for witnesses (including per diem, mileage, and subsistence)
- fees for exemplification and copies of papers necessarily obtained for use in the case
- docket fees
- costs incident to taking depositions

[2]FRCP 79(a).

The prevailing party (through his or her paralegal) will usually file a Bill of Costs form with the clerk of court's office specifying what costs are being claimed. A copy of the Bill of Costs is sent to the counsel for the losing party. If the losing party opposes any or all of the itemized costs, objections can be filed with the clerk of court. If objections are filed, the clerk of court must make a determination of the costs allowable. Once the amount of costs is determined it becomes part of the judgment itself.[3]

Exhibit 11.3 is a copy of both sides of a Bill of Costs form.

**EXHIBIT 11.3**

## Bill of Costs Form

AO133
(Rev 7/82)

**BILL OF COSTS**

United States District Court      DISTRICT

DOCKET NO.

v.      MAGISTRATE CASE NO.

Judgment having been entered in the above action on _____ against
date

_____ the clerk is requested to tax the following as costs:

**BILL OF COSTS**

Fees of the clerk . . . . . . . . . . . . . . . . . . . . . . . . . . . . . . . . . . . . $_____
Fees for service of summons and complaint . . . . . . . . . . . . . . _____
Fees of the court reporter for all or any part of the
transcript necessarily obtained for use in the case . . . . . . . . . _____
Fees and disbursements for printing . . . . . . . . . . . . . . . . . . . . . _____
Fees for witnesses (itemized on reverse side) . . . . . . . . . . . . . _____
Fees for exemplification and copies of papers necessarily
obtained for use in case . . . . . . . . . . . . . . . . . . . . . . . . . . . . . . . _____
Docket fees under 28 U.S.C. § 1923 . . . . . . . . . . . . . . . . . . . . . _____
Costs incident to taking of depositions . . . . . . . . . . . . . . . . . . . _____
Cost as shown on Mandate of Court of Appeals . . . . . . . . . . _____
Other costs (Please itemize) . . . . . . . . . . . . . . . . . . . . . . . . . . . . _____
_____
_____
_____

Total      $_____

---

[3]Title 28 U.S.C. §1920.

**EXHIBIT 11.3**

## Bill of Costs Form (continued)

SPECIAL NOTE: Attach to your bill an itemization and documentation for requested costs in all categories. Briefs should also be submitted supporting the necessity of the requested costs and citing cases supporting taxation of those costs.

### DECLARATION

I declare under penalty of perjury that the foregoing costs are correct and were necessarily incurred in this action and that the services for which fees have been charged were actually and necessarily performed. A copy hereof was this day mailed with postage fully prepaid thereon to:

SIGNATURE OF ATTORNEY _____

For: _____ DATE _____
          Name of claiming party

Please take notice that I will appear before the clerk     DATE AND TIME
who will tax said costs on the following day and time:

Costs are hereby taxed in the following        AMOUNT TAXED
amount and included in the judgment:            $

CLERK OF COURT          (BY) DEPUTY CLERK                    DATE

### Witness Fees (computation, cf. 28 U.S.C. 1821 for statutory fees)

| NAME AND RESIDENCE | Attendance | | Subsistence | | Mileage | | Total Cost Each Witness |
|---|---|---|---|---|---|---|---|
| | Days | Total Cost | Days | Total Cost | Miles | Total Cost | |
| | | | | | | | |
| | | | | | | | |
| | | | | | | | |
| | | | | | | | |
| | | | | | | | |
| | | | | | TOTAL | | |

NOTICE

Section 1924, Title 28, U.S. Code (effective September 1, 1948) provides: "Sec. 1924. Verification of bill of costs."

**EXHIBIT 11.3**

## Bill of Costs Form (continued)

"Before any bill of costs is taxed, the party claiming any item of cost or disbursement shall attach thereto an affidavit, made by himself or by his duly authorized attorney or agent having knowledge of the facts, that such item is correct and has been necessarily incurred in the case and that the services for which fees have been charged were actually and necessarily performed."

**See also Section 1920 of Title 28 which reads in part as follows:**
"A bill of costs shall be filed in the case and, upon allowance, included in the judgment or decree."

**The Federal Rules of Civil Procedure contain the following provisions:**
*Rule 54 (d)*
"Except when express provision therefor is made either in a statute of the United States or in these rules, costs shall be allowed as of course to the prevailing party unless the court otherwise directs, but costs against the United States, its officers, and agencies shall be imposed only to the extent permitted by law. Costs may be taxed by the clerk on one day's notice. On motion served within 5 days thereafter, the action of the clerk may be reviewed by the court."

*Rule 6 (e)*
"Whenever a party has the right or is required to do some act or take some proceedings within a prescribed period after the service of a notice or other paper upon him and the notice or paper is served upon him by mail, 3 days shall be added to the prescribed period."

*Rule 58 (In Part)*
"Entry of the judgment shall not be delayed for the taxing of costs."

## IV. APPEAL

An **appeal** may be taken only from a final judgment, decree, or order of the trial court. Although there are exceptions to this rule, such as in the case of inter-locutory appeals (certain issues may be appealed prior to final judgment), it is beyond the scope of this chapter to elaborate on these specific exceptions. The purpose of an appeal is to have a higher court review the trial court's conduct of the case in the hope that the decision of trial court will be changed. As was stated earlier in this book (Chapter 2), appeals from the United States District Court are usually taken to the United States Court of Appeals for the circuit in which the district court is located. Any party to the lawsuit may appeal the final judgment of the trial court. However, due to expense and time involved, most parties do not file appeals from the decisions of trial courts.

There are certain terms that need to be defined concerning the process of appeal. Most important is the terminology used to define the parties. The party who files the appeal is called the **appellant.** The party who was successful at trial and did not appeal is called the **appellee.** Other terms will be defined as they arise.

## A. Scope of Review

Appellate courts do not determine the facts in a case. The trial court, through the jury or judge, does this. They were the ones who saw the witnesses and can better determine credibility. In some cases, where the jury has made a finding that is unsupported by any evidence presented at the trial, the appellate court may reverse the decision. This is similar to the granting of a motion for judgment n.o.v. In most appeals, the appellate court is asked to review one or more legal conclusions reached by the trial court. Most frequently attacked are the following: (1) rulings concerning the admissibility of evidence; (2) rulings on various motions (for example, motion for a directed verdict); and (3) the judge's interpretation of the applicable law as expressed in the charge to the jury (in a jury case) or the opinion of the judge (in a nonjury case). The appellate court is free to reach its own legal conclusions and totally disregard the reasoning of the trial judge, provided, of course, that its conclusions are consistent with the facts as determined by the lower court.

## B. The Effect of an Appeal on Pending Procedures

To permit the party who prevailed at trial to collect the judgment while the losing party is appealing the decision might be unfair to the losing party if the appeal is successful. On the other hand, it could prove equally unfair to the appellee (the party appealed against) if the appellant were able to deprive the winning party of the court's judgment merely by filing for an appeal to stall for time. These two problems are handled by the use of stays and bonds.

A **stay of judgment** means that no action may be taken by the successful party to enforce the judgment until the appeal is decided. Taking an appeal does not automatically suspend the judgment of the lower court, however. The appellant must affirmatively request this from the trial court.

To protect appellee against loss while the appeal is pending, appellate rules frequently provide that a judgment or order may be stayed only if the moving party files a **bond.** A bond is an obligation, entered into by the appellant and an insurance company or other person (called a surety), pursuant to which the appellant and surety agree to pay to the appellee any damages sustained because of the delay caused by the appeal if the appellant is not successful. A fee is charged by the surety for this service. The amount is set to ensure payment of the judgment as well as to ensure payment of the costs of appeal if the appellant is not successful. In the federal courts, the application for a stay pending appeal is made first to the district court. If the district court denies the request for a stay, application may then be made to the appropriate appellate court.

## C. Decisions of Appellate Courts

If a majority of members of the appellate court panel hearing the case believe that the decision in the lower court was correct, the appellate court will **affirm** the lower court's decision. An appellate court will **reverse** the lower court's decision if it feels that the lower court either misinterpreted the law or applied the wrong law. For example, in a civil case the appellate court might agree with the trial court's finding on the liability question but disagree with the computation of damages. In such a case, it will probably affirm on the issue of liability and reverse on the issue of damages. In that case, it would probably be necessary to **remand** the case, that is, return it to the lower court for a redetermination of the damages. A remand is necessary whenever the appellate court feels that more facts must be determined before it can make a decision to either affirm or reverse. If the error of the trial judge was harmless (in that it did not prejudice the rights of the appellant), the appellate court will probably overlook the error and deny the appeal. And if the appellant did not raise a timely objection to the error or irregularity during the trial, the appellate court may decide that the appellant waived the right to complain and it will deny the appeal (affirm the trial court's decision).

If an appellate court that has an even number of judges is equally divided on whether to affirm or reverse a case, the case is affirmed unless the judges decide to remand the case to the lower court for further findings of fact or to hear further argument from legal counsel for the parties to the case.

After the appellate court has "handed down" its decision, it will usually issue some form of order returning jurisdiction over the case to the trial court. The lower court must carry out all instructions of the appellate court. It may not open (relitigate), vacate, or modify the judgment of the higher court.

## D. Taking the Appeal in Federal Court

An appeal must be taken within the period of time specified by statute or court rules. If an appeal is not taken within the specified time, the right to appeal will be lost. The procedures for taking an appeal vary greatly from jurisdiction to jurisdiction.

### 1. The Notice of Appeal

The first step in the appellate procedure is usually the notice of appeal. In federal courts, the notice of appeal must be filed in the district court that heard the case within thirty days from the date of the entry of the judgment or order appealed from. (In some state court systems, the notice is filed with the appellate court and not the trial court.)

The notice usually contains the caption of the case in the trial court and specifies the party who is taking the appeal, the order of the court appealed from, and the name of the court to which the appeal is taken.

Once the notice of appeal has been filed and the applicable filing fee has been paid to the clerk of the district court, the clerk will notify the other parties in the case (by sending a notice to the attorneys for each party) that an appeal has been filed by the appellant. In addition, the clerk will transmit a copy of the notice of appeal and a copy of the docket entries (of the district court proceedings) to the clerk of the court of appeals named in the notice of appeal.[4] Exhibit 11.4 provides a suggested form for the Notice of Appeal.

### 2. Ordering the Transcript

Within ten days after filing the notice of appeal the appellant must notify and order from the court reporter a transcript of the parts of the proceedings (trial) that are at issue on the appeal.[5]

### 3. Transmission of the Record

The **record on appeal** consists of the pleadings and exhibits received in evidence in the trial court, the transcript of the testimony, if any, and the docket entries certified by the clerk of the district court to be correct.

While it is the duty of the district court clerk to transmit the record to the court of appeals, it is the appellant's duty to be sure that transmission is timely (within forty days after the filing of the notice of appeal) and to be sure that all

---

**EXHIBIT 11.4**

## Notice of Appeal

UNITED STATES DISTRICT COURT FOR
THE _____ DISTRICT OF_____

A.B., Plaintiff
    v.               }      Civil Action No._____
C.D. Defendant              Notice of Appeal

Notice is hereby given that C.D., defendant above named, hereby appeals to the United States Court of Appeals for the _____ Circuit (from the final judgment) (from the order (describing it)) entered in this action on the _____ day of _____. _____ 19____ .

/s/

_____
Attorney for C.D.

_____
(Address)

---

[4]See Rule 3 of the Federal Rules of Appellate Procedure (hereinafter referred to as FRAP).
[5]FRAP 10(b).

the papers that are includible have actually been included in the court's record and transmitted to the court of appeals.[6] For example, a particular pleading or other paper or exhibit may have been handed directly to the judge during a trial and not filed in the clerk's office, and the trial judge may have neglected to send the document to the clerk's office. It is the appellant's duty to track down the document and be sure that it is included in the record on appeal.

### 4. Docket the Appeal

The final step in the appeal in the federal system is the docketing of the appeal with the court of appeals by paying the docket fee and making certain that the record on appeal was transmitted within the prescribed time. The clerk of the court of appeals will then enter the appeal on the docket of that court.

### 5. Brief and Oral Argument

The case is usually presented to the appellate court both orally and in writing. The written briefs will contain a statement of the issues raised on appeal, a statement of the facts of the lawsuit, and a legal argument applying the law to the facts. After all parties have had an opportunity to file briefs, the appellate court will normally schedule oral arguments. Even though counsel will argue the merits of their case orally, it is the brief that will be the permanent record of each party's position on appeal. After oral argument, the court will decide the case either in a written opinion, or merely **per curiam** (a decision without an opinion).

### 6. Postappellate Decision Procedures

If, after the appellate court has decided the case, the losing party is still not satisfied, further appellate steps may be available. In the federal system, for example, after the case has been decided the losing party may petition for a rehearing. It is unusual for an appellate court to grant such a rehearing.

Where the decision has been made by an intermediate appellate court, there may be a right of appeal to the highest court, or the highest court may have discretion as to whether it will permit the appeal.

## V. Enforcing Judgments

A judgment may be looked upon as merely a means to an end, meaning that a successful party is entitled to collect only a certain sum of money (in the case of a money judgment award) or that the losing party is supposed to do or refrain from doing a certain specified act (as in the case of an injunction). If the losing party complies with the judgment by either paying the money owed or by doing the act required, there is no problem with respect to enforcing the judgment.

---

[6]FRAP 11(a).

However, if the losing party does not voluntarily comply with or honor the judgment, steps can be taken to enforce the judgment. The balance of this chapter focuses on the procedures established to enable a party to enforce a judgment.

## A. Enforcing Money Judgments

The process by which a party enforces a judgment for the payment of money is called **execution.** It is a procedure whereby a court officer (the marshal in the federal system) is directed to seize the **judgment debtor's** (losing party at trial) property, and if the debtor does not pay, to sell it at a public sale and distribute the proceeds of the sale to the **judgment creditor** (the successful party at trial) as a way of satisfying (paying) the judgment or to actually turn over the debtor's property (or assets) directly to the judgment creditor as a means of satisfying the judgment. The execution procedure selected by the judgment creditor is directly related to the nature and type of property owned by the debtor or money owed to the debtor by some third party not directly involved in the lawsuit. In other words, the process of execution is dependent on the assets of the judgment debtor.

In the federal court, the procedure used to enforce a judgment for the payment of money (execution) is in accordance with the practice and procedure of the state in which the district court is situated.[7] For example, execution on a judgment in the United States District Court for the Eastern District of Pennsylvania is based on the execution procedures mandated by the practice and procedure of the state of Pennsylvania. Also, in accordance with FRCP 62A, no execution is allowed on a judgment until the expiration of ten days after the judgment is entered on the court docket.

There are three basic concerns that may arise in enforcing or satisfying a money judgment: (1) locating assets; (2) assuring that the assets are not removed from the jurisdiction of the court; (3) getting possession of the assets and forcing their sale, if necessary. Every state has statutory provisions designed to help overcome these problems and permit the enforcement of money judgments.

### 1. Locating Assets

As a matter of public policy, certain basic necessities, such as clothing, may be statutorily **exempt** from being taken from the judgment debtor by the judgment creditor to satisfy a money judgment. Except for such exempt property, a money judgment may be enforced against real property, tangible personal property (jewelry and automobiles, for example), and intangible personal property (bank accounts, for example). In almost every state, persons believed to owe money to the judgment debtor can be questioned by the judgment creditor and can be required to furnish information about the property or money owed to the judgment debtor in his or her possession. This third person is called a **garnishee.**

---

[7]FRCP 69.

In order to facilitate the location of assets belonging to the judgment debtor, almost every state allows the judgment creditor to engage in discovery procedures in aid of execution. This process is similar to the discovery procedure outlined in chapter 7 except that it is confined to locating the existence or whereabouts of any assets belonging to the judgment debtor that might be subject to execution. The judgment creditor can take oral depositions or propound written interrogatories on any person, including the judgment debtor, who may have knowledge concerning assets that may be subject to execution.

### 2. Preventing Transfers of Assets

Every state has a procedure for restraining a judgment debtor or a garnishee from transferring any property of the judgment debtor. The procedure varies from state to state. For example, it may be possible to issue a writ of garnishment to a bank in which the debtor has an account. Upon doing so, the bank is not thereafter permitted to allow any withdrawals from the "garnished" account until the debt to the person holding judgment is satisfied.

Another important step in protecting the judgment creditor's rights is filing the documents necessary to obtain a **lien** against the debtors property. A lien is a claim against real or personal property resulting from a judgment against the owner of the property. Its purpose is to notify prospective purchasers of the property that the property is subject to a claim by a judgment creditor and cannot be transferred without satisfying that claim. In general, recording or filing a copy of the judgment in the appropriate county (or other statutorily specified political subdivision) office automatically creates a lien against all real property owned by the judgment debtor that is located within that county. Therefore, to ensure payment of the judgment, a money judgment might be recorded in all jurisdictions in which the defendant owns property. The methods for doing this vary from state to state but require that a copy of the judgment, certified by the court where it was originally given, be filed in the court in the locale where the property is, together with a simple request to enter judgment in accordance with the judgment of the originating court.

### 3. Getting Possession of the Assets

The procedures for execution, which are governed by statute and court rules, vary widely from state to state. An execution is an order directing the appropriate court officer to **levy,** or take possession of, all or some of the debtor's property. Depending on the jurisdiction, the nature of the property, and who has possession of the property, the court officer may be required to actually seize the property or may be required merely to make a written inventory of the property. Commonly, a notice is posted indicating that the property listed in the notice is now under the court's control and may not be sold or removed (in the case of personal property). See Exhibit 11.5 for an example of the form to be used for a praecipe for writ of execution. Exhibit 11.6 for a writ of execution, Exhibit 11.7 for a notice to the judgment debtor concerning the writ of execution, and Exhibit 11.8 for a claim for exemption.

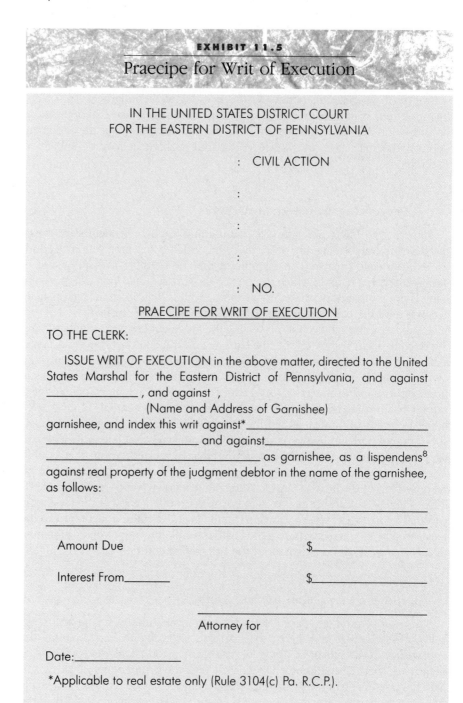

**EXHIBIT 11.5**

## Praecipe for Writ of Execution

IN THE UNITED STATES DISTRICT COURT
FOR THE EASTERN DISTRICT OF PENNSYLVANIA

: CIVIL ACTION

:

:

:

: NO.

PRAECIPE FOR WRIT OF EXECUTION

TO THE CLERK:

ISSUE WRIT OF EXECUTION in the above matter, directed to the United States Marshal for the Eastern District of Pennsylvania, and against _____ , and against ,
(Name and Address of Garnishee)
garnishee, and index this writ against*_____
_____ and against_____
_____ as garnishee, as a lispendens[8] against real property of the judgment debtor in the name of the garnishee, as follows:

_____
_____
_____

Amount Due                                    $_____

Interest From_____                          $_____

_____
Attorney for

Date:_____

*Applicable to real estate only (Rule 3104(c) Pa. R.C.P.).

---

[8]A claim against real property.

**EXHIBIT 11.6**

# Writ of Execution

WRIT OF EXECUTION

To The United States Marshal for the Eastern District of Pennsylvania:

To satisfy judgment, interest and costs against_____

_____ , defendant,

           (Name of Defendant)

(1) you are directed to levy upon the property of the defendant and to sell his interest therein;

(2) you are also directed to attach the property of the defendant not levied upon in the possession of _____ ,

           (Name of Garnishee)

as garnishee,

_____

      (Specifically describe property)

and to notify the garnishee that

    (a) an attachment has been issued;

    (b) the garnishee is enjoined from paying any debt to or for the account of the defendant and from delivering any property of the defendant or otherwise disposing thereof;

    (3) if property of the defendant not levied upon and subject to attachment is found in the possession of anyone other than a named garnishee you are directed to notify him that he has been added as a garnishee and is enjoined as above stated.

Amount Due               $_____

Interest From_____     $_____

[Cost to be added]        $_____

              MICHAEL E. KUNZ

                   (Clerk)

Seal of the Court

          BY:_____

                   Deputy Clerk

Date:_____

MAJOR EXEMPTIONS UNDER PENNSYLVANIA AND FEDERAL LAW

1. $300 statutory exemption
2. Bibles, school books, sewing machines, uniforms and equipment
3. Most wages and unemployment compensation
4. Social Security benefits
5. Certain retirement funds and accounts
6. Certain veteran and armed forces benefits
7. Certain insurance proceeds
8. Such other exemptions as may be provided by law

EXHIBIT 11.7

# Notice to the Judgment Debtor Concerning the Writ of Execution

IN THE UNITED STATES DISTRICT COURT
FOR THE EASTERN DISTRICT OF PENNSYLVANIA

:  CIVIL ACTION
:
:
:
:
:
:
:
:  NO.

WRIT OF EXECUTION
NOTICE

This paper is a Writ of Execution. It has been issued because there is a judgment against you. It may cause your property to be held or taken to pay the judgment. You may have legal rights to prevent your property from being taken. A lawyer can advise you more specifically of these rights. If you wish to exercise your rights, you must act promptly.

The law provides that certain property cannot be taken. Such property is said to be exempt. There is a debtor's exemption of $300. There are other exemptions which may be applicable to you. Attached is a summary of some of the major exemptions. You may have other exemptions or other rights.

If you have an exemption, you should do the following promptly: (1) Fill out the attached claim form and demand for a prompt hearing. (2) Deliver the form or mail it to the United States Marshal's office at the address noted.

You should come to court ready to explain your exemption. If you do not come to court and prove your exemption, you may lose some of your property.

YOU SHOULD TAKE THIS PAPER TO YOUR LAWYER AT ONCE. IF YOU DO NOT HAVE A LAWYER OR CANNOT AFFORD ONE, GO TO OR TELEPHONE THE OFFICE SET FORTH BELOW TO FIND OUT WHERE YOU CAN GET LEGAL HELP.

LAWYER REFERENCE SERVICE

(Name)

2nd Floor, Widener Building
1339 Chestnut Street
Philadelphia, Pennsylvania 19107

(Address)

(215) 686-5698

(Telephone Number)

**EXHIBIT 11.8**

## Claim for Exemptions

IN THE UNITED STATES DISTRICT COURT
FOR THE EASTERN DISTRICT OF PENNSYLVANIA

: CIVIL ACTION
:
:
:
:
:
:
:
: NO.

CLAIM FOR EXEMPTION

To the U.S. Marshal:

I, the above-named defendant, claim exemption of property from levy or attachment:

(1) From my personal property in my possession which has been levied upon,

    (a) I desire that my $300 statutory exemption be

    ☐ (i) Set aside in kind (specify property to be set aside in kind):

    _____ ;

    ☐ (ii) paid in cash following the sale of the property levied upon; or

    (b) I claim the following exemption (specify property and basis of exemption):_____

(2) From my property which is in the possession of a third party, I claim the following exemptions:

    (a) my $300 statutory exemption: ☐ in cash; ☐ in kind (specify property):_____

    (b) Social Security benefits on deposit in the amount of $

    _____ :

    (c) other (specify amount and basis of exemption):
    _____

I request a prompt court hearing to determine the exemption. Notice of the hearing should be given to me at_____

_____, _____
        (Address)        (Telephone Number)

I declare under penalty of perjury that the foregoing statements made in this claim for exemption are true and correct.

Date: _____  _____
                       (Signature of Defendant)

**EXHIBIT 11.8**

## Claim for Exemptions (continued)

THIS CLAIM TO BE FILED WITH THE OFFICE OF THE U.S. MARSHAL FOR THE EASTERN DISTRICT OF PENNSYLVANIA:

2110 United States Courthouse
601 Market Street
Philadelphia, Pennsylvania 19106

(Address)
(215) 597-7272

(Telephone Number)

*Note:* Under paragraphs (1) and (2) of the writ, a description of specific property to be levied upon or attached may be set forth in the writ or included in a separate direction to the United States Marshal.

Under paragraph (2) of the writ, if the attachment of a named garnishee is desired, his name should be set forth in the space provided.

Under paragraph (3) of the writ, the United States Marshal may, as under prior practice, add as a garnishee any person not named in this writ who may be found in possession of property of the defendant. See Rule 3111(a). For limitations on the power to attach tangible personal property, see Rule 3108(a).

(b) Each court shall by local rule designate the officer, organization or person to be named in the notice.

Once the ten days has expired after the judgment has been entered, the execution process is initiated by preparing and completing the praecipe for writ of execution and filing it with the clerk of court. The clerk then issues a writ of execution and attaches the notice form, and the claim for exemption form with the writ. These forms are served upon the judgment debtor by the U.S. Marshal. In addition to the service function, the U.S. Marshal can also be directed to attach the property of a judgment debtor in the possession of a third person (garnishee) upon request of the judgment creditor.

Once the assets of the judgment debtor have been seized and if no settlement is made between the parties concerning the payment of the money owed, the court officer (U.S. Marshal for example) will be directed to hold a public sale to sell off the real property or tangible personal property that has been seized in order to satisfy the judgment.

In order to produce the most money from the public sale and to protect the rights of the parties, notice of the sale in a certain manner and form is required. In general, the notice must be printed and put on the property and/or on a bulletin board or billboard in certain locations for a certain period of time. Notice must also be sent to the debtor. Newspaper advertisement is usually required as well. Advertisements and notices of sale must contain the following information: (1) the date, day of the week, and hour of the sale; (2) the place where the sale will be held; (3) an appropriate and accurate description of the property (and improvements) to be sold; (4) the owner's name; and (5) the judgment of the court that gave rise to the sale.

At the sale, the property is sold to the highest bidder, who must pay a portion of the purchase price at the time of the sale. The purchaser is obligated to pay the balance within a fixed period of time or the property will be resold. The proceeds of the sale are used to satisfy the costs incurred in execution and to satisfy the judgment. If there is a surplus remaining, it is given to the judgment debtor.

If the judgment debtor has an income-producing asset such as an apartment building, the judgment creditor might ask the court to appoint a receiver who will be authorized to manage the property and pay income to the judgment creditor until the judgment is satisfied.

In cases in which the judgment debtor receives a salary but does not have sufficient real or personal property to satisfy a judgment, some states allow the court to issue an attachment against the salary (this is also called garnishment of wages) so that the judgment is paid out to the judgment creditor in installments from the salary of the judgment debtor. Other states, like Pennsylvania, forbid the garnishment of wages. Pursuant to federal law, however, even in those states that allow this form of garnishment there is a limitation (25 percent) placed upon the amount that may be taken out of each wage payment.

## B. Enforcing Nonmoney Judgments

A judgment awarding the possession or recovery of specific property (either real or personal) is generally enforced by an execution procedure similar to that involving a money judgment. However, no public sale is conducted when there is a nonmoney judgment. Where a judgment awards possession of personal property, upon direction of the judgment holder, a court officer (sheriff or marshal) will be directed to actually seize the property and deliver it to the judgment holder. In the case of an ejectment action judgment (landlord/tenant situations where possession of real property is at issue) awarding possession of real property to the owner and dispossessing the tenants, the court officer will be directed to forcibly remove the tenants from the premises if they do not leave voluntarily.

If a judgment directs a party to convey land, by deed or otherwise, or to perform some other specified act, and this party fails to comply, the court can order that the act be performed by some other person with the same effect as if done by the disobedient party.[9] For example, a sheriff or marshal may be authorized to convey land in accordance with the court's order or decree.

In situations in which a judgment calls for the doing or the refraining from doing a certain act (injunctions, for example), another remedy is available to enforce that judgment. The disobedient party may be cited and held in contempt

---

[9]FRCP 70.

of court. Civil contempt of court is a violation of any court order. Therefore a party who refuses to obey a court order (such as an injunction) may subject him- or herself to punishment by the court as a result of the disobedience. Once the court has determined that a party has willfully and deliberately disobeyed its order, it can impose a fine and/or imprisonment as punishment for contempt and to coerce compliance. (Civil contempt is different from criminal contempt in that the main aim of civil contempt proceedings is to coerce compliance with a court order. Criminal contempt is misconduct committed by a person directly to the court that interferes with the business of the court, for example, attorney misconduct during trial.) Obviously, contempt is a very valuable enforcement weapon.

Keep in mind that some judgments do not need enforcement. For example, a divorce decree does not need to be enforced. The judgment itself is self-executing (that is, the parties are divorced by virtue of the order).

## C. Moving and Enforcing Foreign Judgments

As of 1991, thirty-nine states have adopted the Uniform Enforcement of Foreign Judgments Act. These uniform laws allow a judgment creditor in one state to transfer and enforce the judgment in another state where the debtor may be located or have assets. The paralegal should obtain a certified copy of the judgment and docket entries from the court in which the judgment was originally obtained and should file these documents with the court to which the judgment is being transferred. Under these uniform laws, the court receiving the "foreign" or transferred judgment is obliged to treat the judgment in the same manner as a judgment that was originally obtained in the court. This Uniform Act procedurally implements the constitutional provision of the "full faith and credit clause" of the United States Constitution found in Article Four, Section One.

## VI. SUMMARY

This chapter focuses on the procedures that may occur after a jury has reached a verdict. Typically, the party dissatisfied with the result can file post-trial motions and/or an appeal, if appropriate. Post-trial motions are filed with the court that has rendered the decision. An appeal of a court's decision is filed with the appropriate appellate court.

The two post-trial motions are a motion for judgment notwithstanding the verdict and a motion for new trial. A motion for judgment notwithstanding the verdict is based on the wrongful denial of a motion for a directed verdict at the close of all the evidence. In essence, it requests the judge to overturn the jury's decision. A motion for new trial is based on questioning errors of a serious nature that may have occurred during the trial and have rendered the jury's process of deliberation unfair. A motion for new trial can also be used to test the sufficiency of the evidence or the amount of a jury award of damages.

Once judgment has been entered by a court, a dissatisfied party may file an appeal. The purpose of an appeal is to have an appellate court review the proceedings of the trial court to determine whether the trial judge applied the correct law and whether the decision was based on substantial evidence found in the record of the proceedings.

To take an appeal to the federal courts one must file a notice of appeal with the court of appeals, ordering the transcript and ensuring the transmission of the record to the appellate court. Once this has been accomplished, the case is presented to the court by written briefs and oral argument. A party dissatisfied with the result of an appeal may file a further appeal with the highest court. This court typically has discretion to grant the allowance of an appeal.

Court rules also provide a mechanism for winning parties to enforce a judgment called execution. It is often a three-step process: locating the assets, seizing the assets, and selling the assets of a judgment debtor. A judgment from one jurisdiction may be transferred to another jurisdiction in order to facilitate this process. Nonmoney judgments may also be enforced by a court officer in a similar fashion.

## VII. KEY TERMS

| | | |
|---|---|---|
| Affirm | Judgment | Motion for new trial |
| Appeal | Judgment creditor | Per curiam |
| Appellant | Judgment debtor | Record on appeal |
| Appellee | Levy | Remand |
| Bond | Lien | Reverse |
| Execution | Motion for judgment | Stay of judgment |
| Exemptions | notwithstanding | Taxation of costs |
| Garnishee | the verdict | |

## VIII. QUESTIONS

1. What are the two criteria that must be met in order to file a motion for judgment notwithstanding the verdict?
2. What is the difference between a motion for judgment notwithstanding the verdict and a motion for new trial?
3. What is the difference between a verdict and a judgment?
4. What is the purpose of an appeal?
5. What is the scope of review of an appellate court?
6. What is the effect of an appeal upon trying to collect on a judgment?
7. What is the difference between an appellate court reversal and remand?
8. What is the process of execution?
9. What are the three basic concerns in enforcing a money judgment?
10. What is the process by which a judgment creditor attaches a debtor's wages? Are there any limitations placed on this process?

# CHAPTER 12

# SETTLEMENT

**INTRODUCTION**

**SETTLEMENT
DOCUMENTS**

Releases

Stipulations for Dismissal

Consent Agreements

Settlement Agreements

**SUMMARY**

**KEY TERMS**

**QUESTIONS**

# I. INTRODUCTION

Although this chapter has been placed at the end of the book, it was done so for convenience, not for lack of importance. Civil disputes may be resolved by voluntary agreement of the parties as well as by a decision rendered by a court after trial. The overwhelming majority of civil cases are resolved by settlement rather than by judgment after trial. The reasons for this are the time and expense involved in litigating a dispute and the gamble that a trial always presents, no matter how sure the parties feel that their respective positions are the right positions. Furthermore, judges encourage parties to settle their disputes without a trial as this helps to ease the burden on the court system. Many more lawsuits are filed than could ever be heard; the courts depend on the fact that most lawsuits will eventually be voluntarily settled. Even with settlements of large numbers of cases, the courts still encounter the problem of increasing backlogs in civil cases awaiting trial.

Settlement is the successful end result of the process of **negotiation.** Negotiation can be viewed as the exploration by the parties to a dispute to find a way of reaching a mutually satisfactory result on their own, without the necessity of having a judge or jury decide the outcome. Unless the parties have some common settlement range, there can be no agreement. Therefore, before settlement discussions begin, it is advisable for each party to value his or her case in order to make a proper **assessment.** The assessment is based on each party's understanding of the facts of liability and damages (the expected value). Once an assessment has been made, the litigation team engages its client in a counseling session to determine a **bargaining range** for settlement. The bargaining range represents to the plaintiff the least amount of money acceptable in lieu of trial and the maximum figure he or she is likely to receive if successful at trial. This range represents to the defendant the most amount of money he or she is willing to pay and the least amount of money he or she is likely to have to pay if successful at trial.

As a result of the process outlined above, negotiation can be looked upon as the search for the common area in which there is an overlap between the amount that the plaintiff will accept in lieu of trial and the amount that the defendant will pay in lieu of trial. For example, assume that the least amount of money a plaintiff will accept in lieu of trial is $15,000. Now, assume that the most a defendant will pay in lieu of trial is $25,000. The bargaining range for settlement is between $15,000 and $25,000. Any offer of settlement between these figures should be acceptable to both parties. Another way of viewing negotiation is not only the search for this common area but the attempt to maximize the settlement figure within that common area. Since there is a $10,000 range for settlement that is acceptable to both sides, each party may try to settle the dispute at the end of the bargaining range most favorable to him or her. Whether the parties are successful depends on the relative strengths of each party's case and the willingness of both sides to compromise.

There is no precise formula for determining a settlement price. In general settlement prices are reached by weighing factors such as the following:

◆ the ability of the defendant to pay a judgment

◆ the difficulty of proving liability

- the difficulty of proving damages

- the nature of the injury

- the quality and availability of witnesses

- the "horror" factor (any extreme situation that will horrify the fact-finder, for example, defendant's drunk driving caused the automobile accident resulting in permanent disfigurement to plaintiff)

- sympathetic appeal for plaintiff or defendant

- plaintiff's financial status (whether plaintiff can afford to "hold out" or whether money is needed quickly)

- the past record of the trial forum for large or small verdicts

- the experience and ability of counsel

- the amount of defendant's insurance coverage, if any

- present value of money received versus devaluation of future receipt

Negotiation is an ongoing process in civil litigation. There is no one specific time designated as the right time for negotiation. Settlement negotiations may take place at any time: before the lawsuit is filed; after the lawsuit is filed but before trial; during trial; or even after trial when an appeal is pending. Settlement can be effectuated while an appeal is pending if the outcome of the appeal is uncertain or if the financial situation and/or the amount of time spent in resolving the case either raises or lowers the party's expectation level and willingness to compromise further. In addition negotiations usually involve a series of interactions between counsel for the respective parties. These interactions can be in person (meetings), by phone, or by letter. The lawyer or paralegal should always keep the client informed of the progress of the negotiations and communicate all settlement offers to the client. Always remember that it is the client who has the right to decide whether to accept any offer.

## II. SETTLEMENT DOCUMENTS

Once the parties have agreed upon the terms of a settlement, certain documents must be prepared in order to effectuate the settlement. The process of drafting these documents is frequently given to the paralegal. Different forms may be used to accomplish settlement depending on the procedural posture of the case at the time of settlement. These forms are a release, a stipulation for dismissal, a consent decree, or a settlement agreement.

## A. Releases

A **release** is a document by which one party (or parties) relinquishes all or certain claims against another party (or parties). The purpose of a release is to protect against future litigation arising from the factual situation giving rise to the dispute. A release may be general or specific. A general release eliminates all possible claims; a specific release eliminates only certain specified claims.

A release can also be viewed as a written contract drafted to resolve a dispute. It usually has the same elements of a contract:

- names of the parties

- a description of the subject matter giving rise to the original dispute

- a description of the consideration (usually the amount of money paid for the release) upon which the agreement is supported

- a description of the claim that is being released (or given up)

- signatures (with dates) of the parties

If the release is drafted, signed by the parties, and supported by consideration, it is a binding agreement. If a party fails to live up to the terms of the release, the other party can enforce the terms of the agreement to ensure compliance. However, it is customary that a party will not give a signed release form to the other party until the other party has fulfilled the promised obligation (for example, payment of money).

There is one major exception to the general rule that a release must be supported by consideration. This involves a promise made under the Uniform Written Obligations Act adopted by some states, which provides:

> . . . a written release or promise hereafter made and signed by the person releasing or promising, shall not be invalid or unenforceable for lack of consideration, if the writing also contains an additional express statement, in any form of language, that the signer intends to be legally bound.[1]

In states that have adopted this model statute there is no requirement that the release state or describe the consideration upon which the release is based.

Exhibits 12.1 and 12.2 are examples of releases. The first form (mutual release) involves a contract case; the second form involves a tort case.

## B. Stipulations for Dismissal

If a lawsuit has been filed, the parties must file a **stipulation** (written agreement) and order for dismissal of the lawsuit with the court in which the lawsuit is pending. It is often prepared in conjunction with a release. The form of such stipulations is governed by statute or court rules and may be somewhat different in each court system. Exhibit 12.3 is an example of a stipulation to dismiss in federal court.

## C. Consent Agreements

Once a lawsuit has been filed, the parties may decide to settle a case by writing the terms of the settlement on a document and requesting that the judge approve the terms of settlement. The parties are requesting that the judge make the

---

[1]In Pennsylvania this act has been codified at Title 33 P.S. § 6.

## EXHIBIT 12.1

# Mutual Releases

WHEREAS, Gabriel Products, Inc. (hereinafter, "Gabriel") has asserted claims against D. B. Manufacturing Company (hereinafter "D. B.") relating to payment for certain pet supplies sold by Gabriel to D. B.;

WHEREAS, D. B. has asserted claims against Gabriel concerning the delivery date and/or quality or condition of certain pet supplies sold by Gabriel to D. B.;

WHEREAS, the above-mentioned claims have been asserted as the subject matter of Civil Action No. 92-1334 in the United States District Court for the Eastern District of Pennsylvania (hereinafter, Civil Action No. 92-1334);

AND WHEREAS, D. B. has agreed to pay the sum of ten thousand ($10,000) dollars to Gabriel in compromise of those claims asserted by each party against the other;

NOW THEREFORE, Gabriel and D. B., intending to be legally bound hereunder and in consideration for the payment of the sum described above and the mutual releases contained herein, hereby mutually release each other and their respective directors, officers, and employees from all claims or liabilities arising out of the sale by Gabriel to D. B. of certain pet supply products pursuant to a certain letter dated December 5, 1991, including those claims asserted in Civil Action 92-1334.

GABRIEL PRODUCTS, INC.
BY:

Dated: _____   _____ (Seal)
                    President

Attest:

_____
Secretary

D. B. MANUFACTURING COMPANY

Dated: _____   _____ (Seal)
                    President
                    BY:

Attest:

_____
Secretary

**EXHIBIT 12.2**

# Release—Accident Case

WHEREAS, George Smith, of 221 East Mountain Avenue, Coalsville, West Virginia (hereinafter, "plaintiff"), has asserted claims against Mary Jones, of 21 Ocean Drive, Darien, Connecticut (hereinafter, "defendant"), relating to an accident involving defendant's vehicle which allegedly occurred on December 22, 1991, at the intersection of Main and High Streets in Coalsville, West Virginia;

WHEREAS, the above-mentioned claims have been asserted as the subject matter of Civil Action No. 92-1021 in the United States District Court for the District of West Virginia (hereinafter, "Civil Action No. 92-1021");

AND WHEREAS, defendant has agreed and promised to pay plaintiff the sum of $40,000;

NOW THEREFORE, George Smith, intending to be legally bound hereunder and in consideration of the payment of the above-described sum, hereby releases Mary Jones from all liabilities of any type or nature whatsoever and hereby relinquishes all claims of any type or nature whatsoever which she has arising from any events whatsoever which may have occurred at any time to the date of this release, and in particular those claims asserted in Civil Action No. 92-1021.

_____
George Smith

Witness:

_____

agreement an order (or judgment) of the court as if the case had been fully litigated. This is called a **consent agreement.** A court's approval of this agreement is a **consent decree.**

This procedure is similar to a stipulation for dismissal except for the following:

- ◆ The terms of the settlement are made public (in a stipulation for dismissal the actual terms of settlement need not be publicly disclosed).

- ◆ The court must approve the actual terms of settlement.

- ◆ In some instances, if one of the parties breaches the agreement, in addition to contract remedies, the sanction of contempt can be imposed.

In class action cases in which there has been an agreement reached between the named parties, it is quite common for notice to be given to the members of the class as to the terms of the proposed consent decree. Absent

---

**EXHIBIT 12.3**

## Stipulation and Order for Dismissal with Prejudice

IN THE UNITED STATES DISTRICT COURT
FOR THE EASTERN DISTRICT OF PENNSYLVANIA

GABRIEL PRODUCTS, INC.          :
    v.                               :   CIVIL ACTION NO. 92-1334
D. B. MANUFACTURING COMPANY    :

STIPULATION AND ORDER FOR DISMISSAL WITH PREJUDICE

    AND NOW, to wit, this 15th day of April, 1992, it is hereby stipulated and agreed by and between counsel for plaintiff and counsel for defendant that the above-entitled action be dismissed with prejudice with respect to all of plaintiff's claims and all of defendant's counterclaim's and without costs to any party, that an order to that effect may be entered at any time without further notice to any of the parties.

_____
Attorney for Plaintiff

SO ORDERED:

_____          _____
                            J.      Attorney for Defendant
DATED:

---

objections, the court will decide whether to approve the terms of the consent decree. Assuming the court approves, the consent decree will become the order of the court.

Exhibit 12.4 is an example of a consent decree and order approving the same.

## D. Settlement Agreements

In many cases, the parties will not be satisfied with the signing of a release alone. In addition, the parties may not want the terms of the settlement to be made public. Instead, in complex cases or cases involving significant amounts of money, the parties will enter into a contract (settlement agreement) specifying the terms of the settlement. Such contracts, or **settlement agreements,** typically deal with the following issues:

◆ the resolution of the underlying business controversy (such as the terms of a franchise agreement or the conditions of a proposed merger) that led to the lawsuit

**EXHIBIT 12.4**

# Consent Decree and Order

## IN THE UNITED STATES DISTRICT COURT
## FOR THE EASTERN DISTRICT OF PENNSYLVANIA

| | |
|---|---|
| JANE SMITH and JOHN SMITH, | : CIVIL ACTION |
| | : |
| Plaintiffs, | : |
| | : NO. 92-0000 |
| v. | : |
| | : |
| LEHIGH VALLEY HOUSING AUTHORITY, | : |
| | : |
| Defendant, | : |
| | : |
| and | : |
| | : |
| SIDNEY WHITE, in his capacity as Housing Coordinator for the Lehigh Valley Housing Authority, | : |
| | : |
| Defendant, | : |
| | : |
| and | : |
| | : |
| RICHARD NELSON, | : |
| | : |
| Defendant | : |

### STIPULATION AND CONSENT DECREE

The parties hereto, by their counsel, are mutually desirous of disposing of the issues raised by this suit without further litigation, and for that reason Plaintiffs and Defendants are willing to consent to the entry of the following Order. This Consent Decree shall in no way be interpreted as an admission by the Defendants of any violation of Federal law.

EXHIBIT 12.4

# Consent Decree andOrder (continued)

WHEREFORE, the parties hereto, by their counsel, hereby stipulate and agree that this case shall be settled by consent decree as follows:

1. The lease agreement between RICHARD NELSON and MR. & MRS. SMITH and the Housing Assistance Payments Contract between RICHARD NELSON and the LEHIGH VALLEY HOUSING AUTHORITY, the rental under the Section 8 Housing Assistance Payments Program of 1547-B Liberty Street, Allentown, is extended to April 30, 1992.

2. The LEHIGH VALLEY HOUSING AUTHORITY will issue a certificate of family participation to JANE and JOHN SMITH, this certificate to be effective as of the expiration of the extended lease term.

3. JANE and JOHN SMITH will make a good faith effort to find alternate housing prior to April 30, 1992.

4. The LEHIGH VALLEY HOUSING AUTHORITY shall not hereafter terminate or attempt to terminate the tenancy of any tenant whose rent is subsidized under the Section 8 existing Housing Assistance Payments Program, whether in the middle of a lease term or at the expiration of a lease term, without providing any such tenant due process of law, to wit, the LEHIGH VALLEY HOUSING AUTHORITY, will notify the tenant of the reasons set forth by the participating landlord for the eviction, together with notice of the tenant's right to be heard in opposition to the eviction and the reasons set forth.

5. The LEHIGH VALLEY HOUSING AUTHORITY, upon a finding that good cause for the eviction exists, shall have the sole right to issue a notice to vacate to the tenant.

6. The terms of the temporary restraining order issued on this matter on March 3, 1992, shall continue through April 30, 1992.

FOR THE PLAINTIFFS:                    FOR THE DEFENDANTS:

_____                _____
Attorney for Plaintiffs                Attorney for Housing Authority

                                       _____
                                       Attorney for Richard Nelson

                                       DATED: _____

**EXHIBIT 12.4**

## Consent Decree and Order (continued)

IN THE UNITED STATES DISTRICT COURT
FOR THE EASTERN DISTRICT OF PENNSYLVANIA

| | |
|---|---|
| JANE SMITH and<br>JOHN SMITH, | : CIVIL ACTION<br>:<br>: |
| Plaintiffs, | :<br>: NO. 92-0000<br>: |
| v. | :<br>: |
| LEHIGH VALLEY HOUSING<br>AUTHORITY, | :<br>:<br>: |
| Defendant, | :<br>: |
| and | :<br>: |
| SIDNEY WHITE, in his<br>capacity as Housing<br>Coordinator for the<br>Lehigh Valley Housing<br>Authority, | :<br>:<br>:<br>:<br>: |
| Defendant, | :<br>: |
| and | :<br>: |
| RICHARD NELSON, | :<br>: |
| Defendant | : |

<u>ORDER</u>

The Court, having reviewed all aspects of this case to date, having fully considered the desirability of the disposing of the matters contained herein by means of Consent Decree and knowing the same to be freely agreed to by the Plaintiffs and Defendants herein as is evidenced by the signatures of their counsel hereto, does hereby ORDER, ADJUDGE, and DECREE that the Stipulation and Consent Decree annexed hereto be approved by and made an Order of Court this _____ day of _____, 1992.

_____
United States District Judge

◆ the time and terms upon which any monetary settlement will be paid

◆ the form and execution of releases

◆ the form, execution, and filing of stipulations concerning discontinuance of the action and other matters

◆ the destruction, maintenance, or return of confidential documents and copies thereof

◆ the future business relationship of the parties

Exhibit 12.5 is an example of a settlement agreement that could have been used when the parties had resolved their dispute.

---

**EXHIBIT 12.5**

## Settlement Agreement

THIS AGREEMENT, entered into on the respective dates of indicated acceptance, by and among Whiz-ball Publications, Inc. (hereinafter referred to as "Whiz-ball") and Torn Paper Company, (hereinafter referred to as "Torn") and William J. Smith;

WITNESSETH:

WHEREAS, there is now pending in the United States District Court for the District of New Jersey the action captioned Whiz-ball Publications, Inc. v. Torn Paper Company, Civil Action No. 91-0000 (hereinafter referred to as "the action"); and

WHEREAS, the parties hereto now desire to record their agreement pursuant to which they wish to terminate said litigation without the necessity of further proceedings.

NOW, THEREFORE, in consideration of the covenants and agreements hereinafter set forth, the sufficiency of which is hereby mutually acknowledged, and intending to be legally bound hereby, the parties hereto agree as follows:

1. Whiz-ball hereby agrees to accept the sum of $35,963.24 in full satisfaction of all claims set forth in the Complaint in the aforementioned action against Torn;
2. Said $35,963.24 shall be payable at the rate of $2,000 a month plus interest at six percent per annum (6%) on the unpaid balance. Said monthly payments shall commence on December 1, 1992, and the remaining installments shall be paid on the same day of each month thereafter.
3. To secure payment of the aforementioned $35,963.24 Torn shall, upon execution hereof, execute and deliver a Note payable to the order of Whiz-ball, in the form attached hereto as Exhibit A, providing for the payment of said $35,963.24 in the manner aforesaid; and authorizing the holder thereof to confess judgment against Torn for the unpaid amount thereof, plus costs of suit and a reasonable attorney's fee.

**EXHIBIT 12.5**

## Settlement Agreement (continued)

4. To induce Whiz-ball to enter into this Stipulation and Agreement, the aforesaid Note shall be endorsed by William J. Smith, President and principal shareholder of Torn, in the form attached hereto, authorizing the holder of said Note to confess judgment against him for the unpaid amount thereof, plus costs of suit and a reasonable attorney's fee upon default.
5. Upon execution of this agreement and of the Note and Endorsement in the form attached, the parties shall forthwith cause the complaint in the action to be dismissed without prejudice.
6. When the full balance of the aforesaid Note is paid, including all interest due thereon, Whiz-ball will execute and deliver to Torn a release of all claims set forth in the aforementioned Complaint.

(Seal)                                    WHIZ-BALL PUBLICATIONS, INC.

Attest:                                   By:

_____        _____
      Secretary                              President

(Seal)                                    TORN PAPER COMPANY
Attest:                                   By:

_____        _____
      Secretary                              President

_____        _____
      Witness                             William J. Smith

## III. Summary

Most civil litigation cases end in settlement. Settlement is a process that involves making an assessment of the value of a case, counseling a client to determine the client's bargaining range, and negotiating an agreement that is acceptable to all parties concerned. Cases cannot usually settle unless the bargaining ranges of the parties overlap.

Certain documents are used to effectuate the settlement once the parties have agreed upon its terms. A release indicates that a party relinquishes all or certain claims against another party. A stipulation for dismissal requests a court to dismiss a lawsuit. In a consent agreement the parties request the judge to make the terms of the agreement an order of the court (the order based on this agreement is a consent decree). A settlement agreement specifies the terms of settlement and is signed by the parties.

## IV. KEY TERMS

| | | |
|---|---|---|
| Assessment | Consent decree | Settlement agreement |
| Bargaining range | Negotiation | Stipulation for |
| Consent agreement | Release | dismissal |

## V. QUESTIONS

1. What is a bargaining range?
2. When is the right time for negotiation in civil litigation?
3. What elements are typically found in a release?
4. What are the differences between a stipulation for dismissal and a consent agreement?
5. Assume in a car accident case that the least amount of money the plaintiff will settle for is $20,000 and that the most the defendant will pay is $10,000. What is the bargaining range?

# GLOSSARY

**Admission** A statement made in a pleading or in discovery acknowledging the truth of a particular factual allegation of the opponent.

**Affidavit** A sworn statement that facts are true and correct to the best of the knowledge, information, and belief of the person making the affidavit.

**Affirm** The act of an appellate court in upholding the decision of the trial court.

**Affirmative Defense** In federal pleadings, that part of the Answer to the Complaint that goes beyond denying the facts of the Complaint and sets out new facts and arguments that act as a defense or reasons for the defendant to win the case even if everything the plaintiff claims is true (e.g., the defense that an action is barred by the statute of limitations is an affirmative defense).

**Allege** To make a representation of fact either in a pleading or orally.

**Allocatur** The name of the petition used in some states by which the highest appellate court accepts jurisdiction to decide a case appealed from the intermediate appellate court.

**Amend** To add or change. An amended pleading is one that replaces the earlier pleading and may state new facts, omit facts, or change the way facts were presented in the earlier pleading.

**Answer** The response to a Complaint. The document filed to admit or deny allegations made in a claim against a litigant.

**Appeal** The procedure for seeking review in a higher court of a lower court's decision.

**Appearance** Coming into court as a party to a lawsuit. A person who does this "appears." An attorney may enter an appearance on behalf of a client.

**Appellant** The losing party in a trial who seeks review of the case in a higher court.

**Appellate Courts** Courts that review the proceedings of lower (trial) courts and have the power to overturn the decisions of such lower courts.

**Appellee** The prevailing party in a trial who may have to respond to an appeal filed by the losing party.

**Arbitration** The procedure by which a dispute may be resolved at a hearing by a person, or persons, who are not judges.

**Arbitrator** A person who conducts an arbitration.

**Argument** Legal and logical precedents used to show a court why it should take the action requested by a litigant; may be in writing in a brief or orally before a court.

**Asset** Something of value. Either real or personal property. One's belongings and investments.

**Assumpsit** A term frequently used in state courts to designate a lawsuit brought to enforce a contract.

**Assumption of Risk** A doctrine that maintains that if a plaintiff has knowingly accepted the danger of doing something, recovery from the defendant in an action brought for negligence will be barred.

**Attachment** The act of taking or seizing personal property, or issuing an order restricting its disposition.

**Authenticate** To prove that an exhibit is what it purports to be. This is usually done by the testimony of the person who took the photograph, wrote the letter, or kept the business record, for example.

**Averment** A statement of fact made in a pleading.

**Award**   Most typically, the decision rendered by arbitrators after an arbitration hearing.

**Backer**   Colored, heavy-weight paper used as a cover for pleadings.

**Bankruptcy**   The procedure under federal law in which a person may deposit all assets with the court for distribution to all creditors with the accompanying discharge of most debts.

**Bond**   An obligation to pay money if certain circumstances occur. An appeal bond is a guarantee to pay to the appellee any damages sustained by reason of the delay caused by the appellant's appeal if it is not successful in overturning the decision of the trial court.

**Brief**   The document filed with a court to substantiate the position of one of the litigants and give the court legal reasons to accept that position.

**Burden of Proof**   The obligation of one party in a lawsuit to prove all the requirements necessary to show entitlement to recovery. If the burden is not met, the party with the burden will lose the issue or the case.

**Capacity**   The legal ability to do something, for example, to enter into a contract or to bring a lawsuit.

**Caption**   That part of a pleading, immediately at the top of the first page, which contains the names of the parties to the lawsuit, the court in which the case was filed, and the number assigned to the case. Frequently, in state courts, the type of action (e.g., trespass, assumpsit, mortgage foreclosure, etc.) will also appear in the caption. Every pleading in a case must contain the caption.

**Cause of Action**   The basis for a legal dispute. Facts sufficient to support a valid lawsuit.

**Certiorari (Writ or Petition for)**   The procedure of requesting a higher court to hear an appeal when there is no absolute right of appeal to that court. If the writ or petition is granted, the higher court orders the lower court to send the record of the case to it.

**Challenge**   An objection, expressed by an attorney, to someone sitting as a juror in the case.

**Charge to the Jury**   A judge's instructions to the jury on the controlling law of a case that it must apply in reaching its decision.

**Circuit**   Each of twelve geographic divisions of the United States for which there is a Court of Appeals. Except for the District of Columbia circuit, each circuit comprises several states and the federal district courts located in those states.

**Civil Law**   That body of principles governing relationships between people where there is no criminal activity involved.

**Class Action**   A lawsuit prosecuted on behalf of a large group of plaintiffs or against a large group of defendants by naming a representative in place of the entire group.

**Clerk**   The court officer in the federal (and many states') system who maintains documents for the court.

**Code**   1. A set of laws or rules 2. A set of rules concerning procedure before a court.

**Common Law**   That body of law that has grown by decisions of courts. It originated in England and has passed to the United States. The common law is always changing to reflect current needs and desires of society.

**Compensatory Damages**   Damages awarded in order to "make the plaintiff whole," that is, to put the plaintiff in the position he or she would have been if no tort or breach of contract had occurred.

**Complaint**   The initiating document by which a lawsuit is commenced. The pleading that sets forth the cause of action.

**Compulsory Arbitration**   The requirement in certain states or localities that disputes below a specified dollar amount are referred to arbitration for resolution instead of to a judge.

**Compulsory Counterclaim**   A claim that arises out of the same transaction or occurrence that is the subject of a complaint and must be presented in the pending case. If not, its assertion at a later time will be barred.

**Concurrent Jurisdiction**   The right of any of several different types of courts to hear a case.

**Constitution**   The document that sets forth the most basic and most important law of the United States. States also have constitutions but the United States Constitution is the "supreme law of the land" to which all other laws must yield.

**Contempt**   An intentional act designed to obstruct a court's work. The willful disobeying of a judge's order.

**Contingent Fee Agreement**   An arrangement between attorney and client in which the attorney agrees to be paid only out of the recovery the client gets. Thus, if there is no recovery, the attorney gets no fee. If there is a recovery, the attorney gets some agreed-upon amount, typically a percentage of the recovery.

**Contract**   An agreement between two or more persons, containing a promise or mutual promises (sometimes implied) that the law will enforce.

**Count(s)**   When a complaint seeks to allege more than one cause of action, each separate cause of action is set forth in a separate count and labeled as such.

**Counterclaim**   A claim made by the defendant against the plaintiff as part of a lawsuit instituted by the plaintiff.

**Court**   1. The place where lawsuits are resolved before a judge. Also frequently used to refer to a judge in the sense of a dispute "being considered by the court." 2. All the judges who are members of a particular court.

**Court Administrator**   That official who sees to the efficient running of the courts of a certain locale.

**Court of Appeals**   1. The intermediate appellate courts in the federal system. They are divided into twelve circuits based on geographical location (sometimes referred to as Circuit Courts). 2. The name sometimes given to an intermediate or highest appellate court by a state (e.g., New York's highest court).

**Court of Claims**   A court of special competence in the federal system that hears commercial claims made against the United States.

**Creditor**   One to whom money or something else of value is owed by another (known as the debtor).

**Criminal Law**   That body of law concerned with preventing and punishing behavior that society, through its elected representatives, deems to be antisocial or destructive.

**Cross-Claim**   A claim made by one defendant against another defendant based on the same set of circumstances for which the plaintiff originally started the lawsuit against two or more defendants.

**Cross-Examination**   Questioning the witness who has been presented by the opponent at trial or at a deposition.

**Customs Court**   A court of special competence in the federal system that hears cases involving disputes under the customs laws of the United States.

**Damages**   1. Loss sustained by a party for which recovery is sought in a lawsuit. 2. Money that a court orders to be paid to a person who has suffered loss or injury by the person whose fault caused it.

**Debtor**   One who owes money or something else of value (the debt) to another (known as the creditor).

**Default**   Default Judgment—When a defendant in a lawsuit offers no defense by not responding to the complaint. This is a procedure by which the court may render a judgment without the necessity of a trial.

**Defendant**   The person against whom a lawsuit has been commenced.

**Demand**   1. In a pleading, a formal request for relief, usually coming at the end of the pleading. 2. A request from one person to another, asserting a legal right.

**Demeanor**   The appearance made by a witness in giving testimony, e.g., tone of voice, hesitations, sincerity.

**Demurrer**   A response to a complaint claiming that even if what the plaintiff has said is true, there is not any basis for a cause of action against the defendant.

**Denial**   A statement made in a pleading refuting a particular factual allegation made by the opponent.

**De Novo**   The procedure by which a case is retried as if no trial of it had previously taken place. Literally, new; completely new from the start.

**Deponent**   The person who testifies at a deposition.

**Deposition**   A pretrial discovery procedure whereby parties or witnesses are examined by asking questions. A court reporter is present and records all questions and answers. Counsel for all parties are normally present at a deposition.

**Derivative Action**   A lawsuit brought by a stockholder in a corporation seeking a recovery for the corporation, not for the individual personally.

**Digest**   A summary of information obtained during discovery.

**Direct Examination**   The initial questioning of a witness by the attorney calling that person as a witness. Sometimes referred to simply as "direct."

**Directed Verdict**   A request by counsel to the trial judge that a decision be rendered without the case going to the jury. A motion for directed verdict asserts that insufficient evidence has been presented by the opponent to find in his or her favor, even if all the evidence presented by the opponent is true.

**Discovery**   The methods and procedure by which information is made available to parties to a lawsuit prior to trial.

**District Court**   1. The trial court in the federal system. There is at least one federal district court for each state in the United States. 2. The name sometimes given to a trial court in a state.

**Diversity Jurisdiction**   The authority of a federal court to hear a lawsuit between parties who are citizens of different states. Diversity jurisdiction is a type of subject matter jurisdiction: the subject matter being the diverse citizenship of the litigants and an amount in controversy exceeding $50,000.00.

**Divorce**   A court order terminating a marriage.

**Docket**   A summary sheet, page, or index system kept by the clerk's office containing a record of all pleadings, court orders, and other important activities in a case.

**Domicile**   The permanent place of residence of an individual.

**Duty**   An obligation to obey a certain standard of conduct with regard to others.

**En Banc**   A session of all the judges of a court sitting together. The manner in which the U.S. Supreme Court normally hears cases.

**Equity**   1. The system of jurisprudence that arose in England to deal with problems that the courts of law were not empowered to deal with. In modern times in the United States it refers to the authority of a court to give some form of extraordinary remedy. 2. Also used in the sense of what is fair. People should treat each other equitably.

**Evidence**   The body of law concerning the manner of presentation of information to a judge or jury in a trial.

**Exception**   An objection to the charge made by the judge to the jury. It shows that the trial attorney disagrees with something the judge has said and may use this point as an argument to reverse the decision in the case.

**Exclusive Jurisdiction**   The right of a particular type of court to hear a case to the exclusion of any other type of court.

**Execution**   The process of enforcing a final judgment, undertaken by the victorious party, e.g., collecting the amount of money the court says the plaintiff is entitled to as damages.

**Exhibit**   Any piece of physical evidence used at a trial. Photographs and letters are examples of exhibits.

**Expert**   A witness who may give an opinion in court based on the particular competence of that witness.

**Federal Question Jurisdiction**   The authority of federal courts to decide a lawsuit because it involves a dispute over the United States Constitution, or the laws and treaties of the United States.

**Filing**   Placing a document into the possession of the court for inclusion in the file of a case, usually by leaving it with the officer of the court charged with the function of maintaining all documents for the court. (In the federal system, this officer is known as the Clerk.)

**Form of Action**   In medieval England, rights were defined into narrow areas. To bring a lawsuit one had to show that all the requirements of a certain "form of action" were met.

**Forum**   A court. The place where a trial is held or a lawsuit brought.

**Forum Non Conveniens**   An "inconvenient court." A method by which a lawsuit is transferred from one court to another because it is a more convenient forum.

**Garnishee**   A person owing a debt to a judgment debtor or having possession of property in which the judgment debtor has an interest.

**Garnishment**   The method of recovering property belonging to or held by a third person, which property is owed by the third party to the defendant in a lawsuit. The plaintiff may serve the holder of the property (the garnishee) and the court may order that the property be turned over to the plaintiff.

**General Damages**   Damages given to compensate plaintiff for things other than out-of-pocket expenses, e.g., pain and suffering.

**General Jurisdiction**   The authority of a court to hear a variety of cases as opposed to a court that may hear only certain types of cases.

**Habeas Corpus**   An order of a court directing that a person be brought before it. Literally, "you have the body."

**Hearing**   1. A trial-like proceeding, usually without a jury. It may be before a court, an administrative agency, or in arbitration. 2. The portion of a trial, jury or nonjury, in which the actual evidence is presented, as distinguished from picking the jury (in a jury case), opening statements, or closing arguments.

**Impeach**   Attacking the credibility of a witness.

**Implead**   To bring a person into a lawsuit as a third-party defendant.

**Indispensable Party**   When a person's rights would be adversely affected by a lawsuit, and those rights are not being adequately represented in the lawsuit, the person must be allowed to participate in the lawsuit.

**Injunction**   An order of the court requiring a party to do something or refrain from doing something. An injunction limiting labor union picketing is a common example.

**In Rem Jurisdiction**   The authority of a court to bind parties with regard to their rights in certain property (real estate or personal property) because the property is within the geographic jurisdiction of the court.

**Interpleader**   A form of action in which a stakeholder deposits money or property with a court and claimants to the same money or property assert reasons why each should be given it. The stakeholder presents no defense to any claim. The various claimants each try to show why they are entitled, to the complete or partial exclusion of the other claimants.

**Interrogatory—Interrogatories**   A written question asked to an opponent in the lawsuit that must be answered in writing. Use of interrogatories takes place during the "discovery" phase of the lawsuit.

**Intervention**   The process by which a person who is not a party to a lawsuit becomes a party to the lawsuit as either a plaintiff or defendant by their own voluntary act.

**Issue**   1. A point in dispute in a lawsuit. It may be a dispute of law or a dispute of fact. 2. To officially announce. For example, when a court issues a writ.

**Joinder**   1. The process initiated by a party to a lawsuit of adding someone to a lawsuit. 2. The process of joining (consolidating) the various claims between litigants into one lawsuit.

**Judge**   The person who presides at a trial or who sits to review the decision reached by a trial court.

**Judgment**   A final order of a court deciding the rights and claims presented in the case.

**Judgment Creditor**   The person who has been successful at trial and has had a judgment for money damages entered in his or her behalf.

**Judgment Debtor**   The person who has lost the trial and a money judgment has been entered against him or her.

**Judgment Notwithstanding the Verdict (n.o.v.)**   An order by the trial judge entering judgment in a manner contradictory to the jury's verdict. This is granted only when the verdict is unreasonable and unsupportable.

**Jurisdiction**   1. The authority by which a particular court may hear a dispute and make a decision that will be binding upon the parties. 2. The geographic area within which a court has the authority to act.

**Juror**   A person who sits on a jury to decide the facts of a case.

**Jury**   The panel of people who decide the facts in a lawsuit.

**Levy**   To seize the property of a judgment debtor. The seizure is only symbolic in most cases, as by posting a notice that the particular property is now under the control of a court.

**Liability**   The determination by a court that a party is responsible to another. This may mean that the party found liable will have to pay damages for wrongful conduct toward that other person.

**Lien**   A claim against real or personal property resulting from a judgment against the owner of the property.

**Litigant**   A party to a lawsuit.

**Litigation**   Lawsuits. The use of the legal process to settle disputes between people.

**Long-Arm Statutes**   Laws that allow a court to exercise jurisdiction over a party who is outside the geographical territory of a court.

**Marshal**   An officer of the court who does such things as serve papers (like complaints); the title given to the federal officer who enforces orders of a federal court.

**Master**   A person appointed by a court to take testimony on its behalf or otherwise gather information for the court.

**Motion**   A request, either written or oral, made to a court that the judge make some ruling or take some action.

**Negligence**   The failure to act reasonably in a given situation. Doing something carelessly or failing to do something that should be done is negligence. For example, driving without headlights at night is negligent conduct.

**Opinion**   A written explanation of a decision made by a judge prepared by the judge.

**Ordinance**   A law passed by a local or municipal government.

**Original Jurisdiction**   The authority of a court to be the first court to which a legal dispute is referred.

**Overrule**   1. The action of a court in setting aside the decision of a prior case for purposes of having value as precedent but without affecting the result in that case. 2. With regard to objections made at trial, an order of the judge dismissing the objection and allowing the matter objected to be presented. Rejecting the objection.

**Panel**   A large number of prospective jurors from whose number the actual jury members will be selected.

**Peremptory Challenge**   A challenge to a particular juror that requires no reason. Usually strictly limited in number by court rule or statute.

**Permissive Counterclaim**   A claim that may be asserted by the defendant against the plaintiff even though it does not arise out of the same transaction or occurrence that is the subject of the plaintiff's complaint.

**Person**   In legal usage refers to natural and artificial persons. A corporation is an artificial person.

**Personal Jurisdiction**   The authority of a court to make its decision binding over a particular person.

**Petition**   A writing filed with a court or administrative agency requesting that it take particular action.

**Place of Abode**   The regular living place of an individual.

**Plaintiff**   The person who starts a lawsuit against another.

**Pleading**   The process of making formal, written statements by the litigants. A pleading is one of the formal, written papers filed with a court. All the papers filed in a case are frequently referred to as the "pleadings."

**Post-Trial**   That period of time after trial of a case but prior to a final decision being entered by the court.

**Precedent**   1. The value that a decided case has as a guide for deciding future, similar cases. 2. A court decision on a point of law that serves as authority on how to decide a similar point of law in a future case.

**Pretrial**   That period of time after the commencement of a lawsuit but prior to the trial.

**Prima Facie**   Literally, at first sight. At the trial the plaintiff must prove that he or she is entitled to win unless the defendant comes forward with evidence to dispute the plaintiff's claim. Doing this is to establish a prima facie case.

**Procedure**   The way in which a lawsuit is carried on. The rules that govern the handling of cases in courts, for example, rules detailing what a complaint must contain, how much time a defendant has to answer a complaint.

**Proponent**   The person who offers or proposes something.

**Propound**   To set forth, issue, offer, propose, or put something forward. For example, to propound interrogatories is to ask them to another party in a lawsuit.

**Punitive Damages**   Damages given for the purpose of punishing the defendant. This type of damages is rarely allowed, usually only when a statute provides for them.

**Re, In Re**   1. "With regard to" or "concerning." 2. "In the matter of."

**Real Estate**   Land and the buildings on it. Also referred to as real property or realty.

**Reasonable Conduct**   What a person with similar characteristics, skill, or training would do in a particular circumstance to judge whether the conduct of a person has been negligent.

**Rebut**   To dispute or defeat the effect of evidence presented by the opponent at trial.

**Record**   All those proceedings in a lawsuit that have been reduced to writing.

**Reformation**   An equitable remedy whereby a court rewrites a document because it was signed out of mistake or fraud.

**Regulations**   Rules made by administrative agencies that are legislative in effect.

**Release**   A written document by which one party relinquishes a legal claim against another party.

**Relevant**   Evidence that is admissible in a case because it tends to prove or disprove one of the issues in the case. Irrelevant evidence is not admissible because it does not prove or disprove a fact in the case.

**Remand**   The order of a higher court, after an appeal has been taken before it, redirecting the case to a lower court for further proceedings.

**Remedy**   What a party in a lawsuit is asking for, as distinguished from the right to have any relief at all. In most lawsuits the plaintiff seeks the remedy of money damages.

**Removal**   The process of sending a case from state court to federal court when the federal court had jurisdiction to hear the case initially.

**Replevin**   A type of lawsuit brought to recover certain personal property that is held by the defendant. In such a case, the plaintiff must show that the defendant's claim to the property is inferior to the plaintiff's.

**Request for Admission**   A discovery procedure in which one party to a lawsuit requests that another party to the lawsuit acknowledge the truth of certain facts or authenticity of certain written materials.

**Request for Production of Documents**   A discovery procedure in which a written request is made by one party in a lawsuit for the delivery of certain written materials from another party in a lawsuit.

**Rescission—Rescind**   The cancellation of a contract either by the parties to it or by a court. Rescission places the parties back into the position they were prior to the contract.

**Res Judicata (also Res Adjudicata)**   The rendering of a final decision that is forever binding on the particular parties to a lawsuit. Literally, "a thing decided." If a court decides a case, and the appeal period has either expired or all appeals have been exhausted, the subject matter of that case is finally decided between the litigants and no new lawsuit may be commenced on the same subject by any of the litigants.

**Responsive Pleading**   A pleading that directly answers the prior pleading in a case.

**Return of Service**   A verification by the person who has served the complaint in a lawsuit telling where, when, and upon whom service was made.

**Reversal**   The order of an appellate court overturning the decision of a lower court.

**Rules**   1. The requirements established by courts by which lawsuits are processed. Regulations to control the workings of a court. 2. With regard to administrative agencies, regulations adopted that may have the effect of law.

**Sanctions**   A penalty or punishment that may be imposed by a court for failure to comply with an order of the court.

**Service—Service of Process**   The physical act of delivering written papers concerning a lawsuit to an opponent. Where physical delivery is not possible, service may sometimes be accomplished by alternate means, such as publication or mailing.

**Settlement**   The agreement of parties to a lawsuit (or a prospective lawsuit) to amicably resolve their differences without a trial.

**Sheriff**   An officer of a state court who does such things as serving complaints and enforcing orders of the court.

**Special Damages**   Damages reflecting actual out of pocket expenses, e.g., medical bills and costs of repairing damage to a car. Frequently referred to simply as "specials."

**Specialized Jurisdiction**   The limited authority of a court to hear only certain types of cases. For example, the Tax Court of the United States, which may hear only disputes concerning the imposition of federal taxes.

**Specific Performance**   A method of enforcing a contract by requiring the delivery of a unique thing that was the subject matter of the contract.

**State of Incorporation**   The state that has granted a charter to a corporation to operate as such. A corporation always has only one state of incorporation.

**Statute**   A law passed by a legislature.

**Statute of Limitations**   The period fixed by law within which a certain type of action must be brought or it becomes barred. Also referred to as the period of limitations or limitations of actions.

**Stay**   1. A postponement by the court of the right of the winning party to enforce its judgment. 2. Stopping all proceedings for a specified period of time.

**Stipulation**   An agreement between parties to a lawsuit, through their respective attorneys, set forth in writing (in most cases) and filed with the court. If not in writing, the stipulation will be announced in open court. Such, for example, are agreements to extend the time for pleading, to take depositions, or to waive technical requirements of a deposition.

**Subject Matter Jurisdication**   The authority of a court to hear and decide a particular type of case.

**Subpoena**   An order of a court directing that a person appear as a witness at a certain time and place. It may also require that the witness bring documents at the time the testimony is to be given.

**Subpoena Duces Tecum**   An order of the court that the witness who is required to appear and testify also bring along certain documents or other things to be presented at the time testimony is given.

**Subrogation**   When an insurance company pays a claim to its policy holder, the insurance company then stands in the shoes of the policy holder with regard to recovering damages from the person responsible for the injuries or damage to the policy holder. This substitution of the insurance company for the policy holder is known as subrogation.

**Substantive Law**   The basic concepts that determine rights and responsibilities between people. For example, contract law and tort law are areas of substantive law.

**Summary Judgment**   When no essential facts in a case are disputed, no trial is held and the case is decided by the judge alone on the basis of the law involved. Such a procedure is prompted by motion of one or more of the parties to the lawsuit.

**Summons**   In the federal system (and some states), a notice accompanying the complaint informing the defendant that a lawsuit has been commenced and that if an answer to it is not filed within a certain time, judgment may be entered against the defendant.

**Supreme Court**   The highest court in the federal system. Also, frequently, the name given to the highest court in state.

**Surety**   A person or company that agrees to guarantee the obligation of another.

**Sustain**   Recognizing the validity of an objection and thereby disallowing material to be presented as evidence. Granting the objection.

**Tax Court**   A court of special competence in the federal system that hears suits brought by taxpayers to contest tax assessments made by the Internal Revenue Service.

**Term of Art**   A word or phrase that has a certain, special meaning within a particular industry or occupation. (Also called word of art.)

**Third-Part Litigation—Third-Party Defendant**   When a lawsuit is brought against a defendant and that defendant wants to add another party to the lawsuit, the original defendant may file a "third-party complaint" bringing the "third-party defendant" into the lawsuit.

**Tickler System**   An early warning system used to keep track of important dates.

**Tort**   A civil wrong.

**Tortfeasor**   The person who commits a tort. A wrongdoer.

**Trespass**   1. A term frequently used in state courts to designate an action brought for a tort committed against the plaintiff. 2. Also, commonly used to refer to the wrongful entry on land.

**Trial**   A hearing in court to decide a legal dispute.

**Trial Court**   The court that hears witnesses and takes testimony to reach its decision. Generally the first court to which a dispute is referred for a decision.

**Trier of Fact**   The jury in a jury trial or the judge in a trial without a jury who decides disputed questions of fact.

**Venue**   The geographic location where a case is tried or may be tried.

**Verdict**   The decision in a case reached by a jury.

**Verification**   An assertion that the facts contained in a pleading are true and correct. In many states an affidavit of the party must accompany each pleading to "verify" it.

**Voir Dire**   Literally, "to speak the truth." The examination of prospective jurors to determine that they are impartial before allowing them to sit on a jury. The voir dire is usually conducted by the attorneys in the lawsuit but may sometimes be conducted by the trial judge.

**Voluntary Arbitration**   An agreement of parties to submit a dispute to arbitration and, normally, to be bound by the decision reached by the arbitrator.

**Waiver**   Knowingly, or by conduct, relinquishing a right that one may have. For example, failing to object to improper venue within the time allowed will result in a waiver of the right to assert improper venue.

**Warrant of Attorney**   A formal, written notice to the court that an attorney has authority to represent and is representing a party to litigation.

**Witness**   One who testifies at a trial or deposition.

**Writ**   At common law, an order in the name of the sovereign, issued by a court and addressed to an officer of the law, requiring the performance of a specific act. For example, advising a defendant to a lawsuit that the lawsuit has begun and that a responsive pleading is required or a judgment will be given in favor of the plaintiff.

**Writ of Execution**   An order from a court allowing the holder of a judgment to use certain remedies to collect the money owing by reason of the judgment.

# INDEX